ILEX: INTRODUCTION TO LEGAL PRACTICE

VOLUME 1

AUSTRALIA
The Law Book Company
Brisbane • Sydney • Melbourne • Perth

CANADA
Carswell
Ottawa • Toronto • Calgary • Montreal • Vancouver

Agents:
Steimatzky's Agency Ltd., Tel Aviv;
N.M. Tripathi (Private) Ltd., Bombay;
Eastern Law House (Private) Ltd., Calcutta;
M.P.P. House, Bangalore;
Universal Book Traders, Delhi;
Aditya Books, Delhi;
MacMillan Shuppan KK, Tokyo;
Pakistan Law House, Karachi, Lahore

ILEX: INTRODUCTION TO LEGAL PRACTICE

VOLUME 1

Fourth Edition

by

CRAIG OSBORNE, B.A., M.A. (Econ.)
Solicitor
Senior Lecturer in Law, Manchester Polytechnic

Foreword by
Sir Jack I.H. Jacob, Q.C., LLB., Hon. LLD.

Published in Association with
THE INSTITUTE OF LEGAL EXECUTIVES

LONDON
SWEET & MAXWELL
1992

First Edition	1982
Reprint	1983
Second Edition	1985
Revised Reprint	1986
Third Edition	1989
Reprint	1990
Fourth Edition	1992

Published by
Sweet & Maxwell Limited of
South Quay Plaza, 183 Marsh Wall, London E14 9FT
Computerset by
MFK Typesetting Limited
Printed in England by Clays Ltd, St Ives plc

A CIP catalogue record
for this book is available
from The British Library

ISBN 0 421 45820 8

FOREWORD TO FIRST EDITION

The life of the law is the practice of the law, and the practice of the law is the ultimate machinery for giving effective force and reality to the legal rights, duties and interests of the members of society. The practitioners of the law exercise a profound and crucial role in regulating, ordering and dealing with our affairs, however multifarious and multitudinous they may be, at any rate at some time in the life of each of us and in relation to some legal problem or matter in which each may be concerned or become involved. However much we may not relish the prospect, we must all in the end, at some time and for some purpose, turn to the legal practitioners for their services.

For this reason, we require those who practise the law to be persons learned in the law, skilled in its practice, familiar with its procedures, competent and efficient to deal with our needs, to safeguard our interests, to protect us against legal mishaps, and at the same time to be persons of integrity, reliability and responsibility.

These qualities are possessed, in a substantial measure, by members of the Institute of Legal Executives, whether as Fellows or Associates, and they manifest and exert these qualities though they are themselves in the service of Solicitors, who constitute a higher branch of the legal profession as members of the Law Society. In addition, the members of the Institute of Legal Executives have developed a high degree of corporateness and, accordingly, it may fairly be claimed that the body of Legal Executives, members of the Institute, themselves constitute a separate distinct branch of the legal profession.

This claim can perhaps be justified by the fact, *inter alia*, that Fellows and Associates of the Institute of Legal Executives are trained, taught and tested in the study of the law, and its practices, procedures and skills, particularly in the areas in which they are or are going to become specialist experts. This book, *Introduction to Legal Practice*, is eloquent testimony to the high standard and the deep and detailed knowledge, learning and expertise expected to be attained and maintained by legal executives. The Editor is to be congratulated on producing an excellent work, clear, comprehensive and masterly, which is at the same time highly practical and professional as well as instructive, informative and stimulating. As the name of the book implies, the two volumes of this work are intended to introduce students to legal practice, and this volume, to be followed by a second, fulfils this challenge faithfully and admirably. It brings the practice of the law to life, studded as it is with numerous and valuable examples, forms, and true-to-life sketches and precedents. There is abundant and thorough guidance as to the practical steps that have to be taken at each stage of a legal transaction or legal process. The book will, I am sure, be of inestimable value not only to students of legal practice and not only to legal executives, but to all who are devoted and committed legal practitioners.

The scope and coverage of the book are extensive. This Volume deals with several important topics: the legal profession and how its different branches work in the practical sense, the methods and places in which to find the law relevant to the particular matter in hand, the important subject of Legal Aid, and the fundamental areas of practice of Conveyancing, Criminal Procedure, and Proceedings in the County Court. Volume II will cover a wide range of rather crucial subjects of the practice of the law, such as litigation in the High Court, Businesses, Succession, Family affairs, Tribunals and Inquiries, and Arbitration. This work will surely give any student a good and thorough grasp and grounding in the fundamentals of the law and legal practice affecting almost every aspect of human affairs and relationships. It should enable the legal practitioner to render effective and effectual legal service to all who need the assistance of the law.

Introduction to Legal Practice will be exceptionally useful to the legal practitioner. It provides a ready and handy reference to legal practice in a great variety of subjects, which no legal practitioner can safely be without.

Jack Jacob

May 1982

PREFACE TO FIRST EDITION

This is the first of two volumes to be published jointly by the Institute of Legal Executives and Sweet and Maxwell Ltd. The books are to be prescribed reading for the practice and procedure aspects of the first stage of the examination syllabuses the Institute provides for trainee legal executives. Volume 2 will appear in due course.

Together the two volumes will introduce readers to the legal profession and will describe and explain much of the day-to-day work of a solicitor's office. No prior specialist knowledge is assumed and the books may well be of interest and value to those not employed in solicitors' offices, but who wish to have a broad view of the means by which everyday actions and transactions are dealt with by legal practitioners.

Fictional case-studies are used to present transactions of every day occurrence in a solicitor's office and they are supplemented by narrative exposition to give a rounded treatment of each subject. It is hoped the case-studies will bring to life the dry rules of procedures, whilst the accompanying narrative explains their significance and the meaning of any technical terms encountered and sets the specific case in its wider legal and procedural context. For students working in solicitors' offices, the case-studies will bring home the relationship between their studies and their work much more forcefully than hitherto. Throughout, the practical aspects of the work, as experienced at the trainee level, are kept in view.

The cases have been imagined as taking place in the County of Barsetshire, mainly in the town of Barset. The adoption of Anthony Trollope's place names serves to confirm the fictional nature of the events and persons featured in the cases. However, absolute consistency in the names of persons and places used in the cases worked up for the various branches of practice should not be looked for. Two firms of solicitors feature regularly, Messrs. Makepiece and Streiff and Messrs. Rime and Reason. As is the custom in the profession, the names are shortened in practice to Messrs. Makepiece and Messrs. Rime. Also in accordance with common practice in solicitors' offices, the conduct of certain matters is shown as being delegated to legal executives in the firm and trainee legal executives are also shown to be taking a hand.

The case-studies indicate one way of accomplishing the client's objectives. Others, equally valid and effective, may be suggested and it is hoped will be discussed by lecturers with their students.

April 1982   *Grenfell Huddy*

PREFACE TO THE FOURTH EDITION

The need to keep up to date with changes in the law and procedure has led to the need to prepare a fourth edition for publication. The changes to the chapter on County Court are the most significant and important. The shift of a vast amount of work from the High Court to the County Court has led to the need for all practitioners, save those in the most specialised practices, to be aware of the importance of County Court litigation, and the changes in the costs rules relating to it have meant that County Court litigation can become an important part of the earning potential of almost all practices.

The text of the lengthiest chapter, that on Conveyancing, was written by my colleague Lyn Jones LL.B Solicitor, Senior Lecturer at Manchester Polytechnic for whose assistance with that and for a later further re-write I am very grateful indeed. The rest of the text was my responsibility.

The text was largely re-written in the early months of 1992 but it has been possible to include some updating at proof reading stage in particular to take brief note of some changes to Conveyancing in the form of the new Standard Conditions of Sale.

I would like to thank the Education Secretary of the Institute, Ian Watson B.A. for his invaluable assistance throughout the preparation of this edition for publication.

Craig Osborne.

July 1992.

ADDENDUM

It should be noted that the Register shown on pp. 119–120 has now been superseded by a computerised format; although the Register shown may be in use at some district registries it will eventually become obsolete. It should also be noted that the first name and address on the Proprietorship Register (p. 119) should be struck through on the form as follows:

~~PERCY BYSSHE SHELLEY of The Limes, Lemon Terrace, Barset, Barsetshire, Steel Erector registered on 14 August 1965.~~

Form 94D on p. 141 has been superseded by the statutory form which appears in Schedule I to the Land Registration (Official Searches) Rules 1990.

Form A4 on p. 143, Box 2, third column – Fee scale para or abatement should read A and not 4.

ACKNOWLEDGMENTS

Acknowledgments for kind permission for the reproduction of copyright material are due to the following copyright holders:

The Law Society and the Solicitors' Law Stationery Society Ltd. for the Law Society's Standard Conditions of Sale (Second Edition) pp. 115–118;

The Law Society for forms reproduced on pp. 110–113;

Her Majesty's Land Registry for forms on pp. 119–121, 132–133, 137–141, 143–146;

Her Majesty's Stationery Office for Crown copyright material on pp. 62–63, 142;

The Legal Aid Board Head Office for the Legal Aid logo on p. 75 and the Green Form and Key Card on pp. 80–81;

Messrs. Butterworth & Co. (Publishers) Ltd. for the All England Law Report *National Westminster Bank Ltd.* v. *Stockman* [1981] 1 All E.R. 800, reproduced on pp. 52–53;

The author and Stevens & Sons for the table from Glanville Williams, *Learning the Law*, reproduced on p. 58;

David Andrews and Longman Group UK Ltd. for the flow chart reproduced from the chapter "Office Layout and Design" in P. J. Purton, D. Andrews and P. K. Brindley, *Organisation and Management of a Solicitor's Practice*;

Longman Group UK Ltd. for the specimen abstract of title from P. G. Ponder, *The Art of Abstracting*;

The Solicitor's Law Stationery Society Ltd. for forms reproduced on pp. 107–109, 122–125, 130–131, 249–252, 299–300.

CONTENTS

Contents

TABLE OF CASES

TABLE OF STATUTES

Table of Statutes

TABLE OF STATUTORY INSTRUMENTS

COUNTY COURT RULES

RULES OF THE SUPREME COURT

CHAPTER 1

THE PROFESSION

LAWYERS

Law as a profession is one mark of a developed community. Modern society can no more do without lawyers than it can do without doctors.

The English lawyer was from the beginning his client's representative. The first group who can be called professional were attorneys. It was only several centuries later that the title solicitor supplanted the many others that had come into use in the meantime. The professional advocate, as being separate from attorneys, is found in the records a little later than the attorney, and the title barrister much later.

The legal profession is often taken to refer to the body of barristers and solicitors. But there are many noted lawyers who have been neither. The profession, moreover, flourishes by the labours of many who, whilst neither being "called" nor "admitted," are nonetheless skilled in the law and have every justification in calling themselves lawyers.

THE PROFESSION

What exactly is a profession? At some stage in his career a sportsman may "turn professional" and we are also used to seeing the term "professional" applied to an actor, a photographer, etc. In these contexts the use of the term usually means "professional" as opposed to "amateur" that is, someone who is good enough to get a living from something that to other people is simply an enjoyable hobby. In its strict sense however, the term "professional" has other connotations. It usually implies the following:

(1) The acquisition of a body of knowledge and practice covering a defined area of social activity.

(2) The offering of a service to the community within that field of activity.

(3) Independence of the person offering the service and the acceptance of personal responsibility for what he does.

(4) Inevitably, the establishing of some kind of order within the profession especially a governing body which will impose its own training and qualification rules and provide rules of professional conduct and disciplinary powers. Often in the so called "learned professions" that is medicine, the law, etc., the professional bodies and their powers are dealt with expressly in statutes. Inevitably, statute will provide that there is some kind of

1

monopoly on persons who have had proper training and have qualified within a profession, so that nobody who has not may practice that profession.

(5) There is a final point which is in many ways more a distinguishing mark of the professions than any of the others so far considered. In what way does a solicitor differ from say a butcher or a car dealer? The difference is perhaps best considered by taking an example or two; suppose that you go to a butcher and order steak; it is not part of the butchers' duties to point out to you that a cheaper and healthier meal could be provided if you were to go instead to the fishmonger opposite. Similarly, if you walk into a car dealer with £30,000, and tell him that although the longest journey you ever do is 3 miles into town for shopping you have always wanted a Porsche and are determined to have one it is not part of his function to point out to you that your real motoring needs could just as well be catered for by buying a mini for a fifth of the price.

The persons employed in these last two occupations, however skilled, are not in the true sense "professional." The distinguishing mark of a profession which makes the work of a solicitor differ from either of these is that it is always a solicitor's duty to give a client the best advice he possibly can in the client's own interest even where this may conflict with the solicitor's personal interest. As we shall shortly see, all that a solicitor has to sell basically is time and skill. In litigation cases therefore it would always, on the face of it, be in the solicitor's interest to take all cases all the way to court. A case which goes all the way to court obviously will take up more of a solicitor's time than one which he manages to compromise to the client's satisfaction at a very early stage.

It follows therefore that the solicitor will be paid much more for a case that goes all the way to court than for one which does get settled at an early stage. This is where we see the true nature of a profession. For of course, the diligent solicitor will always attempt to get the best possible result for his client at as early a stage as possible. Accordingly if, faced with a client with a difficult litigation problem the solicitor can manage to settle it with perhaps two or three letters and a meeting with the client's opponent without ever going to court at all, that solicitor will have been acting in the best possible way. It will of course follow that the solicitor himself will not make out of the case anything like as much in fees as he would have done had it gone all the way to trial. So in this single instance we can see the vital distinguishing mark of the profession referred to above, namely insistence that the professional always acts in his client's own interests even where this conflicts with his own.

It must of course be pointed out that a solicitor who persistently takes clients' cases all the way to court at great expense will in the end get a poor reputation whereas one who obtains a successful outcome very early will in the end get a good reputation with the consequent improvement in the amount of work attracted to his practice, so in the end acting in one's client's best interest often tends to be acting in one's own best interest as well.

The division between barristers, who are either advocates or specialist advisers, and solicitors, the general practitioners of law, is found only in the United Kingdom and some of the Commonwealth countries. Historically, it rests on convention but now this has the backing of statute, although the rules about appearances in court as advocates still largely rest on the conventions of the courts, as we shall see.

THE WORK OF SOLICITORS

Solicitors are the main agency by which a citizen is able to ensure that he receives his legal rights. There are many other agencies which offer help in explaining the law and advising on it of course. Some are general like the Citizens' Advice Bureaux, and others are specialists like the local Trading Standards Office and Housing Advice Centres. However the role of the solicitor is different. In the first place the scope of the matters on which he will give advice is not restricted. There is no legal topic on which in principle a solicitor will not advise, although in a complex modern society some topics have become so specialised that the ordinary solicitor will candidly admit his ignorance and refer you to someone who specialises in that particular subject. For example if someone walks in off the street into an ordinary suburban solicitor's office requiring detailed advice on say international copyright, the solicitor will almost certainly admit his ignorance of this topic which is only too understandable given the rarity with which he is likely to have encountered it in his professional career.

Another difference between the role of the solicitor and those of the other advisory agencies however is that the solicitor gives more than advice. He will give a service in dealing with the client's whole problem going beyond advice, into correspondence, negotiations and, if need be, litigation. The law in the case may indeed be very plain. Often the law is so obvious that even the client already knows it. What the client does not know is how to go about attaining his legal rights, that is the practice and procedure of the law as opposed to the law itself. The solicitor enters into a relationship with his client in which he undertakes to render a proper professional standard of service. This undertaking is backed by professional, financial and other guarantees and we shall consider this in due course hereafter at page 7.

The legal profession is an entirely *independent* social service even though often a solicitor is paid from public funds, that is to say by way of legal aid for persons who do not have the means to undertake proceedings. Despite legal aid the profession is still truly independent, indeed in many instances legal aid is given so that the citizen may sue the government. In other words the government is directly funding litigation to be brought against itself!

In carrying out his work, a solicitor must necessarily rely on others who with him make up the full staff of his office. These may consist of the solicitor and his partners, if any. But in addition there are persons who are not partners, that is they do not have a share in the total profits of the practice at the year end. These include other solicitors who are not partners but are just employed by the practice and these are known as "assistant solicitors." In addition there are "unadmitted persons," that is people who work in the legal practice but are not qualified as solicitors, or "admitted" to use the correct term. These generally fall into two categories. Some of them are engaged on professional legal work and the most notable example here is the legal executive. The legal executive, whose exact role we shall consider shortly, acts more or less as a solicitor except that traditionally the legal executive special- ises to a greater extent than a solicitor. He will see the clients personally, give advice and conduct their cases. He is bound by exactly the same rules of ethics and etiquette which we shall consider later, as the solicitor himself. The legal executive and the assistant solicitor therefore are the prime example of "fee earners" that is those mem- bers of staff whose time and skill is charged out to the clients and whose work directly brings income into the office.

In addition there are people whose work is just as vital to the practice but who are not "fee earners." These are the back up staff such as accountants, cashiers, office manager, secretaries, telex machine or telephone operators, messengers and receptionists. The proper organ- isation of the office and the creating of a harmonious atmosphere so that all concerned have an enjoyable and stimulating working environ- ment is a vital task in the setting up of a modern legal firm.

We shall in the section on ethics and etiquette hereafter at page 8 consider what solicitors *cannot* do. With regard to what they *can* do, the diversity of practice is so great that it is possible here only to hint at it. The scope of a practice's work will be influenced by its clientele and by its locality. If it is in a big industrial town, London, a suburban residential district, a small village or market town in an agricultural area, in each case the clientele and type of work will differ. These differences lead to specialisation and many firms now will reject legal work of a kind in which they do not specialise.

In London for example there are firms who do not act for private individuals at all but only for limited companies and whose main concern is property development and planning regulation; likewise some specialise in taxation, E.C. law, company formation and admi- nistration and so on. In agricultural areas firms will specialise to some extent in the law as it relates to farming and agricultural holdings.

In medium size and smaller firms that make up the greater part of the profession there is less specialisation. Even though individuals may specialise, the full complement of partners and other fee earners in such firms cover a very broad range of work. So, almost every firm will have one or more persons who do the legal work in buying and selling houses and flats for owner occupation and the granting of leases. Conveyancing, as this work is called, accounts still for a very sub- stantial part of the income of the profession despite the fact that solicitors have recently lost their monopoly on this work and there is now a small specialised sub profession of licensed conveyancers who on qualifying may undertake conveyancing.

Any firm which has as its client a company with a work force of any size is likely to have to deal not merely with company law practice and taxation but also with problems of employment such as dismissal, redundancy and so on which may often take the firm's members into the industrial tribunal. In most urban areas there will be clients with matrimonial problems, not merely separation and divorce as such but maintenance, custody of children and problems to do with ownership of matrimonial property. There will also be more general litigation work, accident claims, breaches of contract and so on to be brought in the County Court and High Court. There will also inevitably be in most firms someone who does for at least part of his time a good deal of work in criminal practice particularly if the firm has an office near a magistrates court. In inner urban areas of big towns a high proportion of the work whether matrimonial, general litigation, or criminal is likely to be legally aided.

For those not in private practice it is possible to receive training in the legal department of a large organisation. There will be a different range of experience here some of which may be highly specialised. In others the scope may not be very different from the general experience of private practice. About a quarter of the students training for qualification as a legal executive are in legal offices in local government for example. In such offices there is a good deal of general experience of conveyancing and some litigation. There will conversely be no opportunity to obtain experience in, say, matrimonial practice. There are also subjects specific to local government such as compulsory purchase orders, traffic regulation orders, public health enforcement orders and those dealing with other legislation for the protection of the consumer.

THE QUALIFICATIONS OF SOLICITORS

A person wishing to become a solicitor must be of good character and have attained the standard of education now needed for admission to university. Almost all entrants to the solicitors' branch of the legal profession today are graduates, although it is still possible for Fellows of the Institute of Legal Executives to qualify as solicitors without having obtained a degree.

A person who wishes to qualify as a solicitor must at present pass the Solicitors' Final Examination and in addition complete a two year training contract which is the name now given to what used to be called "Articles of Clerkship." A training contract must be carried out within the office of a solicitor who must undertake to give experience to the trainee solicitor in a number of the many fields of legal practice.

The great majority of entrants to the profession now have a law degree and in the main go straight from this law degree on to a course of one year at either the College of Law or one of a number of approved Polytechnics offering a course leading to the Solicitors' Final Examination. This is an examination with a heavy practical bias covering most of the areas of mainstream legal practice. After completion of that examination the candidate will then commence his training contract, on fulfilment of which he will be entitled to be "admitted" as a solicitor.

There are two other main routes to qualification. One is for the increasing number of persons who wish to enter the legal profession who have a first degree in some discipline other than law. Such people have already demonstrated their intellectual ability by the acquisition of a non-law degree and therefore all that is required of them is a one year preliminary training in the basic legal subjects. Again the College of Law and many Polytechnics offer this course, which leads to either a Diploma in law or the passing of the so called Common Professional Examination. Thereafter such students proceed to the one year vocational course leading to the Solicitors' Final Examination.

The other route to qualification is available to Fellows of the Institute of Legal Executives. Fellows can go on to qualify as solicitors and indeed currently about one in three of all Fellows do go on to become admitted. Fellows are entitled to exemption from some aspects of the solicitors' qualifying procedure.

With effect from September 1993 the uniform Law Society Finals Course and examination which currently exists will be replaced by the "Legal Practice Course" which will be offered by the College of Law and a number of Polytechnics and Universities. The main differences will be an even greater practical emphasis in the course and the addition of substantial elements of "skills training" in such areas as Advocacy, Negotiation, Drafting and Interviewing. More importantly, as from September 1993 each institution will be responsible for administering examinations and continuing assessment to its own candidates and there will be no centrally run examination. The Law Society will however continue to occupy a supervisory role over the institutions offering the course. Courses are likely increasingly to be offered in a part-time format, probably over two years, in view of the lack of mandatory state grants which have caused students from impecunious backgrounds grave difficulty in qualifying at present, which difficulties are likely to be exacerbated since course fees for the new Legal Practice Course may well be in excess of £4,000 per annum.

On admission as a solicitor, application can be made to the Law Society for a practising certificate, without which a solicitor cannot practice. There is an annual fee, fixed with the approval of the Master of the Rolls, and in addition a compulsory professional insurance premium is payable and a contribution to the indemnity fund. The latter makes it possible to make good losses to clients from defalcations and other risks that are not within the insurance cover. There are restrictions on independent practice in the first three years after admission.

A solicitor who holds a current practising certificate is entitled to practice as a solicitor and to undertake the kind of legal work which is reserved to solicitors (and others, whose numbers are insignificant) by the Solicitors Act 1974. The effect is that at present the transfer of title to land (conveyancing), bringing and defending proceedings in court and certain work in connection with the estates of deceased persons can only be done in a solicitor's office (whether in a firm of solicitors in private practice or wherever else solicitors are employed). The transfer of title to land (conveyancing) is also, at present, reserved to solicitors and licensed conveyancers.

THE LAW SOCIETY

We are going to consider separately the question of ethics and etiquette. The Law Society has a dual role which is sometimes a little uncomfortable, in that it regulates the conduct of the general body of solicitors by virtue of the powers contained in the Solicitors' Act 1974. It also however, acts as a voluntary association which solicitors may join although they do not have to do so. In this capacity it provides professional and social facilities and amenities in return for the membership fee. It also acts in this capacity as something of a "trade union" for solicitors representing the interests of solicitors, in making submissions to government bodies and sometimes in negotiation with those bodies, for example on the question of rates of fees payable for legal aid work, and in proposing various improvements to the solicitor's lot, *e.g.* it has frequently suggested increased rights of audience for solicitors and even the possibility of appointment to the High Court bench. These matters are currently much under consideration in the light of the consultation process that is going on pursuant to the Courts and Legal Services Act 1990, which provides in principle for the extension of rights of audience in the higher courts.

The Council of the Society with the concurrence of the Master of the Rolls makes rules concerning professional practice, conduct and discipline, the maintaining of proper books of accounts, etc. We shall be considering certain of the specific aspects of this later at page 8. For the moment, we can consider three particular monetary matters which affect solicitors and which are overseen by the Law Society.

(1) The accounts rules are particularly strict in relation to money held by a solicitor on behalf of a client. This may be, *e.g.* where a solicitor is acting in the administration of an estate and has to collect in the assets of the estate before distribution; or more commonly it is a regular feature of practice where for example between the signing of a contract to sell a house and the completion of the sale, the deposit (which is usually 10 per cent. of the sale price) is held by the solicitor in his account. Clients' monies must not be mixed up with the practice's own accounts, that is, the money belonging to the partners. Clients' monies must be kept in a separate clients' account and then must never be drawn on for the solicitor's own purposes. At the end of the transaction the solicitor must account to the client for any balance which is due to him, taking into account the solicitor's own charges which can then validly be retained out of the money in the clients' account. The Society has power to inspect a solicitors' books of account and every solicitor must present annually a report from an independent accountant certifying that the accounts are in order. The most frequent cause of the Society having to *intervene* in a solicitors' practice (see later page 9) is where there is difficulty with the administration of a clients' account and default or dishonesty is suspected.

(2) Apart from this supervisory function of the Law Society, another form of protection for the client is compulsory

insurance. Under the Solicitors' Indemnity Insurance Rules all solicitors in practice are required to effect insurance up to one million pounds worth of liability per claim. This insurance is to cover liability in law to the solicitor's client for negligence and for other risks such as failure to account for clients' monies or dishonesty and fraud of the solicitor's staff or loss of documents.

(3) Solicitors are also required to contribute to the Compensation Fund, the purpose of which is to make good losses of clients' monies which have been misappropriated by any solicitor and which cannot be recovered from that solicitor. The fund makes grants to those who have suffered loss by reason of the dishonesty of the solicitor or his employee in connection with the solicitor's practice. The fund is something of a "last resort" so that if there is any insurance covering the matter, then first recourse must be had to that insurance. It will sometimes be that one of several partners has dishonestly made off with the client's money. In such a case the insurance of the existing partners may be adequate to recompense the client who has suffered loss, without having recourse to the fund. Only if this is not possible is there likely to be need for an award out of the fund.

THE CONTROL OF SOLICITORS

PROFESSIONAL MISCONDUCT

(1) *The Solicitors' Complaints Bureau*

The Professional Standards and Development Directorate of the Law Society has responsibility for the maintenance of professional standards and for the provision of advice and assistance to the profession on matters of professional conduct. The Council of the Law Society has delegated its powers for the enforcement of professional conduct to the Solicitors' Complaints Bureau and all complaints about solicitors received by the Society are referred to the Bureau in the first instance. The most important part of the Bureau is its investigation committee, the majority of whom are not solicitors. When a complaint is received it is first referred to an investigation officer on the Solicitors' Complaints Bureau staff. He will investigate the complaint and see whether there is a case to answer. This may include communicating the complaint to the solicitor with a request for an explanation (and a warning that any reply may be used should disciplinary proceedings be necessary). The most common cause of complaint is "breakdown in communications" covering everything from writing incomprehensible letters, to not responding to letters at all, being totally unavailable on the telephone, and so on. More serious charges include negligence, gross delay, unprofessional conduct and conflict of interest. The investigating officer may attempt to conciliate between the solicitor and the complainant. Complainants are not always disgruntled clients; many complaints are received from other members of the public affected by solicitors and sometimes from other solicitors. The investigations committee may then recommend that no further action should be taken. Obviously where many thousands of complaints are received from solicitors' clients many will be in the end discovered to be unfounded. In litigation particularly, somebody has to lose and there are always disgruntled clients who will blame their solicitor. If however the investigation committee thinks the matter should go further it is referred to the *adjudication committee* with a recommendation as to action. This committee comprises nine Law Society Council members, three other solicitors and six lay people. It has powers to take the following action:

(i) Order a refund of fees paid to the solicitor

(ii) To rebuke or reprimand the solicitor

(iii) To impose conditions on the solicitor's practising certificate

(iv) In more serious matters to apply on behalf of the Law Society to the Solicitors' Disciplinary Tribunal (see below).

(2) *The Legal Services Ombudsman*

The Legal Services Ombudsman is appointed under ss.21–26 of the Courts and Legal Services Act 1990. The Ombudsman has powers to investigate the handling of complaints by the Law Society (and indeed by the Bar Council). He may re-investigate the complaint itself and thereafter recommend any proper remedy including the payment of compensation if it is appropriate. In addition the Ombudsman has the power to suggest improvements which he considers necessary for the complaints procedures of professional bodies. He will prepare an annual report for the Lord Chancellor and Parliament. In addition, if his recommendations for a payment of compensation are not met he may publicise the facts wherever he wishes (for example in a local or national newspaper) including giving the reasons why the solicitor concerned has not complied with his recommendation. At present the Ombudsman has a staff of about 12 consisting of a legal adviser, investigating officers and support staff.

(3) *Intervention in solicitors' practice*

The Law Society has the power to *intervene* in a solicitors' practice, that is to take it over and manage it. The most common reason for this is where there is a suspicion of dishonesty on the part of the solicitor or members of his staff or failure to comply with the Accounts Rules. In addition the Society sometimes intervenes where a sole practitioner has died and there is delay in appointing someone else to take over the running of the practice so that existing clients may be suffering.

(4) *The Solicitors' Disciplinary Tribunal*

This body is entirely independent of the Law Society and is established by the Solicitors' Act 1974. Its members are appointed by the Master of the Rolls and are solicitors and laymen. Its hearings are conducted like a court of law and it determines applications in respect of solicitors relating to allegations of conduct unbefitting a solicitor and other disciplinary matters. The vast majority of applications are made on behalf of the Law Society itself following a complaint to the Solicitors' Complaints Bureau, but in some instances it is open to anyone to make an application to the Tribunal directly.

The Tribunal has power to strike off the Roll the name of the solicitor, or to suspend him from practice or to impose a fine. In addition it has the power to order the payment of costs. In relation to legal executives it has the power to make an order prohibiting employment of any legal executive in any solicitor's practice without the prior obtaining of the written permission of the Law Society.

PROFESSIONAL NEGLIGENCE

It will therefore be observed that under the various procedures indicated above, a disgruntled client ought in the end to obtain satisfaction. It must however be indicated that if what is alleged against a solicitor is in effect professional negligence, that the client will be expected to pursue his remedies in the courts and not through these bodies in the first instance. Of course professional negligence may also amount to professional misconduct but neither the Disciplinary Tribunal nor the Solicitors' Complaints Bureau can be seen to be prejudging a matter, especially one in which many thousands of pounds may be involved, where the client really ought to pursue his claim in the ordinary courts which are much better fitted for the necessary investigatory procedures to get at the truth of the allegations.

FORMS OF PRACTICE

Of over 55,000 solicitors who have practising certificates, some 87 per cent. are in private practice. There are roughly 6,500 firms in England and Wales. In London and other large cities there are many large firms with 20 or more partners. Their clients include many of the larger national and multi-national companies. Outside the centre of London the average firm tends to have four or five partners. Many have fewer and there is a sizeable proportion of solicitors (over 3,000) practising single handed, although they will, of course, have supporting staff including legal executives. The solicitors who own a firm are referred to as *principals*. The relationship between principals—their capital contributions, shares of the profits and so on—are regulated by a partnership deed which also says what is to happen if the partners decide to split up.

Apart from practice as partnership or sole practitioner there was a provision in section 9 of the Administration of Justice Act 1985 authorising the Law Society to make rules permitting solicitors to incorporate their practices, that is to practice as a limited company. Recently the Solicitors' Incorporated Practice Rules 1988 have been made under the provisions of the 1985 Act so that the profession may have a chance to consider them. An incorporated practice must be approved by the Law Society and is then known as a "recognised body." Recognition by the Law Society is renewable every 3 years. In general the Rules permit solicitors to practice in the form of limited companies and provide that the shareholders and directors of such companies must all be solicitors with a practising certificate, so that the ban on sharing of fees with non-solicitors is maintained. There are other rules requiring additional insurance to be taken out in respect of claims made against the solicitors practice and requiring the shareholders to enter into covenants with the Council to guarantee any sums paid out from the Compensation Fund to persons who have suffered loss as a result of the solicitors practice or its individual members.

In addition to private practice, solicitors play a prominent part in employment, industry and commerce, in local and central government and in a wide range of statutory and voluntary bodies. Solicitors employed by the principals of a firm in a salaried capacity are called *assistant solicitors* and there are many in industry, commerce, etc., who go under this designation.

There is now a branch of practice which those who work in it call "the public sector" that is, solicitors who work in law centres. These, of which there are over 50, are to be found in some of the older residential areas of our big cities. They offer a free service to persons who will not, or cannot afford to, see a solicitor in private practice. Many of our older inner suburbs are, on the one hand, without many solicitors practising there and, on the other, productive of difficulties and tensions over matters such as housing, matrimonial matters and juvenile crime. It is widely acknowledged that private practice has not hitherto catered in any adequate way for the underprivileged in such areas and the legal aid provisions do not in themselves seem to meet the need fully. There seems to be a psychological barrier in the way of people in such circumstances seeking a solution to their problems by legal action and it is this barrier that the law centres want to break down.

The solicitors who take up the work of law centres are often young and infused with the desire to do all they can to improve the lot of the particular clients they seek to serve. They therefore in many cases go outside the traditional role of solicitors in private practice and actively involve themselves in and foster social movements towards betterment by the various pressure groups that operate in the area. All such centres are dependent on public funds for their support.

RELATIONS BETWEEN SOLICITOR AND CLIENT

The range of work undertaken in private practice will be looked at in some detail below. Here we must refer to the relationship of confidence which exists between the solicitor and his client. It sets its mark on all that goes on in the office and all who work there. No client would leave his business in the care of a solicitor for five minutes if he did not feel sure that his private affairs were a secret between himself, the solicitor or legal executive advising him, and those in the office who must necessarily have knowledge of the client's affairs.

The main characteristic which typifies the solicitor's relationship with his client is its personal character. A solicitor's work starts with a personal interview with his client. It could not be otherwise. The client is going into something that, at best, he imperfectly understands. The solicitor does not know the nature of the client's problem. It is an exploration on both sides (other, of course, than cases where a solicitor has a standing arrangement with a business client to take a series of routine matters all of a similar kind). In this the solicitor is not unlike the doctor who, if he is to diagnose his patient's illness and prescribe correctly, must first physically examine him. The solicitor nowhere demonstrates his abilities more clearly than in his care and skill in probing into the legal basis of his client's problem, picking out the significant from the irrelevant and amassing the detailed informative material required for its solution. He must be able to see his client's problem as a whole. He must put it in the context of the client's financial position and may have to take into his reckoning the delicate personal relationships which swift and drastic legal action will be in danger of disturbing. Life is not lived in compartments—legal, financial, matrimonial and so on—and it is not inapt to think of the solicitor as the man of affairs, the family and business confidant. He needs the academic polish that his professional education ensures, but he needs more than this. He must be shrewd, attentive and painstaking. These qualities need to be shared by those who work for him, not least by those who interview clients and conduct their affairs on the solicitor's behalf.

Solicitors who are employed in industry, commerce or central or local government obviously have a rather different position. They only have one client—their employer. Many such posts have a large administrative or managerial component and indeed many employed solicitors are directors of companies or chief executives of local authorities. We shall consider in due course the special position of such solicitors in terms of ethics and etiquette.

THE BARRISTER AND THE COURT

It is natural to think of lawyers in the courts as being the judges and the barristers in their robes. In the High Court these are the main practitioners, but they could not operate unless the ground had been prepared for them by solicitors and their staffs, nor without the support services provided by the permanent staff of the courts. These exist at a great range of levels, from the Senior Master of Queen's Bench and Queen's Remembrancer to the court ushers. It is not possible to list all these levels here, but when considering the branches of practice before the several courts later in this book it will be necessary to look in some detail at the functions of the court officers who assist the judges and the lay magistrates. It must also be borne in mind that in the lower courts the greater part of advocacy is in the hands of solicitors.

The Bar, as the body of practising barristers is called, still has a largely conventional basis. Bar students join one of the four Inns of Court, Lincoln's Inn, Gray's Inn and the Middle and Inner Temples, survivals of the mediaeval places of residence of the "pleaders" and "apprentices" of former times. The Bar is still largely self-governing (through the Senate of the Inns of Court and the Bar Council) and self-financing. Students still attend the regulation number of dinners in the Hall of their Inn, a symbol of the fellowship which membership of an Inn imparts, and also reflecting the tradition of passing on the learning and wisdom of the profession by precept and example.

Bar students are always university graduates or graduate during their Bar training. The only exceptions are a few "mature" students who transfer from other professions. After passing the Bar examination they are called to the Bar. Before practising they must serve a year in pupillage. That is, they are required to serve an established member of the Bar, assisting him in the preparation of his cases, including researching the law needed for a particular case ("devilling"). In the second six months of pupillage, the pupil may take briefs and appear in court as an advocate.

The number of practising barristers is small compared with solicitors—about 6,400 in 1992. They are essentially individual practitioners. Although they come together in shared accommodation known as Chambers, they are not permitted to join together in partnership. In this, they are not unlike doctors whose responsibility is always that of the individual doctor to the individual patient. So the barrister's responsibility is that of the individual member of the Bar to the individual client. In the case of the barrister, however, there is the additional complication that the responsibility to the client is through the solicitor. Because of the way the profession has developed the business relations of the barrister are unique. He does not enter into a contract with the solicitor "instructing" him. Still less with the client. He does not strictly speaking make a charge for his services. He receives an honorarium and cannot sue if it is not paid. Neither is it possible for a barrister to be sued for negligence in respect of his work as an advocate in court. Of particular importance to the solicitor is the rule that with insignificant exceptions only a solicitor can engage a barrister. The barrister, therefore, has two clients: the professional client (*i.e.* the solicitor) and the "lay" client (the person for whom the solicitor acts). But when engaged he represents not the solicitor who engages him but the lay client. All communications with the barrister go through the solicitor, who (or whose legal executive) is in the great majority of instances present when the client is interviewed by the barrister.

As mentioned above, barristers work in groups in chambers. These are offices, often in a large building in the vicinity of the courts. In London the majority of chambers are still in the four Inns of Court. Each set of chambers has a senior member of the Bar as its head and perhaps 10 to 20 other barristers. The work of the barristers flows to them from solicitors via the senior clerk of the chambers, a person who has considerable influence on the kind of work the barristers for whom he is responsible undertake and the financial reward they obtain. He "combines the functions of office administrator and accountant, business manager, agent, adviser and friend" (Benson Report). The barrister's clerk is remunerated often by a straight commission based on the fees of the barristers he represents. Sometimes his commission is as high as 10 per cent. of each fee note which he delivers on behalf of each barrister whom he represents. Increasingly however there is a move towards salaried clerks in barristers' chambers. Sometimes there is a combination of basic salary and relatively modest rate of commission, (*e.g.* 1 per cent. on all the fees of each barrister). With the growing complexity of court work and the computerisation of court records and an increasing sophistication of the listing processes for court cases, many chambers are moving both to increased size in the interests of efficient administration and expertise, (*e.g.* chambers of up to 40 or more barristers are no longer uncommon) and also to a greater expertise in the administrative backup which they receive. Thus some chambers have sought to engage professional administrators, often with qualifications in other areas such as accountancy or management, rather than taking clerks who have come up by the traditional route (that is who have joined often straight from school and trained as junior clerks under the tuition of an existing clerk to chambers).

Nonetheless, by whatever route a clerk or chambers administrator, has obtained his position his functions are likely to be very similar to those which the barrister's clerk traditionally had. His main duty will be to ensure that each member of his chambers is as fully employed as he is able to arrange, that the important cases in which each member of chambers is engaged do not come into different courts on the same day, and to negotiate the fees for the barristers in his chambers with the solicitor or Legal Executive who wishes to employ the barrister concerned. In addition he may attempt to procure work for his barristers in discussion with solicitors who are uncertain about the relative kinds of expertise of each of the barristers in his chambers, and about whom they should brief for any particular case. His work therefore is entirely taken up in promoting the interests of the barristers by whom he is employed.

Most barristers concentrate on advocacy. Their work in chambers is concerned with preparation for appearances in court, consultations with clients and solicitors or the drafting of documents (pleadings) for use in court proceedings. On the other hand, others, particularly those who choose Chancery work, spend little or no time in court, but specialise in advising on the law or drafting legal documents which may be needed, for instance to record complex business deals or to set up technical, professional or other business relationships.

The Inns of Court cluster around the Royal Courts of Justice in the Strand. There are also six "circuits" based on provincial centres in which High Court cases are heard. Each circuit has its own organisation concerned with such matters as the siting of chambers. On being called to the Bar, a barrister decides whether he will be a member of a circuit or practice in London chambers. He can only be a member of one circuit, but he may appear in court anywhere.

Barristers who have attained the right degree of seniority in practice are able to petition the Queen to be made Queen's Counsel (Q.C.). Every year the Queen, advised by the Lord Chancellor appoints a small number of new Q.C.s who as a body account for perhaps 10 per cent. of the whole number of barristers. Originally Q.C.s (or K.C.s when there is a king) were selected to appear in cases in which the Crown had a direct interest and were in effect the protectors of that interest. Today those who "take silk" as the phrase is, from the silk gown Q.C.s wear, in effect give notice that they will only accept the larger and more complex or important briefs and will not normally do the work which "juniors" (the name applied to all who are not Q.C.s—of whatever age) habitually do in drafting the pleadings necessary in the preparation of cases for trial.

It is from the Bar that the great majority of appointments "to the bench," (*i.e.* of judges) are made, by the recommendation of the Lord Chancellor. Previously all judges were barristers of at least 10 years standing. Now, however, recorders, who are part-time circuit judges, may be appointed from among solicitors of 10 years standing and some of these later become full time circuit judges.

The student's first contact with the Courts is likely to be through the local county court or district registry of the High Court. Here, next to the judge, the most important official is the district judge who is usually a solicitor. His particular functions are described below (see p. 294).

Students whose firms are near the law courts in the Strand, London will learn of the functions of the masters of the High Court. These are lawyers, whose functions correspond roughly to those of the district judges in the county court and district registries of the High Court. Legal executives regularly appear on behalf of their principals before district judges and masters, whose decisions can have a crucial effect on the course of the cases brought before them.

ADVOCACY AND RIGHTS OF AUDIENCE

Advocacy is the prerogative of the barrister and the solicitor. It calls for a balance between the ends of justice and the personal interests and objectives of the client. The barrister and the solicitor, by history and by training, serve both objectives: they are as much servants of the court as they are representatives of the client. Without this dual allegiance, there would be serious dangers of trials being drawn out with insubstantial arguments and unfair advantage being taken of inadequate preparation by opposing lawyers. It is a part of the duty of the advocate not to extend his advocacy beyond the merits of his case and if he is arguing a point of law, he must disclose to the court previous reported cases where they tell against him.

The professional advocate, whether barrister or solicitor, is generally held to be one of the safeguards of the liberty of the subject and a bulwark of his legal rights. Independence and objectivity are essential attributes of the profession and are supported by the traditional rules of conduct and legal principles that apply to both branches. Some of these have been mentioned above, *e.g.* the immunity of the lawyer from liability for negligence in the conduct of a case in court. This leaves him free to act in accordance with principles even where this may conflict with the way the client thinks his case should be conducted. There are rules also to ensure that an advocate does not appear in circumstances in which he would have a conflict of interests.

The way in which advocacy is shared between barristers and solicitors partly depends on the right to appear and conduct cases before the various courts. This is the right of audience. The courts, *i.e.* the judges, have always reserved the right to decide who may appear before them. Obviously, litigants in person cannot be deprived of this right. The rights of lawyers to appear as representatives is still largely based on the traditional practice of the courts, although in the case of the county court the rules have been prescribed by statute.

These traditional practices however are likely to be subject to some changes at least in the early future. The question of rights of audience is now governed by ss.27–33 of the Courts and Legal Services Act 1990. These sections provide for the grant of rights of audience before various courts. They are however subject to rights being granted by appropriate authorised bodies which are the General Council of the Bar, the Law Society and any professional other body which has been designated by Order in Council as an authorised body for the purposes of the sections. At the time of writing there is a substantial consultation process being undertaken to determine precisely how, to whom and when the extended rights of audience should be given before courts where there is at present no right of audience for the class of persons concerned. The debate currently centres on the extent to which solicitors in private practice, and those employed in industry and commerce, should be given extended rights of audience before the higher courts, and similarly the extent to which barristers who are employed in commerce and industry should also be given such rights.

A barrister is able to appear before any court whatsoever and, with very minor exceptions, appearing in the High Court is the exclusive preserve of the Bar. A solicitor can only appear before a High Court judge in open court in certain bankruptcy applications and on one or two other procedural matters. Solicitors also have only very limited rights of audience in the Crown Court at present, *e.g.* on appeals from the magistrates' court where the same solicitor or one from the same firm appeared in the court below.

In the County Court solicitors and barristers have equal rights, and with the increase in the financial jurisdiction of County Courts this will clearly give solicitors the opportunity to practice advocacy in cases of considerably greater substance than hitherto. In addition a number of other representatives are permitted to appear by statute or at the discretion of the County Court Judge.

In the magistrates' court, whilst solicitors and barristers have equal rights, they are shared with a large number of other persons who are by custom allowed to conduct prosecutions and civil applications: central or local government officials and others.

In most tribunals there are no formal restrictions on who may appear as a representative.

The foregoing description does not deal with the applications that take place both in the High Court and the county court in chambers. These hearings in chambers may be of crucial importance to the progress of the case. The more important the nature of the appointment, the more likely it is that a barrister or solicitor will appear, or an experienced legal executive. In more routine procedural matters most cases are dealt with by legal executives of more junior rank or other unadmitted personnel.

THE LEGAL EXECUTIVE

For students who are taking up a career in the law, but who do not have an immediate aim to be either barristers or solicitors, the most important role in the profession is that of the legal executive. There have been unadmitted personnel in the solicitor's profession from the earliest times, but their functions have changed. One of the oldest skills in a solicitor's office was that of engrossing: writing documents in a fair round hand with many embellishments on parchment or parchment paper. Clerks achieved great proficiency in this and many beautiful examples of their work are met as documents still in operation today. It is natural that the more able clerks engaged on this and other comparable duties should in time learn much about the content and significance of the documents they were handling so that they were able to draft the documents themselves. Gradually, as clerks became more knowledgeable and solicitors' practice became wider and more technical, the delegation of legal work to clerks increased so that in time a clerk would be carrying his own case load on behalf of the principal by whom he was employed. The engrossing function gradually became disused as the typewriter came into use in the latter part of the last century, but the unadmitted staff carrying out legal work expanded and increased their seniority, so that many were given the title of managing clerk. In 1892 the Solicitors' Managing Clerks' Association was founded to represent their interests. The managing clerk now had a recognised position in the structure of the profession, which has continued to develop although the title is no longer in general use.

In 1949 the Association introduced examinations leading to the award of certificates in order to establish measurable levels of attainment and so a clearer status for certificated personnel within the profession. Unfortunately, little recognition was given by employers to the existence of certificates and the scheme did not meet with the success anticipated.

In 1955 a fresh approach was made to the problem when the Association came forward with proposals to the Law Society which they hoped would improve the status of managing clerks as well as increasing the number of school leavers joining the profession. A joint committee was set up which worked out a scheme for a new parent body to be formed with membership open to all managing clerks and offering courses of education, training and examination through which solicitors' staff could progress to recognised qualifications. The scheme was approved by the Law Society in 1961.

Because the title managing clerk had come to be used indiscriminately and without regard to qualification or experience a new name was needed which would indicate a connection with the law and at the same time describe the status of the person concerned. A true managing clerk was clearly an executive in legal work and, therefore, "legal executive" was decided upon by the joint committee who recommended that the name of the new parent body should be "The Institute of Legal Executives" and that those clerks who reached fellowship, the highest grade of membership of the Institute, should be called Legal Executives and be entitled to use the letters F.Inst.L.Ex. after their names. The Institute came into being on January 1, 1963 and with it the examination and qualification system. The popularity of the new title was such that its use was permitted and even encouraged in some parts of the profession for persons who were old style managing clerks without formal qualifications and the correct usage is even today often misunderstood.

Legal Executives are regularly entrusted by their principals, that is the partners of the firms that employ them, with the conduct of matters in the office. The distinguishing feature of the legal executive is specialisation in one or other of the branches of solicitors' practice. Within his chosen subject a legal executive may have expertise comparable with that of a solicitor and will expect to have regular and direct contact with clients on matters he is conducting. It has to be borne in mind that his responsibilities are to his principals and that only they have formal responsibility to the client. Hence, the principal will decide how far to delegate the work to his legal executive and how closely his work should be supervised.

The Law Society has given recognition to the particular value to the profession of the Institute's qualifications in several ways, including a measure of recognition of Institute qualifications for the purpose of exemptions from papers in the Law Society's own examinations. Under the Solicitors' Practice Rules a solicitor is required to ensure that every office where he or his firm practises is properly supervised. Apart from a solicitor holding a practising certificate the only person who will in future be authorised to take charge of an office is a Fellow of the Institute confirmed by the Institute as being of good standing and having been admitted as a Fellow for not less than five years. Fellows are authorised to sign cheques on solicitors' clients' accounts. And by the County Courts (Rights of Audience) Direction 1977, Fellows of the Institute engaged in litigation have the right to address the court on:

(a) an unopposed application for adjournment; or

(b) an application for judgment by consent (except where, notwithstanding the consent, a question arises as to the applicant's entitlement to the judgment or its terms).

There are at present about 21,800 members of the Institute including Fellows, Associates and Students.

SOLICITORS' CHARGES

At the end of the case or matter in question a solicitor will present a bill to his client. This bill is often called the solicitor's *costs*. The word "costs" in fact covers two elements; the first of them is the actual out of pocket expenses or disbursements paid on the client's behalf as the matter goes along, such as land registry fees or stamp duty in conveyancing, court fees in litigation, etc. In addition there is the solicitor's own charge. The proper term for this is actually "profit costs." This latter figure is the fee for the only thing which the solicitor in fact has to sell, which is his time and skill. The figure is based largely on the time involved on the client's matter. The accurate recording of the time spent on a client's matter is of great importance and we shall return to this in the next section. The fee paid for the solicitor's time will not of course be entirely profit for the partners. Allowed for in the fee will be a very large element which will only cover the overheads of running the legal office and the salaries of those persons who are not partners. Thus, when the lay public are horrified to find that a solicitor's hourly charging rate is say £75 and they therefore imagine that this person is earning over £3,000 per week they are of course in error. Of an hourly charging rate of £75 in any given practice the amount to be allowed for overheads and office expenses may well be £50 or even more and only the balance over that figure is actually the net profit to the practice.

We shall shortly consider the factors to be taken into account in assessing solicitors' fees. It must be borne in mind however that in the modern world these considerations only apply to certain types of case. In some cases, for example work done under criminal legal aid in the Magistrates' Court or when advising a client under the Green Form Scheme (see page 77) fixed hourly rates are allowed by the state, which pays the fees. In other kinds of cases particularly conveyancing it is becoming increasingly common for the clients to shop around and obtain a fixed price quote from a solicitor for doing conveyancing work, which the solicitor must usually stick to no matter how difficult or time consuming the matter proves to be in the end. In principle however, when deciding on what is a proper rate to charge for legal work the factors which may be taken into account are almost identical whether the case is *non-contentious*, (*e.g.* probate, company formation, taxation advice) or *contentious* that is litigation. A solicitor is entitled to charge what is "fair and reasonable in all circumstances" having regard in particular to the following factors:

(a) The complexity of the cause or matter in question and the difficulty or novelty of the problems involved.

(b) The skills, specialised knowledge and responsibility required of the solicitor and the time and effort expended by him.

(c) The number and importance of the documents (however brief) prepared or perused in connection with the matter.

(d) The place and circumstances in which the business involved is transacted.

(e) The importance of the cause or matter to the client.

(f) Where money or property is involved, its amount or value.

These are common sense categories which assist in judging how much to charge for a given matter. Therefore in a case involving the preparation of complex documents, probably with some urgency, where large sums of money are involved so that the work can only be done by very senior skilled solicitors or legal executives, a much higher hourly charging rate will be permitted than for say advising someone in connection with a dispute with their neighbours over maintenance to a boundary wall, important though this latter problem will of course be for the client who suffers it.

Where a solicitor at the end of a matter delivers a bill to his own client, therefore the client will usually pay the bill. Indeed it is becoming increasingly prudent for solicitors to obtain money on account of costs from clients before ever commencing a matter of any kind for clients. To do this will save any risk of bad debts. If the client wishes to dispute the bill then there are two different procedures depending upon whether the bill is in relation to a contentious matter or non-contentious matter. In relation to a contentious matter the client is entitled to have the bill "taxed" by the court. The word "taxed" should not be misunderstood. It has nothing to do with the Inland Revenue but is an old word meaning "assessed." Where the client insists on this procedure then the solicitor must obtain an appointment with an officer of the court called a "taxing officer" and present the bill in a certain prescribed form. The client and the solicitor will attend and the solicitor will be called upon to justify each item in the bill and the way in which it has been charged, *e.g.* the hourly rate claimed for the work. The taxing officer will listen to the client's objections to the bill either in terms of individual items, or hourly rate charged, etc., and if he agrees with the objection to any item, it will be struck out of the bill or "taxed off" to use the proper term. The taxing officer will then certify what is the total correct charge for the client to have to pay. If the client then refuses to pay, the solicitor may enforce the bill by suing the client. A client is still entitled to have a bill taxed even though he has already deposited with the solicitor in advance sufficient monies to cover it. In such a case, the solicitor, after the bill has been taxed will be obliged to reimburse the client with any amounts that were deducted from the bill by the taxing officer. It must of course be borne in mind that in litigation matters there might well be an order for some other person to pay all or part of the client's bill and indeed there might be an order for the client to pay all or part of some other person's bill and we shall return to this below.

In non-contentious business the charges are calculated by reference to more or less the same factors as in contentious business. Under the regulations, a solicitor and client may fix the fees by agreement in advance. We have already referred to this in the context of a client telephoning to obtain firm quotations for conveyancing work. If the matter is not proceeding on this basis then the client still has the right to have the charges made by the solicitor after the work has been done reviewed. The client is entitled to ask for taxation of the bill by the court, just as in the case of a client in contentious matters but there is a further possible procedure which is swifter and less costly; under the Solicitors' Remuneration Order 1972 a client may ask the solicitor to obtain an assessment of the proper costs by the Law Society. The solicitor is required to obtain a certificate from the Law Society stating its opinion whether the amount charged is fair and reasonable or should be reduced. There is no charge to the client for this certificate. A solicitor may not sue a client to recover his charges in a non-contentious matter until the expiry of one month from the solicitor informing the client of his right to require a remuneration certificate and of the possibility of having the bill taxed by the court.

In litigation as we have indicated above, there is of course the possibility that all or part of the client's bill will be paid by some other person, *i.e.* the loser of the litigation. It is almost unheard of for there to be fixed fees agreed in advance with one's own client in relation to litigation, because the course of litigation is so unpredictable, that is, it is impossible to say how long the case will take or what procedural steps will be involved. It is even difficult to give a realistic estimate in advance of what the costs of the case may be. In ordinary litigation the court usually orders the loser to pay a large proportion of the winner's costs. Indeed, in routine litigation the order may in effect be that the loser pays the whole of the winner's costs. In such a situation where an individual is called upon to pay the costs of someone else's solicitor there must obviously be a fair way of assessing what those costs should be. This procedure is called *taxation* as we have seen. It is more or less the same in both county court and High Court. A detailed bill must be prepared with each item set out and the relevant fees charged against the item. Full indication must be given of the time spent on each aspect of the matter. An appointment before the taxing officer of the court is taken out and both parties attend. The loser may object to each individual item in the bill or the total amount or the hourly rate and the solicitor will be called upon to justify these items. Items will then be either allowed or disallowed. The final total of the bill after taking account of the objections will then be payable by the loser. To short circuit this procedure which is time consuming, in most routine litigation the solicitors for the winner send the loser's solicitors a copy of their bill, or simply a letter setting out the main headings and what the bill will be, and invite them to agree a figure for the costs. In the vast majority of cases it is possible to agree a figure for costs because it is in everybody's interest to do so.

In criminal cases the position is rather different. If one is acting for a client who is acquitted and who was not in receipt of legal aid then an application is usually made for the costs to be paid out of central funds, that is a Government fund established for this purpose. The costs will then be assessed by an officer of the court concerned whether it is a magistrates court or Crown Court. It is not usual to obtain an order that the prosecution themselves pay the costs of acquitted defendants unless there has been some improper conduct by the prosecution.

If a legally aided person is acquitted then there is no need for there to be any other order for costs between the parties or from central funds. The normal order in such a case is that if the legally aided person has not paid any contribution he is not called upon to do so and his solicitor will be remunerated from the Legal Aid Fund in the usual way. If he has paid a contribution then, unless the court thinks that there has been something wrong in the accused's own conduct such as for example, that he brought the prosecution upon himself by behaving foolishly, then his legal aid contribution will be returned to him and any future instalments will be cancelled.

The drawing up of bills of costs especially in litigation matters is an important and complex task. Considerable experience and first hand knowledge of the procedure and practice on taxation is vital. Very few solicitors now prepare their own bills. The need for litigation bills particularly to be in a very detailed form has led to the growth of a specialised sub profession called "costs draftsmen." These are commonly legal executives who have specialised in this area often since joining the firm. Larger firms will have their own costs draftsmen who will draft all the bills both contentious and non contentious. Some large firms may indeed have large costs departments which are often next to the offices of those who perform the cashiers or accounting functions at those firms, to provide easy access to details of clients' and office accounts. Medium sized and small firms however cannot usually afford to have one individual who does nothing but prepare bills all the time. Of course a legal executive may be the specialist draftsman and in addition run some matters of his own but this is probably increasingly rare. For firms who cannot afford to have a full time costs draftsman, freelance costs draftsmen practising alone or in partnership provide the necessary service. The solicitor will send his whole file to the costs draftsman with the request for him to prepare a bill for taxation at court or for delivery for the client as the case may be. This is one reason why it is vital to keep files in neat order so that the costs draftsman, who will never have seen the file before, can make sense of it and see just what was done at every stage. Proper details of the time expended must also be supplied. It is best if a full narrative is set out inside the file detailing exactly what was done for the client and at what stages, and drawing the costs draftsman's attention to anything that is not immediately apparent from the file which might justify a higher charge, or higher hourly rate of charging under any of the factors explained above. For example, suppose that part of the litigation in question involved a very urgent application to the court, so much so that the legal executive dealing with it had to cancel all his other appointments for that day with a good deal of inconvenience. Clearly a higher rate of charging should be allowed for the legal executive's time for that urgent day under the principle of "the importance of the matter to the client." The narrative supplied to the costs draftsman should explain this and the degree of inconvenience to the practice suffered by the need to concentrate on this client's affairs exclusively for one day.

Freelance costs draftsmen usually charge on a percentage basis based on the total of the bill they draft. This percentage is usually between 5 per cent. and 7½ per cent. It will immediately be seen that this will be a very unwelcome further overhead to a solicitor's practice, since this sum is not recoverable from any other person. So for example if one is delivering a bill for say £10,000 in respect of a lengthy and difficult matter, the costs draftsman's fee for preparing it will be perhaps £500 and this sum is therefore immediately lost to the practice. This provides a powerful incentive for the parties in litigation to agree costs rather than going through the procedure of taxation, because where costs can be agreed no detailed bill need be prepared. In such a case the solicitor for the successful party, either over the telephone or in correspondence invites the loser to say whether he will agree the costs and then provides his suggestions for the amount charged and give some details of the work done in a very brief form usually by letter. Agreement of costs is very common therefore.

The topic of costs in Civil cases is further discussed below in the chapter on proceedings in the County Court Act p. 367.

TIME RECORDING

The management of private practice requires concentration on the use of time and the recording of work done on a time basis. As a leading text book on the management of solicitor's offices states, "time, tempered of course by professional knowledge and skill, is the single commodity the lawyer has to sell and it also happens to be the one commodity which he cannot and never will be able to increase."

Time therefore is an important element in knowing how much to charge. The practice of recording time spent on client's matters is therefore a very important aspect of management. Research has shown that fee earners of whatever status in an average year can spend approximately 1,100 hours only which are chargeable directly to individual clients. This may not seem like a very great figure, given that most people think they work a 35 hour week for say 46 weeks of the year taking account of holidays. Indeed senior fee earners of course would think that they worked far longer than a 35 hour week. However a good deal of most fee earners' time will be spent on general work of a kind not attributable to any individual client such as keeping up with the law, general administration, travelling between offices and so on. The 1,100 hours that remain have to bring in sufficient fees to pay all the overheads of the office and to provide a reasonable profit for the partners. How the figure for hourly rate of charging should be computed will be a question of detailed individual calculation for each practice. Of course there are variations in hourly rates of charging, depending on the status of the fee earner so that a senior partner who deals only with substantial matters involving large sums of money can expect to charge his time at a considerably higher rate than that of a junior legal executive who deals mainly with debt collecting of a modest nature. The hourly rate is merely a way of costing time. The actual charge to be made to the client will vary upward from this basic cost rate taking into account the various factors which we have previously discussed.

The first task then is to ensure that all time is recorded against the client concerned. It is vital to remember that it is not merely major chunks of time such as one hour interviews that must be recorded but also phone calls, although here there is no alternative but to "round them up" to the nearest five minutes. Five minutes per phone call minimum is in fact probably quite fair given that there will inevitably be the need to locate a file, locate the place in the file, deal with the inquiry and then put the file away afterwards, having made a note of what was discussed. Time recording should now be a feature of all professional office management. In litigation, particularly where a bill is disputed and the taxation procedure has to be gone through, the taxing officer will inevitably need to be informed of the precise amounts of the time spent on the client's business. Rough guess estimates will no longer do on taxation in court.

The most common method of time recording is for each fee earner to have a daily or weekly time sheet on his desk which is maintained by him as the day goes on. Time in either five, 10 or 15 minutes slots is allotted to the client on whose business the time was spent. In some systems, for each entry a duplicate is pinned inside the client's file to assist in justifying the amount of time should there be a taxation. It is, anyway best to make file notes even of brief telephone calls to establish what has been discussed and/or agreed.

At the end of the day, or week, the master time sheet is sent to the cashier's office who will make a note of the time expended on each client's ledger card or master account. Thus, at the end of a matter it will be possible to have an exact knowledge of the time spent on the client's business as the basis for one element of the bill.

Naturally, completing these records is a time consuming matter in itself and this is the paradox. To keep an accurate and complete record, the constant attention of the fee earner is required and a lot of clerical time involved in processing it. However, there is no real alternative other than an entirely hit or miss method. The fact that filling in forms is unwelcome must not obscure the fact that there is no proper professional alternative. A half-heartedly applied or inefficient system is actually worse than useless. The firm must expect discipline from all the fee earners, from partners to the most junior legal executives in completing their time sheets. Correct habits of time recording from the earliest stages of training will be a good foundation for more senior responsibility.

Staff do sometimes worry about the "big brother is watching" syndrome. Of course it is possible to misuse a time system to make comparisons of the relative efficiency of individual staff members. However this would be very unusual. For example, a junior legal executive may only work for a small proportion of his or her time on his or her own files. A lot of time may be spent helping more senior staff on their files as a manner of training the junior legal executive. That time will therefore be recorded on the senior legal executive's matter. In any event the degree of time which cannot be spent on any client's matters such as for general administration, travel between offices, etc., will vary greatly between individual fee earners. Indeed it may be that the more senior partners are doing less fee earning work because of the time they need to spend in the general administration of the firm. So long as the fee earner is able to justify the time spent reasonably, then no worries need be entertained on this subject. The main purpose is merely to see that the full value of each individual's work is billed.

OFFICE METHODS

The service a solicitor gives to his clients is in every respect personal and will always be so. Perhaps it is on this account that solicitors as a body have in the past not given high priority to matters of organisation and office methods. One of the post-war developments in business life has been the realisation that management is a study in itself and the application of sound management principles is familiarly known as O & M (Organisation and Methods). The economic starkness of the last decade has turned the attention of solicitors to this subject. As the manual *Organisation and Management of a Solicitor's Office* (P. J. Purton and others) states: "it used to be thought that you, the solicitor, could not be both professional and commercial. Today, you cannot be professional unless in terms of management you are commercial."

In a book intended to introduce students to legal practice, it is not appropriate to enlarge on the principles of management. It is, however, important to indicate the kind of office routines at the lower levels that will assist the top managers to make a financial success of the business. But first we need to look at some general considerations affecting solicitors' practices.

Firms vary from individual solicitors practising on their own to partnerships of 20 or 30 solicitors or many more. It is no doubt economic pressure that is leading to an increase in the average size of practices and a reduction in their number. The ability of the larger firms to afford to mechanise their management information by computer, etc., is just one factor in encouraging this trend.

Here we are concerned with private practice firms: legal offices in big organisations, like local authorities and nationalised bodies, tend to rely for support services on the other professional and administrative departments of the organisation. It is in private practice that the way in which resources are used bears directly on success or failure.

Small firms and sole practitioners cannot be expected to have expensive machinery or separate office management staff. Still, they will not thrive without care to make the most effective use of the resources of manpower and equipment available. Hence, O & M is relevant to all sizes of firms. It is also relevant at all levels of work and responsibility, from the bottom to the top.

ADMINISTRATIVE SUPPORT SERVICES

In all but the smallest firms, financial administration will be found to be a separate function. The minimum resource will be a cashier to control the cash, wages and banking and possibly the ordering of stationery and other materials. In a small firm, the fee earners may prepare the bills for the matters they are handling. Some firms have a costs section separate from the cashier. This will comprise a costs clerk and possibly clerical support.

Secretarial assistance may be organised as a separate section supervised by a senior shorthand typist, or secretaries may work individually for the fee earners. Whilst typing pools are operated in very large firms, there is a natural tendency for secretaries to be allotted to fee earners individually. This presents the advantage that if the fee earner is not available, enquiries, messages and so on are received by someone who can get the file and ensure that no step arising from the message is unnecessarily delayed. There are at the same time difficulties in the one to one relationship, as the dovetailing of activities and attendances is necessarily partial. Dictating machines have almost entirely taken over from shorthand typists and where they are employed, one secretary may find it possible to cover for two or three fee earners.

The larger the firm the greater is the need to bring support services under unified management. Indeed in very large firms, one or more of the partners, known as the "managing partner" or "management committee," may virtually give up fee earning activities in favour of running the administration and management of the firm full time. In some cases, rather than partners devoting their time to this, professionals, often with substantial management experience, or from another discipline such as accountancy, have been taken on as practice managers to run the firm and to be accountable only to the senior partner or managing partner. Such firms may also have substantial full-time personnel sections, directors of training, and so on. Although demarcation disputes have rarely intruded into solicitors' practice in the larger firms which are almost invariably departmentalised, each individual may have a highly specific job description and carefully allocated duties in a highly defined structure. Conversely, in small High street firms Legal Executives and Solicitors will often be considerably less specialised and expected to turn their hand to coping with a great variety of the kind of work which comes through the door.

Although many legal executives come into the profession from being legal secretaries, once a certain degree of expertise has been reached a Legal Executive's time is simply too valuable to spend on typing her or his own documents. Paradoxically however, the increasing possibilities of office technology have meant that a lot of fee earners in the bigger firms have their own word processing units on their desks and this applies even to senior solicitors and partners. Thus for example where the firm has a regular precedent, say for a business lease, it is just as easy for the fee earner to call up the precedent on the screen and type in the modest amendments necessary to make it relevant to the specific situation before printing it for use on the client's matter. Thus the acquisition of key board skills can paradoxically now be of significant advantage in processing work for all levels of fee earner.

JUNIOR RESPONSIBILITIES

A trainee taking up duties in a legal office should be watchful to learn how the duties are allocated between the staff with whom he will be working. He should get to see any staff instructions that may have been issued. He will certainly expect to receive a letter or note of his terms and conditions of work, which is his due in law. Early on, he may expect to handle the firm's money, *e.g.* in paying court fees or handling cheques in connection with conveyancing transactions. He will need to know what the firm's procedures are on obtaining cheques and bankers' drafts and on drawing petty cash. Banking hours must be kept in mind, because moneys received must be banked on the day of receipt.

Emphasis has been placed on the personal nature of the service a solicitor offers. This makes personal relations of especial importance at all levels of the office. It hardly needs saying that within the office, acceptance of proper authority and a reasonable tolerance of others' foibles are requisites. In contacts with clients, other firms and so on, the manner of approach can brighten or it can tarnish the image of the firm, it can enhance or it can diminish its standing with the client. Staff at all levels will find themselves in direct personal or telephone contact with clients. For the staff, such contacts are among the things that make the career worthwhile. Care is needed to ensure due courtesy and, when occasion demands, to show an interest in a client's successes and concern for his disasters.

A new client's assessment of the standing and efficiency of a firm is much influenced by the way he is received and the appearance of the reception area. Reception staff can do much to uphold the good image of the firm by close attention to tidiness in the reception area. There should be no clutter and there should be sufficient chairs and tables pleasantly arranged in a pleasantly decorated room. If reading matter is provided, as it should be, this should be kept up to date and clean and be of some interest to the likely clientele. For example, in an inner urban area doing mainly matrimonial and criminal work the provision of magazines such as "Country Life" or exclusively concerned with ocean going yachts would not merely be irrelevant to the clientele's interest but actually promote a feeling that the solicitors' firm was unlikely to be in tune with its client's problems. The provision of Law Society leaflets particularly with regard to legal aid may be useful additions to the collection of reading matter. Equally important is the attitude of reception staff to clients and other callers. They should be friendly, relaxed and welcoming. Requests for details of the type of matter concerning which the client wishes to see someone should be put tactfully. If the reception area fronts on to a crowded waiting room a new client may be somewhat reluctant to give many details about his legal problem. If persons who are waiting need to use the telephone and no call phone can be provided, their needs should be reasonably and hospitably attended to.

Tidiness should be carried through into all the other offices. Eating in offices and where other callers are likely to see it is undesirable.

Cups and plates must be promptly cleared away after use. Perishable food should not be stored in offices.

The confidentiality of a solicitor's relations with his client has been mentioned above. The co-operation of the staff in this requires that they do not chat to colleagues about matters with which they are not concerned. Correspondence and other file papers should not be read on buses or in other public places. Papers not in use are to be kept in their files and the files in their cabinets. Cabinets which are lockable should be kept locked where access is not required.

No member of a solicitor's staff should be without a diary. For the fee earner, the rational planning of his time depends upon it. In his case, the diary will go beyond the entry of appointments for interviews. It will indicate for every matter in hand the dates on or by which particular steps have to be taken. When we deal with the individual subjects, conveyancing, litigation, etc., the vital importance of time limits will become clear. It is not enough merely to make a note of the final day for taking a procedural step. That step will often take time to prepare: it may mean spending a day drawing a brief, or getting essential information by correspondence or an official search. The workload is necessarily made up of a large number of individual matters and diary entries can be valuable in settling work priorities and in planning the days ahead. It must also be borne in mind that client matters can stay current over long periods. Action may be required after a lapse of months or even years, *e.g.* the service of a notice of intention to renew a lease of business property. A long term diary will be needed for such purposes.

For the junior member of staff, the habit of correct and complete diary entry of tasks by date is a valuable part of training for the more senior responsibility that will follow.

A development of the desk diary system is the use of a card index, one card per working day, setting out the tasks for that day. Entries can be fuller, but the practice of taking out the card at the start of the day, or possibly better, at the end of the previous day, is a discipline that must be made a regular routine. It can be shared with an assistant or secretary, so making assurance doubly sure.

THE FILING SYSTEM

The fee earner who has the conduct of the matter, will not only probably feel a proprietary interest in, but even an affection for his or her own file, that is, the file that he or she creates and maintains. Most fee earners have their own filing cabinet handy to their desk and the filing is done by the fee earner or his or her secretary. This system is usually called de-centralised filing. It has the great advantage of convenience for the fee earner where the file will be literally within arms reach of the telephone and so ought always to be available. The main difficulty is that fee earners and their secretaries unfortunately vary in efficiency and care. Any filing system is entirely dependent on the human element for actually ensuring that the file is kept tidy and up to date with all relevant documents being filed immediately. A subsidiary difficulty arises in the case of a file which is being dealt with by more than one person, *e.g.* where an experienced Legal Executive is using the file to help train a junior legal executive by letting him or her have conduct of certain aspects of the matter. The sheer effort in locating a file which may be with any of two or three people or their respective secretaries can cause problems.

The alternative is so called "centralised filing" where all current files are kept in a single filing area under the control of supervisors who do nothing but that task. This ought to ensure that the files go astray less often because they will always be in the central area or en-route to, or actually being used by, the person who wants them. This physical distancing between fee earner and file can be extremely inconvenient particularly in relation to telephone conversations. There is also a certain amount of physical effort required to go and get the file and in very large offices this may involve a journey of several floors and corridors. Probably only in the very biggest organisations is central filing likely to be useful. An alternative is a possible combination with a complete duplicate of everything being kept on a centralised file but this would be prohibitively expensive in terms of the extra photocopying and cost of paper. If word processors are used, master copies of some documents may be stored on disk.

The filing system, of what ever kind, must be methodically and carefully used. In particular it must be well indexed. Many firms still have a system whereby matters are only indexed under the name of client and a general title, *e.g.* "J. Brown, litigation." The problem with this is that when reference is needed to the file in years to come the firm may find it had many clients called J. Brown some or all of whom had one or more litigation matters. Almost certainly in the modern era, a proper numerical indexing system possibly with colour coding ought to be employed. There ought always to be a central index showing the serial file reference for every matter. The opening of a new file can then be the opportunity to notify the cashier or accountant of the need for a new client account or that a new matter has arisen, so that a check can be kept on it as to where the bill is to be delivered. Likewise, for this purpose it is vital that each new matter be given a new file. It is all too tempting if a client has two large conveyancing matters on the go at once and wants a will to be prepared to do the will and keep it in the same file. This can cause confusion and difficulty and may even lead to the billing of the will being overlooked. There must therefore be a clear rule of procedure as to the registering of new files and the maintenance of the filing system. Almost certainly, one individual, possibly the cashier or accountant himself will be made responsible for maintaining the register by way of a book or card index. Matters ought to be indexed by reference to clients name but also cross indexed to a numerical code and subject matter. The card may also indicate the fee earner involved on the client's matter and where the file is held and may even give more details such as of arrangements about fees, *e.g.* "to be paid by employer" or "legal aid."

If a centralised filing system is used then security is also a vital matter. It is obviously essential that there should always be someone present at times when the office is open. Whatever system is used it is vital to remember that it should be possible by the filing system both to locate any document within a file within a matter of seconds and to locate any file, even many years after the matter has been concluded, in a matter of minutes.

All firms have strong rooms or safes for deeds and important papers entrusted to them. The deeds may be held on behalf of the client, indefinitely for safe custody or temporarily as where house deeds are entrusted to the firm by the building society to await the redemption of a mortgage on sale of the property by a client. The firm will give an undertaking to the building society for safe custody of the deeds. In any kind of matter, safety in the handling and storage of deeds is absolutely paramount. A Deeds and Securities register should be kept and entries must identify the date of arrival and the location of each parcel to facilitate retrieval.

DESTRUCTION OF PAPERS

In a profession which produces so much paper as the legal profession, the disposal of unwanted paper is as important as the retention of papers needed for a permanent record. Usually, by the time the matter is concluded and the bill has been paid, deeds, original contracts, insurance policies and important documents will have been separated from a file and conveyed to a person entitled to them or else put in the firm's strong room or safe. There may be other papers the solicitor will wish to retain such as counsel's opinion on which the solicitor's advice in connection with the conduct of the matter has been based. Even, however, if there are not papers of this vital kind in the file and the file merely contains routine correspondence about a matter which never came to litigation, then the firm must not destroy the file immediately the matter is over and the fees are paid. The papers are held on behalf of the client to whom they belong and who may have some reason to wish to see them. There may be cases where a client could be vulnerable to further action or where the matter revives unexpectedly after many years.

Accordingly, files must be retained for some period however routine they may seem. Storage will depend upon the facilities of the firm. Certainly a file is likely to be retained in the premises of the firm for at least a year or so. Thereafter, a file may have to be sent out of the office because the sheer bulk of papers makes storage after this period impossible. In such cases files may be stored several miles away, *e.g.* in a warehouse rented for that purpose, or even in the garage of one of the partners. They must be stored systematically so that they can be recalled at reasonable notice. Thereafter, by using the index of files and updating these when the file is closed, a note can be made as to when the files can be extracted and destroyed. A firm will usually have a policy of leaving files for a set period before destruction. In the case of files to do with land, a period of some 20 years may be required because of the limitation period in substantive law. For other kinds of matter, only three or six years may be needed. The decision to destroy should always be taken by the fee earner who conducted the matter if he is available and details of the destruction should be entered on an index card. If a made up draft of some vital document such as a will is contained in the original file this ought to be extracted and kept separate. If for example the original will has been given to the client for safe keeping and he dies in circumstances where the will cannot be found then it may be possible to use the made up draft in future litigation concerning his estate. In the case of wills particularly therefore, (though also in the case of other kinds of document) properly completed drafts should be retained indefinitely.

THE POST

Arrangements will be found in all offices for the opening of the morning post. This may require the attendance of a partner or senior legal executive. Whoever attends will be responsible for marking letters out to the fee earners. The importance of the consistent use of references on letters will be readily understood. The arrangements will vary with the circumstances of each firm, the status of the persons employed and the trust the principals repose in them. Obviously the quicker letters can be got to the persons who will act on them, the better.

A rather similar point affects the signing of letters. A few firms require all correspondence to be signed by a partner. Others require copies to be presented for scrutiny after despatch. The arrangements must always be suited to the calibre and responsibilities of the fee earners at the various levels, but delegation of signing authority, where consistent with the proper degree of supervision, encourages staff to take full responsibility.

OFFICE MACHINES

The changes in legal office practices that followed the introduction of the typewriter were immense. The slow and painstaking manuscript engrossment of documents was eliminated. The speed of communication was raised and office staff were relieved of both manual labour and freed to take on other tasks and learn new skills. The fusty image of the profession current among the public faded away. The introduction of the photocopier has had a comparable effect. Law is essentially the communication and study of the written word and the speed and accuracy of reproduction are of vital importance in all manner of transactions from straightforward conveyancing to the most complex litigation. Three further recent developments have followed on from the introduction of the typewriter, photocopier and telephone:

(1) *Telexes*

A telex is a particular kind of letter which is instantaneously trans-
mitted and received and printed by a telex in the recipient's office. It
therefore follows obviously that the telex is only of any use as a method
of communication if both sender and recipient have a machine. Where
that is the case however, as it is increasingly in large solicitor's offices
and with commercial or professional clients, it is of enormous use
because of the immediacy of the communication. It is also particularly
important where actual specific wording needs to be communicated
such as a new draft clause in a contract. It is possible to have a number
of exchanges of telex correspondence within a day between solicitors
offices and wording on a contract, lease, etc., might well be hammered
out by the end of the day, when several exchanges of letters, telephone
calls and even meetings might have been necessary otherwise. A telex
is also particularly useful for communication with overseas recipients
where there are different time zones involved. Because of the immediacy of communication, it is usually vital to first have typed a draft of
what one proposes to say and then to check it. If this is not done one
may find oneself, because of the speed of the process, bound by ill
considered wording.

(2) *Fax*

Facsimile machines or telecopies as they are sometimes called,
permit the simultaneous transmission of facsimile copies of letters,
plans, diagrams and all other documents. Again it is essential that both
sender and recipient have one. It is increasingly common for solicitors
firms to have fax machines now. Transmission is down the telephone
line and is relatively inexpensive. It enables urgent documents to be
sent immediately. It is indeed becoming increasingly common for
solicitors faced with the need to instruct counsel urgently for court
applications the next day to transmit the brief via fax rather than by
delivery in paper form.

(3) *Computers*

The greatest revolution in the management of solicitor's practices is
taking place through the agency of computers.
For many years computers were seen as being relevant only to the
scientist. This was because, in their early forms, the most effective use
that could be made of them was to perform mathematical operations at
a speed that far exceeded the capacity of humans. In recent years,
however, computers have become far more powerful, with the result
that it is within the reach of every solicitor's office to afford a computer
that can perform the far more difficult task of dealing with words as
well as numbers. This is not, of course, to say that lawyers have no use
for calculating machines. The accurate recording and control of financial transactions is an essential part of the firm's business, and here too,
computers can make an important contribution.

One difficulty that faces a firm considering the installation of a computer is that its members will usually lack the expertise to distinguish between good and bad computer systems. It is likely that the newest (and youngest) members of the firm will have more knowledge of computers than the longer-established members, and they may find themselves closely involved in the choice and installation of a new system. Solicitors are buying computers at an increasing rate, but at the date of writing substantially less than half of all practices in England and Wales owned or made use of computer systems.

The word "system" is important here. Most uninitiated persons think of computers in terms of the machinery itself—the "hardware." This, however, is only half the system. The other, in some ways the most important, half is the set of programs—the "software." These are the instructions that tell the hardware what it is to do; perform calculations, store or retrieve information, edit documents, etc. Without the software the hardware is useless, and if the software is defective the whole system is worse than useless. Indeed, if defects only become apparent after the system has been installed, the work of the practice may suffer severely. Even working software can cause difficulties if it is not appropriate to the work of the practice, and for this reason any firm considering the purchase of a computer system should look very closely indeed at the software available. An outline of the most common functions for which software is available is set out below.

The physical appearance of the system will depend in the first instance on whether the firm decides to buy its own computer (an "in-house" system) or whether it makes use of someone else's system (a "bureau" system). If a computer bureau is employed there may be no evidence of it in the office. In many cases the firm simply sends off a batch of documents which the bureau types into its own system. The information is then processed and the results sent back to the firm. Clearly this is only possible where the results are not urgently required and where regular batches of information can be assembled, (*e.g.* weekly or monthly accounts). In other cases the firm uses a terminal (a television screen and keyboard) and printer to communicate with the bureau's system over the telephone. This is a fairly slow process as ordinary telephone lines cannot handle large amounts of data, and the telephone charges are surprisingly expensive. However, bureaux do have the advantage that little capital investment is required.

More commonly, though, firms purchase their own system. The smallest system will consist of a terminal, a processing unit (this is, in a sense, the "computing" part of the system), some kind of magnetic data storage system (which may be built into the processing unit) and a printer. Larger systems will have more terminals and printers, and probably more sophisticated data storage. There is no need for all this equipment to be stored in one place—a typical larger system might have one terminal for each secretary and the book-keeper, whilst the main printer would be in a small, fairly soundproof room, and the processor etc. in the basement.

The size and nature of the chosen system will depend very much on what functions it is intended to perform. The most common uses for solicitors are:

(a) *Word Processing*. This is a method of preparing documents that is far superior to conventional typewriting. The information is typed in on a standard keyboard, but instead of being immediately produced on paper it is stored magnetically and appears on a television screen (a "visual display unit" or VDU). The typist may then correct errors, transpose words or paragraphs, or alter the entire format. Until the document is perfect there is no need to print it out. In practice, when dealing with complicated documents intermediate versions will be printed, but even here word processing has advantages. When changes are made there is no need to re-type the rest of the document as the computer automatically re-pages, etc., and of course only the amended part needs to be proof-read again. A further advantage is that standard documents (conveyances, specimen wills, etc.), can be stored permanently in the system, and then called up by the typist and quickly amended to suit the particular case. There are on the market "dedicated" word processors that perform few if any other functions, and a small practice that has no need for other computing facilities might well have one of these. However, the quality of word-processing programs on more general systems has improved dramatically, and such systems can offer a wide range of other facilities that may be useful to the firm.

(b) *Accounts*. The importance of full and accurate accounts cannot be over-emphasised, not only because of the stringent requirements of the Solicitors Accounts Rules but also to ensure efficient management of the firm. Computers are particularly good at performing this function. The books are kept in the ordinary way, but on the computer. From this information the computer can, at a few minutes notice, produce balance sheets, bank reconciliations, etc. In addition, a good accounts program should be able to produce regular management information such as the profitability of different areas of the firm's work. Proper use of this information will assist the efficient running of the business.

(c) *Time Recording*. Many firms already use a manual system of time recording where the fee-earners record the amount of time spent on each matter. This information greatly assists the process of billing clients and also gives a useful insight into the pattern of work in the firm. Time recording programs can speed up the analysis of this information, and indeed, can also be linked to the accounts programs so as to prepare the bills themselves.

(d) *Data Storage*. Provided the system has disk drives or some other form of reliable memory, large amounts of information can be permanently stored on the system. This information could range from lists of names and addresses (the word-processing program could probably cope with these) to complete client files containing copies of all the relevant documents. The main reason for storing data in this way is that, given an efficient program for managing the "database," information can be retrieved very quickly and efficiently. In theory there is no danger of losing important details through mis-filing. However, although many of the paper documents can be disposed of, it will still be necessary to store certain papers in their physical form, *e.g.* wills, conveyances or affidavits, because it is virtually impossible to detect whether a document stored magnetically has been altered.

A further use that can be made of the office computer is to link it via the telephone to other computers. Examples of how legal materials may be found in this way will be given in the next chapter. The Prestel service, run by British Telecom, offers a wide range of information, as do a number of other organisations. In addition, through links with the banks, building societies and the Land Registry, it will soon be possible to use the computer to perform much of the work of conveyancing, and for other financial transactions.

The future of computers in the office is likely to be spectacular. Even now it is possible to use them to control the physical environment; lighting, heating, security, etc. Work is in progress on producing computers that recognise the spoken word—a computer that takes dictation! Perhaps the development that is likely to have the most immediate impact is in the area of "expert systems," systems that give advice and explain their reasoning. Expert systems in legal and financial matters are likely to become available in the near future.

FLOW CHART OF TYPICAL NON-CONTENTIOUS MATTER THROUGH OFFICE

The flow chart on p. 36 is reprinted with permission from David Andrew's chapter, "Office Layout and Design in Organisation and Management of a Solicitor's Practice," by P. J. Purton and D. Andrews (Oyez Publishing Company, 1981). It illustrates graphically some of the essential points on office procedures discussed above.

FLOW CHART OF TYPICAL NON-CONTENTIOUS MATTER THROUGH OFFICE

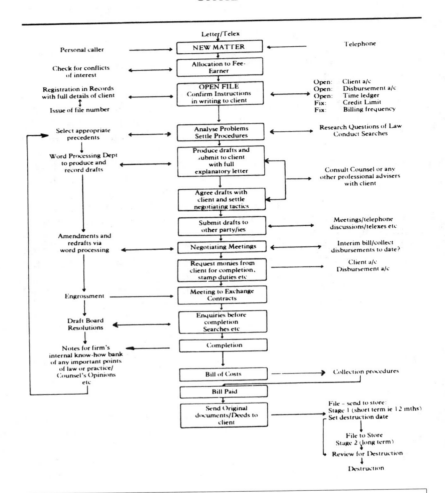

For self-testing questions, see the end of Chapter 3, p. 74.

CHAPTER 2

ETHICS, ETIQUETTE AND PROFESSIONAL CONDUCT

INTRODUCTION

The solicitors' branch of the legal profession is of course subject to the ordinary law of the land. Thus solicitors who are dishonest in handling their clients' money will be subject to criminal law. With regard to the legal relations between solicitors and their clients, these are governed in addition by:

(a) The law of contract. Under the law of contract the solicitor impliedly warrants to act with diligence and competence in the conduct of the client's affairs and the client impliedly consents to pay the solicitor's reasonable charges.

(b) The law of tort. A solicitor who does not act properly in his client's interest may be liable in negligence in tort as well as in contract. Sometimes the measure of damages in tort is different to that in contract and it might well be advantageous for a client who had a cause of action against a solicitor to bring his action in both tort and contract. Thus, for example, in one decided case where a client with an urgent problem which required the obtaining of an injunction (that is an order prohibiting a certain person from doing something to the client's detriment) contacted a firm of solicitors whose employee was entirely incompetent and inexperienced in such litigation, so that gross delay was caused to the client with considerable distress and inconvenience, the court awarded damages in the tort of negligence rather than for breach of contract.

(c) In addition to the law of the land, a solicitor's relationship with his client and indeed with the outside world is also governed by the Rules of Professional Practice. These are rules formulated by the Law Society, breach of which will lead to some disciplinary sanction being taken against the solicitor concerned. We shall now consider these both in so far as they relate to a solicitor's clients and to a solicitor's relationship with the outside world generally.

A SOLICITOR'S DUTIES TO HIS CLIENTS

(1) *Proper skill and care*

A solicitor has a primary duty to act in relation to his clients with diligence and to exercise competence, care and skill. It goes without saying also that a solicitor must behave scrupulously honestly to his client. He must treat the client with courtesy and reply promptly to the client's inquiries and thus keep the client properly informed. In this connection the solicitor's duty of competence also implies that any staff such as assistant solicitors or legal executives whom the solicitor selects to deal with the client's matters will be similarly competent and courteous. We shall return to this more generally under the topic of management of the solicitor's office below.

(2) *Conflicts of interest*

(a) *Between solicitor and client.* As part of his overriding duty of honesty to the client, a solicitor must make absolutely sure there is no possible conflict of interest when he deals with a client's problems. Primarily he must ensure that there is no conflict of interest between the client and himself or any of his firm's employees. Obviously a solicitor is not going to act for a client who actually wants to commence proceedings against that solicitor but conflicts of interest are usually more subtle than this. For example, a solicitor might be a substantial shareholder in a building company which is seeking planning permission to develop certain land and there may be hundreds of local residents who are aggrieved by this and wish to protest and take their objections through the necessary planning procedures. The objectors would of course have little idea that the solicitor might have an interest in the company which stands to gain from the development of the land. Of course in such a situation the solicitor would have to point out to the client the conflict of interest immediately the client commenced indicating to him the nature of the legal problem on which the client was seeking assistance. The solicitor should then ask the client to instruct another firm and if the client has no idea whom to instruct perhaps provide him with a list of local firms. If this is done pleasantly and courteously the client may well wish to return to instruct that solicitor on some other matter subsequently where there is no conflict of interest, *e.g.* a road accident claim, or matrimonial matters.

A specific aspect of the requirement that there be no conflict of interest which is the subject of considerable current legal controversy is the vexed question of *contingency fees*. Contingency fees are fees which are payable, dependent on the outcome of litigation. A crude version would be where a lawyer fixes a fee which he is to have if he wins the litigation for the client but stipulates that there will be no fee or a greatly reduced fee if the client loses in the litigation. More subtle versions exist in the United States where contingency fees are common, whereby, although there is no fee if the client loses, if the client wins, the fee is actually a proportion of the damages recovered. In some kinds of litigation in the United States indeed the fees may be as high as one-third of the damages recovered or even more. Whilst contingency fees may exist in other legal systems, in England they are absolutely prohibited both by the rules of professional practice and by the general law of the land as being contrary to public policy. The reason is said to be that such fees might well lead to a conflict of interest between solicitor and client. A client might wish to settle a case for a modest figure at an early stage and the solicitor whose fees would relate to the actual amount of damages received might be eager to press on in the hope of getting a higher sum after trial. Accordingly, the solicitor would have half an eye to his own interests rather than those of the client throughout the litigation. Such personal involvement in the outcome of the litigation moreover might tempt a solicitor to behave other than with scrupulous honesty towards his opponent and generally might create a less professional and objective atmosphere.

(b) *Between clients.* A solicitor should not of course act for two clients at the same time who have a conflict of interest either. Again, in obvious cases this will cause no difficulty. If two people wish to litigate against each other, then clearly, even if both happen to be old-established clients of the same firm, the firm cannot act for both of them now. Usually, in such a situation the firm will act for the first of the clients to consult it about the new matter. It should be noted, however, that the firm may not even be able to do this, if for example it has relevant confidential information about the other client which it has acquired whilst acting for him. In such a situation it may be better for the firm to tell both clients that they had better instruct other solicitors. The more difficult case arises where, having commenced to act for two people who appeared to be in harmony, a conflict of interest arises. Depending on the circumstances, it may sometimes be possible to invite one of the individuals to go to some other solicitor. Sometimes, however, it will be necessary to send both the clients to different solicitors because the solicitor will have acquired confidential information about each client's position in his capacity as solicitor and it would be wrong to put him in a position where he could use that information. Suppose, for example, that one is instructed by two clients A and B on a criminal charge. Both stoutly maintain their innocence and the solicitor commences acting for both. After a time, as often happens in criminal cases, one changes his story slightly. Suppose, for example, that now A says yes, the crime was committed but that it was actually B who committed it and although he, A, was present at the time, his involvement was entirely innocent. The solicitor is now in an impossible position. It is clear that A is going to attempt to get off by blaming B entirely. So, to conduct A's case as vigorously as necessary the solicitor would have to cross-examine B to try to establish that A's version is correct. This he obviously cannot do whilst B is his client. Likewise, since B is his client, he would have to cross-examine A to show that his story is untrue. Again he cannot do this. Unfortunately therefore, since he will by now have obtained confidential information from both clients whilst he acted in the capacity of their solicitor, this solicitor will now have to tell both A and B to go to separate other solicitors. A solicitor must therefore always be aware of the risk of a conflict of interest when taking on new clients even though there does not appear to be one at the outset of the matter. He should always be alive to the possibility of a conflict of interest arising suddenly.

(3) *Confidentiality*

A solicitor owes a duty of utmost confidentiality to his clients. He must keep confidential the affairs of his clients and he must ensure that all his staff do likewise. The duty to keep a client's business confidential continues even after the death of the client or after the client has taken his business elsewhere, unless the client expressly permits the disclosure of the information. A solicitor may not even reveal his client's address or telephone number without the client's consent. It is absolutely vital in the conduct of a solicitor's office for this to be borne in mind. It is very easy, particularly when responding to apparently innocent telephone enquiries, for junior staff who are trying to be helpful in the absence of the solicitor or senior legal executive dealing with the case to get out the client's file and respond to the telephone enquirer with all manner of information which ought not to be given. To this duty of confidentiality there are some exceptions. In particular, if a court orders that certain information be disclosed this will have to be done. In addition, where a client has legal aid, the solicitor has an overriding duty to the legal aid fund to communicate certain information to the legal aid authorities during the currency of the legal aid certificate even though it may not be in the client's own interest to have this information passed on. Where for example it comes to a solicitor's notice that the client has deceived the Legal Aid Board into granting legal aid and that there are for instance false statements on the Legal Aid application forms, the solicitor must communicate this information. Likewise, where a client who has legal aid wishes a solicitor to behave unreasonably in the conduct of the litigation, the Legal Aid Board must be informed.

SOLICITORS AND THE COURT

A solicitor who is engaged in litigation for a client owes that client the normal duties of competence and diligence and must generally try to do his best for the client. When speaking for the client in court he must say what the client would properly have said for himself if the client possessed the necessary skill and knowledge. However, a solicitor has a duty never positively to deceive or mislead the court. If the client requires the litigation to be conducted unreasonably or dishonestly then the solicitor has a duty to withdraw from acting for that client. It is up to a solicitor to draw any relevant *legal* points to the court's notice but in relation to *factual* matters the solicitor's duty is more complex. When acting for any party in a civil case, or for the defendant in a criminal case, a solicitor has no duty to disclose relevant facts to the court if they harm his client's case. To take an extreme example which always astonishes the layman, suppose that there is a road traffic accident between your client A and another driver B. They are in collision at an unmarked junction and both are injured. A sues B claiming damages and B defends and counterclaims for his own damages contending that the accident was caused by A. Both parties believe that there were no independent witnesses and are happy to go to court on the basis of seeing which person's version the judge believes. Late on in the case you discover that there was in fact an independent eye witness, who gets in touch with you. You take a statement from this witness and the witness tells you unfortunately that from his view point the accident was entirely the fault of your client A. It appears that the other side do not know of this witness's existence. Odd though the position may seem in terms of *general* ethics your *legal* ethical duty is quite clear. You are entitled not to call this witness at trial and not to reveal the existence of the witness to your opponent. In other words you can go to trial hoping that your client's version will be believed and depriving the court of this apparently vital source of information about the accident.

The same would apply if you were acting for a defendant in a criminal matter where you obtained a witness statement from someone who confirmed that your client had committed the crime. Again you would have no obligation to call that witness or to notify the prosecution of his existence. To this principle however, there is one important exception in civil litigation. There is a stage of civil procedure called *discovery of documents* where the client must reveal to his opponent all the relevant documents which he has in his possession. This must be carried out with scrupulous honesty even though one may have to reveal documents which are harmful to one's own case.

(In the example given above, however, the witness statement would not have to be revealed since there is a principle that documents which come into being just for the purpose of the litigation do not have to be disclosed at discovery.) This kind of document is said to be *privileged* from production.

Although as we have seen, a lawyer in litigation does not have a general duty of disclosure to his opponent, this rule has one important exception and that is in the case of a lawyer acting for the prosecution. A solicitor presenting a case for the Crown Prosecution Service has an overriding duty of fairness. He must not press for a conviction at any price and whilst he must ensure that all material points which support the prosecution case are made, he must present the evidence dispassionately and scrupulously fairly. In particular, a prosecuting lawyer has a duty to make available to the defence any evidence obtained which may assist them. Thus if the prosecution came across a witness who was helpful to the defence case they would have a duty to draw this witness's existence to the attention of the defence.

THE SOLICITOR AND HIS OFFICE

(1) *Supervision*

A solicitor has a duty to employ competent and honest staff. A solicitor is responsible for the acts or omissions of his firm as a whole and this extends to his partners and the staff concerned. Each and every duty which a solicitor owes is also owed by legal executives in his employment. We have already mentioned the duty of confidentiality referred to above but the same applies to all the other duties. Thus, if a legal executive has a conflict of interest with the client it will be his duty to draw the matter to the attention of his principal who will in due course have to invite the client to instruct some other solicitor. Where the solicitor's firm has several branch offices each must be managed either by a solicitor holding a practising certificate or by a Fellow of the Institute of Legal Executives who has been admitted as a Fellow for not less than five years. The solicitor or Fellow shall normally be in attendance at that office during all the hours it is open to the public. If an office is managed by a Fellow of the Institute, then a solicitor who has been admitted for at least three years must still attend at the office every working day for at least part of the time.

(2) *The accounts rules*

We have already referred to these in the general text of Chapter 1. It is vitally important that a solicitor does not mix up his client's money with his own money and abides by the provisions of the accounts rules and this duty applies of course to all the staff employed by the solicitor.

(3) *Attracting business*

Until recently no solicitor was allowed to obtain business by direct arrangement with some other person such as an estate agent or an accountant whereby clients were to be introduced to him. All that meant was, however, that there must be no inducement to refer work nor any formal contractual arrangement that work should be channelled to that solicitor. It was of course common and quite proper for solicitors to have good relations with other local professional firms of different kinds and to mutually recommend clients and that was never against any rule. The position now is governed by the Solicitors' Introduction and Referral Code 1988. Under this code persons who wish to refer work to solicitors may only do so if they comply with the code. Any participation by a solicitor in any such referral scheme outside the terms of the code would be a disciplinary matter. The rules require that anyone, such as say a bank or estate agent, referring persons on to a solicitor should inform that person that the solicitor is an independent professional who will give impartial and confidential advice and should also point out that the individual is free to choose another solicitor. No business arrangements must ever come about which undermine the independence or integrity of the solicitor. The code is lengthy and detailed and its rules govern three basic situations. First, there is that of some other person who is referring clients to a solicitor. The rules provide that in such cases no payment or commission must be made other than ordinary hospitality. The code also governs the position of a solicitor agreeing to be paid by a third party to do work for that third party's customers (such as might come about where an estate agent might provide a conveyancing service, or a firm might pay for their employees' conveyancing). The rules relevant to this include a requirement that any such arrangement must be set out in writing and open to inspection by the Law Society. Finally, the rules govern the situation of a solicitor recommending a client to use some other firm, agency or business. The rules again stress the need for a solicitor to act throughout in good faith and in the client's best interest.

(4) *Advertising*

A solicitor may now publicise his practice by proper advertising. The advertising must be in good taste, be accurate and not breach the Solicitors' Practice Rules. In particular, advertisements must not criticise other firms, name famous clients of the firm, or boast about the firm's success rate in litigation. A reference in a firm's publicity material to "legal executives" may only be made if the persons concerned are Fellows of the Institute of Legal Executives.

(5) *Fee sharing*

A solicitor must not share his professional fees with a person who is not a solicitor. What this means is that, whilst it is of course perfectly proper for a solicitor to employ other staff, no other staff such as a Fellow of the Institute of Legal Executives may become a partner in the firm so that he shares in the eventual net profits. This is not to say, however, that it is not perfectly proper to have an arrangement, subject to the approval of the Law Society, whereby a bonus is paid annually depending on the firm's profits. An important provision, however, is that this bonus, if it is to be approved, must not be related to the introduction of clients to the firm by staff. For example, a bonus cannot be paid of say £20 for each client that the legal executive introduces to the firm; if, however, the firm has had a particularly profitable year and the legal executive has by his efforts contributed markedly to that success it would be perfectly proper to give him a bonus based on his performance.

A further aspect of this is that a solicitor may not share his fees with any non-lawyer. So multi-disciplinary partnerships whereby solicitors, estate agents, accountants, etc., might all set up in practice together are prohibited. A solicitor can, if he wishes, employ a chartered surveyor to do work for his property clients and indeed many large firms now do, as indeed they may employ chartered accountants, etc., but these latter can never become partners in the solicitor's firm. In particular a solicitor is prohibited from having any fee-sharing arrangement with a claims assessor in insurance litigation. Exceptionally, if a solicitor who is engaged in selling property instructs an estate agent as his sub-agent for the sale of that property the solicitor may remunerate him on the basis of a proportion of the solicitor's professional fee.

(6) *Property selling*

At one time there was a very firm division between work which a solicitor could properly do and work which he was not permitted to do. Over the years, however, solicitors have seen more and more of their traditional areas of work being taken by other professions. In particular, a lot of the administration of estates has been lost to the Trust Departments of large banks, and a lot of work on taxation has been lost to the accountancy profession. In a partial effort to redress this balance, solicitors have from recent times been permitted to engage in advertising and selling of property. Solicitors sometimes group together locally to set up property centres to offer a full house transfer service. Although such property centres may employ chartered surveyors, etc., to assist with valuations and sale, these latter can never become partners in the venture as we have seen.

THE SOLICITOR AND OTHER PERSONS

(1) *The solicitor's undertaking*

An undertaking is a formal promise by a solicitor, which declares his intent to someone who reasonably places reliance in it. The undertaking may be given by a solicitor or by a member of his staff, but in any case the solicitor becomes personally bound. It is serious professional misconduct not to honour the undertaking. An undertaking, then, is a solemn promise. A great deal of a solicitor's work is facilitated by the giving and receiving of undertakings, because, since the consequences of breaching an undertaking are so serious, a solicitor will always know that he is entitled to place absolute reliance on another solicitor's word given in this way. It is vital for a solicitor when organising his practice to formulate office rules as to precisely who may give written undertakings. Such rules commonly stipulate that undertakings in writing may only be given and signed by either a partner in the firm or a Fellow of the Institute of Legal Executives. Where an undertaking is given by a solicitor's staff the solicitor is still personally bound by it. It therefore is absolutely imperative that no undertaking should be given unless it can be personally fulfilled by the solicitor. For example, a solicitor should never give an undertaking as to something which his *client* will do or as to something which is outside his control. Even if an undertaking has been given in reliance on the fact that, *e.g.* money will be received from a client, the undertaking must still be fulfilled even if the client defaults in providing the money. For this reason it is vital carefully to consider each occasion on which the solicitor is asked to give an undertaking and to ensure that the exact terms of the undertaking are carefully defined.

(2) *Relations with third parties*

A solicitor must not act in any way which is fraudulent or deceitful or which attempts to take advantage in an unfair way for himself or some other person. The clearest example of this is where a solicitor who is acting for a party in litigation or conveyancing is faced with an opposite party who does not choose to have legal representation. As every solicitor and legal executive will know this tends to increase the difficulties. Documents which are received from such persons may be completely wrongly drafted, unrepresented persons may cause gross delays in litigation by incompetence or mismanagement and often will be given great indulgence by the court to the frustration of the lawyer and his own client. Despite this, a lawyer faced with an unrepresented opposite party must always behave courteously and with fairness. This does not mean, however, that one is debarred from taking perfectly legitimate legal points. Everything will depend upon the facts of the situation. Often, frequent suggestions to one's opponent that it would be wise for him to consult a solicitor will be appropriate.

(3) *The solicitor and other solicitors*

All lawyers should act towards each other with courtesy throughout. Even though the litigation has become bitter between the clients (and this is particularly so in the case of matrimonial disputes), the solicitors should always attempt to maintain good relations, which will almost always be in the clients' interests in the end. Indeed, in matrimonial matters solicitors should not view themselves entirely as in an adversarial role but should do what is possible to minimise the bitterness of the situation and to bring about such conciliation as they can. Apart from this, however, solicitors must always act towards other solicitors with frankness and good faith consistent with their duty to their clients. A solicitor who concludes that another solicitor has misconducted himself in some way is under an obligation to report that matter to the Law Society.

EMPLOYED SOLICITORS

A solicitor who is employed by an undertaking such as a large company or a local authority is in a sense acting for only one client. He will actually be in the client's premises and this may bring about a difference in atmosphere and perhaps a certain lack of objectivity in the lawyer. He may tend to identify completely with his employer's interests in every sphere from employment law to taxation and litigation. It is even more vital for such lawyers, however, to remember that they are first and foremost *lawyers* rather than employees. Such lawyers are subject to the same general principles of professional conduct as apply to individuals in private practice and should always attempt to bring a proper legal objectivity to their view of a situation and to attempt, so far as is possible, to treat their employer as their "client."

CHAPTER 3

FINDING THE LAW

INTRODUCTION

The study of law is the study of the written word. Books are the tools of trade, so to speak, of the lawyer. So practitioners must have their books and lawyers' offices are often lined with books. Before we discover how to make use of these books we must look for a moment at the law itself—the material from which the books are compiled.

Law may be laid down in broad precepts or principles, or it may be set out in great detail in an attempt to cover all foreseeable circumstances. The ancients were content with the rule: Thou shalt not steal. But we need to know more. Can you steal electricity, perhaps by a connection which cuts out the meter?

Even today there are two approaches to the creation of law. Some countries use the broad principle approach, others adopt the more detailed exposition. English law is set out in great detail. There are two main reasons. First, the system of judicial precedent by which the common law has been built up over the centuries rests on countless decisions of the judges in individual cases. Secondly, Parliament has adopted the principle that if law is to be certain in its application to particular circumstances, if the citizen is to know where he stands under law, statutes must be as comprehensive as possible. Hence, we have voluminous Acts of Parliament, with numerous schedules. These moreover give rise to a mass of orders and regulations of great detail and complexity. Even when Parliament has enacted the law on a subject, that is not the end, because it is the task of the judges to clarify by their decisions any points a statute may leave in doubt.

The problems of setting down the law are therefore largely problems of bulk and space. There is more than a grain of truth in the saying: a lawyer does not have to know the law, but he must know where to find it. Because the law itself is so vast, many of the books a law library contains do not set out the law but describe it, summarise it or indicate where we must look to find an authentic statement of it. Such authentic statements are referred to as "sources" and we must be careful to distinguish between sources and other statements of what the law is. A judge will listen to what is found in the sources. Only rarely will he be prepared to receive the views of writers on the law, however eminent they may be.

There are two main sources of English law: statute (which must be taken to include all orders and regulations and even bylaws made with the authority of statute) and the decisions of the judges or case law. What we need to know in using the library is how these sources are made accessible by the books a modest law library can contain. We will start with case law.

CASE LAW

In a system in which a large part of the law depends on what a judge decided in a particular case, lawyers are necessarily dependent on the publication of reports of cases. As the judgment can itself only be fully understood by reference to the facts of the case the reports need to set out the way the case arose, that is, the names of the parties, and a statement of the relevant facts as established by the court in the course of the trial. In the five centuries during which cases have been reported, conditions of publication and standards of reporting have varied, as we shall see.

CURRENT SERIES OF REPORTS

There are many series of reports now available. Some of them are general; others specialise in particular subjects, like tax law, patents and so on. Some reports are produced commercially by general law publishers. The method is to issue reports periodically, usually in monthly parts which contain the most recent cases made available for publication. At the end of the year these are bound together to form part of the series of annual volumes. The number of reports is now so large that the year's total in a non-specialised series may require two or three bound volumes. Of course, only those cases considered to have value as precedents are selected for publication, a point supported as much by economics as by common sense.

Today the most important series of reports is referred to simply as The Law Reports. This is a non-commercial series published under the auspices of a body set up by the judiciary and the profession itself called the Incorporated Council of Law Reporting. Reports for publication in The Law Reports are seen and approved before being printed by the judges whose decisions are being reported. They are therefore the most authoritative reports. They are divided up into four sub-series reflecting the organisation of the work of the High Court: Appeal Cases, Chancery, Queen's Bench and Family. The Appeal Cases volume contains the decisions of the Court of Appeal and the House of Lords.

The Law Reports are also the most useful to the practitioner because they usually include not merely the judgments but the arguments put forward by Counsel and it is therefore, for both academic and practical purposes, possible to see which arguments found favour, and which did not, with the judge concerned. A number of Practice Directions have required that if a case is available in a variety of reports the version in The Law Reports should be the one to be cited and used in court.

The next most important series of reports for the practitioner is the All England Reports, the only remaining commercial *general* series, published by Butterworth & Co. (Publishers) Limited. Started in 1936, this series provides a wide coverage of reports of high standard. If a solicitor's office has a series of general reports it is likely to be the All England Reports.

The system of precedent, which is explained more fully below (p. 50) makes it possible for a lawyer to support his viewpoint on any legal issue by reference to any judicial decision that appears to confirm his reasoning. This is called "citation" or the "citing" of a case. Of course, the contribution a case makes to settling a point must itself be evaluated: is the case recent or old; is it truly "in point" or "on all fours," *i.e.* does it really apply to the facts of the issue under examination and so on. For the system to work, there must be a unique means of identifying each case and indicating where it can be found. This is called the reference. Thus, you will find references like the following:

Northey Stone Co. v. *Gridney* [1894] 1 Q.B. 99.
Norton v. *Knowles* [1967] 3 All E.R. 1061.

The first is to be found in the Queen's Bench volumes of The Law Reports. Scanning the shelves in this series one finds the Queen's Bench series and locates the two volumes that appeared in 1894, labelled 1 and 2. The first of these is 1 Q.B. and the report will be found on page 99. The All England Report series works on the same principle and in the instance quoted the case will be found at page 1061 in the third volume published in 1967.

Libraries that have The Law Reports may also take the Weekly Law Reports (W.L.R.), also published by the Incorporated Council of Law Reporting. Published since 1953, this series takes the place of Weekly Notes (W.N.) a series of reports which will be found in some libraries. W.L.R. is published in two sections. One section contains the reports to be published later by the same publishers in The Law Reports. The other section contains reports of cases that for whatever reason will not be republished by them. The advantage of taking W.L.R. is therefore that not only does it come out earlier than other reports (other than the short reports in *The Times* newspaper and the weekly law journals), but it contains reports which may not be found elsewhere.

There are many specialised series of reports, such as Cox's Criminal Cases (Cox) and the Justice of the Peace Reports (J.P.), Taxation Reports (T.R.) and Tax Cases (T.C.). Other specialised branches of the law have their own series of reports. These are more likely to be found in the libraries of firms which specialise in a particular branch.

Reference is made above to the reports appearing in *The Times* newspaper and in the law periodicals. One has to be guarded about treating these as reports in the true sense. The most important thing about a judicial decision is the words the judge uses in giving his judgment. All modern series of reports set out the judgment so far as possible verbatim. It is the judge's reported words that will be quoted by advocates as authority for their submissions. Any condensation of a judgment will tend to obscure the finer shades of meaning. Of course there are decisions the general significance of which can be expressed effectively in a few words. Such a judgment may be referred to as a "short point of law." But there are others where the effect of the judge's words will be argued over in case after case. Therefore, short reports in journals are best treated as introductions to the full reports, to be looked for when they appear in one of the series mentioned above.

The Times reports are valuable because they can be read the day after the judgment is given. Moreover, the arguments of counsel are often summarised and the judgments, whilst condensed, are still quite lengthy and salient points are given verbatim. The law periodicals giving a general service of reports are *The New Law Journal* and the *Solicitors' Journal*. Students may also find help from the brief summary reports in *The Legal Executive* or *Law Notes*.

PRECEDENT

We have seen how the common law has developed out of countless decisions of the judges in individual cases—the "wilderness of single instances" (Tennyson). In his study of the law, the student will meet many cases that illustrate how general principles arise by the system of precedent. To guide the search for relevant cases in the law reports, we need to know something of how precedent works.

Precedent implies that where the facts of a case are comparable with those of a previously decided case, the court's decision in the new case will be consistent with its previous decision. But what is "comparable"? No two cases are exactly alike. Suppose I have a client who has been involved in a car accident and claims damages for his injuries. My search for a comparable case leads me to a report in which the facts seem closely comparable except that the reported case involved a horse and carriage. I must decide whether the difference in the mode of transport is important: if in the reported case a car had been involved, would the decision have been different? Another way of putting this question is to ask whether the difference in the vehicle was "material" or whether the fact that it was a horse-drawn vehicle was "necessary" to the decision; if it was, the case does not form a precedent for my case. So, when using a case as a precedent we must be satisfied that the *material* facts are comparable.

The significance of a reported case as a precedent is referred to as the *ratio decidendi* of the case. This may be simply translated as "the reason for the decision." For the parties fighting the case, the important point is who wins: whether the defendant is or is not liable. In using the case as a precedent we must know by what process of reasoning the particular facts led to the decision.

Sometimes, the court in delivering judgment will enunciate 'a general principle as the basis of its decision. *Donoghue* v. *Stevenson* ([1932] A.C. 562), the snail in the bottle case, was decided on the broadest of principles: that a man has a duty to consider the effect of what he is doing on his "neighbour." In many cases, however, the court carefully refrains from setting the decision in the context of general principles. The judge says that the facts are in all material respects comparable to those of a particular case cited to him and he is "bound" by the previous decision.

Where the court does not express a general principle, the lawyer must extract this for himself. By taking all the available reported decisions that appear to bear on the facts of the matter in hand, he hopes to find a thread of consistency and logic running through them. This enables him to extract the general principle on which the court appears to be acting, although it may nowhere be stated.

A succession of cases all of which tend to establish a particular point of law is referred to as a "line" of cases.

Where a reported decision is used by a judge as authority for his decision in the case in hand, he is said to "follow" the earlier decision or to "apply" that decision. Where he rejects the authority of a reported case because although comparable in some respects it is different in others—which he specifies—he is said to "distinguish" the reported case. Where the court rejects the authority of a reported decision altogether, it is said to be "over-ruled." The circumstances in which this can happen are now to be mentioned. The general principle is that the decision of the higher court binds all lower courts. This is inherent in allowing a right of appeal through the hierarchy of courts up to the House of Lords. However, the principle is not as rigidly applied as formerly. Historically, the House of Lords has been bound by earlier decisions of the House, but for some years it has taken freedom to depart from its own precedents. The Court of Appeal generally accepts the authority of its previous decisions, but not where it is satisfied that a previous decision was defective. The lowest tier of the High Court (the Divisional Court) is bound by its own previous decisions.

Cases in the county court and magistrates' court are not now regularly reported and their decisions have no authority over any other court.

Where a litigant appeals to a higher court, his appeal is either "rejected" or "allowed." If it is allowed, the decision of the lower court is "reversed." In a criminal case, when an appeal against conviction is successful, the conviction is said to be "quashed."

THE CONTENT OF REPORTS

On pp. 52–53 is set out the report of the case of *National Westminster Bank Ltd.* v. *Stockman* [1981] 1 All E.R. 800. The letters in the inner margin are a feature of the All England and other series and are repeated on every page. They are a great help in pinpointing a judicial statement (or "dictum") that needs to be quoted in support of an argument. The numbers overprinted in the outer margin indicate the different elements that usually make up a modern report. Their explanation is as follows:

1. Series, reference and page number.

2. Case title giving the names of the parties to the proceedings. "v" represents the Latin versus (against). In a civil case between a plaintiff and defendant at first instance (*i.e.* when the claim, etc., comes before the court for the first time) the plaintiff's

1.   800   **All England Law Reports**   **[1981] 1 All ER**

2.   # National Westminster Bank Ltd v Stockman   *a*

3.   QUEEN'S BENCH DIVISION
      RUSSELL J
      18th AUGUST 1980

4.   *Execution – Charging order – Land – Interest in land – Property held legally and beneficially by* *b*
      joint tenants – One of joint tenants a judgment debtor – Whether charging order may be made in
      respect of debtor's interest in land – Charging Orders Act 1979, s 2.

5.   Section 2(1)[a] of the Charging Orders Act 1979 extends the availability of charging orders
      for securing payment of money due under a judgment or order to beneficial interests in
      the proceeds of sale of land held under trusts for sale and accordingly permits a charging *c*
      order to be made on the debtor's interest in real property, such as an interest in a
      matrimonial home, which is held under a trust for sale (see p 801 *f*, post).

6.   *Irani Finance Ltd v Singh* [1970] 3 All ER 199 distinguished.

      Notes
7.   For charging orders on land and interests in land, see 17 Halsbury's Laws (4th Edn) para *d*
      557.
            For the Charging Orders Act 1979, s 2, see 49 Halsbury's Statutes (3rd Edn) 769.

      Case referred to in judgment
8.   *Irani Finance Ltd v Singh* [1970] 3 All ER 199, [1971] Ch 59, [1970] 3 WLR 330, 21 P &
      CR 843, CA, Digest (Cont Vol C) 342, 1628Aa.   *e*

      Interlocutory appeal
9.   The plaintiffs, National Westminster Bank Ltd, appealed against the order of Master
      Ritchie on 19th June 1980 refusing their ex parte application for a charging order nisi to
      be made against the beneficial interest of the defendant, Hugh Stockman, in the property
      known as 12 Priory Gardens, Old Basing, Basingstoke, Hampshire to satisfy a judgment *f*
      dated 30th August 1978 obtained by the plaintiffs against the defendant for £11,604 and
      £49 costs. By an order made by Mustill J on 11th July the notice of appeal was served on
      the defendant. The appeal was heard in chambers but judgment was given by Russell J
      in open court. The facts are set out in the judgment.

10.   *G A Mann* for the plaintiffs.   *g*
      David G M Marks for the defendant.

11.   **RUSSELL J.** This is an appeal against the refusal of Master Ritchie to make a charging
      order nisi in respect of property at 12 Priory Gardens, Old Basing, Basingstoke. The
      plaintiffs obtained judgment against the defendant in default of defence in the sum of
      £11,604·10 together with costs on 30th August 1978. The ex parte application for the *h*
      order nisi was dismissed by the master on 19th June 1980. I was told that apparently he
      was not satisfied that the provisions of the Charging Orders Act 1979, and in particular
      s 2 of that Act, enabled the order to be made. On 11th July 1980 the matter came on
      appeal before Mustill J, who ordered that notice of appeal should be served on the
      defendant. Consequently I have had the advantage of argument from counsel for the
      defendant as well as from counsel for the plaintiffs.   *j*
            The facts can be stated very shortly. The judgment was in respect of moneys owing
      by the defendant to the plaintiffs in an overdrawn bank account. The defendant's
      matrimonial home was held by him and his wife, as so often happens, under a trust for

      _____
      a   Section 2, so far as material, is set out at p 801 *e*, post

sale. The conveyance of the house to the defendant and his wife was a conveyance to
a them as joint tenants both legally and beneficially.

I have been referred to s 35 of the Administration of Justice Act 1956 and to the
judgments of the Court of Appeal in *Irani Finance Ltd v Singh* [1970] 3 All ER 199, [1971]
Ch 59. Section 35(1) of the 1956 Act provided:

> 'The High Court and any county court may, for the purpose of enforcing a
b > judgment or order of those courts respectively for the payment of money to a
> person, by order impose on any such land or interest in land of the debtor as may be
> specified in the order a charge for securing the payment of any moneys due or to
> become due under the judgment or order.'

The judgment of the court in the *Irani* case, delivered by Cross LJ, traced the history
of charges in favour of judgment creditors on the land of judgment debtors. I need not
c do so. The ratio of the judgment was that the words 'interest in land' to be found in s 35
did not include interests under trusts for sale of land. Such interests were not interests
in land but interests in the proceeds of the sale of land. Those equitable interests,
therefore, were not caught by the provisions of s 35 and no charging order could be
made.

Section 35 of the 1956 Act has now been repealed by s 7 of the Charging Orders Act
d 1979. The short point for my consideration is whether s 2 of the 1979 Act has removed
the limitations of s 35 of the 1956 Act, as interpreted by the Court of Appeal in the *Irani*
case, so as to permit charges on the interests of those, such as the defendant in the instant
case, who hold real property under the terms of a trust for sale. Section 2 of the 1979 Act,
so far as it is relevant, provides:

> '(1) . . . a charge may be imposed by a charging order only on—(a) any interest
e > held by the debtor beneficially—(i) in any asset of a kind mentioned in subsection
> (2) below, or (ii) under any trust . . .
> '(2) The assets referred to in subsection (1) above are—(a) land . . .'

Is the defendant caught by these words? In my judgment it was plainly the intention
of Parliament that the availability of charging orders should be extended to cover cases
f in which the interest sought to be charged is a beneficial interest in the proceeds of sale
of land held under a trust for sale. I think that that object has been achieved by the plain
wording of s 2, despite the interesting arguments to the contrary advanced by counsel for
the defendant. There are various safeguards available to the debtor when application is
made to make the order absolute and to his wife whose position can be protected in the
event of any application by the creditor which would have the effect of defeating the
g purpose for which the trust was established. These, however, are not matters before me.
I shall allow the appeal and grant the charging order nisi.

Appeal allowed. Charging order nisi granted.   **13.**

Solicitors: *Wilde Sapte* (for the plaintiffs); *Ward Bowie*, Basingstoke (for the defendant). **14.**

K Mydeen Esq   Barrister. **15.**

name comes first. In appeals the practice until 1975 was to put the name of the appellant first. This led to the names being switched around, sometimes more than once where there was a further appeal. The present practice is to retain the original title unaltered. The point needs to be watched in searching for the latest report of a pre-1975 case, although most indexes list the parties separately.

There are other forms of case name, *e.g. In the Matter of the Estate of Brown (deceased)* or simply *Re Brown's Will Trusts.* This form is often found where trustees are involved in disputes with beneficiaries under a trust. A case in which the subject-matter is a ship will be titled with the name of the ship: *The Moorcock* (1889) 14 P.D. 64.

A report of a criminal case is headed *R.* v. *Fagin*, etc., where R. stands for Regina or Rex; (*i.e.* Queen, or conveniently enough for King also). Where there is an appeal from the magistrates' court to the High Court in a criminal case on a point of law, the name is changed. R. is replaced by the name of the prosecutor, who may have been a policeman or other person authorised to bring the proceedings. Here, it is the name of the appellant, whether prosecutor or defendant, that comes first in the title of the appeal.

At a criminal trial, when the clerk announces the case he usually says "The Queen versus Fagin." In citing a criminal case the advocate says "The Queen against Fagin." But on appeal to the High Court and in all civil proceedings it is "Fagin and Black."

3. The court by which the case was heard, the judges who sat and the date(s) of hearing. In speech, the judge is "Mr. Justice Russell." In reports this becomes Russell J. Two judges would be Russell and Lawson JJ. Other contractions will be readily understood, *e.g.* LCJ: Lord Chief Justice.

4. A brief synopsis of the subject-matter dealt with in the case. It is strictly an editorial insertion intended to shorten the work of finding out the relevance of the case without actually reading it, but it cannot be relied upon to be comprehensive.

5. The headnote. Necessarily a short case has been selected for illustration. Reference to other reports will show that in nearly all cases the headnote is in two parts.
    (a) the reporter's précis of the facts of the case and the stage reached in any earlier litigation
    (b) introduced by the word "Held," a summary, also in the words of a reporter, of the court's decision and reasons for the decision. In a case heard by several judges, if one or other dissents the decision of the majority will appear here and the views of the dissenting judge or judges are given underneath.

The headnote, being editorial, has no value in itself other than to indicate to the reader whether the case and judgment are likely to help him.

Occasionally it is followed by a note headed "Per curiam" (by the court) containing a summary of observations made by a judge in the course of his judgment, but which were not strictly part of the reasoning on which his conclusion was based. He might for instance say that if the facts had been different in such and such respects his conclusion would have been different. Such observations, whilst being of interest to the lawyer, do not bind judges in future cases. They are referred to as *obiter dicta* (statements by the way: singular, *obiter dictum*).

In the older All E.R. reports the headnote was followed by an Editorial Note explaining the point of law at issue and its possible implications in the wider legal context.

6. A note of a particular decision found to have direct relevance to the case now reported. In this instance reasons were found for saying that the facts did not quite tally in all respects and the case cited was therefore distinguished (see above). In another case the reported decision might be found to be exactly analogous. If so it would be followed or applied. This is also the place to refer to any reported decision that is overruled.

7. Notes on the law, comprising cross references to relevant law in *Halsbury's Laws and Statutes* and relevant cases in the Digest (The English and Empire Digest: see p. 54).

8. As indicated, the cases referred to in the judgment. In other reports it is followed by a complete list of all the cases cited by counsel, but not used in the judgment. In this case there were none.

9. The heading gives the category of the proceedings: Application for Injunction, Appeal or whatever it may be. The note that follows states the previous stages of the litigation by which it has reached the trial now reported.

10. The names of counsel for the parties. In The Law Reports, following the naming of the counsel there is an account of the arguments presented by them respectively to the court.

11. The judgment. This is reported as near as possible verbatim and usually follows this pattern:
    (a) exposition of the facts as established by the pleadings and evidence with, so far as necessary, an evaluation of the weight attached to disputed evidence. If there is more than one judgment, this section is usually not found in those that follow;
    (b) the arguments advanced by counsel on each side and the reasons for the judge's acceptance or rejection of them respectively. This will include the judge's opinion on the application to the case of reported decisions submitted by counsel on either side as precedents;

Finding the Law

    (c) the judge's general statement of the law applying to the case and the decision.

12. The title of the case and the judge. This is repeated at the top of every subsequent page of the case.

13. A succinct statement of the outcome as it will be recorded in the court records and notified to the parties.

14. The solicitors acting for the parties.

15. The name of the reporter.

Other series of reports will naturally follow a slightly different pattern, but the head note is an invariable part of a report and to be authoritative the report of the judgment must be or purport to be verbatim.

THE OLDER LAW REPORTS

The student will become familiar from his law studies with some of the many leading cases of the common law decided many decades or even centuries ago:

Armory v. *Delamirie* (1722) 1 Stra. 505.
Felthouse v. *Bindley* (1863) 7 L.T. 835.
Hadley v. *Baxendale* (1854) 9 Exch. 341.
Paradine v. *Jane* (1647) Aleyn. 26.
Rylands v. *Fletcher* (1868) L.R. 3 H.L. 330.

As in theory an advocate can quote any decision recorded over the whole period of five centuries or so over which reports have been published, the importance of a means of identifying every case by a unique number and letter reference will be understood: when counsel quotes from a case in court he invariably opens his quotations by giving the name and reference, as set out above for the cases mentioned. This enables the court usher to go to the court library (which in the case of the High Court is complete) and pick out the volume containing the case. To facilitate this there is a standard form of abbreviation for every series of reports. Alphabetical lists of these will be found in *Halsbury's Laws* and *Halsbury's Statutes* and in such annual publications as the Lawyer's Remembrancer.

Until 1865, the publication of reports had to rely on the enterprise of the individual publishers, whose competence varied from good to bad. Professor Glanville Williams (*Learning the Law*) quotes the case of *Slater* v. *May* (1704) in which a report was being cited from which a material fact had been omitted. Holt C.J. burst out: "see the inconveniences of these scrambling reports, they will make us appear to posterity for a parcel of blockheads."

Reference is rarely required today to cases before 1865, but the reports of the preceding three centuries have been brought together and reprinted in a series called "The English Reports," which will be found in some very large libraries. More readily accessible is the All

England Law Reports Reprint which reproduces a selection of cases from the reports of all earlier periods to the commencement of its own series in 1936. Those selected are mainly cases that have been referred to in the current All E.R. series or in *Halsbury's Laws*.

With the publication of The Law Reports in 1865, the position was transformed as it was possible to rely on reports of a high and consistent standard. At that time and until the reorganisation of the High Court by the Judicature Act 1875, there were 11 different courts to be covered. Since then, progressive simplification of the organisation of the High Court has made it possible to reduce The Law Reports to the four series: Queen's Bench, Chancery, Family and Appeal Cases.

The changes of series over the years have complicated the system of referencing. The table set out on page 58 gives the titles of the various series current at the different dates and the references for each. It will be noticed that until 1891 the year of publication was not an essential part of the reference. The volumes of each series were numbered consecutively, though usually they represent annual publication. Where the year is given in the reference to these cases, it is put in round brackets: (1890), to distinguish it from the essential inclusion of the year of publication of later reports: [1891].

As publishers and their reporters make their own selection of cases for publication, it is usual to find more than one report of any case. The following is a case taken at random from the County Court Practice (1991):

Stanton v. *Southwick*, [1920] 2 K.B. 642; 89 L.J.K.B. 1066; 123 L.T. 651; 84 J.P. 207; 36 T.L.R. 567; 64 Sol.Jo. 498; 18 L.G.R. 425; 31(1) Digest (reissue) 477.

The references are as follows:

[1920] 2 K.B. 642: The Law Reports series. The earliest reports in this series had L.R. in the reference, but this is omitted from 1875. Where there is a report in the series it is usually put first. The last figure is always the page number.

89 L.J.K.B. 1066: Vol. 89, Law Journal Reports series (1822–1949); printed separate from the Journal.

123 L.T. 651: Vol. 123. The Law Times Reports (1859–1947); also printed separate from the Journal.

84 J.P. 207: Vol. 84, Justice of the Peace Reports (1837—still published); printed separate from the Journal.

36 T.L.R. 567: Vol. 36, Times Law Reports (1884–1952); printed separate from the newspaper. Note that law reports still feature in *The Times* newspaper and usually appear the day after the case is decided. These reports, which are of course selected for their interest either to the public generally, or sometimes for their interest to the legal profession dealing in particular with points of procedure or practice, have the formal features of a full report, but the judgments are necessarily brief and a considerable précis of the judge's words. They make valuable additional reading for a law student but it is always imperative to wait for the report to come out in a fuller version before it can be relied on authoritatively. Occasional misprints and omissions, caused no doubt by the speed of publication, sometimes mean that the true point of the

1866–1875	1875–1880	1881–1890	1891–present
House of Lords, English and Irish Appeals (L.R. ... H.L.) House of Lords, Scotch and Divorce Appeals (L.R. ... H.L.Sc. or L.R. ... H.L.Sc. and Div.) Privy Council Appeals (L.R. ... P.C.)	Appeal Cases (...App.Cas.)	Appeal Cases (...App.Cas.)	Appeal Cases ([ ] A.C.)
Chancery Appeal Cases (L.R. ... Ch. or Ch. App.) Equity Cases (L.R. ... Eq.)	Chancery Division (...Ch.D.)	Chancery Division (...Ch.D.)	Chancery Division ([ ]Ch.)
Crown Cases Reserved (L.R. ... C.C., or, ... C.C.R.) Queen's Bench Cases* (L.R. ... Q.B.) Common Pleas Cases (L.R. ... C.P.) Exchequer Cases‡ (L.R. ... Ex.)	Queen's Bench Division (...Q.B.D.) Common Pleas Division (...C.P.D.) Exchequer Division (...Ex.d.)	Queen's Bench Division (...Q.B.D.)	Queen's (or King's) Bench Division ([ ]Q.B. or K.B.)†
Admiralty and Ecclesiastical Cases (L.R. ... A. & E.) Probate and Divorce Cases (L.R. ... P. & D.)	Probate Division (... P..)	Probate Division (...P.D.)	Probate Division ([ ]P.) Since 1972 Family Division ([ ]Fam.)

* Note that there is also a series called Queen's Bench Reports in the old reports (113–118 E.R.).
† After 1907 this includes cases in the Court of Criminal Appeal, later the Court of Appeal, in place of the previous Court for Crown Cases Reserved.
‡ Note that there is also a series called Exchequer Reports in the old reports (154–156 E.R.).

case is not always fully conveyed. Law Reports now also appear in *The Independent* and *The Guardian.*

64 Sol.Jo. 498: Vol. 64 of the Solicitor's Journal (1856—still published). Short summaries only.

18 L.G.R. 425: Vol. 18 of the Local Government Reports (1902—still published).

31(1) Digest (Reissue) 426: Vol. 31(1) of the English and Empire Digest, which draws together under subject-matter headings reports previously published elsewhere. They are in short summary form and serve as a subject index to the original reports. Reissue refers to replacement volumes. The first replacement set has a broad blue band across the spine of the volume, the later set has a green band.

AVAILABILITY OF REPORTS

It will be clear from what is said above that the average solicitor's firm can only carry a small part of the whole of reported cases. What these will be will depend on the size and also on the age of the firm. One must beware also of incomplete series on the shelves, where an office subscription lapsed or volumes have been lost in use.

It will be noticed also that many of the old series, particularly before 1865, flashed across the legal scene like meteors. They appeared when their publisher had the necessary money and initiative and disappeared when these faded. Some lasted only a very few years. Even many of the longer-lived series that started in the last century (Law Times Reports, Times Law Reports and many others) have disappeared under the stress of commercial pressures since the war.

In these circumstances an office is fortunate to possess the English and Empire Digest referred to above. Where only the name of a case is known, it can be found in this series by reference to the alphabetical list of cases in Vols. 52–54, which includes cases to 1966. For later cases there is a cumulative Supplement. The Digest can also be used where no reported case on a particular point is known: to find out whether any useful decisions exist the reader should turn directly to the relevant subject heads and sub-heads.

All the main series of reports have their own index volumes, *e.g.* All England Law Reports, Tables and Index (1936–1976). This is in the standard dark blue binding and is supplemented by the Current Cumulative Tables and Index, which has a light blue cover and is regularly reissued. The Law Reports series has a digest series (Digests, 1865–1949) and Index volumes have come out at intervals since.

The preliminary pages of law textbooks and works of reference invariably contain an alphabetical list of all the cases cited in the volume with their references. The standard layout is: Contents—Table of Cases—Table of Statutes—Text.

STATUTE LAW

Acts of Parliament or statutes which bring in changes in the general law are called Public and General Acts. Parliament also passes Local Acts which are initiated by local authorities and other public bodies charged with statutory functions. Local Acts affect the law in the geographical area served by the body concerned. Personal Acts are occasionally initiated by private individuals to overcome legal obstacles, often in relation to property matters. Neither Local nor Personal Acts are printed with the Public General Acts.

Statutes are published in many series by different publishers. Some are simple copies of the original statutes. Others are annotated. Only one print is authentic: that published by the Comptroller of Her Majesty's Stationery Office and Queen's Printer of Acts of Parliament. This is the first to appear and all others are taken from it by licence. Noticeable among these are the Law Reports Statutes published like the reports by the Incorporated Council of Law Reporting. The courts take judicial notice of the contents of the Queen's Printer's copy of an Act. This means that the court will conclude without further evidence that what is there printed is correct. It is a point of more practical significance for Personal and Local Acts, which are of course not widely available, than for Public General Acts. The latter are available on sale individually, shortly after the Royal Assent has been given, at Her Majesty's Stationery Office (HMSO).

For those who must know in advance what legislation is being prepared in Parliament, HMSO provides a service by publishing Bills as they are presented and follow this by issues of new versions as the Bill proceeds on its several stages through the Parliamentary process.

The bound annual volumes of statutes printed by HMSO contain all the Public General Acts passed in the year. Up to 1939, however, the annual volume contained all the statutes passed by the session of Parliament that commenced in the autumn of the preceding year and ended in the autumn of the year of publication. So a statute passed in, say, December of one year is to be found in the volume for the next year.

As most textbooks and works of reference list statutes by their short title and date, it is usually possible to go straight to the table of statutes at the beginning of the volume and find what you are looking for. But not always has this been so. Until 1963, the official way of citing a statute was by reference to the year of the sovereign's reign and the number giving the order in which it was passed in the Parliamentary session—the chapter number. Whilst regnal years are no longer used in citing statutes, many of the old case reports give only these references. Turning to the schedule of repeal at the end of any statute you will see that the old references are given as well as the short title and date in all statutes before 1963. Some textbooks still list statutes in order of enactment, under the old references. Thus you will find references like "15 & 16 Geo. 5 c. 20," which cloaks a statute students are very familiar with: Law of Property Act 1925. The regnal year is reckoned from the date of accession of the sovereign and as a Parliamentary session invariably covers parts of two regnal years, there are normally two successive years in the reference. Thus, 38 and 39 Vict., c. 77 is the proper citation for the Judicature Act 1875. It was the 77th statute passed in the session of Parliament that commenced in the 38th year of Victoria's reign and terminated in her 39th year.

Since 1962, chapter numbers refer to the order of enactment in the calendar year.

THE FORM OF A STATUTE

Statutes follow a standard pattern of layout, preceded in the Queen's Printer's copy by a list of parts and sections. In the example reproduced on pp. 62–63 the elements that make up the Act are numbered alongside.

They are:

1.   Short title, chapter number and page

2.   Sovereign, followed by royal arms

3.   Year and chapter number

4.   Long title

5.   The standard words of enactment expressing the constitutional authority of the Queen in Parliament

6.   Section

7.   Subsection

8.   Marginal note: for information only, not part of the enactment

9.   Amendment of previous legislation. In a longer Act this is likely to be in a schedule

10.   Short title, commencement and geographical operation.

A statute introducing legislation covering a general field of business or activity will be divided into Parts by the subject matter, as indicated in the heading of each Part. The last Part is often "Miscellaneous and General." It is in this Part that one must look for:

1.   An interpretation section. This lists all the words used in the Act which have a special meaning in the context of the Act; when using an Act it is always wise to scan through the interpretation section before reading any of the operational sections.

2.   Consequential amendments and repeals of other Acts. Where there are several they will be found in a schedule.

3.   As our illustration shows, the last section usually gives
     (a) the short title, *e.g.* "This Act may be cited as the Solicitors Act 1974";
     (b) arrangements for bringing the Act into force. This may be to bring the various Parts or sections in force on different

Misrepresentation Act 1967 Ch. 7 1 **1.**

ELIZABETH II 2.

[*Royal Arms is inserted here*]

1967 CHAPTER 7 3.

An Act to amend the law relating to innocent mis- **4.**
representations and to amend sections 11 and 35 of the
Sale of Goods Act 1893. [22nd March 1967]

BE IT ENACTED by the Queen's most Excellent Majesty, by and **5.**
with the advice and consent of the Lords Spiritual and
Temporal, and Commons, in this present Parliament
assembled, and by the authority of the same, as follows:—

6. **1.** Where a person has entered into a contract after a mis- Removal of **8.**
representation has been made to him, and— certain bars
to rescission
    (*a*) the misrepresentation has become a term of the contract; for innocent
    or misrepre-
sentation.
    (*b*) the contract has been performed;

or both, then, if otherwise he would be entitled to rescind the
contract without alleging fraud, he shall be so entitled, subject
to the provisions of this Act, notwithstanding the matters
mentioned in paragraphs (*a*) and (*b*) of this section.

    2.—(1) Where a person has entered into a contract after a Damages for
misrepresentation has been made to him by another party thereto misrepresenta-
and as a result thereof he has suffered loss, then, if the person tion.
making the misrepresentation would be liable to damages in
respect thereof had the misrepresentation been made fraudulently,
that person shall be so liable notwithstanding that the misrepresentation was not made fraudulently, unless he proves that he had
reasonable ground to believe and did believe up to the time the
contract was made that the facts represented were true.

7.   (2) Where a person has entered into a contract after a
misrepresentation has been made to him otherwise than fraudulently, and he would be entitled, by reason of the misrepresentation,
to rescind the contract, then, if it is claimed, in any proceedings
arising out of the contract, that the contract ought to be or has
been rescinded, the court or arbitrator may declare the contract
subsisting and award damages in lieu of rescission, if of opinion

(*continued overleaf*)

that it would be equitable to do so, having regard to the nature of the misrepresentation and the loss that would be caused by it if the contract were upheld, as well as to the loss that rescission would cause to the other party.

(3) Damages may be awarded against a person under subsection (2) of this section whether or not he is liable to damages under subsection (1) thereof, but where he is so liable any award under the said subsection (2) shall be taken into account in assessing his liability under the said subsection (1).

Avoidance of certain provisions excluding liability for misrepresentation.

3. If any agreement (whether made before or after the commencement of this Act) contains a provision which would exclude or restrict—

(a) any liability to which a party to a contract may be subject by reason of any misrepresentation made by him before the contract was made; or

(b) any remedy available to another party to the contract by reason of such a misrepresentation;

that provision shall be of no effect except to the extent (if any) that, in any proceedings arising out of the contract, the court or arbitrator may allow reliance on it as being fair and reasonable in the circumstances of the case.

9.

Amendments of Sale of Goods Act 1893.

1894 c. 71.
(56 & 57 Vict.)

4.—(1) In paragraph (c) of section 11(1) of the Sale of Goods Act 1893 (condition to be treated as warranty where the buyer has accepted the goods or where the property in specific goods has passed) the words " or where the contract is for specific goods, the property in which has passed to the buyer " shall be omitted.

(2) In section 35 of that Act (acceptance) before the words " when the goods have been delivered to him, and he does any act in relation to them which is inconsistent with the ownership of the seller " there shall be inserted the words " (except where section 34 of this Act otherwise provides) ".

Saving for past transactions.

5. Nothing in this Act shall apply in relation to any misrepresentation or contract of sale which is made before the commencement of this Act.

10.

Short title, commencement and extent.

6.—(1) This Act may be cited as the Misrepresentation Act 1967.

(2) This Act shall come into operation at the expiration of the period of one month beginning with the date on which it is passed.

(3) This Act, except section 4(2), does not extend to Scotland.

(4) This Act does not extend to Northern Ireland.

specified dates or to provide for commencement dates to
be fixed by statutory instrument;

(c) extent, *i.e.* whether the Act operates over the whole of the
United Kingdom or only say in England and Wales.

Numbered sub-divisions of sections are of course subsections. Numbered sub-divisions of subsections are paragraphs. The contents of
Bills in course of passage through Parliament are similarly named
except that instead of section we refer to clause. Schedules to Acts and
Bills have paragraphs and sub-paragraphs.

The naming of numbered divisions of statutory instruments varies
with the type of instrument. Regulations and Rules use these same
words: "Regulation" or "Rule 1 . . . ." Orders (including Orders in
Council) on the other hand are divided into articles.

Subdivisions in all statutory instruments are paragraphs and
sub-paragraphs.

ANNOTATED EDITIONS

Annotation is invariably needed for a full understanding of the effect
of a statutory provision. There are two main series: *Halsbury's Statutes*
and *Current Law Statutes*. Annual volumes maintain these series up to
date and *Halsbury's Statutes* has a Cumulative Supplement Service
showing the impact the current legislation has had on previous volumes. This function is provided in the case of *Current Law* by the
Statute Citator.

Full annotation of a section will include cross references to other
sections, sub-sections, schedules, etc., relevant word definitions,
effect on other legislation, relevant cases and statutory instruments
made under the power conferred by a section.

DELEGATED LEGISLATION

Delegated or subordinate legislation is law made by an authority on
which or on whom power has been conferred by an Act of Parliament.
Authority is usually conferred on the Minister of the Government who
heads a Ministry or Department: Secretary of State for the Environment, etc. The power is in most cases exercised by bringing before
Parliament a draft statutory instrument which may take the form of
Rules, Regulations or Orders. When approved by Parliament (or in
some cases if not disapproved within a specified time) they have the
force of law. Orders in Council made by the Queen on the advice of the
Privy Council are a form of statutory instrument.

The content of Rules, etc., must be within the statutory power and
must have been made in conformity with the particular procedure
specified by the statute. Otherwise it may be void as being *ultra vires*.
Hence, when a case is based upon a Rule, etc., it is wise to refer first to
the power it is made under before going to the statutory instrument
itself.

Statutory Instruments (S.I., formerly S.R. & O.) are numbered in sequence through the year as they appear. They are cited by the year and number: S.I. 1975 No. 727 is The Solicitors (Disciplinary Proceedings) Rules 1975, the 727th Statutory Instrument to be made in that year. As there are over two thousand of them made annually and as they may deal for instance with the most abstruse technicalities of industry and commerce, they are for practical purposes obtained individually as and when required. It is the lawyer's responsibility when dealing with a problem to search out all relevant subordinate legislation and obtain copies where necessary from HMSO.

All statutory instruments are notified in the daily lists of publications issued by HMSO, which also publishes monthly and annual lists of statutory instruments, also bound volumes of these instruments. All are listed in *Current Law* and the most important are referred to in the legal periodicals. *Halsbury's Statutory Instruments*, a continuing series, gives full lists under subject headings and copies of the important ones.

TEXTBOOKS

One should bear in mind the distinction between textbooks for students and those for practitioners. It is only the latter with which we are concerned here. Practitioners' textbooks usually cover their subject as thoroughly and comprehensively as the corresponding subject in *Halsbury's Laws*, sometimes more so. In using a textbook it is important to note its date and to see that you are using a reasonably up to date book and in any case the latest edition. With the date in mind one can limit the search for subsequent developments, without which no research is thorough and complete.

HALSBURY'S LAWS OF ENGLAND

Unquestionably the most comprehensive and the most respected textbook of English Law is *Halsbury's Laws of England*. This is, in fact, an encyclopedia covering virtually every aspect of the law. The latest *complete* edition, the fourth, comprises 40 volumes bound in green covers and a general index in Vols. 41 and 42. There is also an index in each volume. The law is set out in all essentials, subject by subject, the first and last subjects in each volume being listed on the spine of the volume. Copious notes at the foot of the page lead the reader on to the statutory provisions summarised in the text, to orders and regulations that cannot there be contained and to relevant case law.

The fifth edition is now in course of publication. As may be expected with such a work, complete publication takes several years and in the meantime the old and new editions must be used together with the aid of the correlating indexes supplied by the publishers.

To bring the combined series up to date, two annual cumulative supplements are published. One covers the 4th edition volumes not yet replaced and the other covers the 5th edition volumes so far published. It will be found that these supplements are arranged to cover changes in the original text, volume by volume, numbered paragraph by numbered paragraph. The volume number referred to is·repeated at the top of each page of the supplement.

We now look at an example of how reference to the *Laws* and the *Statutes* (as the two Halsbury series are generally referred to) is made in a particular matter in the office.

Example

Our local solicitors Messrs. Rime and Reason have had an inquiry from a client who is concerned about the possible fire hazard created for his neighbour by the storage of a drum of petrol in his garage. The petrol is needed for a motor mower to mow a large lawn. The principal, Mr. N. Wisdom, has told his client that he believes the amount that can be stored in residential property without a licence is quite small—possibly two gallons—but he will need to check on this before advising because there are other aspects, such as storage in vehicle fuel tanks and the material of which containers must be made. Mr. Wisdom asks his trainee legal executive, Miss Stella Muse, to look out the references in the *Laws* and *Statutes*.

As the law relating to the storage of petrol is likely to be in regulations made under statute, Stella looks first at the brown-covered Statutes volumes, of which there are 39, brought out between 1968 and 1972. The subjects are listed on the spine, so if she were sure of the heading under which the subject-matter would come it might short-circuit the search to pick out the volume with the appropriate subject and look at the separate index devoted to that subject in its volume. But under which heading will petrol storage come? There is on the spines no subject "Petrol" nor the word from which it comes: "Petroleum."

From 1972 annual continuation volumes of the Statutes are published, containing the statutes for each year and among these there is an index to the whole series to 1975. This index is by no means as full as the general index to *Halsbury's Laws*, but it is worth a try. Stella turns to "PETROLEUM AND PETROLEUM SPIRIT." A search through this does not disclose any entry clearly pointing to petrol storage.

She turns to the *Laws* volumes where the subject may be expected to be found in complete form and logical order. The only complete index is that in the green volumes 41/2 of the 3rd edition. Turning to "Petroleum," she first pauses at "spirit," as this is what the client is storing. Looking at the sub-entries under this word she pauses again at "storage" and she sees:

"legislation	31, 395
use of motor vehicles	31, 406–408
without licence	31, 406–408"

This seems near enough to the target to be worth a try. She turns to Vol. 31 and finds that Petroleum is a subdivision of the subject "Public Health." On p. 395 she finds that storage of petrol and other inflammable substances is regulated under a series of Petroleum (Regulations) Acts 1928–1936. Glancing through the paragraphs she pauses next (as the index directed) at p. 406. Here she finds that no petroleum spirit licence is needed to keep petroleum spirit either for private use or for sale if it is kept in certain kinds of container in quantities of not more than one pint and to the total quantity of three gallons. Can this be all? How then do we keep our cars in the garage? Looking further down the same page she finds an answer under the heading "Petrol for motor vehicles, etc."

From this paragraph and the notes she learns that the statutory provisions regarding the keeping of petrol for, *inter alia*, motor-mowers are contained in the Petroleum (Consolidation) Act 1928; that petrol must be kept in secure metal vessels and that, apart from petrol kept in the fuel tank of a "motor vehicle, motorboat, aircraft or engine," the quantity must not exceed two gallons. She is referred to the Petroleum Spirit (Motor Vehicles, etc.) Regulations 1929, S.R. & O. 1929 No. 952, Schedule.

She flags p. 406 of the *Halsbury's Laws* volume as the first reference Mr. Wisdom will want to see. To go further than this, she would need to refer to the regulations themselves. But the library does not have the only summary compilation of statutory instruments: *Halsbury's Statutory Instruments*, or a copy of the regulations themselves. The only course for Mr. Wisdom if he needs to see the regulations is to order a copy from H.M. Stationery Office.

Stella does, however, think it worthwhile to give Mr. Wisdom the statute under which the regulations are made. To locate this, she turns to the Index volume to Vols. 1–45 of the brown-covered series of *Halsbury's Statutes*. In this she turns at once to the alphabetical table of statutes at the beginning of the volume. The Petroleum (Consolidation) Act 1928, as in the *Laws*, is under the heading "Public Health," in volume 26. This is also taken out and flagged for Mr. Wisdom to look at.

But this is not quite the end of the task. One most important step remains. The title page of Vol. 31 of the *Laws* shows that it was published in 1960. Stella must find out what, if anything, has happened to change the law as stated in paragraphs 592–595. She turns to the Cumulative Supplement for the latest year—the one containing the commentary on the volumes of the 3rd edition that have not yet been replaced. Knowing that she will find the volume numbers printed boldly at the top of each page she has no difficulty in finding the page where paragraphs 592–595 are commented on. This gives her the law to the end of the previous year and she flags this page also to give to her principal.

There remains unexplored now only the years or month since the Supplement was published. To cover the possibility of changes in this period she might turn to the *Halsbury's Laws* Current Service where the Monthly Review issues are collected with a cumulative index. As this is rather selective in its operation and not so quickly published as the monthly issues of Current Law, Stella prefers to look at the latest monthly issue of that series. However, she finds nothing on the subject in the cumulative index which covers all issues to date in the current year.

Her task is now completed.

CURRENT LAW

Stress has been placed above on careful regard to the date of publication of any book consulted on a point of law and the importance of using the latest edition. In the case of *Halsbury's Laws* and *Statutes*, as has been explained, the continuation volumes and supplements will provide information on all changes since the main volumes in each series were published. But only up to a certain date, perhaps some 12 months or so previously. It is essential to bridge the gap to the time of search so far as possible. This is the main function of Current Law, to which several references have already been made. It comes out monthly in the first week of the month and includes everything of importance arising in the preceding month. Necessarily, entries are condensed to a short paragraph or two so that the law is pointed to rather than expounded. But room is found, for instance, for digests of decided cases similar to the head note of a full report. The cases reported in practically all the series of general and specialist law reports are included, as well as a selection of cases relating mainly to personal injuries not included in any published report. A summary of new statutes and statutory instruments is given, all of which are listed in separate cumulative tables.

The aim to serve the practising lawyer is seen in the list of dates of commencement of new legislation and in the section headed "Damages," which extracts from court decisions cases that are of interest and use to solicitors and others negotiating settlements of personal injuries claims. The "Case Citator" guides the practitioner to the fullest report or transcript of a case and enables him or her to see at a glance whether a reported decision he may be using in an office matter has been overruled, confirmed or otherwise affected by a later decision. The section "Words and Phrases" gives an alphabetical list of words the meaning of which has been commented on by judges in the preceding month with a cross-reference to the digest of the relevant case.

The use of the monthly issues is simplicity itself. Apart from the general index, which is cumulative throughout the year, the text is organised under an alphabetical series of topics. The titles of the topics are those that are in common use: Legal Aid, Practice, Company Law and so on.

At the end of each year, the publishers consolidate the monthly entries in a Year Book. This is indexed cumulatively over several years. There are other ancillary indexes and compilations. This is truly a magnificent addition to the lawyer's resources of knowledge. Every practising lawyer needs access to it. Students should start by closely examining a recent monthly issue and noticing the way it is made up and how the items are indexed.

The conventional Current Law service is now supplemented by an electronic publication, Current Law Year Books on CD-Rom, which allows the user to search through five years of Year Books using a simple word search. The user can then print out a reproduction of the actual Year Book page for reference.

PRECEDENT BOOKS

Precedent here does not refer to the judicial precedent in case law but to the form and content of documents having legal effect. It is a basic skill of the lawyer to express in written form the business, social and family relationships of everyday life. Wills, contracts, conveyances, writs and a hundred and one other documents pour from legal offices in a never-ending stream. At one stage or another, a document has to be prepared in nearly every matter a solicitor handles and precedent books are an aid to him, shortening the labour of composing the more formal parts of the document and, in the commoner kinds of transaction, providing a complete blueprint for the most likely contexts. Before looking at the books available, we will turn aside briefly to consider the place of drafting in legal practice.

In earlier times, the drafting of documents and the production of the fair copies for signature ("engrossments") took up a bigger proportion of a lawyer's time than it does today. Partly this was due to the inordinate length of the old documents. Lawyers went to extraordinary lengths to express their subject-matter in as many words as possible for fear that something might be omitted. Whereas today we express the transfer of ownership of land in one word "convey" or "assign," until the earlier years of this century this was "grant, bargain, sell, alien, release, confirm and enfeoff" or some equally long string of words. The fact that the length of the document largely determined the charge no doubt delayed the reform of the language of drafting. Today, even if brevity had not been accepted as a virtue in itself, commercial pressures would long since have curtailed drafts.

Other features of the old drafting were the absence of division into paragraphs and the sparsity of punctuation. The avoidance of punctuation within sentences is still looked on as a virtue on the hypothesis that a sentence should be so constructed that its meaning is clear without resort to commas or other pauses. This principle is still exemplified in the sections and subsections of Acts of Parliament. In modern documents, sentences are shorter and the content is divided into numbered paragraphs. Names and words which must recur many times are defined: "Hereinafter called the vendor," etc.

In drafting a document, a solicitor has several objectives:

(1) comprehensiveness: often the draft will uncover connections and possibilities the client had not thought of;

(2) clarity of language: clarity here includes exactness. The protection of the client's interests demands that the lawyer be

successful in giving precise expression to the instructions he has received so that no argument can arise from ambiguity of expression—a counsel of perfection, but still an objective;

(3) brevity: this as we have said is desirable for its own sake, but must often be sacrificed to the first two aims.

It is strongly arguable that skill in drafting is the lawyer's greatest accomplishment. Skill, however, in devising expressions and clauses to give effect to complex relationships is not in itself enough. He must at the same time take meticulous care in the simple matters, spelling, punctuation and so on. One of the less attractive tasks in a solicitor's office is the checking over of drafts and finished documents, comparing new typescripts with the drafts from which they were typed. At other times, original documents have to be compared word by word with duplicates or with copies (even photocopies) which then have to be certified as true copies of the original. It would be disingenuous to say that the "calling over" of documents, etc., is not done as quickly as the tongue can be made to work. At worst the typescript is gabbled through with scant regard to the dangers of mishearing. This is a bad mistake. Such tasks are to be treated with the seriousness they require. The consequences of overlooking an obtrusive "not" or "be" may be drastic, perhaps even an action for damages against the firm.

The importance of success in drafting is nowhere more clearly perceived than in the number of reported cases where the decision "turns" on a disputed interpretation of a word or phrase in a document. One has only to think of the long line of cases on phrases in contracts for the sale of land: "subject to contract," "subject to survey," etc.

For the busy practitioner no volumes are more valuable than those in which he can find samples of documents of the particular kind he happens to require. Drafting to meet the case in hand is bound to be individual. Still, there are aspects of documents which are common to all: the layout, the sequence of parts and in many cases operative clauses that will fit into many situations. It is a great saving of time if the basic pattern can be extracted from a book and worked up into a finished draft to fit the case.

Fortunately there is an excellent compilation which meets the lawyer's requirements in most matters. Published by Butterworth & Co. (Publishers) Limited, the publishers of the two Halsbury works, it is now in its fourth edition, comprising 23 volumes: "Butterworth's Encyclopaedia of Forms and Precedents." The aim is to provide a form for at least every ordinary transaction that occurs in practice and for all others except such as are purely academic; to present them in a simple and straightforward form so that the nature and effect can be understood at a glance; to collect and arrange them so that they can be found with the utmost facility. There is an annual Service containing new forms to meet new legal situations: perhaps a change in the law or in business practice. A cumulative Noter-up, published yearly, gives a ready check on the contents of the main volumes for changes since the date of publication. A most important aspect of the work is the

Preliminary Note to the forms under each subject setting out the legal context, but strictly from the point of view of the practical implications and pitfalls for the draftsman. Each volume of the series has its subject headings listed on the spine and it will be found very easy to use. For firms which do not have the Butterworth work, a short but valuable substitute is Kelly's Draftsman, a book that covers many of the more regularly used document forms.

The Encyclopaedia and Kelly do not cover court forms. There are, however, several excellent compilations of these. "Oke's Magisterial Formulist" gives what is required in the magistrates' court. Chitty and Jacob's "Queens Bench Forms" covers much of the High Court practice and there are others. Atkin's "Court Forms" is the most comprehensive set of those in common use.

INDICES

Indexing may refer to two different things: the index or indices to a book or series of books and the cataloguing of books in a library.

The latter is of more practical relevance for research in one of the large law libraries or in a public library where law books form a subject heading in a general classification system. General libraries and large law libraries invariably have two catalogues: a name or author index and a subject index. They are normally to be found in card-index form in cabinets. Increasingly, however, these are being replaced by micro-film or micro-fiche. This requires a "reader," *i.e.* an appliance for showing the entries on a screen. The subject-matter of each micro-film or fiche will be indicated on the film. Having located the book required in the card index or on the screen, the reader must note down the classification reference and, unless he is already familiar with the library layout, consult a librarian on where the volume is kept.

The indexing of books is of more immediate importance, because the proper use of an index is often the only guarantee that a reference will not be missed. There are two common methods of indexing: word by word (like the telephone directory) or letter by letter. Compare the following lists:

Letter by letter	*Word by word*
Law	LL.B. (Degree)
Lawabiding	Law
Law Court	Law Courts
Lawful	Law Lords
Law Lords	Law, Prof. J.
Lawmaker	Law Times
Law, Prof. J.	Lawabiding
Law Times	Lawful
Lawyer	Lawmaker
LL.B Degree	Lawyer

The point should be borne in mind particularly when searching a card-index catalogue in a library because the system used will not be evident at a glance.

It has also to be borne in mind that indexes vary in their thoroughness. One should not be content to take the first blank as conclusive that the point sought is not to be found in the text. The student should look for another word under which it might be indexed. Suppose you wish to know whether the police were entitled to stop your client when driving his car and require him to have a breath test. Assume we have a textbook on the Road Traffic Acts, we may start looking under "breathalyser" or "police" or under "offences" or "summary offences." The exercise of imagination will often yield results.

INFORMATION RETRIEVAL

A comparatively new way of finding legal information, and one which works in a very different way from written indices, is to make use of computerised databases that can be connected to a terminal in the office via the telephone. These are generally known as "information retrieval" or IR systems. As we have already seen (Chapter 1, p. 31) there is a wide variety of databases of commercial material. However, the number of databases of legal information is small, reflecting both the limited number of potential users and the high costs of providing the information.

These legal IR systems can be classified under two headings. The first type runs on Prestel. The major service here is Lawtel. This is a closed user group service (*i.e.* a subscription must be paid annually) it covers English case and statute law from 1988 and includes summaries of significant decisions, awards and statutes. There is also an index to articles published in the Law Society Gazette. The information can be obtained by subscribers through a special television set or a computer terminal connected to Prestel via the telephone.

As opposed to the Prestel system there is also "full text" information retrieval. Under this system there is a database which covers the full text of a large number of cases and statutes.

The main "full text" information retrieval system is LEXIS. This has a dedicated terminal linked by telephone line to the Lexis data bank. A person who wishes to make some inquiry formulates a "search" giving certain key words and these are typed into the system on a more or less ordinary typewriter keyboard. There is a visual display unit which looks much like a television screen which provides the reply.

The legal texts which are available on Lexis are arranged in "libraries" and each library is subdivided into "files" which consist of materials of particular types such as cases or statutes. All the main series of Law Reports since 1945 are fully recorded in Lexis. The advantage of a system such as Lexis is that if one has only partial or inadequate information and wishes to look something up the system operates with quite astonishing speed. If a search is properly formulated the very answer can be provided in an on-screen display within seconds. Suppose, for example, that one had a client whose house was near a large lake and who was persistently troubled by the noise of power boat racing at weekends. She wonders whether anything can be done. You are not yourself greatly experienced in this area of the law of nuisance and you doubt whether there has ever been a nuisance case to do with power boat racing noise. Accordingly you decide to search Lexis. You ask for the main library which is called the English General Library. This gives you access to cases since 1945 in England and Wales, and statutes. You decide that it is unlikely that any statute will have dealt specifically with power boat racing so you decide to search through cases. All you need do is key in the words "power boat" and "noise" and perhaps the further word "nuisance" and Lexis will then find for you every case in which those words were mentioned since 1945. You may be pleasantly surprised to find that there is in fact a number of such cases and that the leading case accepts that noise from power boat racing, even occasionally at weekends, can amount to nuisance. Of course, in fields like nuisance and negligence factual similarities cannot be taken too far but you can now obtain a full print-out of the case concerned, which is called *Kennaway* v. *Thompson* [1981] Q.B. 88. Alternatively, instead of getting a print-out of the case on Lexis, which can be expensive, one can simply now turn to the Law Reports in the office and look up the case there. Accordingly one can go on to advise the client properly.

Lexis is not at all difficult to use. Training courses are provided by Butterworth's Telepublishing who operate the Lexis system and the courses usually last one day. As a tool for legal research, Lexis is invaluable. Large firms of solicitors and an increasing number of barrister's chambers now have access to it although the cost is probably disproportionate for smaller firms of solicitors for the time being. It must be remarked, however, that a solicitor who did not have access to Lexis, nor a great deal of time to spare, might very well decide to take counsel's opinion on the point mentioned above which would cost his client a considerable sum. Where the answer is easily available to such a brief inquiry it would arguably be more profitable for the solicitor to have Lexis and do the research work himself, charging an appropriate rate to the client for his skill and expertise even though a comparatively short amount of time was involved. By using Lexis in such a case, counsel's fees and the lengthy delay in the preparation and dispatch of documents to counsel and the receipt of his advice would be saved.

CONCLUSION

The quickest way to learn about finding the law is to use the library. It is hoped that the explanations given here will help, but there is no substitute for actual experience in the use of the books. Students should make a point of browsing in the library. They will find that the interest their reading generates will be a help in their general studies.

Self-Testing Questions
(Chapters 1, 2 and 3)

1. What is a legal executive and what does he or she do?
2. Why and how are computers used today in solicitors' offices?
3. What is a law report and what series of law reports exist?
4. What are the reasons for making attendance notes?
5. How is the solicitor's profession governed and regulated?
6. Explain what problems can be caused by conflicts of interest.
7. How are a solicitor's charges regulated?
8. What are the governing marks of a profession?
9. What methods exist for discovering the law on a particular topic?
10. What is a statute and how does it differ from case law?
11. How can a solicitor's staff best keep up to date with the law?

CHAPTER 4

LEGAL AID AND ADVICE

INTRODUCTION

Lawyers have throughout history usually had a bad press. In part, this is the profession's own fault. Until very recently it has been notoriously poor at public relations, that is, publicising the good it does. It is certainly true that the media find stories of lawyers' incompetence or dishonesty considerably more newsworthy than stories of the thousands of daily transactions which are carried out efficiently. In addition, there is the factor that many people consult lawyers only at times of trouble in their lives, that is after they have suffered accidents, bereavement, been troubled by defective workmanship or other breaches of contract, been unfairly dismissed or made redundant, or even charged with a criminal offence. Accordingly, the need to see a lawyer often has unpleasant connotations. Moreover this is even true of non-contentious situations such as house sale and purchase. Indeed psychologists tell us that moving house is one of the most stressful experiences of a person's life, on a par with bereavement or divorce.

Apart from the nature of the occasions on which the layman needs to see a lawyer, another undoubted cause of the lawyer's possible unpopularity is the expense of his services. It has been said by one cynic that a poor man is no more likely to be surrounded by a crowd of lawyers than he is by a crowd of pick pockets. So long as poverty impeded access to legal services people were prone to say that there was one law for the rich and one for the poor. For centuries poor people were only able to obtain legal assistance from public spirited lawyers who might give their services cheaply or free for meritorious cases. However, one of the major social advances after the Second World War was the Legal Aid and Advice Act 1949 whereby the state provided finance for litigation to be brought by persons of modest means. The working of the system has changed a number of times since it started in 1950. The scheme was always means tested and when it was initiated about two-thirds of the population were eligible for legal aid. A rather smaller proportion is eligible today.

The present system of legal aid and advice has three different aspects: The first of these is a system of advice and assistance given by solicitors in their own offices known as "the Green Form" Scheme from the colour of the form which needs to be filled in. We shall consider shortly the limitations on this and on something which has evolved from it known as "assistance by way of representation." The second aspect of the scheme is civil legal aid which is available to persons who wish to bring or defend actions in the ordinary civil courts. Finally, there is a quite separately administered system of legal aid for criminal cases which we shall consider below.

The funding for legal aid is voted annually by Parliament. Until very recently the responsibility for dispensing and administering legal aid was in the hands of the Law Society. Since the Legal Aid Act 1988 came into force, however, a new Legal Aid Board has been responsible for the overall management of the legal aid system. It acts through the previous machinery whereby England and Wales is divided into 15 areas and each area has an Area Director who is in charge of his area. Each area director has a substantial supporting clerical and administrative staff including a number of lawyers, to process the enormous number of legal aid applications which are received. These persons are in effect civil servants. In addition there are legal aid area committees in each area consisting of barristers and solicitors in private practice who give up their time on a rota basis to consider some matters to do with the administration of legal aid.

We are now going to consider the various kinds of legal aid. Exact figures are given in some places so as to give a clear picture of how the system really works. The figures are those current from June 1989. The reader should bear in mind however that it is pointless learning the figures by heart for any purpose. They are reviewed annually and any practising lawyer will have to hand the Legal Aid Guide which sets out the relevant figures.

THE GREEN FORM SCHEME

Under the Green Form Scheme a solicitor may give a client who qualifies under it advice and assistance about almost any matter to which English law applies. This matter may generally be either contentious or non-contentious and it may with certain exceptions cover any work a solicitor may properly do for a client.

A solicitor must not take a step in court proceedings under a Green Form, nor may he give advice and assistance in respect of conveyancing matters other than in very limited circumstances. Finally, a solicitor may not give advice and assistance in respect of making a will unless the client concerned falls into one of certain special categories, including in particular persons aged over 70 and persons with serious disabilities. Other than this, however, the Green Form can cover advice in connection with contracts, conducting correspondence for a client, entering into negotiations on behalf of a client, drafting documents, interviewing witnesses, giving a client advice relating to future proceedings, and, particularly, helping the client complete an application form for full legal aid.

A Green Form client therefore comes to the solicitor's office just as a fee paying client does. The solicitor will normally ask if the client has heard of the Green Form Scheme; most people today have heard something about its nature and appreciate that there are means of receiving legal advice without having to pay the full rate. The solicitor will then work out whether the client is eligible for assistance under the scheme. The test is entirely financial and there is no investigation of the merits of the client's case. Thus even a client who appears to have a hopeless case on some matter is entitled to receive advice under this scheme.

The Scheme covers work done by the solicitor up to a total of two hours in an ordinary case or three hours in divorce and judicial separation cases. Solicitors are paid for their work on a fixed hourly rate which is adjusted from time to time. As a matter of interest the hourly rate at the time of writing is £43.25 per hour, except in London where the rate is £45.75 per hour. Thus the limit of the work which a solicitor can do outside London at the moment in an ordinary case other than matrimonial is £86.50. Moreover the solicitor is not restricted in his use of this amount of money to receiving it as his own costs. He may himself incur disbursements on the client's behalf and pay for them out of the total sum if he likes. So for instance if he wished to take counsel's advice on a difficult point on a client's behalf he could do so provided the overall maximum fee were not exceeded. There is also a provision permitting a solicitor to apply to the area office for an extension of the Green Form to allow him to do more work for a client than the basic limit.

The assessment of financial eligibility is carried out immediately by the solicitor in his own office and is a very easy task. The solicitor uses a "Key Card" which enables him to take financial details from a client and to assess at once whether the client qualifies under the scheme. The key card is used to compute the client's net disposable capital after certain fixed allowances for dependants; in addition the client's net disposable income needs to be computed after making allowances for tax, national insurance contributions, and certain fixed allowances for dependants. No allowances are made, odd though it may seem, for such outgoings as rent, rates or mortgage repayments because the allowances for these are inbuilt into the other allowances. If the client's income and capital are then below a certain figure the client qualifies for legal assistance without any payment on his part. If the client however has a disposable income above the minimum figure but still below a certain higher limit then he may obtain legal advice but will need to pay a contribution towards it, assessed by reference to a scale shown on the key card. The current key card is Number 24 and is illustrated below at p. 81. The solicitor uses it by lining it up alongside the Green Form in the way shown so that the arrows meet and then writing down the necessary figures. The computation only takes a minute or so to do. Let us now consider in more detail the various matters shown on the key card.

CAPITAL

"Capital" includes the value of all savings whether in cash, investments, money in the bank or in the post office and articles of substantial value such as furs or jewellery. However things that do not have to be taken into account are the value of the house in which the person lives, household furniture and effects, clothing and tools of the person's trade. Neither does the value of the thing itself that is in dispute have to be taken into account so, *e.g.* if the whole problem concerns the ownership of an antique clock, the value of the clock is left out. Having taken details of capital from the client it is a simple matter to see whether the client qualifies. As can be seen at letter "A" on the key card, a client who has no dependants qualifies if he has £1,000 capital or less; if a client has more than £1,000 then the client will be expected to pay for the initial advice. Of course if the client has say £1,010 and chooses to go out and spend the extra £10 this does bring him within the limit. As will also be seen, a client with one dependant may have as much as £1,335 capital, a client with two dependants £1,535 and thereafter a further £100 is allowed for every other dependant.

INCOME

Assuming that the client does not have excessive capital the solicitor must then look at income. If the client receives income support or family credit or disability working allowance (these are types of bene-fits payable basically to people on low incomes) then there is no need to investigate income any further. The client qualifies for assistance under the scheme. Suppose however, the client has earnings. From these need to be deducted income tax, national insurance contribu-tions and a fixed allowance for a spouse or cohabitee which at present is £40.69 so long as the parties are living together. In addition there are certain fixed allowances for children which vary with the age of the child between £18.19 for each child under 11 years to £42 for each dependent child or relative of 18 years or over. These allowances are totalled up and deducted from the gross income. What is left is then the "net disposable income." As can be seen from the form if this is £75 per week or less the client qualifies without paying any contribution. There is then, a sliding scale up to a disposable income of £145 per week and between the figures of £75 and £145 per week a contribution has to be paid by the client. If the client's disposable income is over £145 then he does not qualify for Green Form Assistance.

If the solicitor is then satisfied that the client is eligible for assistance he completes the Green Form (GFI) and gets the client to sign it to confirm the accuracy of the figures. We shall now show a worked example of the Green Form as illustrated.

Example

Messrs Rime & Reason are consulted by Mrs. Fiona Johnson who is a widow who lives with her twin 12-year-old daughters in her own house. Mrs. Johnson is having some difficulty with a neighbour over the question of the boundary of the property where she lives and the repair of the fence which divides the property from her neighbour's. She needs advice on ownership of this fence and repairing obligations.

The solicitor therefore knows that he will have to obtain the title deeds to her property (which are currently kept by the building society to whom the property is mortgaged) and inspect the deeds to determine this question and give her advice. He may then need to write letters on her behalf to the neighbour setting out Mrs. Johnson's position and asking for co-operation in repairing the boundary fences. The letters to and from the building society, the work of inspecting the deeds and advising her and then writing to the neighbour may well cost £40 to £50. Accordingly Mr. Reason explains the Green Form scheme briefly and takes her financial details. He ascertains that she has no substantial assets apart from her house but does have savings of £1,000. Since she has two dependants (her daughters) she is well within the capital limits. He now passes to her income. She is a supply teacher whose income varies somewhat from week to week. In such a situation only the income in the last 7 days needs to be taken into account. He finds out that her income last week, when she was only able to work for 3 days, amounts to £90 gross. In addition she receives child benefit for each child, a total of £16.45. Her total gross income for the last 7 days therefore was £106.45. Deductions for income tax and national health contributions were £10 last week. In addition she is entitled to the fixed allowance for each of her 12-year-old daughters which amounts to £53.50. After making these deductions it is obvious that she qualifies for the Green Form without any contribution because her income is substantially below £75 per week. He can now go ahead to advise her, write the necessary letters and obtain the title deeds with a view to assisting her. We must however consider three other matters:

(1) *Extensions*

As indicated above, basically a solicitor is only entitled to do two hours' worth of work for a client. If the work is more complicated or becomes more long drawn out then a solicitor may apply to the legal aid area office for an extension of this figure. The solicitor should indicate the nature of the matter and why it is necessary to do further work. If the area office give permission, they will fix a higher figure, say £100, or £150, up to which the solicitor may now go. He may then therefore continue acting for the client in relation to the problem up to that higher figure. Sometimes extensions very much higher than this are given, *e.g.* up to £400 or £500 in an appropriate case.

Because of the nature of Mrs. Johnson's problems, probably ordinary legal aid would not have been available since this in effect only covers litigation in the courts. Accordingly it might well be that her problem was an appropriate case on which to obtain an extension if more work needed to be done. If however, the case is one which ought to come to ordinary litigation such as a road accident, or breach of contract claims, then usually an extension will not be granted and the area office will insist that the solicitor applies for full legal aid to which we shall come below.

GF 1

LEGAL AID BOARD
LEGAL AID ACT 1988

GREEN FORM

Key Card

Surname	JOHNSON	PLEASE USE BLOCK CAPITALS Forenames FIONA	Male/Female	AREA REF. No.
Address	11 KEELEY RD	GARSET		

CAPITAL		CLIENT	£ 1000
TOTAL SAVINGS and OTHER CAPITAL		SPOUSE OR COHABITEE	£ ✓
		TOTAL	£ 1000

Ⓐ

Ⓑ

NOTES FOR SOLICITORS

1. Advice and assistance may only be given in relation to the making of **wills** in the circumstances set out in The Legal Advice and Assistance (Scope) Regulations 1989. In such circumstances your client must complete **Form GF 4**

2. Where advice and assistance are being given in respect of **divorce or judicial separation proceedings** and the work to be carried out includes the preparation of a petition, the solicitor will be entitled to ask for his claim for costs and disbursements to be assessed up to an amount referred to in The Legal Advice and Assistance Regulations 1989.

INCOME
State whether in receipt of Income Support, Family Credit or Disability Working Allowance.
YES/NO   If the answer if YES ignore the rest of this Section.

Total weekly Gross Income

Client	£	106—45
Spouse or Cohabitee	£	✓
TOTAL	£	

Allowances and Deductions from Income

Income tax	£ 5 — 00	
National Insurance Contributions, etc.	£ 5 — 00	
Spouse	£	

Dependent children and/or other dependants — Number

Under 5		£
5 but under 11		£
11 13	2	£ 53 —50
13 16		£
16 18		£
18 and over		£

LESS TOTAL DEDUCTIONS	£ 63 — 50
TOTAL WEEKLY DISPOSABLE INCOME	£ 42 — 95

Ⓒ
Ⓓ
Ⓔ

Ⓕ

TO BE COMPLETED AND SIGNED BY CLIENT

I am over the compulsory school-leaving age.

I have/have not previously received help from a solicitor about this matter under the Legal Aid and Advice Schemes.

I am liable to pay a contribution not exceeding   ..   .. £ NIL

I understand that any money or property which is recovered or preserved for me may be subject to a deduction if my contribution (if any) is less than my Solicitor's charges.

The information on this page is to the best of my knowledge correct and complete. I understand that I may be prosecuted for giving false information.

Date 28-1-1993   Signature F. Johnson

**GREEN FORM KEY CARD
(NO. 24)**
Effective from 6th April 1992

ENGLAND and WALES

Green Form

Please see over for
further explanatory notes.

N.B. The green form (GF 1) should not
be used for advice to suspects at police
stations.

CAPITAL means the amount or value of every resource of a capital nature
In computing Disposable Capital disregard
(i) the value of the main or only dwelling house in which the client resides, and
(ii) the value of household furniture and effects, articles of personal clothing and tools or implements of the client's trade, and
(iii) the subject matter of the advice and assistance.

Maximum Disposable Capital for Financial Eligibility (dependant = partner, child or relative)

Advice and Assistance*	ABWOR**
£1000 – client with no dependants	£3000 – client with no dependants
£1335 – client with 1 dependant	£3335 – client with 1 dependant
£1535 – client with 2 dependants	£3535 – client with 2 dependants
Add £100 for each additional dependant	

*Capital must be assessed for advice and assistance even if client is on income support, family credit or disability working allowance. See note 3.

**Capital is disregarded if client is on income support. See note 3.

INCOME means the total income from all sources which the client received or became entitled to during or in respect of the seven days up to and including the date of this application.

The capital and weekly income of both partners must be taken into account unless:
(a) they have a contrary interest
(b) they live apart
(c) it is inequitable or impractical to aggregate their means

Some types of income are ignored. See note 3.

In computing Disposable Income deduct:-

(i)   Income Tax

(ii) Contributions paid under the Social Security Acts 1975-88

(iii) £40.69 in respect of the client's partner (if living together) whether or not their means are aggregated. Where they are separated or divorced, the allowance will be the actual maintenance paid by the client in respect of the previous 7 days.

These deductions also apply to the partner's income if there is aggregation.

(iv) £18.19 for each dependent child or dependent relative of the household under 11 years of age
£26.75 for each dependent child or dependent relative of the household of 11 but under 16 years of age
£31.94 for each dependent child or dependent relative of the household of 16 or 17 years of age
£42.00 for each dependent child or dependent relative of the household of 18 years of age or over

Where the child or dependent relative is not a member of the household the allowance will be the actual maintenance paid by the client in respect of the previous 7 days.

There is no deduction in relation to a foster child.

Client's Contributions

Disposable Income	Maximum Contribution	Disposable Income	Maximum Contribution
Not exceeding £75 a week	nil	Not exceeding £110 a week	£38
„ £80 „	£5	„ £116 „	£45
„ £86 „	£12	„ £122 „	£51
„ £92 „	£19	„ £128 „	£58
„ £98 „	£25	„ £134 „	£64
„ £104 „	£32	„ £140 „	£70
		„ £145 „	£75

Note

The green form must be signed by or on behalf of the client at the initial interview as soon as his/her eligibility has been determined except in the case of an authorised postal application.

(2) *Contribution*

As we have seen, Mrs. Johnson did not have to pay a contribution. Suppose however that after the figures have been worked out her net disposable income had been rather larger, say £85. As can be seen by the list of figures on the Green Form key card, with an income of £85 she would have had to pay a contribution of £12. The solicitor should take this sum from her at the outset, or arrange for her to bring it in subsequently. This means in effect that of the £86.50 worth of advice she pays £12 and a claim can then be made to the legal aid area office for the balance of £74.50. Moreover in such a case it is up to the solicitor to exhaust the client's contribution first. Suppose therefore that Mrs. Johnson's problem had been rather different and had been a very simple one which could be resolved with say 15 minutes' advice. Suppose that the solicitor's charge for this was almost exactly £12, he should then retain the contribution he has received and not make any further claim to the Legal Aid Board. Only if the work he does exceeds this figure of £12 would he make a claim for the balance.

(3) *Money or property recovered*

Suppose that a solicitor, assisting someone in correspondence in negotiations under the Green Form succeeds in recovering money or property. In principle the money or the property must be used to pay the solicitor's fees before there is any call at all on public funds. Suppose for example that there was dispute over a sum of £300 owed to a client and that a solicitor advising that client under the Green Form Scheme was able to obtain this money by writing letters. The solicitor's charges should then come out of the money recovered and the balance be given to the client. It would obviously be quite wrong in such a situation for the tax payer to pay, where the client had now received sufficient funds to enable him to bear the legal costs.

There are however exceptions to this principle so that in appropriate circumstances the solicitors do not need to insist on the money or property recovered being used to bear his bill.

   (i) If it would cause hardship or distress for example if a pensioner has been overcharged in rent and the solicitor writes letters for the pensioner and recovers say £50. It would cause hardship to put that money to the solicitor's bill and therefore the money could be returned to the pensioner without deduction and a claim made for the solicitor's bill from the Legal Aid Board.

   (ii) If it would be difficult to pay the bill out of the property recovered because of the type of property, for example if there is a dispute over ownership of a pet dog. The dog is recovered for the person who is receiving assistance under the Green Form but clearly it would be inappropriate for the solicitor to insist on the dog being sold to obtain monies with which to pay his bill. Again in such a situation the solicitor can simply make his claim for payment under the Green Form.

The solicitor claims payment by completing the back of the Green Form which is divided into a number of boxes in which the solicitor can fill in the types of work done and a summary of exactly what has been done under each so as to justify his claim for fees. Usually solicitors' offices save their Green Forms and send them in a few at a time with a composite claim for costs forms.

LEGAL AID FOR CIVIL PROCEEDINGS

Legal aid for civil proceedings includes everything which may be done in court by a solicitor and if necessary a barrister. It consists of pre-action work such as finding out the facts, visiting the site of an accident, interviewing witnesses, etc., right up to enforcement of any judgment obtained. Usually where a client comes to see a solicitor in connection with civil proceedings the initial interview will be conducted under the Green Form Scheme and part of the time spent with the client will be used for filling in an application for full legal aid.

Legal aid proper is available for proceedings in the County Court, High Court, and the Court of Appeal and the House of Lords and also in some tribunals, particularly the Lands Tribunal and the Employment Appeals Tribunal. It is not generally available in the Industrial Tribunal nor for undefended divorce or for proceedings before a Coroner's Court or for actions for defamation. Full legal aid is granted on two tests, namely financial eligibility and on the test of whether the applicant can show that he has reasonable grounds for taking or defending or being a party to proceedings. Unlike with the Green Form therefore the client must show that he has some prospect of winning the case. Legal aid would not therefore be available for example where a defendant admitted liability for a debt but merely wished to be represented in court on an application to the court for time to pay by instalments. It is generally essential that a client should show that he is likely to win. Despite this requirement it is by no means unusual for both parties to a case to receive legal aid for the same matter. This is because in essence when applying one is only obliged to submit one's own version of the facts on one's legal aid application. Thus, each party may just produce a version of facts which favours himself.

The way in which the means (that is disposable capital and disposable income) are worked out is not unlike that for the Green Form Scheme except that the assessment is considerably more sophisticated. An assessment is carried out by an assessment officer of the D.S.S. and is much more detailed. The client will often have to attend for interview and bring with him documentary evidence of gross and net income, dependants and mortgage, rent, rates, etc. Where a solicitor ascertains financial eligibility under the Green Form Scheme no evidence of means was required to be produced, a solicitor was entitled to act on the basis that the client was telling him the truth about his means without demanding to see wage slips or bank statements. The D.S.S. interview will be considerably more demanding. The monetary limits for legal aid are however much wider than for the Green Form. The limit of disposable capital (that is the capital a client has after deducting the value of his house, etc.) is currently £6,750. If the client has £3,000 or less then there will be no contribution at all out of capital and between £3,000 and £6,750 there will be a contribution of the excess over £3,000. Disposable income is worked out by taking expected gross income over the next 12 months and making various allowances for dependants at prescribed rates. In addition, for legal aid, proper rent and rates, mortgage payments and other items such as fares to work and trade union membership may be deducted from gross income. If what is left as disposable income is £3,060 per annum or less no contribution will be payable. Between £3,060 and £6,800 a contribution on a sliding scale will be payable, usually a quarter of the disposable income between those figures.

Where contribution is to be paid from capital it must normally be paid at the outset in one lump sum. If it is to be paid out of income it can be paid in instalments usually over 12 months.

The above figures are for ordinary claims by persons in employment. Persons in receipt of income support are eligible for civil legal aid regardless of capital. In addition, pensioners applying for legal aid have certain figures of capital disregarded in differing bands depending on how much income they have. So for example a pensioner whose annual disposable income is only £350 will have any capital up to a value of £35,000 disregarded and so on in reducing bands. In addition, legal aid for personal injury cases is available to persons of greater means than for any other kind of case. So, for example, legal aid is obtainable up to an upper income limit of £7,500 and upper capital limit of £8,560 in personal injury cases.

There are four types of application form, namely:

Form A1 General.
Form A2 Matrimonial.
Form A3 Emergency application.
Form A4 Application for courts of summary jurisdiction.

Each form requires the applicant to make a statement of his case to enable the Legal Aid office to decide whether there are reasonable grounds for the proceedings to be taken. There is also a form L1 "applicant's statement of circumstances" which requires a detailed statement of the applicant's means. The form is signed in two places. This form is then forwarded to the Legal Aid office who forward the statement of means to the D.S.S. for assessment by an assessment officer. As we have noted above, often there will be a need for an interview. However, if the applicant is already receiving welfare benefits, the D.S.S. will already have a file on the person concerned and may make the assessment without the need for personal attendance. Once financial eligibility has been determined the forms are returned by the D.S.S. to the Legal Aid office who then consider whether on the legal merits the case should have legal aid. If it is decided that legal aid should be granted without any financial contribution being required the Legal Aid Certificate is then sent out to the person's solicitor. If a contribution is required however, then first, an offer of legal aid is sent to the applicant informing him of the contribution which has been assessed. He then has an opportunity to decide whether he will accept legal aid subject to paying that contribution.

The form of application for emergency legal aid is dealt with much more swiftly than any of the others by the Legal Aid area office. Other forms of application for legal aid generally take at least a month to be dealt with and sometimes rather longer than that. The application form for emergency legal aid is only appropriate where some step needs to be taken urgently to protect the applicant's position. A good example would be where an injunction is necessary to restrain somebody else from doing an act to the detriment of the person applying for legal aid, or where some time limit is about to run out and the applicant needs to apply to the court very swiftly before this happens. In such a situation the emergency application will usually be granted but legal aid is only given, limited to the single step necessary to protect the applicant's position. It is always necessary to submit an application for ordinary legal aid at the same time as the emergency legal aid application. The full application will then be considered for any proceedings subsequent to the further step.

Because a client receives legal aid it does not mean that he will never be called upon to pay any part of the costs of the case. Legal aid is only a guarantee that his own solicitor's fees will be met out of public funds. If a legally aided party (called "an assisted person") loses a case it is always open to the court to order that he pays his opponent's costs. However, in such a situation the court can only award the assisted person's opponent any costs which it is reasonable for the assisted person to have to pay bearing in mind the means of both parties and all the other circumstances including their conduct in relation to the case. In regard to his own solicitor's costs, of course the legally aided person does not have to pay anything whilst the litigation goes on over and above any contribution to which he has been assessed. However if the litigation is successful and the assisted person receives damages or recovers property from an opponent, then this property has to be made available to satisfy any costs to the Legal Aid Board. Of course, where a party wins a case, usually one's opponent is ordered to pay all or part of the costs. If the opposing party is ordered to pay all the costs then the legally aided person will suffer no call on any damages recovered. Indeed he may receive a refund of his contribution if all the net cost to the legal aid fund is met by his opponent. If however, for any reason the opponent does not pay the costs but money or property is recovered, then the legal aid fund has a "charge" on this property to the extent of any monies it has expended in respect of the assisted person's own solicitor's costs. Two examples may be helpful.

Example 1

An assisted person obtains legal aid to sue a small builder D in respect of some defective workmanship. The assisted person wins the litigation and is awarded £1,000 damages and costs. The builder manages to pay the damages, but before the costs are assessed he goes bankrupt because of other claims against him for defective work-manship, consequently the costs are not paid. Unfortunately in this situation the amount of the assisted person's own solicitor's bill will be deducted from the damages recovered and the assisted person will only get the balance. Had the builder D managed to pay the costs as well as the damages then the assisted person would have received the £1,000 intact and indeed had returned to him any contribution which he had had to pay.

Example 2

A and B are in dispute about ownership of a piece of land. A is in occupation of the piece of land. B sues A claiming that the land is his. A obtains legal aid to defend the proceedings. In the proceedings A is held to be the true owner of the piece of land and is awarded costs against B. However B has no money to pay the costs and the Law Society reluctantly decide it is not worth the trouble of attempting to enforce the order for costs. The amount of solicitors costs that had been paid to A's solicitor by the legal aid fund is £1,000. The Legal Aid Board will accordingly have a *charge* on the land which has been "recovered or preserved" in the litigation. Their charge on this land will be registered as a mortgage at the Land Charges Registry and, as and when the land may be sold in the future A will be required to reimburse the Legal Aid Board the £1,000 out of the proceeds of the sale of the land.

As we can see therefore legal aid should ordinarily be regarded as something like a loan to be repayable out of any monies recovered in litigation. Unlike the position with the Green Form, where it will be recalled a solicitor may waive the charge on the grounds of hardship or inconvenience, there is no discretion to waive the charge where full legal aid is granted and property is recovered or preserved in court proceedings. There are a few exceptions to this principle of the legal aid fund's charge in particular on payments of up to £2,500 in matrimo-nial property disputes; payments of maintenance of various kinds; and *interim payments* recovered in High Court or County Court proceed-ings, on account of damages.

The final thing to note about civil legal aid is that while the legal aid certificate is in force the solicitor must not accept fees from the assisted person for the case. Of course the assisted person may have a normal fee-paying relationship with the solicitor in relation to other matters. For example a client who has legal aid for the purposes of litigation may have a will prepared by a solicitor on a fee paying basis.

ASSISTANCE BY WAY OF REPRESENTATION (ABWOR)

Assistance by way of representation covers the cost of a solicitor preparing a case and representing a person in most civil cases in magistrates' courts. These include separation, maintenance, custody, affiliation, defended adoption proceedings, etc. It is also available to patients appearing before the Mental Health Review Tribunal and to some prisoners who face disciplinary charges before Board of Visitors in prisons.

The Application is made by filling in a Green Form and another form of application. Unlike the case with the Green Form where there was no investigation of the merits of the situation this latter form requires the applicant to give a statement of his case and show why it is reasonable for him to receive assistance from public funds in this way. This form is then submitted to the Area Office. They will consider whether it is reasonable for a person to have assistance under the ABWOR Scheme for the proceedings in question. If approval is granted then the whole of the solicitor's costs are covered without any limit on them. The application for solicitor's costs eventually is made by the solicitor completing the normal Green Form and submitting it.

In qualifying for assistance by way of representation therefore, there is a test of merits of the case. There is also a financial test. The same income conditions apply as in the case of the Green Form but the capital limit is higher so that one may have up to £3,000 in savings and still qualify. An applicant will qualify however much capital he has if he receives income support. A contribution may be asked for in the same way as under the Green Form. The same provisions apply also in respect of any money or property recovered or preserved in the litigation subject to the provisions of the Green Form Scheme so that there is *prima facie* a charge on such property to recover fees paid out of public funds to a solicitor. The same exceptions however apply in the case of hardship, inconvenience, etc., as apply in relation to things recovered under the Green Form Scheme itself.

LEGAL AID FOR CRIMINAL PROCEEDINGS

A quite different scheme applies in relation to legal aid for criminal proceedings although in respect of the magistrates' court, part of such proceedings payment is made by the Legal Aid office just as with civil legal aid. We shall consider the various stages at which legal aid and advice might be provided for someone charged with a criminal offence.

(1) *The Green Form scheme*

If a person has been charged with a criminal offence, or even just been questioned and released having been told that he may be further questioned and charged later then that person is free to go to a solicitor and obtain advice under the Green Form scheme if he qualifies. As we have seen, the Green Form covers any matter of English law and there is therefore no problem with wanting to get advice under it about a criminal offence even if no charge has as yet been brought. Assistance under the Green Form of course presupposes that the client is at liberty. We must now therefore consider the position if he is not.

(2) *Duty solicitor schemes*

If the police are questioning an individual about an offence at the police station, whether they have arrested him or whether he is there of his own free will to help them with their enquiries, such a person has a right to free legal advice without any means test. A person has the right to see a duty solicitor. The current duty solicitor scheme provides a solicitor who is available on call to all police stations in a defined area over a 24-hour period. Such solicitors are not employees of the court service and certainly not of the police. They are solicitors in ordinary private practice who agree to be available on a rota basis for this service. The solicitor is paid via the Legal Aid office from public funds. Accordingly a person in custody should ask to see the duty solicitor. Indeed the police must tell a person in custody of his right to see a solicitor. If a person in custody has his own solicitor who he thinks will come out to see him, he can ask for that solicitor instead of the solicitor on duty. Of course there may be a little delay in seeing a solicitor, particularly in large conurbations where only one or two solicitors may be on duty to cover several police stations.

If a person has to go to court, either because he has just been taken into custody by the police or where a person has been charged, released on bail to appear before a court at some future date and turns up at court without having previously contacted a solicitor, it is also possible for such persons to see the court duty solicitor. He will be available at court, usually for a couple of hours before the court business begins at 10 a.m. to give free advice and representation on a first appearance again without a means test. Of course where a person has been released on bail and told to appear at court at some future date it would be much more prudent for that person to go and see a solicitor privately in advance of the court hearing. If a person, having had some weeks to consider the matter only decides to see the duty solicitor on the morning of the case, then if there is any complexity in the matter at all, the duty solicitor is bound to have to ask for an adjournment so that proper instructions can be taken, witnesses contacted, etc. This may lead to delay and inconvenience and perhaps to the displeasure of the court.

(3) *Criminal Legal Aid*

As we have seen therefore, a person can obtain preliminary advice on a Green Form if not in custody or if at the police station under the duty solicitor scheme. For actual work in court, after the first appearance where one may be represented by the duty solicitor, an application for full legal aid must be made. Here the application is not made to the Legal Aid office but to the court in question. There is an application form to complete in which the applicant states his means. The test is two-fold: First there is a means test. This is not however worked out by the D.S.S. as with civil legal aid, it is actually worked out by the court staff. This is because of the greater speed and urgency of criminal proceedings. It may be necessary to decide a legal aid application on the day it is submitted. Indeed, often such applications are made just before a case starts and are dealt with in a few minutes. The court looks at a person's income, capital and outgoings and decides whether legal aid should be granted either without a contribution or subject to payment of a contribution. No contribution will be asked for from income if the person is receiving income support or family credit or if the disposable income which the applicant has left after allowing tax, national insurance contribution, housing expenses, travel to work and dependants and other reasonable living expenses is £65 per week or below. If that figure works out at more than £65, then a weekly contribution over six months will be asked for of a quarter of the amount over £65. So, for example, if a person's net income after taking all these matters into account is £77, a quarter of the excess over £65 per week will be required, that is £3 per week for six months. If the applicant has disposable capital of £3,000 or less then no contribution from capital will be called for. If more than £3,000, then it is likely that the court will estimate the cost of the case and demand an immediate payment from capital. However, if the applicant is receiving income support then no contribution from capital can be asked for.

If a person does not keep up instalment payments of contribution the court must be immediately informed of the reason for this (*e.g.* job change or job loss). The contribution may then be reassessed.

That deals with the means test aspect but there is also a merits test for criminal proceedings. This test is not however the same as that for civil legal aid so that the test is not "will the applicant win the case." Indeed it is very often the case that an applicant is granted legal aid even though he indicates that he proposes to plead guilty. In such a situation he may need legal aid so that, *e.g.* a bail application can be made or so that argument can be presented to the court as to why he should not receive a sentence of imprisonment. The further test is expressed in the phrase "do the interests of justice require" that the person should receive legal aid. In deciding what "the interests of justice" are, there is a helpful series of categories which are known as the "Widgery Criteria" from the name of the former Lord Chief Justice who chaired a committee which was concerned with legal aid. These criteria are now contained in section 22 of the Legal Aid Act 1988. They are also included on the application form for legal aid so that an applicant may indicate which applies to him. The criteria are as follows:

(i) Is the applicant in real danger of receiving a custodial sentence? In other words whether because the present offence is very serious, or because the applicant has a bad criminal record is he likely to be sent to prison for this offence? If so then he should normally be granted legal aid.

(ii) Is the applicant in real danger of losing his livelihood or suffering serious damage to his reputation? This would therefore apply in the case of someone who might lose his driving licence in the criminal proceedings where a driving licence was essential for his job; or for someone who might be exposed to public humiliation in some way (such as a vicar accused of shop lifting).

(iii) Where a substantial question of law is involved. Obviously it would not be proper to invite a layman to argue a difficult question of law to the court and in such a situation, even though none of the other reasons apply it may be proper for legal aid to be granted.

(iv) Where the applicant would be unable to follow the proceedings because of inadequate knowledge of English or where he suffers from some disability.

(v) Where a solicitor's special skills are needed particularly in relation to the tracing and interviewing of witnesses or expert cross examination of prosecution witnesses or where the case is a complex one.

(vi) Where legal aid should be granted in the interests of someone other than the applicant. For example, suppose that a man is accused of some sexual offence on a small child. It would be desirable in *the child's* interest that the defendant be granted legal aid because if he were not, then the defendant himself would have to cross examine the child in the witness box which might be a very distressing experience for the child.

The application is considered by the clerk to the magistrates and in some cases by the magistrates themselves. It is fair to say that around the country the policy of magistrates' courts in granting or refusing legal aid varies tremendously. Some courts are notoriously mean in granting it, others are considerably more liberal. If legal aid is refused on the grounds of "the interests of justice" then sometimes this is the case because the applicant did not give sufficient information on his application form. For example a person may not have given details of his own previous criminal record so as to indicate how likely it was that he might receive a custodial sentence. In such a situation, if legal aid is refused the best procedure is to reapply to the court on another legal aid application form giving more detail. If this is refused then if necessary an oral application can be made to the court either by the applicant personally on his first appearance or by the solicitor whom he wishes to represent him.

There is a further route of appeal in the cases of offences which are triable *either way*. These are offences of sufficient seriousness that they may be tried either in the magistrates' court or the Crown Court. Examples are; theft, some kinds of burglary, etc. (see later page 259 for fuller explanation). In the case of such offences, if the court itself refuses legal aid, the applicant can appeal outside the court system to the Criminal Legal Aid Committee. This is a committee of barristers and solicitors who give up their time to sit on a rota basis at the Legal Aid Area Office to decide such applications and appeals. They may grant legal aid even though the court has refused it.

Where a person is granted criminal legal aid it will usually be so that he may be represented by the solicitor he himself nominates on the form. Where a legal aid application form is completed in a solicitor's office with the help of a solicitor, then obviously it will be that solicitor nominated. If an applicant does not know a solicitor, he may choose one from a list kept by the court or the court will itself assign a solicitor to him. If two or more persons are charged with committing the same offence jointly usually the court will attempt to assign all legal aid applicants to the same solicitor in the interests of saving time, trouble and costs. However, just because the court assigns everyone initially to the same solicitor it does not necessarily follow that each applicant cannot have his own solicitor. In particular, when acting for clients in criminal cases a solicitor must be very vigilant to see that there is no conflict of interest or potential conflict of interest between the clients. If there is, then he must tell the court and request that one or more of the defendants be assigned to some other solicitor.

LEGAL AID IN THE CROWN COURT

Almost all criminal proceedings commence in the magistrates' court and the overwhelming majority are dealt with there. For the small proportion that go to the Crown Court after the magistrates' court, legal aid may be obtained either from the magistrates' court itself or by application to the Crown Court on a simple written form. Since only more serious cases are dealt with in the Crown Court it is usually easier to persuade the court that "the interests of justice" require that the applicant should have legal aid.

PAYMENT OF SOLICITOR'S FEES IN LEGAL AID CASES

For work done in the magistrates' court, application is made for payment to the Legal Aid office on an application form giving details of the work done, the number of court attendances and the time spent on the matter. Payment is then allowed at various fixed hourly rates so that there are different rates for interviewing the client, waiting at court, actual advocacy in court, etc. In relation to work done at the Crown Court, application is made for payment to the Crown Court office itself and payment is made by them out of Home Office funds.

PUBLICISING LEGAL AID

The Legal Aid Board goes to considerable trouble to publicise the availability of legal aid. Firms which are willing to offer legal aid facilities display the logo shown at the commencement of this chapter usually in their office windows. In addition Citizens' Advice Bureau and other welfare bodies have details of legal aid schemes and lists of local solicitors who are willing to act under the schemes. In addition, the Legal Aid Board publishes a number of very helpful leaflets explaining the operation of the schemes generally for civil and criminal legal aid.

Self-Testing Questions

1. What is the Green Form scheme?
2. How are means assessed under this scheme?
3. What is the purpose of the "Key Card"?
4. When is legal aid not available?
5. How are means assessed for legal aid?
6. What is meant by "assistance by way of representation"?
7. How is legal aid for criminal proceedings given?
8. What are duty solicitor schemes?
9. How are they organised?
10. What is the best way of finding a solicitor willing to do legal aid work?

CHAPTER 5

CONVEYANCING

LAND AND PROPERTY

That land is a marketable commodity is a commonplace of everyday life. It is, in fact, the single most important commodity we have. Industrial, commercial and domestic life are all directly dependent on the use, occupation and ownership of land. More money is invested directly and indirectly in land and the buildings erected on it than in anything else.

Whilst it is a saleable commodity, it is different from every other commodity in its fixity and indestructibility. It is these characteristics that set land apart from other commodities in the ways in which it is valued, used and passed from owner to owner.

There is no stock market quotation for land. Instead there is a profession of valuers who work within established principles of valuation, but who must apply those principles to the particular locality of the piece of land being valued, its available uses, its amenities, the local population able to service it, work on it, and so on.

For the lawyer, however, it is the varieties of legal occupation and interest that mark land off from all other ownerships. The fact that land is capable of such infinitely variable uses, that it can be developed by the construction of buildings capable of occupation by many different persons, families or organisations—these features call for a corresponding variety in the forms and extent of ownerships.

Because land is and always has been a vital economic resource, the forms of land owning have to match the economic needs of the day. But since land is also basically unchanged over the centuries there is a continuity of legal forms and concepts which distinguish the way lawyers today handle land transactions. To a large extent this is now a matter of terminology, but in spite of all the changes there are many kinds of interest in land which have stood the test of time and are required as much or more now as they were, say, in the agricultural economy of the eighteenth century.

In studying land law the student will learn how the feudal system of land holding has moulded the development of legal concepts of land ownership. It is not our function here to explain the history of land law, but we must occasionally refer to the past to explain the present.

One feature which makes land ownership different from owning other things is its indestructibility. If I buy some other thing, I can destroy it at will, even a Rembrandt portrait! With land I can pull down the buildings erected on it (although there are important restrictions on the freedom to do this in modern statute law), but the underlying space and subsoil will remain, whatever I extract from, or add to it. In effect the right of ownership is not quite so complete in land as in other things. The highest form of ownership of land in English law is the freehold which, subject to two things, can be equivalent to outright ownership. The two things are first, the limits of what man and his machines can do to the land, and to what is underneath or on top of it, and secondly, the vast range of statutory restrictions on land use and development that are imposed "for the social good."

THE USE OF LAND

Land can be not only used and developed, it can be shared. It is this feature of different people having an interest in the same land that brings into being the forms of partial ownership that exist, as it were, under the freehold. Principal among these is the leasehold. The essential characteristic of this is that the lease owner has rights of use and occupation for a fixed period (a "term of years"). It may be for only a very brief period, perhaps three years, or it may be a very long period: 99 years is a very common term. The life span and the changing patterns of life being what they are, such a period gives the lessee virtual ownership of any buildings on the site and this is reflected in the particular terms of the lease.

For the rights granted by the lease, the lessee will pay an annual rent to the person from whom he acquired it. The amount of the rent will be based on a careful assessment of the economic benefits the lease confers and the amenities that will be enjoyed by the lessee. In the case of a very long lease of land and buildings, as for practical purposes the benefits of full ownership of the buildings are being transferred, the transaction will usually involve the payment to the lessor of a large capital sum, reflecting the value of the buildings and a small annual rent called a ground rent, reflecting the value of the land. This is payable throughout the term.

As we find in common experience, the buildings on land can be leased off in whatever divisions or parts the landowner wishes. So we have leases of flats which can only exist so long as the parts of the building that support it continue in existence. It is also common experience to find that the leaseholder grants a sub-lease, which must be for a period at least one day less than the term he has been granted and this process of sub-leasing can be repeated by the grant of a sub-sub-lease and so on without legal limit.

The co-existence in one piece of land of the freehold and a lease and other forms of partial ownership shows that ownership in land is, as it were, bundles of rights over land and what is on it (generalised in commercial and general usage in the term "property"), the nature of those rights depending partly on the category of ownership, of which the lease is a primary example, and partly on the particular terms agreed between the parties when the rights are granted. It is common knowledge that a lessor has wide, but not complete, freedom to say what rights a person to whom he grants a lease shall have in his land. The freeholder is also free, within limits, to impose his own conditions when he grants other partial or subordinate interests out of his ownership. For the duration of his lease, the leaseholder can do the same.

When the freeholder has granted a lease he may, of course, still sell his freehold, but the purchaser takes subject to the lease, so that he has for the time-being only the rights of the landlord under the lease, including the right to payment of the rent. However, when the period of the lease expires he may expect to have the full rights of the freehold once again. Those rights, in effect, revert back to him and whilst the lease lasts he is said to have a "reversion." In fact the law now confers on leaseholders statutory rights that may enable them to extend their period of occupation. Thus, a business tenant may be able to apply for a new lease and a residential leaseholder under a long lease may be able to compel the lessor to sell his interest to him. The latter is called enfranchisement.

The lease has led on to the idea of the tenancy which in some ways is a kind of mini lease but, in its most common usage for family residences, is hedged about by statutory rules and restrictions on the freedom of the landlord to decide for himself what the tenant's legal position shall be.

OTHER RIGHTS OVER LAND

Leases and tenancies carry with them the right of exclusive possession, though if the lease allows it the leaseholder may have parted with this right to a sub-leaseholder or tenant. The right to exclude all others is of course also enjoyed by the freeholder. However, there are other subordinate interests which do not carry the right of exclusive use and occupation of a piece of land and to the extent that a freeholder grants such rights, his own use and occupation are diminished.

One example of this kind of ownership is the right of way. This enables a landholder to use in whatever way may be specified a small part of his neighbour's land as an adjunct to the enjoyment of his own land. There may be nothing to show on the land that such a right exists: no boundary walls or fences, perhaps nothing more than the worn-down grass of a footpath in a field, perhaps not even that. Rights of way are the commonest variety of a kind of ownership called the easement, which takes many forms. Easements include, for instance, rights to light—ensuring that your neighbour cannot build on his land so as to obstruct the light to your windows; rights of support, ensuring that your neighbour does not alter his own building so as to weaken the stability of yours; the right to take water from a stream and many others. Lawyers say the list of easements is not closed. As different land uses—methods of industrial production, etc.—arise, new easements will be recognised by law. Easements, being in essence rights in another's property rather than property in its everyday sense of a thing owned, are referred to as "intangible" or "incorporeal" rights.

One other kind of ownership which is part of our everyday awareness is the mortgage. In a society in which over 60 per cent. of families live in houses, etc., that have been, or are being, bought with the aid of a loan from a lender, or "mortgagee," the usefulness of this kind of property right needs no emphasis. Compared with the other forms of ownership mentioned above, it is in a sense incorporeal in that, if all goes well there will be no intervention by the mortgagee (whether it be a building society, bank, or individual lender) in the borrower's use and occupation. However, it is in law a form of substantive ownership in that if the borrower defaults on his repayments the mortgagee can exercise a power to sell the full rights of the borrower to recover the amount of his loan and interest.

There are other minor rights in land, amounting in many cases to no more than contractual rights. An example is the licence, which is either granted expressly in writing, which may be quite formal, such as a letter. Or it may arise by implication from the way in which a person (the licensee) is allowed to enter and stay on the land. No one who can claim the grant of a licence can be treated as a trespasser. Usually, the grant is subject to termination on short notice. There are circumstances, however, when the rights of use conferred by the licence are equivalent to full occupation rights. Then complications can arise because the licensee may claim that a tenancy has been granted. If the case is one where the licensee is residing on the property, this may bring him within the statutory protection for residential tenants and eviction may present big difficulties.

Of all the varieties of ownership mentioned above, there are two which the law has singled out as "legal estates." These are the freehold (technically, the "fee simple absolute") and the leasehold (technically the "term of years absolute"). All other forms of legal ownership are "legal interests." This does not quite exhaust the list, because we must add that there are also equitable interests.

JOINT OWNERSHIP OF LAND

The ownership of land can be shared, in that a variety of legal estates, interests and rights can, in a sense, be carved out of the freehold and vested in separate owners, each having a different interest. This must be distinguished from co-ownership, where two or more persons jointly own the same estate, interest or rights: joint lessees, joint freeholders, joint mortgagees and so on.

The most common example of co-ownership is that of joint tenants. Here the word "tenant" must not be thought of as related to a tenancy under a landlord, but to its earlier meaning derived from the Latin "tenens," which means "holding." Joint tenants are, in fact, simply joint holders or owners of a legal estate or interest. When a house is bought for family use, it is more often than not conveyed to husband and wife as joint tenants.

The law places a limit on the number of persons who can be the co-owners of a legal estate in land. That limit is four. But this does not stop other persons, without limit of number, having a beneficial interest in the land, except that their interest must be through and by virtue of the legal estate of the joint tenants. The latter are, in effect, trustees for those beneficially entitled. The interest of the beneficiaries is equitable.

There are at the same time two ways in which the equitable interest of the beneficiaries can be held: they can have a beneficial joint tenancy or a tenancy in common—also called undivided shares. The practical difference lies in what is called the right of survivorship that applies to the joint tenancy, but not to the tenancy in common. The practical difference is seen by taking the familiar case of husband and wife. When they hold the property as beneficial joint tenants and one dies, the survivor becomes the sole owner and can dispose of the property to a purchaser. If they hold the property as tenants in common in equal shares and one dies, a half share in the property only remains with the survivor. The interest of the deceased tenant in common passes to his personal representative. This may well be the survivor of them, but even so his duty will be to deal with the share in accordance with the wishes of the deceased joint owner as expressed in his will or in accordance with the rules of intestacy. In the outcome, the share may not, or may not all, pass to the survivor. Moreover, if the estate of the deceased is substantial, inheritance tax may have to be borne on the value of the share.

For practical purposes husband and wife are almost invariably joint tenants. In business relationships, on the other hand, a tenancy in common is often the appropriate form of ownership, because here if the retirement or death of a business partner causes the termination of the relationship, each co-owner will seek the return of the capital he has contributed to the joint venture. If on the death of a partner the partnership continues, his family will stand to benefit, not his business partners. It will be understood that the shares of tenants in common will vary, depending on the terms of the business arrangement, whereas joint tenants always have equal interests.

The function of transferring estates, interests and rights in land from seller to buyer—on which the market in land depends—is the practice of conveyancing. Whilst buying and selling account for the majority of transactions, conveyancing is also required when land is given by one person (the donor) to another (the donee) and where land is left by a person on his death. Conveyancing calls for a range of skills in which the solicitor and his staff are proficient. For many years solicitors had a statutory monopoly over paid conveyancing work. This led to criticism and in 1983 the government announced that non-solicitor conveyancers would be permitted to undertake this work subject to suitable safeguards to protect consumers. Indeed in 1984 the Farrand Committee on Conveyancing was established and as a result of its First Report, the Administration of Justice Act 1985 introduced the new profession of licensed conveyancer.

CONVEYANCING

For many centuries the ownership of land and property has been transferred—conveyed, granted, and so on—by deed. The particular features of a deed are dealt with later. In the case of the passage of ownership on death, the way the heir or beneficiary has obtained his rights has varied over the years and need not be described for our present purposes. The essential point is that until this century, and to a considerable extent even now, the evidence of ownership is wholly contained in the documents by which the land has passed from owner to owner. Therefore the skills of conveyancing have for the most part been concerned with the creation and examination of deeds and documents relating to a piece of land (lawyers speak of a "parcel" of land) or property. The conveyancer must be able to satisfy himself that the land described in the documents and the rights conferred by them are exactly those his client proposes to buy.

Moreover, he must not merely examine the deed by which the latest transaction was carried through: he must go through all the transactions affecting the land for at least the last 15 years. All must be in order and the first one, called the root of title, should, preferably, be of the outcome of a bargain struck between persons negotiating freely and independently (negotiating at "arm's length," as the phrase expresses it) or at least an outright disposal in the natural course of events.

The deeds and other documents by which ownership is established are called documents of title and to satisfy a purchaser that the title is a sound one, it has to be "proved." This is the kernel of the conveyancer's work. So long as the traditional method of proving title remains, physical possession of the deeds is crucial.

The traditional system of conveyancing is, however, giving way before the spread of registered land conveyancing. Acts providing for voluntary registration of title were passed in 1862 and 1875 but not until the Land Transfer Act 1897 made registration of title compulsory in the County of London were any substantial number of titles registered. The present principal Act is the Land Registration Act 1925, as amended. Under the registered land system the evidence of ownership is not the deeds of the property but the entries in the register maintained by the Chief Land Registrar of Her Majesty's Land Registry. The document of title held by the owner is merely a copy of the contents of the register in relation to that property. This is called the Land Certificate or, where held by a mortgagee, the Charge Certificate.

Compulsory registration of title has been spreading over the country since it was introduced, at first slowly, but with increasing pace until by 1978 it applied in all the main centres of population. As from December 1990 the whole of England and Wales has become an area of compulsory registration. It is intended that there be computerisation of the system by 1993.

When an area was made subject to an order for compulsory registration, unregistered titles were not immediately affected: conveyancing by deed proceeds as before, but when a property changes hands on sale the new owner is obliged to apply for the first registration of his title within two months.

THE ADVANTAGES OF REGISTRATION

The object of registration is, as the Land Registry explains in Explanatory Leaflet No. 1, to provide a safe, simple and economic system of land transfer. The main advantages of the system are stated as follows:

1. Registration of title gives finality and certainty by providing an up-to-date record of land ownership. The need to examine the past history of the title on each successive transaction is thus eliminated.

2. A registered title is guaranteed because there is express provision for indemnity should any person suffer loss through any error or omission that occurs in the register.

3. Registration can cure defects in title which may, up to the time of first registration, have been the subject of recurrent conditions of sale and enquiries. In addition, many unregistered titles have been successfully re-established by registration after the title deeds have been lost or destroyed.

4. For each title, there is provided an official plan which clearly identifies the extent of the registered land. These title plans are based on the large scale maps of the Ordnance Survey with the result that a common, unifying and accurate base is provided for all registered titles.

5. The proprietor of registered land (when it is not in mortgage) is issued with a land certificate which contains a copy of the entries in the register and of the official plan identifying the land. This certificate, unlike the often numerous and bulky deeds of an unregistered property, is a comparatively simple and compact document from which a proprietor can readily see and understand what he owns. If he should lose the certificate it can be replaced so that, even if this happens, he will still be able to deal with the land.

6. When unregistered land is mortgaged to secure a loan, the mortgagee holds the title deeds as part of his security. In the case of a mortgage of registered land, the mortgagee holds a charge certificate which is a document similar in form to a land certificate and to which is annexed the mortgage deed. This can be particularly helpful to mortgagees because it helps to reduce the costs of handling and storing bulky documents. So far as the mortgagor is concerned, he is always able to obtain an up-to-date record of his title without having to go to his mortgagee because he can obtain from the Land Registry an official copy of the register of his title.

7. A proprietor registered with an absolute title has a title to the land together with all its appurtenant rights which is subject only to such mortgages and other burdens as are set out on the register or are declared by the Land Registration Act 1925 to be overriding interests. Overriding interests are matters which do not normally appear in the abstract of an unregistered title. They may, for example, be local land charges which can be discovered by means of enquiries of the local authority or short-term occupation leases which will be revealed by inspection of the property or by enquiry of the occupier.

8. Registration of title eliminates the need for the deduction by the vendor and the examination by the purchaser of proof of ownership originating from a satisfactory root of title at least 15 years old as is necessary on each successive transaction with unregistered land. Should the proprietor of registered land wish to sell his property, he can speedily offer proof of his title by obtaining an official copy of the register and the title plan without normally any problems arising from defects in the title or in the identity or extent of the land.

9. In his turn, the purchaser can quickly and safely accept the evidence of title offered by the vendor without the need to investigate the past history of the title. He can then protect himself (without the need for a personal visit to any land registry office) by making an official search of the register immediately before the completion of the purchase. This will ensure that no other entries have been made on the register since the date of the official copy which the vendor has supplied to him and it will also have the effect of reserving priority for the subsequent registration of his transfer. Under the Land Registration Act 1988 open inspection of the registers of title, filed plans and documents referred to on the register (other than mortgages and leases or copies of either) has been possible since December, 1990. There is no need for a purchaser (or anyone else interested in the land) to obtain the registered proprietor's formal authority to inspect a particular register.

The highest form of ownership recognised by the Land Registration Acts is "absolute title." It is virtually a state guaranteed title (subject to any overriding interests, such as are referred to in clause 7 set out from the explanatory leaflet above). Lesser forms of ownership are possible. For example, it may happen that after a transfer on sale a landowner applying for first registration cannot produce any of the earlier deeds because they have been destroyed or lost or because the vendor is a squatter. In such a case, a possessory title is appropriate, *i.e.* the guarantee given is limited and the proprietor and subsequent proprietors take the land subject to any interests existing at the date of registration. A further example of where a "limited" guarantee is given is where a lease is registered without investigation of the freehold title out of which it is granted, and the leaseholder is given a "good leasehold title." It is possible for these lesser grades of title to be upgraded in due course. For example, once a squatter(s) has been in adverse possession for more than 12 years, an Absolute title can be given.

The Land Registry publishes a series of explanatory leaflets for the general public and solicitors' practice notes. Students would be well advised to obtain these free issues from which they may supplement their knowledge. The leaflets, for instance, will indicate the areas served by the District Registries and provide particulars of their addresses.

THE NATURE OF CONVEYANCING

Before looking in detail at a simple conveyancing transaction arising from a sale of house property, a word should be said about the basic elements of the work involved.

Initially, the seller and buyer reach a bargain on the price, with or without the help of the seller's estate agents. It is not unknown for the solicitor to negotiate a sale or purchase but it is unusual.

The respective solicitors receive the details of the property and the proposed terms of the transaction either from the estate agents, or from their own clients. The first stage is concerned with the drawing up of a formal contract. In this stage, the buyer's solicitor must make wide and detailed enquiries into possible snags or shortcomings that might affect the use and full enjoyment of the building itself, and the surrounding garden or other land (called the "curtilage"). By enquiries of the seller's solicitor, he checks on the state and condition of the property and the services. He asks about the seller's legal rights, his title, and any restrictions or obligations attaching to it. At this time, he will not expect to have full proof of all he learns, but the representations and copy documents supplied will enable him to conclude that, unless there is some omission, error or deception, the vendor has what he purports to sell. These enquiries are supplemented by enquiries of the local authority as to whether any of the array of statutory powers that affect land, its use and development, could prejudice the full enjoyment of the owner.

Having satisfied himself on all points, and agreed with the seller's solicitor a form of contract that accurately expresses the terms of the purchase and the details of the title, etc., the buyer's solicitor can proceed to the next stage: the formalities of entering into the contract by which the parties will be bound to complete the transaction. This is referred to as exchange of contracts. At the next stage the seller's solicitor must bring proof of the representations he has made as to the legal position of the seller. Then the document by which the ownership is to be transferred must be prepared and agreed between the solicitors and all remaining enquiries and investigations are carried out by the buyer's solicitor. The final stage comprises the formalities by which the transaction is brought to its conclusion and which we shall learn to recognise under the name of "completion."

These elements will now be looked at in detail by following through a transaction being handled by our two firms of Barset solicitors. (It will be recalled that conveyancing work may now be carried out by licensed conveyancers as well as by solicitors.)

THE SALE AND PURCHASE OF A REGISTERED FREEHOLD HOUSE

Butler to Burton

Mr. Amity, the partner in charge of the conveyancing department at Messrs. Makepiece has many long-established clients. One of them,

Mr. Butler, telephones to say that he is shortly to retire from work, and has decided to move North to live with his daughter and her family. This means that he will be selling his house and he has already taken the initial steps. He has placed the property in the hands of estate agents, Messrs. Sellars, Wright, Quick. They have been marketing the house for some time and have now found a buyer. Mr. Amity should therefore be hearing from them shortly.

In due course, the firm hears from the agents, who have agreed a sale "subject to contract." They write enclosing their Notification of Sale, a type of pro-forma employed by most agents to confirm the details of the sale to the parties and to inform their solicitors.

Sellars, Wright, Quick

Chartered Surveyors, Estate Agents & Valuers

23 Market Street
Barset
5th January 1993
Tel. 00765 6789

Dear Sirs,

Butler to Burton

"The Limes," Lemon Terrace, Barset

We have negotiated a sale of the above property subject to contract and set out the details in the following Notification of Sale.
Will the Seller's solicitor please submit a draft contract to the Buyer's solicitors as soon as possible?
Please let us know when contracts have been exchanged.
Yours faithfully,
J. Burden
pp. Sellars, Wright, Quick

THE TRANSACTION TAKES SHAPE

Mr. Amity has asked John Black, his conveyancing legal executive, to deal with the matter. He too knows Mr. Butler, and the matter has been marked out to him in the post room. The letter is passed to him when it arrives. It is accompanied by a copy of the agent's sale particulars, a circular they hand out to prospective buyers giving details of the house and its main points. Mr. Black finds this useful and, when read in conjunction with the Notification, it gives a good impression of what is to be involved. However, he thinks it will be prudent to make it clear in the contract that the description of the property and its amenities in the agents' particulars (not here reproduced) does not create any binding obligations as to its state and condition. The agents do not pretend to have drawn up a legal description and the buyer must take what he sees.

Sellars, Wright, Quick

<u>NOTIFICATION OF SALE</u>
Subject To Contract

Proposed sale of:	"The Limes," Lemon Terrace, Barset.
Purchase Price:	£42,000
Possession:	Vacant possession on completion
Tenure:	Freehold
Seller:	Mr. Bernard Oliver Butler
Address:	in residence *Tel. No.:* 00765 5432
Seller's solicitors:	Messrs. Makepiece & Streiff, Bank Chambers, Barset. Ref.: C. Amity
Buyer:	Miss M. Burton
Address:	c/o Royal Hotel, Market Square, Barset. *Tel. No.:* 00765 2345
Buyer's solicitors:	Messrs. Rime & Reason, Invicta House, Market Street, Barset.
Location of Deeds:	Please refer to Seller's solicitors
Deposit:	£250
Buyer's Mortgage Requirements:	None
Inclusions:	as attached Particulars Fixtr Futongs
Completion date:	None agreed by us. Both parties are in a position to proceed and want it as soon as possible.
Special conditions:	There is a right of way for pedestrians across the adjoining allotments in favour of the owner of the property.
Further information:	Miss Burton is arranging a survey and her surveyor will make the appointment to inspect direct with the vendor. The parties are negotiating the sale/purchase of carpets, curtains and other items. Details will be supplied direct by the clients in due course.

easement

A copy of this letter has been sent to the parties and to their respective solicitors. If any further information or clarification is required, please contact the undersigned who will give the matter his personal attention.
pp. Sellars, Wright, Quick
Signed
James Burden, ANAEA
4th January 1993

He notes that in addition to the house itself, the carpets and curtains now there are to be purchased by Miss Burton. He telephones Mr. Butler to confirm that he has heard from the agents, and that he will be dealing with the matter. He enquires whether the price has been agreed for the carpets, curtains and light fittings and Mr. Butler says that these have still to be discussed between himself and Miss Burton. He asks whether they would also be dealt with by the solicitors, as he had assumed that they were not part of the property. Mr. Black confirms that this is correct, that the ownership will pass "on delivery," that is, when Miss Burton takes possession of them on payment. However, it is well to include such agreements in the contract of sale of the house, as it is then a more readily enforceable term of the agreement as a whole, and also leaves no party in any doubt.

Mr. Butler appreciates this and says that he will speak to Miss Burton as soon as he can and let Mr. Black know the outcome. Mr. Black mentions the agent's statement that the parties want completion as soon as possible, but explains that the enquiries he must make before the contract is signed will take a week or two and it is too early to try to agree with the purchaser a date for the move.

Mr. Black then enquires of the whereabouts of the deeds, and learns that they are held for safe-keeping by Mr. Butler's bank. There is no mortgage on the house. Mr. Butler promises to call at the bank the next day and to authorise them to send the deeds on to the firm.

When he rings off, Mr. Black calls in Thomas, his trainee assistant and, handing him the papers, asks him to start the matter off in the usual way. This Thomas does when he returns to his own office. He prepares a letter to Mr. Butler thanking him for his instructions and an acknowledgment to the agents, thanking them for their letters. Then he writes briefly to Messrs. Rime to establish contact formally, and to state that a draft contract will be forwarded in due course.

Mr. Black's secretary opens a file and the copy letters are incorporated. When it is ready, Thomas takes his work to Mr. Black for him to check and for signature. All is in order, and the letters go off that evening.

Mr. Black adds to the file a copy of a standard pro-forma used by the office, and which sets out, for reference purposes, the details of property and parties that will be needed in the course of the transaction. This serves to disclose the particulars of the transaction at a glance, and an example is reproduced at the end of this chapter. An additional copy is made for Mr. Amity, who keeps a file for the forms and is consequently aware from the beginning of what matters are in hand.

He has also prepared an attendance note or "minute" of the work he has done so far, as has Thomas. This is a simple record of what has occurred, and the time taken. It will both inform anyone dealing with the file during his absence of the stage reached, and will also inform the cashier's department of the time expended so that, on its conclusion they may draw their bill to reflect all such steps and charge accordingly. If the firm uses a computer for accounting purposes the appropriate instructions must be given to the computer operator confirming the time spent on that file, so that he or she can record time spent on a daily basis on the computer. When the transaction is completed and the file is ready for billing the computer will, on request, produce a billing guide summarising the total time spent on the matter. The bill can then be drawn on that basis. "Time costing," as it is called, is coming increasingly into use, though in conveyancing, where part of the charge is based on the value of the transaction, its use is far from universal. (In areas where conveyancing is particularly competitive firms have to give quotations on a fixed fee basis to obtain instructions. If this has been done, time costing is immaterial and the agreed fee must be adhered to.) Though it will not be mentioned again, it may be assumed that each step hereafter taken by the firms of solicitors respectively will be so recorded. The minutes are added to the file, and Messrs. Makepiece can do nothing further for the moment.

In the offices of Messrs. Rime however, work is in hand for the buyer now, as they have also received the Notification of Sale from the agents. Messrs. Rime have never acted for Miss Burton before, so Mr. Reason telephones to confirm her instructions. She tells him that she is a health service employee moving into the area and has been recommended to the firm by one of their established clients. She confirms that she has no house to sell and will not need a mortgage. She gives her full name as Miss Molly Burton. He asks whether the surveyors referred to in the agents' notification are advising on the structural condition as well as the value. She replies that she has had a full survey carried out and the surveyors' report is awaited.

She would like to proceed as soon as the formalities permit, but she has heard from Mr. Butler that day that he will be retiring in about two weeks, and may need another four weeks or so thereafter to arrange his move. Mr. Reason explains that eight weeks is a fairly average time from instructions to completion.

Miss Burton has seen that there is a gate at the end of the garden and is curious about the right of way that the agents have referred to. Mr. Reason has to tell her that until he receives the contract from Messrs. Makepiece he really cannot comment. He will, of course, let her know.

He mentions the carpets and curtains to her, and she tells him that no price has been agreed, but that she has now arranged to call on Mr. Butler later in the week to discuss this point. Mr. Reason says this will no doubt be included in the contract and she promises to ring him as soon as she is able.

When they conclude the call Mr. Reason calls in James, his trainee legal executive, as, whilst he will deal with the matter himself, James will assist. He explains their instructions and leaves it to James to take the initial steps. James open his file, writes to the agents and dictates a short letter to Messrs. Makepiece whose letter has not yet arrived:

RIME & REASON
Solicitors

C. Reason
N. Wisdom BA
R. E. Verse

Invicta House
Market Street
Barset
Tel: 00765 1234

Messrs. Makepiece & Streiff,
Bank Chambers
Barset
Our Ref: CR/JC/Burton

6th January 1993

Dear Sirs,

Burton from Butler

"The Limes," Lemon Terrace, Barset

We are instructed to act for Miss Molly Burton, who we understand has agreed to purchase the above property from Mr. Butler, at the price of £42,000 subject to contract.
We believe you have the details from the Estate Agents, Messrs. Sellars, Wright, Quick. Will you therefore please let us have a draft contract for approval as soon as possible.

Yours faithfully,

(signed)

Rime & Reason

James's first step can be taken immediately. He fills in, in duplicate, the Requisition for Search in the Register of Local Land Charges (LLC 1 p. 109). This is a request to the local authority for the District in which the property is situated for them to search in the register and to give a certificate either that there are no entries that may affect the property, or giving particulars of any found therein. To send with it he makes out a form of Enquiries of District Councils (Form Con. 29, p. 110) also in duplicate, filling in the name of the road "Lemon Terrace," in question 1 on page 2. This enquires into matters not contained in the register but over which any local authority has control. Notes on the content and significance of these local searches are set out below (pp. 154).

These are sent off with a cheque for the fee for a single parcel of land, as are his letters which have been checked and signed by Mr. Reason, together with a letter from him to Miss Burton thanking her for instructions and at the same time pointing out that he feels it is advisable for "The Limes" to be insured by her from the time the contract is entered into. He asks her to let him know if she would like the firm to arrange the insurance cover at the right time and if there are particular insurers she would prefer.

Messrs. Rime's letter is duly received by Messrs. Makepiece and on the same day Mr. Black receives the title deeds from the bank, which he acknowledges by letter. As he is checking them through Mr. Butler rings. He can confirm that the price for the carpets and curtains has been agreed at £800 and Mr. Black says that he has just received the deeds and will now prepare and submit the contract, including a clause for the chattels.

The deeds consist of the Land Certificate and various other documents, including the deeds which led to the first registration of the title. The principal document for consideration is the Land Certificate, which is a copy of the details of the property and ownership contained in the land register at the time when the Certificate was last returned to the Registry—in this case when Mr. Butler purchased. He notes that the right of way gives right of passage on foot over a path that provides a short cut to the shops. A copy of the Land Certificate is set out on pp. 119–121.

Duplicate
Form LLCI

Official Number_____
(To be completed by the registering authority)

Register of local land charges

Requisition for search and official certificate of search

fold

Requisition for search

An official search is required in *Part(s)*_____of
the register of local land charges kept by the above-named
registering authority for subsisting registrations against the land
[defined in the attached plan and] described below.

Description of land sufficient to enable it to be identified

Name and address to which certificate is to be sent

Signature of applicant (*or his solicitor*)

Date

Telephone number

Reference

Enclosure
Cheque/Money Order/Postal Order/Giro

Official certificate of search

To be completed by authorised officer

It is hereby certified that the search requested above reveals
no subsisting registrations

*or the*_____registrations described in the Schedule
hereto up to and including the date of this certificate.

Signed ....

On behalf of ....

Date

Form LLCI. (*Local Land Charges Rules 1977 Schedule 1, Form C*)

The duplicate of this form must also be completed: a carbon copy will suffice

For directions, notes and fees see overleaf

Insert name and address of registering authority in space below

⌐   ¬

BARSET DISTRICT COUNCIL
12/18 RIVER ST
BARSET

Official Number 69143/B
(*To be completed by the registering authority*)

Register of local land charges

Requisition for search

and official certificate

of search

---

fold

Requisition for search
(*A separate requisition must be made in respect of each parcel of land except as explained overleaf*)

An official search is required in *Part(s)*_____of[1] the register of local land charges kept by the above-named registering authority for subsisting registrations against the land [defined in the attached plan and][2] described below.

Description of land sufficient to enable it to be identified

"THE LIMES"
LEMON TERRACE
BARSET

Name and address to which certificate is to be sent

⌐   ¬

MESSRS RICE AND REASON
SOLICITORS
INVICTA HOUSE
MARKET STREET
BARSET

Signature of applicant (*or his solicitor*)

Date
         7 January 1993

Telephone number
         007651234

Reference
         CR/JC/BURTON

Enclosure
Cheque/~~Money Order/Postal Order/Giro~~ £7.50

To be completed by authorised officer

Official certificate of search

It is hereby certified that the search requested above reveals no subsisting registrations[3]

~~or the xxxxxxxxxxxxx registrations described in the Schedule hereto xxxxxxx xxxx xxxxxxxxxxx the xxxx xxxxx xxxxxx xxxxx~~

Signed ....
Local Land Charges Registrar

On behalf of .... BARSET DISTRICT COUNCIL[4]

Date   14 January 1993

---

1 Delete if inappropriate. Otherwise insert Part(s) in which search is required.

2 Delete if inappropriate. (A plan should be furnished in duplicate if it is desired that a copy should be returned.)

3 Delete inapplicable words. (The Parts of the Schedule should be securely attached to the certificate and the number of registrations disclosed should be inserted in the space provided. Only Parts which disclose subsisting registrations should be sent.)

4 Insert name of registering authority.

Directions and notes

1 This form and the duplicate should be completed and sent by post to or left at the office of the registering authority.

2 A separate requisition for search should be made in respect of each parcel of land in respect of which a search is required except where, for the purpose of a single transaction, a certificate is required in respect of two or more parcels of land which have a common boundary or are separated only by a road, railway, river, stream or canal.

3 'Parcel of land' means land (including a building or part of a building) which is separately occupied or separately rated or, if not occupied or rated, in separate ownership. For the purpose of this definition an owner is the person who (in his own right or as trustee for any other person) is entitled to receive the rack rent of land, or, where the land is not let at a rack rent, would be so entitled if it were so let.

4 The certificate of the result of an official search of the register refers to any subsisting registrations, recorded against the land defined in the application for search, in the Parts of the register in respect of which the search is requested. The Parts of the register record:

Part 1	General financial charges.
Part 2	Specific financial charges.
Part 3	Planning charges.
Part 4	Miscellaneous charges.
Part 5	Fenland ways maintenance charges.
Part 6	Land compensation charges.
Part 7	New towns charges.
Part 8	Civil aviation charges.
Part 9	Opencast coal charges.
Part 10	Listed buildings charges.
Part 11	Light obstruction notices.
Part 12	Drainage scheme charges.

5 An office copy of any entry in the register can be obtained on written request and on payment of the prescribed fee.

Fees

Official search (including issue of official certificate of search)
in any one part of the register	£1.40
in the whole of the register	£3.70

and in addition, but subject to a maximum additional fee of £11.00, in respect of each parcel above one, where several parcels are included in the same requisition (see notes 2 and 3 above) whether the requisition is for search in the whole or any part of the register ... 60p

Office copy of any entry in the register (not including a copy or extract of any plan or document filed by the registering authority) ... £1.00

Office copy of any plan or other document filed by the registering authority ... Such reasonable fee as may be fixed by the registering authority according to the time and work involved.

All fees must be prepaid

oyez The Solicitors' Law Stationery Society plc, Paulton House, 8 Shepherdess Walk, London N1 7LB

6.89 BM
5063019

LLC1 ★ ★

CON. 29 (1991)
To be submitted in duplicate

Search No........69143/B.

ENQUIRIES OF
LOCAL AUTHORITY
(1991 EDITION)

Please type or use BLOCK LETTERS

A.

To

BARSET DISTRICT COUNCIL
12/18 RIVER STREET
BARSET

A. Enter name and address of District or Borough Council for the area. If the property is near a Local Authority boundary, consider raising certain Enquiries (e.g. road schemes) with the adjoining Council.

B.

Property

THE LIMES
LEMON TERRACE
BARSET

B. Enter address and description of the property. A plan in duplicate must be attached wherever possible, and may be insisted upon by some Councils. Without a plan, replies may be inaccurate or incomplete. A plan is essential if Optional Enquiry 18 is raised.

C. Enter name and/or location (and mark on plan, if possible) any other roadways, footpaths and footways (in addition to those entered in Box B) to which Enquiries 3 and (if raised) 19 are to apply.

C.

Other roadways, footpaths and footways

D. Answer every question. Any additional Enquiries must be attached on a separate sheet in duplicate, and an additional fee will be charged for any which the Council is willing to answer.

E. Details of fees can be obtained from the Council or from the Association of District Councils, 26 Chapter Street, London SW1P 4ND.

D.

A plan in duplicate is attached — ~~YES~~/NO

Optional Enquiries are to be answered (see Box G) — YES/~~NO~~

Additional Enquiries are attached in duplicate on a separate sheet — ~~YES~~/NO

F. Enter name and address of person or firm lodging this form.

G. Tick the Optional Enquiries to be answered.

E.

Fees of £ 40.00 are enclosed.

Signed: *Rime and Reason*

Date: 7 January 1993

Reference: CR/JC/BURTON

Tel. No.: 00765-1234

Please read the Notes on page 4.

F.

Reply to

MESSRS RIME AND REASON
SOLICITORS
INVICTA HOUSE
MARKET ST
BARSET

G. Optional Enquiries

17	21	25	29	33
18	22	26	30	
19	23	27	31	
20	24	28	32	

OYEZ The Solicitors' Law Stationery Society Limited, Oyez House, 7 Spa Road, London SE16 3QQ
Conveyancing 29(1991)

LAW SOCIETY COPYRIGHT
4.91 F19619 5033379
* * *

PART I—STANDARD ENQUIRIES

(APPLICABLE IN EVERY CASE)

DEVELOPMENT PLANS PROVISIONS

Structure Plan

1.1.1 What structure plan is in force?

1.1.2 Have any proposals been made public for the alteration of the structure plan?

Local Plans

1.2 What local plans (including action area plans) are adopted or in the course of preparation?

Old Style Development Plan

1.3 What old style development plan is in force?

Unitary Plan([1])

1.4.1 What stage has been reached in the preparation of a unitary development plan?

1.4.2 Have any proposals been made public for the alteration or replacement of a unitary development plan?

Non-Statutory Plan

1.5.1 Have the Council made public any proposals for the preparation or modification of a non-statutory plan?

1.5.2 If so, what stage has been reached?

Primary Use and Provisions for the Property

1.6 In any of the above plans or proposals:
   (a) what primary use is indicated for the area?
   (b) what provisions are included for the property?

Land required for Public Purposes

1.7 Is the property included in any of the categories of land specified in Schedule 13 paras 5 and 6 of the T&CP Act 1990?

DRAINAGE

Foul Drainage

2.1.1 To the Council's knowledge, does foul drainage from the property drain to a public sewer?([2])

2.1.2 If so, is the connection to the public sewer effected by:
   (a) drain and private sewer, or
   (b) drain alone?

Surface Water Drainage

2.2.1 Does surface water from the property drain to a public sewer?

2.2.2 Does surface water from the property drain to a highway drain or sewer which is the subject of an agreement under s.21(1)(a) of the Public Health Act 1936?

2.2.3 If the Reply to either 2.2.1 or 2.2.2 is "Yes", is the connection to that sewer or highway drain effected by:
   (a) drain and private sewer, or
   (b) drain alone?

Combined Private Sewer

2.3 Is there in force in relation to any part of the drainage of the property an agreement under s.22 of the Building Act 1984?

Adoption Agreement

2.4.1 To the Council's knowledge, is any sewer serving, or which is proposed to serve, the property the subject of an agreement under s.18 of the Public Health Act 1936?([3])

2.4.2 If so, such an agreement supported by a bond or other financial security?([4])

Potential Compulsory Drainage Connection

2.5 If the Reply to either Enquiry 2.1.1 or 2.2.1 is "No", to the Council's knowledge is there a foul or surface water sewer (as appropriate) within 100 feet of the property and at a level which makes it reasonably practicable to construct a drain from the property to that sewer?([5])

Sewerage Undertaker

2.6 Please state the name and address of the sewerage undertaker.

MAINTENANCE OF ROADS ETC.

Publicly Maintained

3.1 Are all the roadways, footpaths and footways referred to in Boxes B and C on page 1 maintainable at the public expense within the meaning of the Highways Act 1980?

Resolutions to make up or adopt

3.2 If not, have the Council passed any resolution to:
   (a) make up any of those roadways, footpaths or footways at the cost of the frontagers, or
   (b) adopt any of them without cost to the frontagers?
   If so, please specify.

Adoption Agreements

3.3.1 Have the Council entered into any outstanding agreement relating to the adoption of any of those roadways, footpaths or footways? If so, please specify.

3.3.2 Is any such agreement supported by a bond or other financial security?([4])

ROAD SCHEMES

Trunk and Special Roads

4.1.1 What orders, draft orders or schemes have been notified to the Council by the appropriate Secretary of State for the construction of a new trunk or special road, the centre line of which is within 200 metres of the property?

4.1.2 What proposals have been notified to the Council by the appropriate Secretary of State for the alteration or improvement of an existing road, involving the construction, whether or not within existing highway limits, of a subway, underpass, flyover, footbridge, elevated road or dual carriageway, the centre line of which is within 200 metres of the property?

Other Roads

4.2 What proposals of their own([6]) have the Council approved for any of the following, the limits of construction of which are within 200 metres of the property:
   (a) the construction of a new road, or
   (b) the alteration or improvement of an existing road, involving the construction, whether or not within existing highway limits, of a subway, underpass, flyover, footbridge, elevated road or dual carriageway?

Road Proposals Involving Acquisition

4.3 What proposals have the Council approved, or have been notified to the Council by the appropriate Secretary of State, for highway construction or improvement that involve the acquisition of the property?

Road Proposals at Consultation Stage

4.4 What proposals have either the Secretary of State or the Council published for public consultation relating to the construction of a new road indicating a possible route the centre line of which would be likely to be within 200 metres of the property?

OUTSTANDING NOTICES

5. What outstanding statutory notices or informal notices have been issued by the Council under the Public Health Acts, Housing Acts or Highways Acts?
(This enquiry does not cover notices shown in the Official Certificate of Search or notices relating to matters covered by Enquiry 13.)

BUILDING REGULATIONS

6. What proceedings have the Council authorised in respect of an infringement of the Building Regulations?

---

(1) This enquiry relates only to London Boroughs and other metropolitan authorities.
(2) Any reply will be based on information supplied to the Council by the sewerage undertakers.
(3) The enquirer should also make similar enquiries of the sewerage undertaker even if the Council reply to this enquiry.
(4) The enquirer should satisfy himself as to the adequacy of any bond or other financial security.
(5) If the Council cannot reply in the affirmative, the enquirer must make his own survey.
(6) This enquiry refers to the Council's own proposals and not those of other bodies or companies.

PLANNING APPLICATIONS AND PERMISSIONS

Applications and Decisions

7.1 Please list:
(a) any entries in the Register of planning applications and permissions,
(b) any applications and decisions in respect of listed building consent, and
(c) any applications and decisions in respect of conservation area consent.

Inspection and Copies

7.2 If there are any entries:.
(a) how can copies be obtained?
(b) where can the Register be inspected?

NOTICES UNDER PLANNING ACTS

Enforcement and Stop Notices

8.1.1 Please list any entries in the Register of enforcement notices and stop notices.

8.1.2 If there are any entries:
(a) how can copies be obtained?
(b) where can that Register be inspected?

Proposed Enforcement or Stop Notice

8.2 Except as shown in the Official Certificate of Search, or in reply to Enquiry 8.1.1, has any enforcement notice, listed building enforcement notice, or stop notice been authorised by the Council for issue or service (other than notices which have been withdrawn or quashed)?

Compliance with Enforcement Notices

8.3 If an enforcement notice or listed building enforcement notice has been served or issued, has it been complied with to the satisfaction of the Council?

Other Contravention Notices etc.

8.4 Have the Council served, or resolved to serve, any other notice or proceedings relating to a contravention of planning control?

Listed Building Repairs Notices, etc.

8.5.1 To the knowledge of the Council, has the service of a repairs notice been authorised?

8.5.2 If the Council have authorised the making of an order for the compulsory acquisition of a listed building, is a "minimum compensation" provision included, or to be included, in the order?

8.5.3 Have the Council authorised the service of a building preservation notice?[7]

DIRECTIONS RESTRICTING PERMITTED DEVELOPMENT

9. Except as shown in the Official Certificate of Search, have the Council resolved to make a direction to restrict permitted development?

ORDERS UNDER PLANNING ACTS

Revocation Orders etc.

10.1 Except as shown in the Official Certificate of Search, have the Council resolved to make any Orders revoking or modifying any planning permission or discontinuing an existing planning use?

Tree Preservation Order

10.2 Except as shown in the Official Certificate of Search, have the Council resolved to make any Tree Preservation Orders?

COMPENSATION FOR PLANNING DECISIONS

11. What compensation has been paid by the Council under s.114 of the T&CP Act 1990 for planning decisions restricting development other than new development?

PRE-REGISTRATION CONSERVATION AREA

12. Except as shown in the Official Certificate of Search, is the area a conservation area?

COMPULSORY PURCHASE

13. Except as shown in the Official Certificate of Search, have the Council made any order (whether or not confirmed by the appropriate Secretary of State) or passed any resolution for compulsory acquisition which is still capable of being implemented?[8]

AREAS DESIGNATED UNDER HOUSING ACTS ETC.

Clearance

14.1 Has any programme of clearance for the area been —
(a) submitted to the Department of the Environment, or
(b) resolved to be submitted, or
(c) otherwise adopted by resolution of the Council?

Housing

14.2 Except as shown in the Official Certificate of Search, have the Council resolved to define the area as designated for a purpose under the Housing Acts? If so, please specify the purpose.

SMOKE CONTROL ORDER

15. Except as shown in the Official Certificate of Search, have the Council made a smoke control order or resolved to make or vary a smoke control order for the area?

CONTAMINATED LAND

16.1 Is the property included in the Register of contaminated land?

16.2 If so:
(a) how can copies of the entries be obtained?
(b) where can the Register be inspected?

PART II—OPTIONAL ENQUIRIES

(APPLICABLE ONLY AS INDICATED ON PAGE ONE)

RAILWAYS

17. What proposals have been notified to the Council, and what proposals of their own have the Council approved, for the construction of a railway (including light railway or monorail) the centre line of which is within 200 metres of the property?

PUBLIC PATHS OR BYWAYS

18. Has any public path, bridleway or road used as a public path or byway which abuts on or crosses the property been shown in a definitive map or revised definitive map prepared under Part IV of the National Parks and Access to the Countryside Act 1949 or Part III of the Wildlife and Countryside Act 1981? If so, please mark its approximate route on the attached plan.

PERMANENT ROAD CLOSURE

19. What proposals have the Council approved for permanently stopping up or diverting any of the roads or footpaths referred to in Boxes B and C on page 1?

TRAFFIC SCHEMES

20. In respect of any of the roads referred to in Boxes B and C on page 1, what proposals have the Council approved, but have not yet put into operation, for:
(a) waiting restrictions,
(b) one-way streets,
(c) prohibition of driving,
(d) pedestrianisation, or
(e) vehicle width or weight restrictions?

ADVERTISEMENTS

Entries in Register

21.1.1 Please list any entries in the Register of applications, directions and decisions relating to consent for the display of advertisements.

21.1.2 If there are any entries, where can that Register be inspected?

Notices, Proceedings and Orders

21.2 Except as shown in the Official Certificate of Search:
(a) has any notice been given by the Secretary of State or served in respect of a direction or proposed direction restricting deemed consent for any class of advertisement?
(b) have the Council resolved to serve a notice requiring the display of any advertisement to be discontinued?
(c) if a discontinuance notice has been served, has it been complied with to the satisfaction of the Council?
(d) have the Council resolved to serve any other notice or proceedings relating to a contravention of the control of advertisements?
(e) have the Council resolved to make an order for the special control of advertisements for the area?

COMPLETION NOTICES

22. Which of the planning permissions in force have the Council resolved to terminate by means of a completion notice under s.94 of the T&CP Act 1990?

---

(7) The Historic Buildings and Monuments Commission also have power to issue this type of notice for buildings in London Boroughs, and separate enquiry should be made of them if appropriate.

(8) This enquiry refers to the Council's own compulsory purchase powers and not those of other bodies.

PARKS AND COUNTRYSIDE

Areas of Outstanding Natural Beauty

23.1 Has any order under s.87 of the National Parks and Access to the Countryside Act 1949 been made?

National Parks

23.2 Is the property within a National Park designated under s.7 of the National Parks and Access to the Countryside Act 1949?

PIPELINES

24. Has a map been deposited under s.35 of the Pipelines Act 1962, or Schedule 7 of the Gas Act 1986, showing a pipeline within 100 feet of the property?

HOUSES IN MULTIPLE OCCUPATION

25. Is the property included in a registration of houses scheme (houses in multiple occupation) under s.346 of the Housing Act 1985, containing control provisions as authorised by s.347 of that Act?

NOISE ABATEMENT

Noise Abatement Zone

26.1 Have the Council made, or resolved to make, any noise abatement zone order under s.63 of the Control of Pollution Act 1974 for the area?

Entries in Register

26.2.1 Has any entry been recorded in the Noise Level Register kept pursuant to s.64 of the Control of Pollution Act 1974?

26.2.2 If there is an entry, how can copies be obtained and where can that Register be inspected?

URBAN DEVELOPMENT AREAS

27.1 Is the area an urban development area designated under Part XVI of the Local Government Planning and Land Act 1980?

27.2 If so, please state the name of the urban development corporation and the address of its principal office.

ENTERPRISE ZONES

28. Is the area an enterprise zone designated under Part XVIII of the Local Government Planning and Land Act 1980?

INNER URBAN IMPROVEMENT AREAS

29. Have the Council resolved to define the area as an improvement area under s.4 of the Inner Urban Areas Act 1978?

SIMPLIFIED PLANNING ZONES

30.1 Is the area a simplified planning zone adopted or approved pursuant to s.83 of the T&CP Act 1990?

30.2 Have the Council approved any proposal for designating the area as a simplified planning zone?

LAND MAINTENANCE NOTICES

31. Have the Council authorised the service of a maintenance notice under s.215 of the T&CP Act 1990?

MINERAL CONSULTATION AREAS

32. Is the area a mineral consultation area notified by the county planning authority under Schedule 1 para 7 of the T&CP Act 1990?

HAZARDOUS SUBSTANCE CONSENTS

33.1 Please list any entries in the Register kept pursuant to s.28 of the Planning (Hazardous Substances) Act 1990.

33.2 If there are any entries:
(a) how can copies of the entries be obtained?
(b) where can the Register be inspected?

GENERAL NOTES

(A) Unless otherwise indicated, all these enquiries relate to the property as described in Box B on page 1, and any part of that property, and "the area" means any area in which the property is located.

(B) These enquiries will not necessarily reveal (i) matters relating to properties other than the Property specified in Box B on page 1, or (ii) matters relating to land outside the area of the Council to whom these enquiries are sent, or (iii) matters which are outside the functions of that Council (although, under arrangements made between District Councils and County Councils, the replies given to certain enquiries addressed to District Councils cover knowledge and actions of both the District Council and the County Council).

(C) References to "the Council" include references to a predecessor Council and to a Committee or Sub-Committee of the Council acting under delegated powers, and to any other body or person taking action under powers delegated by the Council or a predecessor Council.

(D) References to an Act, Regulation or Order include reference to (i) any statutory provision which it replaces and (ii) any amendment or re-enactment of it.

(E) References to any Town and Country Planning Act, Order or Regulation are abbreviated, eg "T&CP Act 1990".

(F) The replies will be given after the appropriate enquiries and in the belief that they are in accordance with the information at present available to the officers of the replying Council(s), but on the distinct understanding that none of the Councils, nor any Council officer, is legally responsible for them, except for negligence. Any liability for negligence shall extend for the benefit of not only the person by or for whom these Enquiries are made but also a person (being a purchaser for the purposes of s.10(3) of the Local Land Charges Act 1975) who or whose agent had knowledge, before the relevant time (as defined in that section), of the replies to these Enquiries.

(G) This form of Enquiries is approved by the Law Society, the Association of County Councils, the Association of District Councils and the Association of Metropolitan Authorities and is published by their authority.

The Replies are given on the attached sheet(s)

Signed ....

                Proper Officer

Date..

Mr. Black also checks through the other papers and documents. Some are of no practical use now, being old search certificates and enquiries long outdated. But he finds a Deed of Covenant entered into by Mr. Butler five years previously with his neighbour when Mr. Butler removed the fence for which he was responsible on the North boundary to make way for a demountable garage along that boundary. At his neighbour's insistence Mr. Butler entered into a covenant to the effect that if the garage should be removed at any time a new fence would be erected to the right specification along the boundary.

Such a covenant may exist although it is not referred to in the register. In law the obligation to carry out some positive act such as building a fence can still be enforced against the covenantor, even after he has sold the land; it does not automatically become the obligation of the buyer. Mr. Black, must, therefore, ensure that if the fence is not rebuilt when it should be Miss Burton will indemnify him against any action by the adjoining owner. The Standard Conditions Contract (see below) covers this point at general condition 4–5–3, which provides that where a seller remains bound by an obligation affecting the property and no indemnity is implied by law, the buyer will give an indemnity covenant in the transfer.

The Contract

Mr. Black is now able to prepare the draft contract in compliance with the requirements of section 2 of the Law of Property Act (Miscellaneous Provisions) 1989. In this, the description of the property and the rights that go with it, including the right of way, must exactly correspond to the particulars in the register. He must put in a provision regarding the covenant and deal with the chattels. It is the practice of the firm to use the Standard Conditions of Sale (2nd Edition) 1992 and Mr. Black completes the outer pages of the form (pp. 115 and 118). The inner pages (see pp. 116 and 117 below) contain the general conditions of contract which apply to all contracts drawn up on the form unless expressly varied or excluded.

To enable Messrs. Rime to decide whether they can properly approve the draft contract on behalf of their client or, if not, what changes to request, they must have full particulars of the registered title and of any unregistered rights or obligations affecting the property, its use and enjoyment. Under the general conditions of contract they will, in due course, be entitled to receive an office copy of the entries in the register and the filed plan. That is, a copy issued by the District Registry in which the property is registered. This is marked with the date of issue and discloses whether any charges have been created or other changes made from the time of the seller's acquisition to the date of issue. It is invariably obtained by the seller's solicitor at the commencement of a conveyancing transaction. Had the firm been able to obtain an office copy earlier, they would have done so and sent it with the draft contract. However, rather than hold up the submission of the draft, a photocopy made in the office is sent with it. This, of course, only shows the position at the time of Mr. Butler's purchase, but there is no reason to think there has been any change.

AGREEMENT

(Incorporating the Standard Conditions of Sale (Second Edition))

Agreement date	:	
Seller	:	BERNARD OLIVER BUTLER OF "THE LIMES", LEMON TERRACE BARSET.
Buyer	:	MOLLY BURTON OF ROYAL HOTEL, MARKET SQUARE, BARSET.
Property **(freehold/leasehold)**	:	THE LIMES, LEMON TERRACE, BARSET, BARSETSHIRE REGISTERED AT H.M. LAND REGISTRY UNDER TITLE No BA 19834
Root of title/Title Number	:	THE SELLER'S TITLE IS REGISTERED WITH ABSOLUTE TITLE UNDER TITLE No BA 19834 IN THE BARCHESTER DISTRICT LAND REGISTRY
Incumbrances on the Property	:	A THE PROVISIONS OF THE A DEED OF COVENANT MADE 3RD APRIL 1977 BETWEEN THE SELLER AND ALPHA BEN OMEGA A COPY OF WHICH IS SUPPLIED HEREWITH. B THE MATTERS SET OUT IN THE CHARGES REGISTER OF THE ABOVE TITLE
Seller sells as	:	BENEFICIAL OWNER
Completion date	:	
Contract rate	:	4% ABOVE NORTHERN BANK PLC BASE RATE FOR THE TIME BEING IN FORCE
Purchase price	:	£42,000
Deposit	:	£4,200
Amount payable for chattels	:	£800
Balance	:	£38,600

The Seller will sell and the Buyer will buy the Property for the Purchase price.
The Agreement continues on the back page.

WARNING	Signed
This is a formal document, designed to create legal rights and legal obligations. Take advice before using it.	
	Seller/Buyer

STANDARD CONDITIONS OF SALE (SECOND EDITION)

(NATIONAL CONDITIONS OF SALE 22nd EDITION, LAW SOCIETY'S CONDITIONS OF SALE 1992)

1. **GENERAL**

1 1 **Definitions**

1.1.1 In these conditions:

(a) "accrued interest" means:

(i) if money has been placed on deposit or in a building society share account, the interest actually earned

(ii) otherwise, the interest which might reasonably have been earned by depositing the money at interest on seven days' notice of withdrawal with a clearing bank

less, in either case, any proper charges for handling the money

(b) "agreement" means the contractual document which incorporates these conditions, with or without amendment

(c) "banker's draft" means a draft drawn by and on a clearing bank

(d) "clearing bank" means a bank which is a member of CHAPS and Town Clearing Company Limited

(e) "completion date", unless defined in the agreement, has the meaning given in condition 6.1.1

(f) "contract" means the bargain between the seller and the buyer of which these conditions, with or without amendment, form part

(g) "contract rate", unless defined in the agreement, is the Law Society's interest rate from time to time in force

(h) "lease" includes sub-lease, tenancy and agreement for a lease or sub-lease

(i) "notice to complete" means a notice requiring completion of the contract in accordance with condition 6

(j) "public requirement" means any notice, order or proposal given or made (whether before or after the date of the contract) by a body acting on statutory authority

(k) "requisition" includes objection

(l) "solicitor" includes barrister, duly certificated notary public, recognised licensed conveyancer and recognised body under sections 9 or 32 of the Administration of Justice Act 1985

(m) "transfer" includes conveyance and assignment

(n) "working day" means any day from Monday to Friday (inclusive) which is not Christmas Day, Good Friday or a statutory Bank Holiday.

.1.2 When used in these conditions the terms "absolute title" and "office copies" have the special meanings given to them by the Land Registration Act 1925.

.2 **Joint parties**

If there is more than one seller or more than one buyer, the obligations which they undertake can be enforced against them all jointly or against each individually.

.3 **Notices and documents**

.3.1 A notice required or authorised by the contract must be in writing.

.3.2 Giving a notice or delivering a document to a party's solicitor has the same effect as giving or delivering it to that party.

.3.3 Transmission by fax is a valid means of giving a notice or delivering a document where delivery of the original document is not essential.

.3.4 Subject to conditions 1.3.5 to 1.3.7, a notice is given and a document delivered when it is received.

.3.5 If a notice or document is received after 4.00pm on a working day, or on a day which is not a working day, it is to be treated as having been received on the next working day.

.3.6 Unless the actual time of receipt is proved, a notice or document sent by the following means is to be treated as having been received before 4.00pm on the day shown below:

(a) by first-class post:	two working days after posting
(b) by second-class post:	three working days after posting
(c) through a document exchange:	on the first working day after the day on which it would normally be available for collection by the addressee.

.3.7 Where a notice or document is sent through a document exchange, then for the purposes of condition 1.3.6 the actual time of receipt is:

(a) the time when the addressee collects it from the document exchange or, if earlier

(b) 8.00am on the first working day on which it is available for collection at that time.

4 **VAT**

4.1 An obligation to pay money includes an obligation to pay any value added tax chargeable in respect of that payment.

4.2 All sums made payable by the contract are exclusive of value added tax.

FORMATION

1 **Date**

1.1 If the parties intend to make a contract by exchanging duplicate copies by post or through a document exchange, the contract is made when the last copy is posted or deposited at the document exchange.

1.2 If the parties' solicitors agree to treat exchange as taking place before duplicate copies are actually exchanged, the contract is made as so agreed.

2 **Deposit**

2.1 The buyer is to pay or send a deposit of 10 per cent of the purchase price no later than the date of the contract. Except on a sale by auction, payment is to be made by banker's draft or by a cheque drawn on a solicitors' clearing bank account.

2.2 If before completion date the seller agrees to buy another property in England and Wales for his residence, he may use all or any part of the deposit as a deposit in that transaction to be held on terms to the same effect as this condition and condition 2.2.3.

2.3 Any deposit or part of a deposit not being used in accordance with condition 2.2.2 is to be held by the seller's solicitor as stakeholder on terms that on completion it is paid to the seller with accrued interest.

2.4 If a cheque tendered in payment of all or part of the deposit is dishonoured when first presented, the seller may, within seven working days of being notified that the cheque has been dishonoured, give notice to the buyer that the contract is discharged by the buyer's breach.

3 **Auctions**

3.1 On a sale by auction the following conditions apply to the property and, if it is sold in lots, to each lot.

3.2 The sale is subject to a reserve price.

3.3 The seller, or a person on his behalf, may bid up to the reserve price.

3.4 The auctioneer may refuse any bid.

3.5 If there is a dispute about a bid, the auctioneer may resolve the dispute or restart the auction at the last undisputed bid.

MATTERS AFFECTING THE PROPERTY

Freedom from incumbrances

.1 The seller is selling the property free from incumbrances, other than those mentioned in condition 3.1.2.

3.1.2 The incumbrances subject to which the property is sold are:

(a) those mentioned in the agreement

(b) those discoverable by inspection of the property before the contract

(c) those the seller does not and could not know about

(d) entries made before the date of the contract in any public register except those maintained by HM Land Registry or its Land Charges Department or by Companies House

(e) public requirements.

3.1.3 The buyer accepts the property in the physical state it is in at the data of the contract, unless the seller is building or converting it.

3.1.4 After the contract is made, the seller is to give the buyer written details without delay of any new public requirement and of anything in writing which he learns about concerning any incumbrances subject to which the property is sold.

3.1.5 The buyer is to bear the cost of complying with any outstanding public requirement and is to indemnify the seller against any liability resulting from a public requirement.

3.2 **Leases affecting the property**

3.2.1 The following provisions apply if the agreement states that any part of the property is sold subject to a lease.

3.2.2 (a) The seller having provided the buyer with full details of each lease or copies of the documents embodying the lease terms, the buyer is treated as entering into the contract knowing and fully accepting those terms

(b) The seller is to inform the buyer without delay if the lease ends or if the seller learns of any application by the tenant in connection with the lease; the seller is then to act as the buyer reasonably directs, and the buyer is to indemnify him against all consequent loss and expense

(c) The seller is not to agree to any proposal to change the lease terms without the consent of the buyer and is to inform the buyer without delay of any change which may be proposed or agreed

(d) The buyer is to indemnify the seller against all claims arising from the lease after actual completion; this includes claims which are unenforceable against a buyer for want of registration

(e) The seller takes no responsibility for what rent is lawfully recoverable, nor for whether or how any legislation affects the lease

(f) If the let land is not wholly within the property, the seller may apportion the rent.

3.3 **Retained land**

3.3.1 The following provisions apply where after the transfer the seller will be retaining land near the property.

3.3.2 The buyer will have no right of light or air over the retained land, but otherwise the seller and the buyer will each have the rights over the land of the other which they would have had if they were two separate buyers to whom the seller had made simultaneous transfers of the property and the retained land.

3.3.3 Either party may require that the transfer contain appropriate express terms.

4. **TITLE AND TRANSFER**

4.1 **Timetable**

4.1.1 The following are the steps for deducing and investigating the title to the property to be taken within the following time limits:

Step	Time Limit
1. The seller is to send the buyer evidence of title in accordance with condition 4.2	Immediately after making the contract
2. The buyer may raise written requisitions	Six working days after either the date of the contract or the date of delivery of the seller's evidence of title on which the requisitions are raised whichever is the later
3. The seller is to reply in writing to any requisitions raised	Four working days after receiving the requisitions
4. The buyer may make written observations on the seller's replies	Three working days after receiving the replies

The time limit on the buyer's right to raise requisitions applies even where the seller supplies incomplete evidence of his title, but the buyer may, within six working days from delivery of any further evidence, raise further requisitions resulting from that evidence. On the expiry of the relevant time limit the buyer loses his right to raise requisitions or make observations.

4.1.2 The parties are to take the following steps to prepare and agree the transfer of the property within the following time limits:

Step	Time Limit
A. The buyer is to send the seller a draft transfer	At least twelve working days before completion date
B. The seller is to approve or revise that draft and either return it or retain it for use as the actual transfer	Four working days after delivery of the draft transfer
C. If the draft is returned the buyer is to send an engrossment to the seller	At least five working days before completion date

4.1.3 Periods of time under conditions 4.1.1 and 4.1.2 may run concurrently.

4.1.4 If the period between the date of the contract and completion date is less than 15 working days, the time limits in conditions 4.1.1 and 4.1.2 are to be reduced by the same proportion as that period bears to the period of 15 working days. Fractions of a working day are to be rounded down except that the time limit to perform any step is not to be less than one working day.

4.2 **Proof of title**

4.2.1 The evidence of registered title is office copies of the items required to be furnished by section 110(1) of the Land Registration Act 1925 and the copies, abstracts and evidence referred to in section 110(2).

4.2.2 The evidence of unregistered title is an abstract of the title, or an epitome of title wit· photocopies of the relevant documents.

4.2.3 Where the title to the property is unregistered, the seller is to produce to the buyer (without cost to the buyer):

(a) the original of every relevant document, or

(b) an abstract, epitome or copy with an original marking by a solicitor of examination either against the original or against an examined abstract or against an examined copy.

4.3 **Defining the property**

4.3.1 The seller need not:

(a) prove the exact boundaries of the property

(b) prove who owns fences, ditches, hedges or walls

(c) separately identify parts of the property with different titles

further than he may be able to do from information in his possession.

4.3.2 The buyer may, if it is reasonable, require the seller to make or obtain, pay for and hand over a statutory declaration about facts relevant to the matters mentioned in condition 4.3.1. The form of the declaration is to be agreed by the buyer, who must not unreasonably withhold his agreement

4.4 **Rents and rentcharges**

The fact that a rent or rentcharge, whether payable or receivable by the owner of the property, has been or will on completion be, informally apportioned is not to be regarded as a defect in title.

4.5 Transfer

4.5.1 The buyer does not prejudice his right to raise requisitions, or to require replies to any raised, by taking any steps in relation to the preparation or agreement of the transfer

4.5.2 The seller is to transfer the property in the capacity specified in the agreement, or (if none is specified) as beneficial owner.

4.5.3 If after completion the seller will remain bound by any obligation affecting the property, but the law does not imply any covenant by the buyer to indemnify the seller against liability for future breaches of it:
(a) the buyer is to covenant in the transfer to indemnify the seller against liability for any future breach of the obligation and to perform it from then on, and
(b) if required by the seller, the buyer is to execute and deliver to the seller on completion a duplicate transfer prepared by the buyer.

4.5.4 The seller is to arrange at his expense that, in relation to every document of title which the buyer does not receive on completion, the buyer is to have the benefit of:
(a) a written acknowledgement of his right to its production, and
(b) a written undertaking for its safe custody (except while it is held by a mortgagee or by someone in a fiduciary capacity).

5. PENDING COMPLETION

5.1 Responsibility for property

5.1.1 The seller will transfer the property in the same physical state as it was at the date of the contract (except for fair wear and tear), which means that the seller retains the risk until completion.

5.1.2 If at any time before completion the physical state of the property makes it unusable for its purpose at the date of the contract:
(a) the buyer may rescind the contract
(b) the seller may rescind the contract where the property has become unusable for that purpose as a result of damage against which the seller could not reasonably have insured, or which it is not legally possible for the seller to make good.

5.1.3 The seller is under no obligation to the buyer to insure the property.

5.1.4 Section 47 of the Law of Property Act 1925 does not apply.

5.2 Occupation by buyer

5.2.1 If the buyer is not already lawfully in the property, and the seller agrees to let him into occupation, the buyer occupies on the following terms.

5.2.2 The buyer is a licensee and not a tenant. The terms of the licence are that the buyer:
(a) cannot transfer it
(b) may permit members of his household to occupy the property
(c) is to pay or indemnify the seller against all outgoings and other expenses in respect of the property
(d) is to pay the seller a fee calculated at the contract rate on the purchase price (less any deposit paid) for the period of the licence
(e) is entitled to any rents and profits from any part of the property which he does not occupy
(f) is to keep the property in as good a state of repair as it was in when he went into occupation (except for fair wear and tear) and is not to alter it
(g) is to insure the property in a sum which is not less than the purchase price against all risks in respect of which comparable premises are normally insured
(h) is to quit the property when the licence ends.

5.2.3 On the creation of the buyer's licence, condition 5.1 ceases to apply, which means that the buyer then assumes the risk until completion.

5.2.4 The buyer is not in occupation for the purposes of this condition if he merely exercises rights of access given solely to do work agreed by the seller.

5.2.5 The buyer's licence ends on the earliest of: completion date, rescission of the contract or when five working days' notice given by one party to the other takes effect.

5.2.6 If the buyer is in occupation of the property after his licence has come to an end and the contract is subsequently completed he is to pay the seller compensation for his continued occupation calculated at the same rate as the fee mentioned in condition 5.2.2(d).

5.2.7 The buyer's right to raise requisitions is unaffected.

6. COMPLETION

6.1 Date

6.1.1 Completion date is twenty working days after the date of the contract but time is not of the essence of the contract unless a notice to complete has been served.

6.1.2 If the money due on completion is received after 2.00pm, completion is to be treated, for the purposes only of conditions 6.3 and 7.3, as taking place on the next working day.

6.1.3 Condition 6.1.2 does not apply where the sale is with vacant possession of the property or any part and the seller has not vacated the property or that part by 2.00pm on the date of actual completion.

6.2 Place

Completion is to take place in England and Wales, either at the seller's solicitor's office or at some other place which the seller reasonably specifies.

6.3 Apportionments

6.3.1 Income and outgoings of the property are to be apportioned between the parties so far as the change of ownership on completion will affect entitlement to receive or liability to pay them.

6.3.2 If the whole property is sold with vacant possession or the seller exercises his option in condition 7.3.4, apportionment is to be made with effect from the date of actual completion; otherwise, it is to be made from completion date.

6.3.3 In apportioning any sum, it is to be assumed that the seller owns the property until the end of the day from which apportionment is made and that the sum accrues from day to day at the rate at which it is payable on that day.

6.3.4 For the purpose of apportioning income and outgoings, it is to be assumed that they accrue at an equal daily rate throughout the year

6.3.5 When a sum to be apportioned is not known or easily ascertainable at completion, a provisional apportionment is to be made according to the best estimate available. As soon as the amount is known, a final apportionment is to be made and notified to the other party. Any resulting balance is to be paid no more than ten working days later, and if not then paid the balance is to bear interest at the contract rate from then until payment.

6.3.6 Compensation payable under condition 5.2.6 is not to be apportioned.

6.4 Amount payable

The amount payable by the buyer on completion is the purchase price (less any deposit already paid to the seller or his agent) adjusted to take account of:
(a) apportionments made under condition 6.3
(b) any compensation to be paid or allowed under condition 7.3.

6.5 Title deeds

6.5.1 The seller is not to retain the documents of title after the buyer has tendered the amount payable under condition 6.4.

6.5.2 Condition 6.5.1 does not apply to any documents of title relating to land being retained by the seller after completion.

6.6 Rent receipts

The buyer is to assume that whoever gave any receipt for a payment of rent or service charge which the seller produces was the person or the agent of the person then entitled to that rent or service charge.

6.7 Means of payment

The buyer is to pay the money due on completion in one or more of the following ways:
(a) legal tender
(b) a banker's draft
(c) a direct credit to a bank account nominated by the seller's solicitor
(d) an unconditional release of a deposit held by a stakeholder

6.8 Notice to complete

6.8.1 At any time on or after completion date, a party who is ready able and willing to complete may give the other a notice to complete.

6.8.2 A party is ready able and willing:
(a) if he could be, but for the default of the other party, and
(b) in the case of the seller, even though a mortgage remains secured on the property, if the amount to be paid on completion enables the property to be transferred freed of all mortgages (except those to which the sale is expressly subject).

6.8.3 The parties are to complete the contract within ten working days of giving a notice to complete, excluding the day on which the notice is given. For this purpose, time is of the essence of the contract.

6.8.4 On receipt of a notice to complete:
(a) if the buyer paid no deposit, he is forthwith to pay a deposit of 10 per cent
(b) if the buyer paid a deposit of less than 10 per cent, he is forthwith to pay a further deposit equal to the balance of that 10 per cent.

7. REMEDIES

7.1 Errors and omissions

7.1.1 If any plan or statement in the contract, or in the negotiations leading to it, is or was misleading or inaccurate due to an error or omission, the remedies available are as follows.

7.1.2 When there is a material difference between the description or value of the property as represented and as it is, the injured party is entitled to damages.

7.1.3 An error or omission only entitles the injured party to rescind the contract:
(a) where it results from fraud or recklessness, or
(b) where he would be obliged, to his prejudice, to transfer or accept property differing substantially (in quantity, quality or tenure) from what the error or omission had led him to expect.

7.2 Rescission

If either party rescinds the contract:
(a) unless the rescission is a result of the buyer's breach of contract the deposit is to be repaid to the buyer with accrued interest
(b) the buyer is to return any documents he received from the seller and is to cancel any registration of the contract.

7.3 Late completion

7.3.1 If there is default by either or both of the parties in performing their obligations under the contract and completion is delayed, the party whose total period of default is the greater is to pay compensation to the other party.

7.3.2 Compensation is calculated at the contract rate on the purchase price, or (where the buyer is the paying party) the purchase price less any deposit paid, for the period by which the paying party's default exceeds that of the receiving party, or, if shorter, the period between completion date and actual completion.

7.3.3 Any claim for loss resulting from delayed completion is to be reduced by any compensation paid under this contract.

7.3.4 Where the buyer holds the property as tenant of the seller and completion is delayed, the seller may give notice to the buyer, before the date of actual completion, that he intends to take the net income from the property until completion. If he does so, he cannot claim compensation under condition 7.3.1 as well.

7.4 After completion

Completion does not cancel liability to perform any outstanding obligation under this contract.

7.5 Buyer's failure to comply with notice to complete

7.5.1 If the buyer fails to complete in accordance with a notice to complete, the following terms apply.

7.5.2 The seller may rescind the contract, and if he does so:
(a) he may
(i) forfeit and keep any deposit and accrued interest
(ii) resell the property
(iii) claim damages
(b) the buyer is to return any documents he received from the seller and is to cancel any registration of the contract.

7.5.3 The seller retains his other rights and remedies.

7.6 Seller's failure to comply with notice to complete

7.6.1 If the seller fails to complete in accordance with a notice to complete, the following terms apply.

7.6.2 The buyer may rescind the contract, and if he does so:
(a) the deposit is to be repaid to the buyer with accrued interest
(b) the buyer is to return any documents he received from the seller and is, at the seller's expense, to cancel any registration of the contract.

7.6.3 The buyer retains his other rights and remedies.

8. LEASEHOLD PROPERTY

8.1 Existing leases

8.1.1 The following provisions apply to a sale of leasehold land.

8.1.2 The seller having provided the buyer with copies of the documents embodying the lease terms, the buyer is treated as entering into the contract knowing and fully accepting those terms.

8.1.3 The seller is to comply with any lease obligations requiring the tenant to insure the property.

8.1.4 The transfer is to record that no covenant implied by statute makes the seller liable to the buyer for any breach of the lease terms about the condition of the property. This applies even if the seller is to transfer as beneficial owner.

8.2 New leases

8.2.1 The following provisions apply to a grant of a new lease.

8.2.2 The conditions apply so that:
"seller" means the proposed landlord
"buyer" means the proposed tenant
"purchase price" means the premium to be paid on the grant of a lease.

8.2.3 The lease is to be in the form of the draft attached to the agreement.

8.2.4 If the term of the new lease will exceed 21 years, the seller is to deduce a title which will enable the buyer to register the lease at HM Land Registry with an absolute title.

8.2.5 The buyer is not entitled to transfer the benefit of the contract.

8.2.6 The seller is to engross the lease and a counterpart of it and is to send the counterpart to the buyer at least five working days before completion date.

8.2.7 The buyer is to execute the counterpart and deliver it to the seller on completion.

8.3 Landlord's consent

8.3.1 The following provisions apply if a consent to assign or sub-let is required to complete the contract.

8.3.2 (a) The seller is to apply for the consent at his expense, and to use all reasonable efforts to obtain it
(b) The buyer is to provide all information and references reasonably required.

8.3.3 The buyer is not entitled to transfer the benefit of the contract.

8.3.4 Unless he is in breach of his obligation under condition 8.3.2, either party may rescind the contract by notice to the other party if three working days before completion date:
(a) the consent has not been given or
(b) the consent has been given subject to a condition to which the buyer reasonably objects.
In that case, neither party is to be treated as in breach of contract and condition 7.2 applies.

9. CHATTELS

9.1 The following provisions apply to any chattels which are to be sold.

9.2 Whether or not a separate price is to be paid for the chattels, the contract takes effect as a contract for sale of goods.

9.3 Ownership of the chattels passes to the buyer on actual completion.

SPECIAL CONDITIONS

1. (a) This Agreement incorporates the Standard Conditions of Sale (Second Edition). Where there is a conflict between those Conditions and this Agreement, this Agreement prevails.

   (b) Terms used or defined in this Agreement have the same meaning when used in the Conditions.

2. The Property is sold subject to the Incumbrances on the Property and the Buyer will raise no requisitions on them.

3. ~~The chattels on the Property and set out on any attached list are included in the sale~~ xxxx
The chattels hereby sold comprise all curtains, carpets and light fittings at the property

4. The Property is sold with vacant possession on completion.

(or) 4. The Property is sold subject to the following leases or tenancies:

Note: It is not necessary for the contract to make specific provision for the Buyer to enter into a covenant indemnifying the seller from any breaches of the Deed of Covenant of 3 April 1977 as this is provided for in standard condition 4-5-3.

Seller's Solicitors   :   Makepiece and Streiff, Bank Chambers, Barset.
                                    Ref: CA/WB/JE

Buyer's Solicitors   :   Rime and Reason
                                    Invicta House
                                    Market St
                                    Barset   Ref CR/JC/BURTON

©1992 **OYEZ**   The Solicitors' Law Stationery Society Ltd,
Oyez House, 7 Spa Road, London SE16 3QQ

4 92   F22381
5065046
* * * * *
2nd Edition

1992   **THE LAW SOCIETY**

Standard Conditions of Sale

H.M. LAND REGISTRY

SPECIMEN

Edition 1 opened 14.8.1965

TITLE NUMBER BA19834

Map Reference SF6205C

This register consists of 4 *pages*

A. PROPERTY REGISTER
containing the description of the registered land and the estate comprised in the Title

COUNTY	DISTRICT
BARSETSHIRE	BARSET

The Freehold land shown and edged with red on the plan of the above Title filed at the Registry

registered on 14 June 1951 known as The Limes Lemon Terrace together with a right of way on foot only over the land tinted brown on the filed plan.

B. PROPRIETORSHIP REGISTER
stating nature of the Title, name, address and description of the proprietor of the land and any entries affecting the right of disposing thereof

TITLE ABSOLUTE

Entry number	Proprietor, etc.
1.	PERCY BYSSHE SHELLEY of The Limes, Lemon Terrace, Barset, Barsetshire, Steel Erector registered on 14 August 1965.
2.	BERNARD OLIVER BUTLER of The Limes, Lemon Terrace, Barset, Barsetshire, Engineer, registered on 10 February 1970.

Any entries struck through are no longer subsisting

	C. CHARGES REGISTER	
	containing charges, incumbrances etc., adversely affecting the land and registered dealings therewith	
Entry number	The date at the beginning of each entry is the date on which the entry was made on this edition of the register	Remarks
1.	14 August 1965-A Transfer of the land in this title dated 12 July 1965 by John Smith (Transferor) to Percy Bysshe Shelley (Transferee) contains the following covenant:- "The Transferee hereby covenants with the Transferor for the benefit of the Transferor's adjoining land that he the Transferee will not at any time use the land hereby transferred or permit the same to be used for any purpose other than as the site for a single private dwellinghouse with the usual garages outbuildings and appurtenances."	

Printed in the United Kingdom for Her Majesty's Stationery Office by Multiform Printing 8188068 4/89 1507

R25

Any entries struck through are no longer subsisting

	TITLE NUMBER		
H.M. LAND REGISTRY	**BA 19834**		
ORDNANCE SURVEY PLAN REFERENCE	SF 6205	SECTION C	Scale 1/1250
COUNTY BARSETSHIRE	DISTRICT BARSET		© Crown copyright

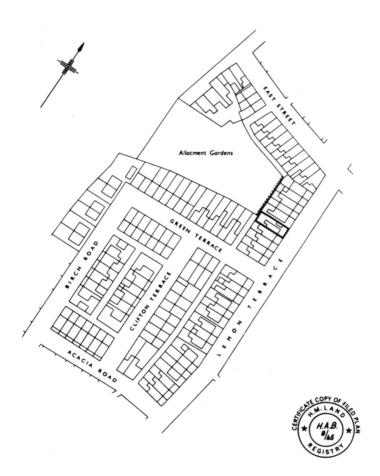

Short description
of the property

re .... THE LIMES, LEMON TERRACE, BARSET ....

Parties .... BUTLER ....

to .... BURTON ....

In cases of property subject to a tenancy, forms **Con 291** (general business and residential tenancies) *or* **Con 292** (agricultural tenancies) should also be used.

These enquiries are copyright and may not be reproduced

Please strike out enquiries which are not applicable

Replies are requested to the following enquiries.	The replies are as follows.
RIME AND REASON	*Makepiece & Streiff*
Proposed buyer's solicitors.	*Proposed seller's solicitors.*
Date ...... 7 January 19 993	Date ...... 11 January ...... 19 93.
GENERAL ENQUIRIES	REPLIES

These replies, except in the case of any enquiry expressly requiring a reply from the Seller's solicitors, are given on behalf of the proposed Seller and without responsibility on the part of his solicitors their partners or employees. They are believed to be correct but the accuracy is not guaranteed and they do not obviate the need to make appropriate searches, enquiries and inspections.

1. Boundaries

(A) To whom do all the boundary walls, fences, hedges and ditches belong?

(B) If no definite indications exist, which has the Seller maintained or regarded as his responsibility?

The land certificate does not show ownership.

The fences on the North and East boundaries have been maintained by the Seller and previous owners.

2. Disputes

(A) Is the Seller aware of any past or current disputes regarding boundaries, easements, covenants or other matters relating to the property or its use?

(B) During the last three years, has the Seller complained or had cause to complain about the state and condition, or the manner of use, of any adjoining or neighbouring property? If so, please give particulars.

a)
b)   The Seller knows of none

3. Notices

Please give particulars of all notices relating to the property, or to matters likely to affect its use or enjoyment, that the Seller (or to his knowledge, any predecessor in title) has given or received.

There are none so far as the Seller is aware.

4. Guarantees etc.

(A) Please supply a copy of any of the following of which the Buyer is to have the benefit:

agreement, covenant, guarantee, warranty, bond, certificate, indemnity and insurance policy,
relating to any of the following matters:
the construction of the property, or any part of it, or of any building of which it forms part;
any repair or replacement of, or treatment or improvement to the fabric of the property;
the maintenance of any accessway;
the construction costs of any road (including lighting, drainage and crossovers) to which the property fronts, and the charges for adopting any such road as maintainable at the public expense;
a defective title;
breach of any restrictive covenant.

(B) (i) What defects or other matters have become apparent, or adverse claims have been made by third parties, which might give rise to a claim under any document mentioned in (A)?
(ii) Has notice of such defect, matter or adverse claim been given? If so, please give particulars.
(iii) Please give particulars of all such claims already made, whether or not already settled.

a) There are none with the deeds and the Seller believes there are none.

None to the Seller's knowledge but no guarantee or warranty is given and the Buyer must rely on an inspection and survey.

5. Services

(A) Does the property have drainage, water, electricity and gas services? Which of them are connected to the mains?

Yes all are connected.

(B) Is the water supply metered?

No.

(C) Do any of the services (except where part of the mains) pass through or over property not included in the sale?

No.

(D) If so, please give details of route and particulars of any easement, grant, exception, reservation, wayleave, licence or consent authorising this.

)
) These do not arise
)
)

(E) Please supply a copy of any licence to abstract water and of any consent or licence relating to drainage, issued in respect of the property or the activities carried on there.

6. Facilities

(A) Except in the case of public rights or where particulars have already been given, what rights are there for the use of the following facilities, whether enjoyed by the owner or occupier of the property, or over the property for the benefit of other property:

— Access for light and air;
— Access for pedestrians and vehicles;
— Emergency escape routes;
— Pipes and wires for services not dealt with in Enquiry 5.
— Access and facilities for repair, maintenance and replacement.

Please supply copies of any relevant documents.

The Seller believes there are none save as respects the passage way at the rear.

(B) Has any person taken any action to stop (whether immediately or at some future time) the use of any facility? If so, please give particulars.

No.

(C) In respect of maintenance, repair or replacement work on any land or fixtures affording any facility:

None of these matters arise.

(i) What work has been done by the Seller (or, to his knowledge, any predecessor in title), and when?

(ii) What work has the Seller been called upon to do which has not yet been done?

(iii) What sums has the Seller contributed to work done by others, and when? Is any demand for such sums still outstanding?

(iv) What sums has the Seller called upon others to contribute, and when? Is any demand still outstanding?

7. Adverse Rights

(A) Is the Seller aware of any rights or informal arrangements specifically affecting the property, other than any disclosed in the draft contract or immediately apparent on inspection, which are exercisable by virtue of an easement, grant, wayleave, licence, consent, agreement relating to an ancient monument or land near it, or otherwise or which are in the nature of public or common rights?

No, but the property is sold subject to any there may be.

(B) (i) Please give the full names, and ages if under 18, of all persons in actual occupation of the property.

The Seller is a widower living alone.

(ii) What legal or equitable interest in the property has each of those persons?

(C) Is the Seller aware of any other overriding interests as defined by the Land Registration Act 1926, s. 70(1)?

No.

8. Restrictions

(A) Have all restrictions affecting the property or its use been observed up to the date hereof? If not, please give details.

The Seller believes so.

(B) Where such restrictions have in the past required any person's consent or approval of plans, does the Seller have written evidence of that consent or approval?

No.

9. Planning etc.

(A) (i) When did the present use of the property commence?
(ii) Has this use been continuous since it commenced?

The Seller believes the house was built in 1930. So far as the Seller knows.

(B) During the four years immediately prior to receipt of these enquiries:

(i) Were any of the buildings on the property erected, or have any been altered or added to?

No.

(ii) Have any other building, engineering, mining or other operations been carried out in, on, over or under the property?

No.

(iii) Has any condition or limitation on any planning permission not been complied with?
If so, please give details.

The Seller has not obtained any planning permission.

(C) Please supply a copy of:

    (i) Any planning permission authorising or imposing conditions upon the present use of the property, and the erection or retention of the buildings now on it.

    (ii) Any bye-law approval or building regulation consent relating to those buildings.

    (iii) Any, current fire certificate.

> There are none.

10. Fixtures, Fittings etc.

(A) Does the sale include all of the following items now on the property, and attached to or growing in it?

    Trees, shrubs, plants, flowers, and garden produce. Greenhouses, garden sheds and garden ornaments. Aerials. Fitted furniture and shelves. Electric switches, points and wall and ceiling fittings.

> All such items as are at present on the property are included.
> See the contract as to carpets, curtains, and light fittings.

(B) What fixtures and fittings affixed to the property are not included in the sale?

> None.

(C) If the property has any fixed oil burning appliance, what arrangements are proposed for the sale to the Buyer on completion of any stock of oil?

> Not applicable.

11. Outgoings

(A) What is the current annual water charge?

> £90 per annum.

(B) What other periodic charges affect the property or its occupier, apart from the community charge?

> None so far as the Seller is aware.

12. Completion

(A) How long after exchange of contracts will the Seller be able to give vacant possession of the whole of the property?

> To be arranged on exchange.

(B) The Buyer's solicitors wish to complete by adopting the Law Society's Code for Completion by Post (1984 edition). Do the Seller's solicitors agree?

> The Seller's solicitors would prefer personal completion if possible.

13. New Properties

(A) Will the Seller pay all charges for construction and connection of the drainage system and the services?

> Not applicable.

(B) Are all the following included in the purchase price: fencing all boundaries, laying all paths and drives, and levelling and clearing the garden area? If not, please give particulars.

ADDITIONAL ENQUIRIES

14. Please confirm that the items referred to in the contract special condition no. 3 are not subject to any lien charges or hire purchase or loan agreement.

> The Seller so confirms.

15.(a) Does the porperty have central heating?

> Yes.

   (b) If so please:-

      i) Give details and particulars of service arrangements and the date of the last service.

> Serviced annually by the Gas Board under their 3 star service plan (copy herewith). Last service took place in September 1992.

      ii) Confirm that the system is the property of the Seller and not subject to any hire purchase or loan agreement.

> The Seller so confirms.

16. When was the property last rewired?

> 1973

For Leasehold Enquiries and further Additional Enquiries see over

LEASEHOLD ENQUIRIES

I. General

(A) Is the lease under which the property is held a head lease or an underlease?

(B) Please state the names and addresses of the lessor, any superior lessors, their respective solicitors, and the receivers of the rent.

(C) Please supply copies of all licences granted by the lessor, other than licences to assign.

(D) What steps have been taken to obtain the lessor's consent to the proposed assignment? Please supply a copy of any licence granted.

II. Covenants

(A) Has the lessor complained of any breach of covenant?

(B) Has any obligation in the lease to paint or do any other work by or at a particular time been strictly fulfilled? If not, please give details.

(C) Has the Seller had cause to complain of any breach of the lessor's covenants?

III. Service Charge

(A) Please give details of service charge payments for the last three years, with any supporting accounts or vouchers that the Seller has.

(B) Has the Seller, or to his knowledge any predecessor in title, exercised a statutory right to obtain information? If so, with what result?

IV. Insurance

(A) Who effected the insurance policy currently covering the property?

(B) Please give particulars: insurers' and any insurance brokers' name and address, policy number, insured's name(s), risks covered, for what amount, premium, and date to which the property is insured.

V. Reversionary Title

Is there with the title deeds a marked abstract or office copy of the freehold title and of any superior lease?

ADDITIONAL ENQUIRIES

17. (a) With Whom is the use of the footpath to the West of the property shared?

    The Seller believes that the properties further North in Lemon Terrace have access but does not know the extent of the legal entitlement.

    (b) Has the Seller ever been asked to contribute to the maintenance of the path at the rear of the properties in East St?

    No.

18. To whom do the telephone instruments on the property belong? Will they be left at the property on completion?

    They belong to British Telecom PLC and will be left at the property on completion.

19. Has the property ever been flooded?

    Not to the Sellers's knowledge.

(Revised 6.90) 11.90 F18532
5033010
★ ★ ★ ★ ★

Messrs. Rime must also have a photocopy of the Deed of Covenant relating to the fence. Thomas prepares a covering letter to them enclosing, with the photocopies, the draft contract with a carbon copy: "copy for your use," a courtesy invariably extended to opposite solicitors in respect of documents that must pass to and fro between them. At the same time he prepares a form of application to the Barchester District Land Registry for office copy entries (Form 44). The letter and form are signed by Mr. Black and sent off with the appropriate fee.

On receipt, Mr. Reason examines the papers, and prepares a form of Enquiries before Contract. The content of the form is described below (p. 148–150).

To the standard inquiries he adds some additional queries on the title, etc., which arise from his examination of the papers. The form is typed and sent to Messrs. Makepiece, again with the courtesy copy for their convenience in replying. He cannot approve the draft contract until he has satisfactory replies to these enquiries and also a clear certificate of search from the local authority together with satisfactory replies to the inquiries he has put to them.

When Mr. Black receives the form he makes an appointment for Mr. Butler to call and supply the answers to enquiries that can only be answered from the personal knowledge of the seller. Following their meeting, he is able to reply, and the completed form he now returns to Messrs. Rime (pp. 122–125).

TOWARDS EXCHANGE

Mr. Reason receives and examines the replies with care. He is satisfied with them. Shortly after he receives from the District Council the certificate of search disclosing that there are no subsisting entries and replies to enquiries. He now telephones Miss Burton and makes an appointment for her to call.

When she calls he tells her that the search is clear, *i.e.* that there are neither any adverse entries in the local land charges register nor any unsatisfactory replies to questions in Form Con. 29. He is, therefore, satisfied that the local and public authorities for the area have taken no action that would impose a financial burden on the owner and that there are no plans which might affect the property. He goes over the replies to his inquiries and is able to satisfy her earlier enquiry on the right of way. As he does not need to make any alterations to the draft contract, the matter can safely proceed when she has a satisfactory report from the surveyors she has instructed. In fact she has brought the report with her. It shows that, no structural defects, infestation or rot, etc., having been discovered, the purchase can be recommended at the price agreed.

Mr. Reason discusses the question of property insurance with Miss Burton. He tells her that under the contract the risk of physical damage to the property passes to her on completion. However, the seller, Mr. Butler, is not obliged to insure the property but is obliged to transfer the property in the same physical state as it was at the date of the contract (fair wear and tear excepted).

This means that Miss Burton would be able to rescind, (*i.e.* cancel) the contract if at any time before completion the physical state of the property makes it unusable for its purpose at the date of the contract. Mr. Reason explains that there could be problems in deciding what state the property actually was in at the date of the contract, as Miss Burton will only have had a brief view of the house. He is also concerned that the seller might have the property under-insured. His advice is for Miss Burton to arrange insurance upon exchange of contracts, even though this could give rise to double insurance of the house. He explains that if the property is damaged then Miss Burton will have a claim for damages against Mr. Butler. However, Mr. Butler may only be able to pay those damages if he has kept the property fully insured to its appropriate reinstatement value. The conditions of contract do not require him to do this, and so Mr. Reason advises Miss Burton that he feels she should arrange her own insurance so as to avoid running the risk of claiming damages against Mr. Butler which Mr. Butler might be unable to pay. She agrees to take his advice and says that she is content to leave it to him to obtain cover.

Up to this point the negotiations and correspondence have been "subject to contract" and Mr. Butler and Miss Burton have both been free to cry off the deal at any time. The point has now been reached at which the contract can be entered into that will bind both of them to carry the transaction through to its conclusion. The only outstanding point on the terms of contract is the date for completion: the day on which possession of the keys of the property will be handed over: the day on which ownership will pass to Miss Burton. This is a practical matter, a matter of the convenience of the two parties and their solicitors. Mr. Reason tells her he will need 7–14 days from the date of the contract to carry through the remaining stages and thinks completion could be in the second or third week of February. She suggests February 19. This is acceptable to him and he promises to get in touch with her again when he has agreed the date with Messrs. Makepiece.

The contract can, however, now be signed. To save unnecessary typing, one copy of the draft is made to serve as a fair copy and Mr. Reason gets Miss Burton to sign it. He also obtains her cheque for the 10 per cent. deposit, less the £250 already paid to the agents and asks her to let him have her cheque for the balance of the purchase price on February 15. The deposit cheque is paid into the firm's clients' account.

The contract is entered into by the exchange of the copies or "parts" signed respectively by the parties and the payment of the deposit by a cheque drawn on Messrs. Rime's clients' account, the client's cheque having in the meantime been cleared.

Mr. Reason writes to Messrs. Makepiece enclosing the other, unsigned, part of the contract, telling them that the draft is approved and that exchange can take place when the completion date is agreed. He suggests February 19.

On receipt of the letter Mr. Black telephones Mr. Butler and arranges for him to call later that day to sign the contract. When he arrives he signs the contract and also agrees the completion date. When he has left Mr. Black speaks to Mr. Reason on the phone and confirms the date. It is agreed that the contracts shall be dated that date, January 25, with a completion date of February 19 inserted in the respective copies. Mr. Reason arranges to send James around to exchange within half an hour.

When James arrives he hands over Miss Burton's part of the contract and the firm's cheque for the deposit. He then carefully inspects Mr. Butler's part which Mr. Black hands over and Mr. Black looks over Miss Burton's part to check that they both accord. It is essential that each part of the contract incorporates all the terms agreed between the parties, in compliance with section 2 of the Law of Property (Miscellaneous Provisions) Act 1989. If this is not done then there will be no binding contract in existence.

On receiving the contract, Mr. Reason, having checked it, telephones Miss Burton to tell her that exchange has taken place and the completion date is confirmed. He also telephones the local agent of the insurers with whom he normally deals, and arranges immediate all risks cover on the property in the name of Miss Burton and in the sum of £42,000. He writes to tell her and to confirm the exchange.

Mr. Black has also reported exchange to his client and it is shortly after this that the estate agents, who have made several telephone calls to ascertain progress, call again and learn of the exchange. They follow this up by sending to Messrs. Makepiece their bill for the commission payable by Mr. Butler.

AFTER EXCHANGE

The greater part of the work in preparing for completion will be for Mr. Reason as the buyer's solicitor. There is more time than he would need if there were grounds for urgency. In this time he must (a) prepare and obtain Messrs. Makepiece's approval to the document formally transferring the ownership to his client (the Transfer, Form 19); (b) put his final questions to Messrs. Makepiece covering all unresolved details and confirming that nothing has happened to change the answers given in replies to Enquiries before Contract. These are the requisitions; (c) search in the District Land Registry and obtain the certificate of the Land Registrar that no adverse entries have been made since the date of issue of the office copy entries now in his possession and (d) ensure that the money required to be handed over on completion is available on February 19 in a form acceptable to Messrs. Makepiece. These steps are now related in more detail.

Mr. Reason drafts the transfer on Form 19, the draft receipt for fixtures and fittings and the requisitions on title. He has these typed in duplicate and dispatched to Messrs. Makepiece with a covering letter. When they are to hand Mr. Black telephones Mr. Butler to inquire about the payment of water rates. He learns that these are paid to March 31, 1993. He points out that these will have to be apportioned so that Miss Burton pays the proportion from completion to March 31. One way of doing this is to ask the Water Board to make the split. They will then charge Miss Burton for the period and make a corresponding refund to Mr. Butler. He undertakes to write to the Water Board to request this. He asks about Mr. Butler's removal arrangements and is told that the loading of his furniture and effects should be completed by mid-morning. Mr. Butler will find it convenient to bring in the keys and his offer is accepted.

Mr. Black is now able to dictate his replies to the requisitions, together with a letter to Messrs. Rime approving the draft transfer without amendment. He returns to them the top copy of the draft transfer and the completed requisition form (pp. 130–133).

Towards Completion

On receipt of the letter, Mr. Reason notes from replies to requisitions that the water rates are to be apportioned by the water authorities to the date of completion and, there being no other outgoings, no adjustment is required in the amount payable on completion. He notes also where completion will take place and how the keys are to be handed over. He gives the transfer out for retyping on the version of Form 19 printed on stout paper. This is the engrossment, a term derived from the time when deeds were hand-written or "engrossed" on parchment. As the transfer contains a covenant by Miss Burton as the transferee, it requires her signature as well as Mr. Butler's. Although it bears no outward resemblance to the old deeds, the transfer is technically a deed, provided it complies with the provisions of the Law of Property (Miscellaneous Provisions) Act 1989 and:

1. Describes itself as a deed or expresses itself to be executed or signed as a deed.

2. The signatures of parties to the deed are witnessed by a person who attests to the signature.

A note on these formalities will be found below (p. 151).

Mr. Reason telephones Miss Burton asking her to call to sign the document. He does not delay in arranging an early appointment because the transfer must be sent to Messrs. Makepiece so that Mr. Black can obtain Mr. Butler's signature before completion day.

She calls the next day when Mr. Reason presents the transfer for her signature. He gives her a moment to read it and mentions the obligation which she is to take over under the covenant. He exchanges a word with her about the balance of the purchase money (including the price of the chattels), together with £420.00 for the stamp duty and £60 for registration fees. He politely declines her offer to give him a cheque now, because such moneys should be held only long enough to clear the cheque before completion.

The transfer is duly signed as a deed by Miss Burton and Mr. Reason adds his name, address and occupation as witness to the signature. He sends the signed transfer to Messrs. Makepiece and Mr. Butler calls by arrangement to sign it and to finalise the arrangements for February 19. The transfer is signed by him and the signature is witnessed by Mr. Black. It is confirmed that the keys are to be brought in and Mr. Butler

Short
description
of the
property *re* ...... THE LIMES, LEMON TERRACE, BARSET

Parties ...... BUTLER

to ...... BURTON

oyez

REQUISITIONS

ON TITLE

*(For use where Enquiries before Contract have
already been answered)*

Please strike out any requisitions not applicable.

---

1. PREVIOUS ENQUIRIES

If the enquiries before contract replied to on behalf of the
Vendor were repeated herein, would the replies now be the
same as those previously given? If not, please give full
particulars of any variation.

Confirmed insofar as they had not been
varied by subsequent correspondence.

---

2. OUTGOINGS AND APPORTIONMENTS

(A) On completion the Vendor must produce receipts for the
last payments of outgoings, of which either he claims
reimbursement of an advance payment or arrears could be
recovered from the Purchaser.

(B) (i) In the case of a leasehold property or property
subject to a legal rentcharge, the receipt for rent due
on the last rent day before the day of completion, as
well as the receipt for the last fire insurance
premium, must be produced on completion.

(ii) Does the former receipt contain any reference to a
breach of any of the covenants and conditions
contained in the lease or grant?

(c) Please send a completion statement.

The Seller will deal with the local
authority direct regarding the Community
Charge — Council Tax and will inform the
authority of the date your client takes
possession. The Seller is arranging for
the water rates to be apportioned by the
water authority and the receipt will be
produced on completion. Sofaras the
Seller is aware there are no other outgoings.

We will require only the amount shown due
on the contract.

---

3. TITLE DEEDS

A. ~~Unregistered land~~ xxx

(i) Which abstracted documents of title will be
delivered to the Purchaser on completion?

(ii) Who will give to the Purchaser the statutory
acknowledgment and undertaking for the
production and safe custody of those not handed
over?

(iii) Why will any documents not handed over be
retained?

B. *Registered land*

(i) When was the land or charge certificate last officially
examined with the register?

(ii) If the Land Registry has approved an estate lay-out
plan for use with official searches of part of the land
in the title, on what date was it approved?

(iii) If the Vendor's land certificate is on deposit at the
Land Registry, what is the deposit number?

19 May 1970, although Office Copy
subsequent to this have been supplied.

)
)
) Inapplicable
)

---

4. MORTGAGES

(A) All subsisting mortgages must be discharged on or before
completion.

(B) In respect of each subsisting mortgage or charge:

(i) Will a vacating receipt, discharge of registered
charge or consent to dealing, entitling the Purchaser
to take the property freed from it, be handed over on
completion?

(ii) If not, will the Vendor's solicitor give a written
undertaking on completion to hand one over later?

(iii) If an undertaking is proposed, what are the suggested
terms of it?

Inapplicable

5. POSSESSION

(A)   (i) Vacant possession of the whole of the property must be given on completion.

      Yes

  (ii) Has every person in occupation of all or any part of the property agreed to vacate on or before completion?

  (iii) What arrangements will be made to deliver the keys to the Purchaser?

       Only the Seller is in occupation and the contract provides he will give vacant possession.

       The keys will be handed over by us on completion.

Or

(B) The Vendor must on completion hand over written authorities for future rents to be paid to the Purchaser or his agents.

6. NOTICES

Please give the name and address of any solicitor, residential tenant or other person to whom notice of any dealing with the property must be given.

    Not applicable

7. COMPLETION ARRANGEMENTS

Please answer any of the following requisitions against which X has been placed in the box.

☒ (A) Where will completion take place?

    At our offices

☐ (B) We should like to remit the completion monies direct to your bank account. If you agree, please give the name and branch of your bank, its sorting code number, and the title and number of the account to be credited.

☐ (C) We should like to remit the completion monies by Speedsend. If you agree, please give the address of the most convenient Trustee Savings Bank branch and state whether you maintain an account there.

☒ (D) In whose favour and for what amounts will banker's drafts be required on completion?

    We require only the amount shown in the contract in one banker's draft payable to ourselves.

The deeds and documents of title remain to be examined and the right is reserved to make further requisitions which may arise on such examination, the replies to the above, the usual searches and enquiries before completion, or otherwise.

Note.—The Requisitions founded on the Abstract of Title or Contract must, of course, be added to the above.

DATED 12 February   19 93   DATED   15 February   1993.

Rime and Reason   Purchaser's Solicitor.   *Makepiece & Streoff*   Vendor's Solicitor.

oyez   The Solicitors' Law Stationery Society plc, Paulton House, 8 Shepherdess Walk, London N1 7LB   7.89 BM

Conveyancing 28B   5032056

Transfer of Whole [1]

HM Land Registry

Form 19

(Rules 98 or 115, Land Registration Rules, 1925)

Stamp pursuant to section 28 of the Finance Act 1931, to be impressed here.	*When the transfer attracts Inland Revenue Duty the stamps should be impressed here before lodging the transfer for registration.*

[1] *For a transfer by a Company or Corporation form 19(Co) is printed. For transfer to joint proprietors form 19(JP) is printed.*

County and district (or London borough)   BARSETSHIRE – BARSET

Title number(s)   BA 19834

Property   THE LIMES, LEMON TERRACE, BARSET.

Date   19   In consideration of   £42,000

[2] *Delete the words in italics if not required.*

[3] *In BLOCK LETTERS enter the full name(s) postal address(es) (including postcode) and occupation(s) of the proprietor(s) of the land.*

[4] *If desired or otherwise as the case may be (see rules 76 and 77).*

[5] *In BLOCK LETTERS enter the full name(s) postal address(es) (including postcode) and occupation(s) of the transferee(s) for entry in the register.*

[6] *On a transfer to a company registered under the Companies Act, enter here the company's registration number if entry thereof on the register is required.*

[7] *Enter any special clause here.*

[8] *A transfer for charitable purposes should follow form 36 in the schedule to the Land Registration Rules, 1925 (see rules 121 and 122).*

pounds (£   ) *the receipt of which is hereby acknowledged* ([3])

I/We ([3])   BERNARD OLIVER BUTLER of the Limes, Lemon Terrace,

Barset, Barsetshire (the Transferor).

as beneficial owners hereby transfer to ([4])

([5])   MOLLIE BURTON of the Royal Hotel Market Square, Barset, the aforesaid District Nurse (the Transferee).

([6]) (Company registration number...)

the land comprised in the title(s) above mentioned ([7])([8])   and the Transferee hereby covenants with the Transferor by way of indemnity only that in the event of the garage at present erecged on the Northern boundary of the land hereby transferred being removed a close boarded fence 6' high will be erected along the said Northern boundary such fence to be erected and maintained at the expense of the transferee.

(continued overleaf)

(9) *If a certificate of value for the purpose of the Stamp Act. 1891 and amending Acts is not required, delete this paragraph.*

(*) It is hereby certified that the transaction hereby affected does not form part of a larger transaction or series of transactions in respect of which the amount or value or the aggregate amount or value of the consideration exceeds £ xxxx ....

Signed as a deed by

BERNARD OLIVER BUTLER ....   }   B Butler

....

in the presence of

Name   JOHN BLACK   Signature of witness   J. Black

Address   BANK CHAMBERS BARSET

Occupation   LEGAL EXECUTIVE WITH MESSRS MAKEPIECE AND STREIFF

Signed as a deed by

....MOLLIE BURTON..............   }   M. Burton

....

in the presence of

Name   COLIN REASON   Signature of witness   Colin Reason

Address   INVICTA HOUSE, MARKET STREET BARSET

Occupation   SOLICITOR , MESSRS RIME AND REASON

oyez The Solicitors' Law Stationery Society Ltd., Oyez House, 27 Crimscott Street, London SE1 5TS

1990 Edition
6.90 F17347
5061083
★ ★ ★ ★ ★

says he can deliver them by 11.30 a.m. latest. In reply to Mr. Black's question he states that he has asked the gas and electricity board offices to have the meters read on the morning of the 19th and for the accounts to that date to be sent on to him. Mr. Black tells Mr. Butler that Messrs. Makepiece will account to him for the net proceeds of sale within a day or two after completion and will let him have a financial statement. He enquires whether, as usually happens, Messrs. Makepiece should pay the account of the estate agents and Mr. Butler agrees that this shall be done, Mr. Black is able to give Mr. Butler a very rough idea of what his firm's charges are likely to be, but carefully points out that the actual amount will be for the cashier's department to work out in the light of the amount of work and disbursements involved on the case. Mr. Butler agrees that the charges may be deducted from the proceeds of sale before the balance is paid over to him.

Following this Mr. Black telephones Mr. Reason and arranges for completion to take place in his office at 12.00 noon on the 19th.

Mr. Reason writes to his client to let her know that the appointment for completion has been made, to enclose a financial statement and the firm's bill and to request a cheque for the total amount on February 15.

Ten days before completion James dispatches the Application for Official Search (Form 94A) to Barchester District Land Registry by first class post (p. 137). Three days later Mr. Reason duly receives the certificate which shows that no new entries have been made since the date of issue of the office copy entries (p. 141). He notes that the priority period by which he must lodge the transfer and supporting papers for the registration of the new owner expires on March 21—30 working days after the date of issue.

On February 15 Miss Burton brings in her cheque for the balance of the price and Mr. Reason passes it to his cashier's department requesting them, subject to clearance of the cheque, to draw a banker's draft for that amount made payable to Messrs. Makepiece early on the morning of February 19.

On that day, one of the cashiers, having confirmed with the bank that Miss Burton's cheque has been cleared, draws the banker's draft and hands it personally to Mr. Reason. The latter calls in James and asks him to undertake the formalities of the completion appointment, giving him the following check list of items to deal with:

The Limes   Barset

Burton from Butler
Completion 19 February 1993 12.00 noon
at the offices of Messrs. Makepiece & Streiff, Bank Chambers, Barset.

1. Examine Land Certificate against office copy entries
2. Examine transfer for vendor's signature and witness name, address and occupation
3. Examine Deed of Covenant (Duplicate) against copy
4. Inspect water rates receipts

5. Look through pre-registration deeds, search certificates and any other papers to be handed over and report back anything unexpected

6. Date and take over transfer, land certificate, duplicate Deed of Covenant and papers

7. Hand over banker's draft

8. Hand over letter to estate agents—if requested

9. Take over receipt for £800.00, the agreed price for the chattels

10. Take over keys.

The letter to the estate agents referred to is the authority to them to release the deposit to their client and is not now often called for. It is made out by James on a pro-forma letter the firm use for the purpose. The money will in fact be retained by the agents towards their fee and only the balance will be paid by Messrs. Makepiece.

Strictly speaking, the production of rates receipts is necessary only if the rates have been apportioned, when it must not be overlooked.

James attends at the offices of Messrs. Makepiece at 12 noon and completion is carried through without hitch. He returns to the office with the bundle of documents and papers and the keys in his briefcase. He reports the success of his mission to Mr. Reason who checks through all he has brought back. He calls Miss Burton at her hotel to confirm completion and asks her to call to collect the keys. She is relieved to know that the purchase is completed and comes in the same afternoon when in a short interview with Mr. Reason she thanks him and takes the keys. He mentions that the title must now be registered and that he will be in touch with her as soon as possible.

AFTER COMPLETION

In Messrs. Makepiece's offices, Mr. Black telephones Mr. Butler to report that completion has taken place and to say that he will be writing within a post or two with a financial statement and a cheque for the amount shown to be due to him. Mr. Butler says he will be spending one last night in Barset with friends before he leaves for good. Thanking Mr. Black for his work, he gives him his daughter's address so that the statement and cheque can be sent on. He passes the file to the cashier's department requesting them to prepare the bill. A day later the bill is drafted and is checked by Mr. Black. It is then approved and signed by Mr. Amity. Mr. Black is now able to pay the estate agent's commission, and he sends them the letter from Messrs. Rime releasing the deposit of £250 held by them and enclosing the firm's cheque for the balance. He is now able to complete the financial statement and send to Mr. Butler a cheque for the net amount due, which he does.

In Messrs. Rime's offices essential post-completion steps have to be taken. On February 22 James makes out a Particulars Delivered form (STAMPS L(A) 451 p. 142). James takes the form, the transfer and a cheque for £420.00 (as one of a batch of documents) to the Barchester Inland Revenue stamp office on his next visit. He first hands the transfer to one of the clerks whose function it is to scrutinise all newly executed conveyances, transfers, leases and so on and assess what stamp duty, if any, is payable. The clerk pencils on the document the figure of £420.00. James next takes the transfer to the counter where the clerks check and receive the Particulars Delivered form. James hands this over and the clerk hands back the transfer marked as examined and the carbon copy of the form. He now takes the transfer to the stamp counter with the cheque. The latter is made payable to Inland Revenue and crossed. After the words Inland Revenue the cashier's department have added Messrs. Rime's registered number, which enables the firm to have documents stamped without waiting for the cheque to be cleared. In addition to the registered number the name of Miss Molly Burton has been typed just below the signature. At one of the service points he hands in the transfer and cheque. The clerk receiving the document impresses the Particulars Delivered Stamp and the *ad valorem* stamps to the value of the cheque.

The documents are now ready to be submitted to the Land Registry so that the register may be brought up to date and a revised certificate issued which will show Miss Burton as the registered proprietor. James prepares an application on form A4 (pp. 143–146) and dispatches it to the Barchester District Land Registry with the documents listed in Panel 1 of the form.

James now passes the file to the cashier's section to prepare the bill for the firm's costs. When prepared it is approved by Mr. Reason and dispatched to Miss Burton, who duly pays it.

The registration of the new owner and preparation of the new Land Certificate takes several weeks, perhaps even a few months depending on the backlog of work at the District Land Registry. (First registrations can take much longer to process.) In due course, the Certificate is received and examined by Mr. Reason who scrutinises it to ensure that there are no clerical or other errors. Subject to this, he dispatches the Certificate to Miss Burton saying that this satisfactorily concludes the matter.

THE DEPOSIT

The buyer is usually required on exchange of contracts to pay a deposit of 10 per cent., including any small deposit he may have given to the estate agent. Whether a deposit is paid to the estate agent is entirely at the discretion of the prospective purchaser, but it has value in giving earnest of his serious intention in making his offer. The Standard Conditions of Sale prescribe 10 per cent., but this can be varied by agreement. The cheque for this sum, which is handed over on exchange of contracts, should be the solicitor's cheque or a banker's draft (as, although clients' cheques are sometimes accepted, the recipient accepts the risk). Normally, where there is no related purchase the contract requires that the deposit be held by the seller's solicitor as "stakeholder." This puts him in a neutral position pending completion, as he becomes in effect a trustee for both parties. This ensures that if something goes wrong which makes the deposit refundable, he will return it to the buyer's solicitor without question. Payment to the

Application by **Purchaser**[(a)] for
Official Search with priority
in respect of the whole of the
land in either a registered title
or in a pending first registration

Small raised letters in **bold** type refer to explanatory notes overleaf.

PRIORITY STAMP

BARCHESTER _____ District Land Registry[(b)]

CENTURY HOUSE
BARSET
BARSETSHIRE

HM Land Registry

Form

94A

(Land Registration (Official Searches) Rules 1990)

For official use

Please complete the numbered panels.

1 County and District or London Borough:–

BARSETSHIRE – BARSET.

2 Title number (one only per form) of the registered property or that allotted to the pending first registration:–

BA 19834

3 Full names of the registered proprietor(s) of the land[(c)] or of the person applying for registration of the property specified below:–

BERNARD OLIVER BUTLER

4 Full name(s) of applicant(s) (ie. purchaser, lessee or chargee):–

MOLLIE BURTON

5 I certify that the applicant(s) intend(s) to:–

| X | P | purchase | | L | take a lease of | | C | lend money on the security of a registered charge on |

[X] the **whole** of the land in the above registered title or

[ ] the **whole** of the land in the pending first registration application referred to above

6 Address including postcode or short description of property:–

THE LIMES
LEMON TERRACE
BARSET

10 Key number[(e)]

00354763

Complete this panel using BLOCK LETTERS and insert the name and address (including postcode) of the person to whom the official certificate of result of search is to be sent.

MESSRS RIME AND REASON
INVICTA HOUSE
MARKET ST
BARSET.

| Reference[(f)] | J/BURTON |

7 If search is against the whole of the land in a registered title enter below the date on which an office copy of the subsisting entries in the register was issued or the last date on which the land or charge certificate was officially examined with the register:–

7 January 1993

8 Enter X in box as appropriate:–

[X] Application is made to ascertain whether any adverse entry[(d)] has been made in the register or day list since the date shown in 7 above.

OR

[ ] Application is made to ascertain whether any adverse entry has been made in the day list since the date of the pending first registration application.

9

Signed *Rime & Reason*

Date 9 February 1993

Telephone No. 00765–1234

Official Certificate of Result of Search

It is hereby certified that the official search applied for has been made with the following result:

[ ] **A** Result of search against the whole of the land in a registered title:–

Since_____ 19_____

[ ] No adverse entries have been made.

[ ] Entries have been made. Details of these and of pending applications (if any) are annexed to and form part of this result.

[ ] No adverse entries have been made but there are pending applications details of which are annexed to and form part of this result.

[ ] **B** Result of search against the whole of the land in a pending first registration application:–

The property specified is the subject of a pending first registration application. Details are annexed to and form part of this result.

Note:
To obtain priority, the application for registration in respect of which this search is made must be delivered to the proper office at the latest by 9.30 am on the date when priority expires: see priority stamp at the head of this form.

Explanatory Notes

(a) 'Purchaser' means any person who, in good faith and for valuable consideration, acquires or intends to acquire a legal estate in land, and includes a lessee or chargee but not a depositee of a land or charge certificate. An official search made by such depositee or by any person other than a 'purchaser', as so defined, should, provided the land is registered, be made in Form 94C.

(b) The application must be sent to the district land registry serving the area in which the land is situated. A list of addresses of the district land registries is set out below.

(c) The name(s) of the registered proprietor(s) of the land must be entered as set out in the register of the title.

(d) Any entry made in the register since the date of commencement of this search but subsequently cancelled will not be revealed.

(e) Where a key number has been allocated it should be used.

(f) This should be restricted to a maximum of 10 digits including oblique strokes and punctuation.

(g) Fuller information about the official search procedure is contained in Practice Leaflet No. 2, entitled 'Official Searches of the Register', and Practice Leaflet No. 7, entitled 'Development of Registered Building Estates' which are obtainable free of charge from any district land registry.

● **Complete both the original form and the duplicate.**

● **For an official search of part of the land in a registered title use Form 94B.**

● **For an official search of part of the land in a pending first registration application use Form 94B(FR).**

● **If when issued the official certificate of result of search states that details of entries and/or of pending applications are annexed but such is not the case, it is important that without delay you contact the district land registry which issued the result of search.**

Addresses of District Land Registries

District Land Registry	Address	DX No./Exchange
Birkenhead	Old Market House, Hamilton Street, Birkenhead, Merseyside L41 5FL	14300 Birkenhead (3)
Coventry	Greyfriars Business Centre, 2 Eaton Road, Coventry CV1 2SD	18900 Coventry (3)
Croydon	Sunley House, Bedford Park, Croydon CR9 3LE	2699 Croydon (3)
Durham	Southfield House, Southfield Way, Durham DH1 5TR	60200 Durham (3)
Gloucester	Bruton Way, Gloucester GL1 1DQ	7599 Gloucester (3)
Harrow	Lyon House, Lyon Road, Harrow, Middx. HA1 2EU	4299 Harrow (4)
Kingston Upon Hull	Earle House, Portland Street, Kingston Upon Hull, Humberside HU2 8JN	26700 Hull (3)
Leicester	Thames Tower, 99 Burleys Way, Leicester LE1 3UB	11900 Leicester (5)
Lytham	Birkenhead House, East Beach, Lytham St. Annes, Lancs. FY8 5AB	14500 Lytham St. Annes (3)
Nottingham	Chalfont Drive, Nottingham NG8 3RN	10298 Nottingham (3)
Peterborough	Touthill Close, City Road, Peterborough PE1 1XN	12598 Peterborough (4)
Plymouth	Plumer House, Tailyour Road, Crownhill, Plymouth PL6 5HY	8299 Plymouth (4)
Portsmouth	St. Andrew's Court, St. Michael's Road, Portsmouth, Hants. PO1 2JH	83550 Portsmouth (2)
Stevenage	Brickdale House, Swingate, Stevenage, Herts. SG1 1EG	6099 Stevenage (2)
Swansea	**For titles falling within the Principality of Wales:** Tŷ Cwm Tawe, Phoenix Way, Llansamlet, Swansea SA7 9FQ	82800 Swansea (2)
	For the remainder of areas served by Swansea: Tŷ Bryn Glas, High Street, Swansea SA1 1PW	33700 Swansea (2)
Telford	Stafford Park 15, Telford, Salop TF3 3AL	28100 Telford (2)
Tunbridge Wells	Curtis House, Forest Road, Hawkenbury, Tunbridge Wells, Kent TN2 5AQ	3999 Tunbridge Wells (2)
Weymouth	1 Cumberland Drive, Weymouth, Dorset DT4 9TT	8799 Weymouth (2)

Application by **Purchaser for**
Official Search with priority
in respect of the whole of the
land in either a registered title
or in a pending first registration

HM Land Registry **Form** **DUPLICATE**

PRIORITY STAMP

94A

(Land Registration (Official Searches) Rules 1990)

———————— District Land Registry

For official use

Please complete the numbered panels.

1 County and District or London Borough:–

2 Title number (one only per form) of the registered property or that allotted to the pending first registration:–

3 Full names of the registered proprietor(s) of the land or of the person applying for registration of the property specified below:–

4 Full name(s) of applicant(s) (ie. purchaser, lessee or chargee):–

5 I certify that the applicant(s) intend(s) to:–

☐ P purchase ☐ L take a lease of ☐ C lend money on the security of a registered charge on

☐ the **whole** of the land in the above registered title or

☐ the **whole** of the land in the pending first registration application referred to above

6 Address including postcode or short description of property:–

10 Key number

Complete this panel using BLOCK LETTERS and insert the name and address (including postcode) of the person to whom the official certificate of result of search is to be sent.

Reference

7 If search is against the whole of the land in a registered title enter below the date on which an office copy of the subsisting entries in the register was issued or the last date on which the land or charge certificate was officially examined with the register:–

8 Enter X in box as appropriate:–

☐ Application is made to ascertain whether any adverse entry has been made in the register or day list since the date shown in 7 above.

OR

☐ Application is made to ascertain whether any adverse entry has been made in the day list since the date of the pending first registration application.

9
Signed

Date

Telephone No.

Official Certificate of Result of Search

It is hereby certified that the official search applied for has been made with the following result:

☐ **A** Result of search against the whole of the land in a registered title:–

Since_____ 19_____

☐ No adverse entries have been made.

☐ Entries have been made. Details of these and of pending applications (if any) are annexed to and form part of this result.

☐ No adverse entries have been made but there are pending applications details of which are annexed to and form part of this result.

☐ **B** Result of search against the whole of the land in a pending first registration application:–
The property specified is the subject of a pending first registration application. Details are annexed to and form part of this result.

Note:
To obtain priority, the application for registration in respect of which this search is made must be delivered to the proper office at the latest by 9.30 am on the date when priority expires: see priority stamp at the head of this form.

● For explanatory notes and the addresses of district land registries, see the back of the original form.

FOR OFFICIAL USE ONLY

ACTION RECORD

☐ Referred to..

Signed...................................... Date...................

Remarks:

☐ Applicant contacted

Signed...................................... Date...................

Search drafted

Search checked

OYEZ The Solicitors' Law Stationery Society Ltd. Oyez House. 27 Crimscott Street. London SE1 5TS

1990 edition 10.90 F18191
5061693

Official Certificate **HM Land Registry** **Form 94D**
of the Result of Search

(Land Registration (Official
Searches) Rules 1988)

This page is to be completed only by HM Land Registry

It is hereby certified that the official search applied
for has been made with the following result:

Since .... 7th January ....19 .....93.....

NO ADVERSE ENTRY HAS BEEN MADE THEREON

```
Date of  ♛  Priority
certificate     expires
            11 a.m. on
10 Feb 93–21 Mar 93
THE BARCHESTER DISTRICT
   LAND REGISTRY
    See note below
```

Note:
To obtain priority (⁷), the application for registration in respect of which this search is made must be delivered to the proper
office at the latest by 9.30 a.m. on the date when priority expires.

EXPLANATORY NOTES

(1) "Purchaser" means any person who, in good faith and for valuable consideration, acquires or intends to acquire a legal estate in land, and includes a lessee or a chargee but not a depositee of a land or charge certificate. An official search made by such a depositee or by any person other than a "purchaser", as so defined, should be made on form 94C.

(2) The application should be sent to the district land registry serving the area in which the land is situated. A list of addresses of the district land registries is set out on page 4 of this application form.

(3) A separate form must be used for each title number to be searched.

(4) The name(s) of the registered proprietor(s) should be entered as they appear on the evidence of the registered title supplied to the applicant. If there has been a change of name(s) the new name(s) should also be entered in brackets.

(5) Any entry made in the register since the date of commencement of this search but subsequently cancelled will not be revealed.

(6) Where a key number has been allocated it should be used.

(7) The period of priority reserved for the registration of the disposition protected by the official search certificate will be shown either by a stamp impressed in the result of search above or on a separate computer printed result.

(8) Where the land is subject to a pending first registration application an official search by a 'purchaser' will only be accepted if made on form 94A(FR).

(9) Fuller information about the official search procedure is contained in Practice Leaflet No. 2, entitled "Official Searches of the Register", and Practice Leaflet No. 7, entitled "Development of Registered Building Estates" which are obtainable free of charge from any district land registry.

Inland Revenue

PARTICULARS OF INSTRUMENTS TRANSFERRING OR LEASING LAND

SECTION 28 FINANCE ACT 1931
as amended by the Land Commission Act, 1967
and Section 89 Finance Act 1985

	FOR OFFICIAL USE
VO No.	....
PD No.	....
ANALYSIS CODE	....
DESC.	....
GV/NAV	....
DW. CODE	....
	....
RETURN	....
O.S. No.	....
OTHER	....

1. Description of Instrument
   Transfer

2. Date of Instrument
   19 February 1993

3. Name and Address of Transferor or Lessor: *(Block Letters)*

   BERNARD OLIVER BUTLER
   THE LIMES,
   LEMON TERRACE,
   BARSET

4. Name and Address of Transferee or Lessee: *(Block Letters)*

   MOLLIE BURTON
   THE ROYAL HOTEL,
   MARKET SQUARE,
   BARSET

5. Situation of the Land. Sufficient information must be given to enable the land to be identified accurately, e.g., by including any dimensions stated in the instrument and by attaching a plan to this form or by describing the boundaries in full. For premises the full postal address including the post code is required. Please indicate whether a plan is provided in the appropriate box.

   THE LIMES,
   LEMON TERRACE BARSET

   Plan attached to this form   Yes ☐

   Plan attached   No ☑

   COUNTY. BARSETSHIRE

   RATING AUTHORITY. BARSET DISTRICT COUNCIL

6. Estate or Interest Transferred. Where the transaction is the assignment or grant of a lease, or the transfer of a fee simple subject to a lease, the terms of the lease, the date of commencement of the term and the rent reserved must be stated.

   FREEHOLD

7. Consideration   State separately:

   (a) any capital payment, with the date when due if otherwise than on execution of the instrument: £42,000

   (b) any debt released, covenanted to be paid or to which the transaction is made subject:

   (c) any periodical payment (including any charge) covenanted to be paid:

   (d) any terms surrendered:

   (e) any land exchanged:

   (f) any other thing representing money or money's worth:

8. Any Minerals, Mineral Rights, Sporting Rights, Timber or Easements reserved: (on a separate sheet if necessary).

9. Any Restrictions, Covenants or Conditions affecting the value of the estate or interest transferred or granted: (on a separate sheet if necessary).

10. Signature of Transferee or Lessee or person on his behalf:

    Rime & Reason   Date 22.2.93.

11. Name and Address of Transferor's or Lessor's Solicitor: *(Block Letters)*

    MAKEPIECE AND STREIFF
    BANK CHAMBERS
    BARSET

12. Name and Address of Signatory if other than Transferee or Lessee: *(Block Letters)*

    RIME AND REASON
    INVICTA HOUSE
    MARKET STREET
    BARSET

STAMPS L(A) 451

Printed in the UK for HMSO. D 8259531 750m 8/90. 36625.

Application to register **dealings with the whole of titles**

HM Land Registry

Form A4

Code	Received stamp	Ackd. by
		Postcard ☐
		Chargee ☐ Postcard
		Initials
Application number		Date
	Record of fees paid	

Please complete the white boxes on pages 1, 4 and 2 in typescript or BLOCK CAPITALS.

Enter District or London Borough

BARSET

1 Title numbers. Enter title number(s) in this panel. If there are more than five, attach a list in alpha-numeric order e.g. 6342, AV4613, AV7542, BD1567 etc.

1

Title numbers	Pending application numbers
BA19834	

2 Fees. Make sure you have enclosed the correct fee: refer to the current Land Registration Fees Order. Cheques and postal orders should be made payable to "HM Land Registry." Fees are payable on delivery of the application.

2

Nature of applications in priority order	Value £	Fee scale para or abatement	Fees paid £	Particulars of over/under payment
TRANSFER	£42,000	4	£70	
		Total	£70	

3 Documents lodged. Treat each original and copy as a separate item.

3

List of all documents lodged

LAND CERTIFICATE/TRANSFER

4 Person or firm lodging application. Name and address (including postcode) of person or firm lodging this application to whom any requisitions will be sent and to whom documents (including land or charge certificate) will be returned unless special directions are given in panel 5.

4

Key No. (if any) 00354763	Requisitions to be sent to and documents returned to	Type
		S. Code
R IME AND REASON INVICTA HOUSE BARSET BARSETSHIRE		

Reference	Telephone No.
CR/JB/AC	00765-1234

5 Special directions. Special request to the Land Registry to issue a document to a person or firm not mentioned in panel 4.

5

Description of document and addressee

Please turn to page 4 and complete panels 6 and 7.

Page 1

Before signing the
certificate in section 12
please complete page 4.

**Please supply the following information where applicable.
All applicants should complete section 12.**

**8 Transfer or assent to
joint owners of the land.**

8

Can the survivor of them give a receipt for capital
money arising on a disposition of the land?   *State yes or no in box.*

**9A Application to
register a company as
proprietor of the land.**
†One or other of the
alternative certificates at
(a) must be given in full.
No alteration of the
certificates is acceptable.
   If the company is **not**
incorporated in England
and Wales or Scotland the
first alternative **cannot** be
used and a copy of the
document(s) of
constitution **must** be
lodged. Failure to do this
will delay your application.

*Cross out if not applicable.

9

A   *(insert Company name)*

We, solicitors to:.. PLC/Limited

certify that:

†(a) *the company is a company trading for profit and is incorporated in England and Wales
or Scotland** under the Companies Acts and its memorandum and articles of association
contain provisions entitling the company to hold and sell, mortgage, lease and otherwise
deal with land:
**where the company is incorporated in Scotland please specify.

or

†(a) *a copy of the company's memorandum and articles of association or other document(s)
of constitution certified as a true copy of the original(s) by the company's secretary or
solicitor accompanies this application.

(b) *the charge(s) by the company do(es) not contravene any part of the memorandum and
articles of association.

(c) *the company's registered no. is as stated in panel 6B on page 4.

**Signature of
company's solicitors**

**9B Application to
register a company as
proprietor of a charge.**
†One or other of the
alternative certificates at
(a) must be given in full.
No alteration of the
certificates is acceptable.
   If the company is **not**
incorporated in England
and Wales or Scotland the
first alternative **cannot** be
used and a copy of the
document(s) of
constitution **must** be
lodged. Failure to do this
will delay your application.

B   *(insert Company name)*

We, solicitors to:.. PLC/Limited

certify that:

†(a) *the company is a company trading for profit and is incorporated in England and Wales
or Scotland under the Companies Acts and its memorandum and articles of association
contain provisions entitling the company to hold and sell, mortgage, lease and otherwise
deal with land and to lend money on mortgage:

or

†(a) *a copy of the company's memorandum and articles of association or other document(s)
of constitution certified as a true copy of the original(s) by the company's secretary or
solicitor accompanies this application.

(b) *the company's registered no. is as stated in panel 7 on page 4.

**Signature of
company's solicitors**

**10 Application to
discharge the last
remaining charge.**

10

As solicitors or licensed conveyancers for the registered proprietors of the land
I/we apply for a land certificate to be issued to me/us.

Signature

11 Reminders.

11

(a) Have you enclosed the appropriate fee? ☐
(b) Have all dates and details been put in charges or mortgages? ☐
(c) Are copy charges certified by a practitioner (or in the name of the firm) as true copies? ☐
(d) Is evidence of change of name or death lodged where required? ☐
(e) Is the original lease lodged in support of an application for merger? ☐
(f) Have full names and addresses been given on page 4? ☐
(g) Have you enclosed Inland Revenue form L(A)451 duly completed (if appropriate)? ☐
(h) Have you enclosed a certified copy of the constitution of a foreign company and
provided an address for service **in the United Kingdom**? ☐
(i) Have you enclosed any consent(s) required by restriction(s) entered in the
proprietorship/charges register(s)? ☐
Delays may be caused when page 4 is not completed fully and accurately

**12 Signature of applicant
or practitioner.**

12

I/We certify that the information required has been supplied and is correct and apply for
registration of the dealings in the order or priority shown in panel 2 on page 1.

A cheque or postal order for £   accompanies this application

**Signature of applicant
or practitioner**   *Rime ₀ Rason*   Date   1.3.93.

For official use. Settlers panel (additional).

For official use	TITLE NO.			Send out after		Type after		
☐ Additions to existing register ☐ New edition of register model	APPLN NO.			SETTLED BY	Name		Stn	Date
Drafted Name		Stn	Date					
				Subject to				
Checked				REVIEWED BY				

Instructions to type	Requisitions
Documents needed for copying	C set on
☐ enter	Enclosing for return
☐ make up	Action required on reply
☐ prepare	
LC CC No. (Xerox form)	
	Repro Instructions
☐ prepare	☐ Make a copy of
☐ comb	☐ and plan tinted/untinted
☐ comp	☐ Make copy of
CC No. (Xerox form) for this and titles	☐ and plan tinted/untinted
☐ prepare A54 & duplicate	
☐ make up A54 & duplicate	**To settler**
☐ type on C2 'refund of fees of to follow'	
☐ prepare envelope label for name & address-panel 4	
☐ prepare envelope label for name & address-panel 5	
Typed by Stn. Date	(Cont. on page 2)

Instructions to compare	Instructions to despatch
☐ sew outside	Issue to name & address in panel 4
☐ sew inside	☐ LC
CC No. original charge dated	☐ CC
Sew up in certificate	☐ C43
☐ new edition	☐
☐ new plan	Documents not marked * on page 1
☐ (office copy) transfer conveyance and plan dated	
☐ (office copy) transfer conveyance and plan dated	Issue to name & address in panel 5
☐ abstract dated	☐ LC
☐ existing SRC	☐
☐ original A54	
☐ sew up in CC No. Xerox sheets and original	Issue
☐ charge dated	☐ Documents as directed in
	Retained
☐ mark copy as an office copy	☐ all documents in panel 3 marked with a *
☐ make copy an office copy	☐ charge dated
☐ mark dated Notice registered	☐ Cancelled LC cover
☐ mark lease dated Lease determined	☐ Cancelled CC
	Register closed	☐ on deposit
☐ Ensure duplicate A54 contains new covenant and replace	☐ After despatch please carry out C167 procedure.
in RR file.	
☐ See that has not been resewn up in certificate and	Instruct daylist to mark off
cancel it.	☐ this application
☐ Stamp old register 'Closed see new edition'	☐ official searches
☐ Cancel LC cover	☐ deposit D
☐ Cancel CC No.	Compared &
See that any cancellations appear on both thin sheets and register.	Despatched by Stn. Date

Instructions to filing branch	Notices
	Form no. R.D. No. to
☐ Add to RR file (original) (duplicate) (copy) dated	
☐ Remove from C/P/E/RR file copy charges dated	

Please complete the white boxes using BLOCK CAPITALS for all names and addresses.

Entry No.

Edition No.

Opened

A

6 New proprietors of the land.
For single proprietors enter as follows:—
"KIM JOYCE of 7 PARK ROAD, BURTON, BEDS. BU1 2PM, Cook."
For joint proprietors enter as follows:—
"KIM JOYCE, Cook, and HILARY JOYCE, her husband, both of 7 PARK ROAD, BURTON, BEDS. BU1 2PM."
If the applicant is a company its registration number should be given here for entry on the register.
NB1 If the proprietor(s) is/are about to move into the property that address should be entered here.
NB2 All addresses for service must be **in the United Kingdom.**

6 **B** (Cancel)

MOLLIE BURTON
THE LIMES
LEMON TERRACE
BARSET
BARSETSHIRE BX1 3PT   (Co. Regn. No.   )

C (Cancel   and insert date)

7 New chargee(s) /mortgagees.
If there is a single new charge enter as follows in the white box:—
THE MONEY BANK PLC of 2 HIGH STREET, WATFORD, HERTS. WD2 3PS.
If there are two charges please enter the first chargee above the white box opposite the asterisk and the second chargee in the white box.
If the chargee is a company its registration number should be given here for entry on the register.
NB1 Check that the names of the borrower(s) agree with those of the registered proprietor(s) of the land or, where there is a transfer, the transferee(s).
NB2 All addresses for service must be **in the United Kingdom.**

*

(Date) Charge dated   registered on

to secure { the moneys   therein mentioned
         { the moneys including the further advances }

7 Proprietor

(Co. Regn. No.   )

registered on

OYEZ The Solicitors' Law Stationery Society Ltd, Oyez House, 7 Spa Road, London SE16 3QQ   11.91 F21441
5061596
* * * * *

SALE/PURCHASE OF DOMESTIC PROPERTY
without mortgage
SIMPLIFIED OUTLINE OF STEPS
Sale agreed subject to contract

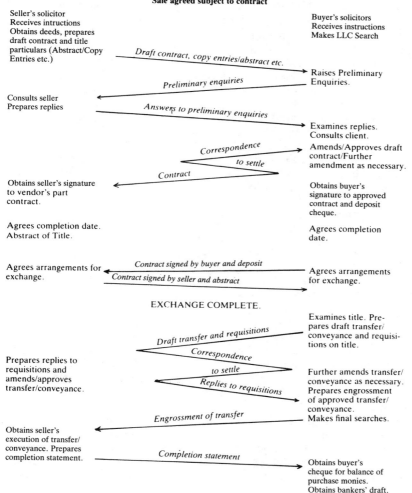

Seller's solicitor
Receives intructions
Obtains deeds, prepares
draft contract and title
particulars (Abstract/Copy
Entries etc.)

Draft contract, copy entries/abstract etc.

Buyer's solicitors
Receives instructions
Makes LLC Search

Preliminary enquiries

Raises Preliminary
Enquiries.

Consults seller
Prepares replies

Answers to preliminary enquiries

Examines replies.
Consults client.

Correspondence
to settle

Amends/Approves draft
contract/Further
amendment as necessary.

Contract

Obtains seller's signature
to vendor's part
contract.

Obtains buyer's
signature to approved
contract and deposit
cheque.

Agrees completion date.
Abstract of Title.

Agrees completion
date.

Agrees arrangements for
exchange.

Contract signed by buyer and deposit
Contract signed by seller and abstract

Agrees arrangements
for exchange.

EXCHANGE COMPLETE.

Draft transfer and requisitions

Examines title. Pre-
pares draft transfer/
conveyance and requisi-
tions on title.

Correspondence
to settle

Prepares replies to
requisitions and
amends/approves
transfer/conveyance.

Replies to requisitions

Further amends transfer/
conveyance as necessary.
Prepares engrossment
of approved transfer/
conveyance.
Makes final searches.

Engrossment of transfer

Obtains seller's
execution of transfer/
conveyance. Prepares
completion statement.

Completion statement

Obtains buyer's
cheque for balance of
purchase monies.
Obtains bankers' draft.

COMPLETION IN SELLER'S SOLICITORS OFFICE (or otherwise as agreed, *e.g.* by post).

buyer's solicitor as agent for the seller is provided for by Standard Condition of Sale general condition 2.2.2 which provides that if before the completion date the seller agrees to buy another property in England and Wales for a residence the seller may use all or part of the deposit as a deposit in that transaction. The deposit can be passed further along the conveyancing chain by the seller's buyer provided general condition 2–2–2 is complied with, but it must ultimately be held by a seller's solicitor as stakeholder. As there is a degree of risk involved, a buyer's solicitor may not wish to allow Condition 2.2.2 to apply.

In exceptional circumstances the 10 per cent. deposit may be paid to an estate agent, although this involves possible dangers for a buyer and is not recommended. The Estate Agents Act 1979 lessens the risk of entrusting the deposit to the agent. Estate agents, like solicitors, are required to pay deposit monies into a separate account and to provide insurance cover to guarantee the client against failure to account for the deposit.

Where the seller is a trustee, which includes where he is selling as the personal representative of the deceased owner, his solicitor will usually require the deposit to be held by him as agent for the vendor, because the deposit is then trust money and should be under the sole control of the trustee.

The difficulty for many buyers in raising the standard 10 per cent. deposit should not be underestimated, particularly in this present era of ever escalating house prices. One approach is to negotiate for a reduced deposit to be paid, but this will not always be accepted. Alternatively a "bridging" loan from the buyer's bank may be considered where there is a linked sale. The buyer would need to be advised of the cost of this and whilst a standard form of undertaking is often used by banks, the buyer's solicitor should ensure that it is in an acceptable form—and in particular that it is limited to sending the ultimate net proceeds of the sale as and when received. An increasingly popular alternative to bridging finance is for a buyer (or more usually his solicitors) to arrange a deposit guarantee scheme with an insurance company. Under such a scheme, no deposit is paid to the seller, but on payment of a premium by the buyer the insurance company guarantees to pay the specified deposit to the seller should the buyer fail to complete. If the insurance company does have to pay out it can recover it from the buyer.

ENQUIRIES BEFORE CONTRACT

This is the title of the form normally used for these enquiries. They are also referred to as preliminary enquiries or pre-contract enquiries. Invariably a standard printed form of enquiries is used as a basis. The one most commonly used (and reproduced on pp. 122–125) is Conveyancing 29 by Oyez Stationery, though in recent years many other firms have introduced printed forms with slight variations. When he raises these enquiries, the buyer's solicitor invariably has before him his notes of the instructions received from his client and when the sale is through an estate agent a copy of the agent's particulars. He will normally have received the draft contract and copy entries in the land register together with such other documents as the seller's solicitor has a duty to disclose about the title to the property or its condition.

Pre-contract enquiries give the buyer's solicitor the opportunity to ascertain all that can be gleaned from the seller about the fabric of the property and its amenities, also about possible legal snags that may not previously have been disclosed. A perusal of the form used in Butler to Burton will show the great range of the questions. The solicitor will adapt the printed form as necessary in the circumstances as it is discourteous and time wasting to allow questions to remain that do not apply to the case. He will add at the end any questions arising from the particular circumstances and from the papers he has perused. This will include questions concerning any technical points on the title, including minor flaws which the draft contract may require the buyer to accept without further question. The replies in the Butler case show that answers are not always helpful—particularly where the buyer can get information from some other source—and that there is a general disclaimer of liability printed at the head of the answers. Nonetheless, this is a most important stage, requiring the fullest liaison with the client on the answers received.

The need for care in all representations made by or on behalf of a seller before contract, whether in the preliminary enquiries, the agent's particulars or in correspondence, is underlined by the remedies available in the case of a misrepresentation. An actionable misrepresentation is constituted if the seller or his agent makes a material false statement of fact which induces the buyer to enter the contract. Misrepresentation can be categorised as fraudulent, negligent or innocent, *i.e.* unwitting.

If fraudulent, the buyer can claim rescission (*i.e.* the contract is cancelled and the parties revert to their position before it was entered into) and damages in the tort of deceit. A negligent misrepresentation is one which is not fraudulent, but where the seller cannot prove that he had reasonable grounds for believing in the truth of the statement. The buyer can rescind and/or claim damages under the Misrepresentation Act 1967. Many errors by sellers or their agents are innocent and the 1967 Act has improved the remedies available—rescission is again available and whilst there is no right to damages the court has a power to award damages in lieu of rescission. Further, the right to rescission is not lost merely because the mis-statement subsequently becomes a term of the contract.

Many of the guarded and vague replies given to preliminary enquiries are made with the object of avoiding misrepresentation liability. "Not so far as the seller is aware" and "to the best of our knowledge and belief" are commonly encountered. However, the case of *Walker* v. *Boyle* (1982) emphasises that such qualified replies may still be actionable. In that case, the seller's solicitor in answering a preliminary enquiry as to the seller's awareness of boundary disputes answered that there were none to the seller's knowledge. After exchange of contracts the buyer became aware of the existence of a long-standing dispute. Liability for misrepresentation was established because the seller was aware of a dispute and the guarded reply was to no avail.

The careful solicitor will wish to protect his seller client so far as he can and it is to be noted that there is a disclaimer at the head of the replies column in the answers to the preliminary enquiries (p. 122). However, doubts have been expressed (in *Walker* v. *Boyle*, for example) as to the effectiveness of such disclaimers in law. The current version of the Conveyancing 29 form also purports to protect the seller's solicitor against liability to the buyer. Liability may exist in negligence (not misrepresentation for which the principal, *i.e.* the vendor, is liable and not his agent, *i.e.* the solicitor) and again the effectiveness of the disclaimer is uncertain, particularly if it cannot be shown to be reasonable.

Returning to the issue of the seller's liability for misrepresentation, Standard Condition 7.1 stipulates the remedies available to a buyer for misdescription and misrepresentation, thus limiting the remedies available. However, these conditions would appear to be void under the Misrepresentation Act unless the seller can show them to be reasonable and this may not be easy to do.

There is a danger that the process of raising and answering preliminary enquiries can become a stereotyped charade but the seller's potential liability as indicated above shows the need to treat the process seriously. The seller's solicitor should take full instructions from his client and try to be as informative as possible in giving replies. The buyer's solicitor for this part needs to read the replies carefully and follow up on any which are unsatisfactory.

DEEDS

A deed is a legal document entered into by set formalities, recording a transaction between two or more people, often concerning the ownership of land or any rights in land. Rights in land are created by deed and cancelled by deed as well as being simply transferred. In its oldest form it was written on parchment. Often each party would require an identical copy and the document would be written twice in identical terms, or even three or more times, on the same sheet of parchment. The sheet would then be cut off with an indented or wavy line between each part. In Henry IV Part I, Shakespeare makes Mortimer say "The indentures tripartite are drawn." This method was of course a protection against fraud, as bringing the severed parts together demonstrated their genuineness. Deeds are still referred to as indentures.

When only a minority of the population was literate the signature of the parties to a document was not essential—a cross or other mark often served, but there was always a wax seal. This would be impressed whilst still hot with an identifiable symbol of the party, perhaps a coat of arms or a signet ring. The action of authenticating the document in this way was naturally called "sealing" it. It was also called "executing" it. However, the formalities were not complete without delivery of the sealed document and, to acknowledge that he was by delivery giving effect to his execution, the party would press his index finger on the seal and say "I deliver this as my act and deed." A deed which is in all other respects complete but has been delivered conditionally, that is, to take effect only if and when the condition is performed, is called an escrow. When the condition is satisfied, the deed automatically becomes legally effective.

It should also be remembered that, unlike the contract, the legal force of which depends on the mutuality of the promises made by the parties, the legal force of a deed depends only on its form and content. No reference to the circumstances in which it was entered into is necessary or appropriate.

Today, a deed will be expressed to be "signed as a deed" and be signed by the parties to the deed and by the witnesses who attest to the signatures of the parties. Deeds made by individuals are no longer required to be sealed. However, the physical possession of deeds is still of great importance, particularly in the case of unregistered land.

The transfer, by which the ownership of registered land is transferred, is technically a deed, but the Land Certificate is not.

If the seller's solicitor is not already in possession of the deeds for safe custody, his first act is to obtain them. If, as frequently happens, they are held by a building society, the society will usually release them to the solicitor on request in return for his undertaking to keep them safely on behalf of the society pending redemption of the mortgage.

The importance of careful handling of deeds in the office cannot be overstressed. This particularly applies to all documents of title to land and property, which are commonly referred to as deeds, even when the title is registered. To mislay essential documents in the course of a conveyancing transaction can have the most embarrassing and possibly serious consequences for the solicitor. This is particularly the case where a conveyance or other deed forms an essential link in proving the title of the owner. In the case of registered land the position is not so critical, because the title in that case is established by the contents of the registers held at the district land registry. The Land Certificate held by the owner is merely a copy of those entries. Even so, the loss of a Land Certificate can be a serious matter.

For the purpose of informing the buyer's solicitor of the content of the documents of title, copies or abstracts are prepared (see below) and the inspection of the documents to ensure that they conform to the copies supplied is an essential part of the conveyancing transaction. This is now usually done at the completion, when the deeds are handed over.

THE CONTRACT

A contract for the sale of land or any interest in the land must be in writing and must be signed by or on behalf of the parties. The requirements relating to contracts for the sale of land are set out in section 2 of the Law of Property (Miscellaneous Provisions) Act 1989. If there is to be one contract document, then this document must set out in writing all the terms that the parties have expressly agreed and be signed by all the parties to the contract. If there is to be an exchange of contracts, then each part of the contract must set out in writing the terms that the parties have expressly agreed, making provision for the signatures of the buyer and seller to be on their respective parts of the contract. Non-compliance with the requirement that the contract must be in writing makes the contract void. In everyday conveyancing we are unlikely to need to refer to the rules on the formation of land contracts, because the established practice and procedure ensures that there is a proper contract in existence.

Where the parties reach a binding agreement for sale and purchase, and incorporate it in a document setting out only the basic details required by law, it is called an "open contract." Even so, when as usually occurs the bargain is made by correspondence, the relationship between the parties is not entirely "open," because conditions are implied by law, known as the Lord Chancellor's Conditions. Invariably, however, solicitors use conditions contained in a printed form: the Standard Conditions of Sale (currently the (2nd edition) 1992). The detailed conditions are printed on the inside pages of the form (as set out the case of the Butler contract). These are the Standard Conditions that provide a standard set of rules covering most of the contingencies that can arise. Solicitors may well make out and reproduce their own form of contract in the office, but if so invariably the Standard Conditions of contract are incorporated by reference. It must be borne in mind that the Standard Conditions may be varied by special conditions drawn up to suit the particular transaction and typed on the outer pages of the form. In the event of conflict between these and the Standard Conditions the special conditions prevail. The student should obtain a copy of the contract form and make a point of reading the Standard Conditions.

Matters regulated by the Standard Conditions include: time limits for the successive stages of the transaction and the information to be furnished by the seller; errors, omissions and mis-statements in plans and representations; the definition of the boundaries of the property; insurance cover; procedure on completion. There are also provisions covering exceptional eventualities, such as the failure of the seller to prove his title or of the buyer or seller to be ready to complete on the due date and the payment of interest on unpaid purchase monies.

One special condition of contract should be briefly explained. In Butler to Burton the seller is expressed to convey as "beneficial owner." This is important because section 76 of the Law of Property Act 1925 gives the buyer from one who conveys as beneficial owner warranties that the seller has a good right to convey the property, that he knows of nothing whereby the purchaser's possession may be disturbed, that the property is free from incumbrances and that if it transpires that some further document is needed to complete the title, the seller will do everything he legally can to supply it. The buyer from someone selling as "trustee" or "personal representative" of a deceased owner cannot be expected to give the full extent of such protection, because he has not necessarily personally possessed or enjoyed the property. His sole warranty is that he has done nothing to impose any charge or incumbrance on the property.

For the practitioner, the conditions of most immediate practical importance are those setting the time limits for the several formal stages between exchange and completion. The Standard Conditions provide the following limits:

Delivery of Abstract—Epitome of Title or Office Copy entries	Immediately after making the contract.
Requisitions on title	6 working days after either the date of the contract or the day of delivery of the seller's evidence of title on which the requisitions are raised—whichever is the later.
Replies to requisitions	4 working days after receiving the requisitions.
Observations on seller's replies	3 working days after receiving the replies.
Delivery of draft conveyance—transfer on behalf of buyer	At least 12 working days before contractual completion date.
Return of draft approved or revised	Within 4 working days of delivery of draft transfer or conveyance.
Delivery of engrossment	At least 5 working days before the contractual completion date.

In conveyancing transactions some latitude is often needed in the time taken on both sides to prepare for completion. Time limits for the most part are, therefore, not strictly enforced. As we shall see this applies for instance to the contract date for completion: as practical hitches can arise in arranging removals, etc., the parties cannot be held to the contract completion date within a few days. This position is expressed by saying that in relation to the date for completion, time "is not of the essence." However, this merely means that the "innocent" party cannot rescind (*i.e.* cancel) the contract but a buyer who delays completion may have to pay interest on the balance of the purchase price due. Furthermore, any delay in completion can lead to a claim for damages. In the standard form of contract the time allowed for delivery of requisitions and observations on replies must be strictly adhered to. In these cases it is expressly provided that time is of the essence. Failure by the buyer's solicitor to deliver either on time deprives the client of the right to take the particular step and so of the protection that step affords.

Finally, two points of professional practice should be borne in mind at this early draft contract stage: first, the Law Society Council Direction with its obligatory steps governing contract races. In view of the inevitable delay before any exchange of contracts and the ever-present possibility that a prospective buyer may withdraw, the seller may give instructions to send out draft contracts to more than one prospective buyer so that exchange can be with the first one ready to proceed. Many firms will not be prepared to act under such instructions because of the ill-feeling and heartache that can be engendered, not to mention the wasted expenditure incurred by those prospective buyers who lose out on the race after having requisitioned surveys, local searches, etc. However, the Council Direction does not prohibit contract races but rather requires disclosure of the existence of the race to all the buyers (where acting alone) or their solicitors. An oral disclosure should be confirmed in writing immediately. Only if the seller refuses to author- ise such disclosure must the solicitor refuse to act. A solicitor must not accept instructions from more than one prospective buyer in a contract race and only exceptionally should he act for both the seller and one prospective buyer.

Secondly, on the general issue of acting for seller and buyer in the same transaction, there should be borne in mind the general rule against acting for separate clients where their interests conflict or there is a significant risk of conflict. This is underpinned by a specific practice rule (Solicitors Practice Rule 6 of 1990) which applies equally to prohibit acting for lessor and lessee on the grant of a lease or for a lender and borrower in a private mortgage. However, Rule 6 does permit of exceptions but all are subject to the overriding criteria of no conflict of interest. The principal exceptions are where both parties are related or are established clients, where the consideration is small (less than £5,000) or where there are no other firms in the vicinity whom a client can reasonably be expected to consult.

LOCAL SEARCHES

Besides obtaining the deeds, one of the first acts of the buyer's solicitor is to make his "local searches." This is done promptly as the Local Land Charges Department of the District Council (or London Borough) to which the search application is made takes varying periods to reply, often up to three weeks and in the case of some authorities substantially longer. There are two parts to the search: 1. Requisition for official search in the Register of Local Land Charges (Form LLC 1), which is the search proper; 2. Enquiries of District Councils—or London Boroughs, for which a separate form is required—(Form Con 29). The first leads to the issue of a certificate which has precise legal effect, in that if the responsible authority either fails to register a registrable charge or fails to reveal a registered charge in a certificate of search the person who relies on the certificate in entering into a contract for the purchase of the land affected can claim compensation from the authority for any loss or damage sustained in consequence of the existence of the charge.

The headings of the matters included in the 12 parts of the register are set out on page 2 of the Requisition for Search Form (LLC 1). They include most of the matters on which the local and public authorities in the area (The District Council answers for all of them, as the register is kept solely by that Council) have statutory powers to intervene in the development, use or occupation of land, the buildings upon it and the surrounding land, including the roads. The solicitor searching is at pains to ascertain that no charges are outstanding for road construc- tion; that there are no inconvenient rights over the land to drain the neighbouring properties; in the older residential districts, that there is no order limiting the number of families in a house or requiring its compulsory improvement; that the local statutory plans will not restrict the use or redevelopment of the site; that no compulsory purchase order that might affect the property has been made by any competent authority; that the property is not included in slum clearance proposals or other action under the Housing Acts and so on.

The Enquiries accompanying the Requisition for search of the register extend the scope of the search to cover matters not registered as charges but which might still adversely affect the property. They include matters that may result in a charge in the register at a later date, but which have not yet reached that stage, *e.g.* a proposal of the Council to make a compulsory purchase order but where the operative resolution has not yet been made. (A formal resolution would be registered.) An important question in these enquiries is as to whether the adjoining road has been made up and taken over by the District Council. The name of the road must always be inserted in the space provided. This question is of particular importance where a new property is being sold by estate developers, or shortly after development. The responsibility for providing the roads is primarily that of the developer as part of the costs of development. He usually enters into an agreement with the local highway authority (the District Council) under which he guarantees by a bond to provide the money for laying, paving and lighting all the new roads on the estate. If no such arrangement is entered into, or is broken, and in the end the local authority is obliged to make up the road at its own expense, it has the power to recover the cost from the adjoining owners—the frontagers—in proportion to the respective lengths of their frontages.

Equally important in some areas is the question whether there has been any ministerial order or proposal to build a new trunk road or other highway within 200 metres of the property. There are also important and detailed questions to establish how the property and the area in which it is situated is affected by development plans. In Part II of the form there are some rather more specialised questions which may affect particular buildings or situations. If the building is old, has it been listed as a building of architectural or historic interest? If so, has permission to alter the building ever been refused, or have any steps been taken to require the owner to carry out restoration work? These questions are only answered if a particular request is made by placing the solicitor's initials against a question and a separate fee is payable. A solicitor enquiring can also frame his own additional questions, but these are only replied to at the local authority's discretion.

These enquiries are rather like the Enquiries before Contract of the seller's solicitor: the local authority does its best to give the information requested, but does not guarantee its accuracy. The particular questions included in Form Con 29 and the terms on which the information is given are those agreed between the Law Society and the local authority associations from time to time. Reference should be made to the terms including the disclaimer of legal liability set out on page 4 of the form (p. 113). There are two versions: Con 29A, for land outside Greater London and Con 29D, London only, where some of the law is different, particularly that affecting building construction.

In particular localities, other enquiries may be needed and for these local knowledge may be required. For instance, if the land is in an area known to be an area of extensive coal mining, enquiries should be made by letter to the central office of British Coal to ascertain whether there is any danger that the property being purchased could be affected. The Board will supply information about any past workings under or near the site and any subsidence that has occurred in consequence, the Board's plans for future extensions of their mines and how far the surface could be affected and whether there are any open-cast workings in the vicinity. The Board will charge a fee for the information.

In a rural or green belt area, thought must be given to the possibility of rights over common land, such as rights of way, and commoner's rights to take wood or growing things from the land. In such areas, the solicitor acting for the buyer of land not yet built on has the duty to search in the Commons Register in which all such rights are registered. The Register is kept by the County Council (Commons Registration Act 1965).

As will be seen when we deal with unregistered land, on the purchase of such land, the buyer's solicitor must search in the General Index Map kept in the District Land Registry to satisfy himself that there will be no obstacle to registering the title on completion of the purchase.

It will be clear that the local searches are vital to the protection of the interests of the purchaser.

EXCHANGE OF CONTRACTS

The exchange of contracts is the most critical point in the progress of a conveyancing transaction. Before it, the parties are entirely free to break off negotiations at their own sweet will. After it, they are bound to hard legal obligations to carry the transaction through to finality.

The moment to choose and the way in which the exchange is conducted are of importance, particularly where there is a succession of sales and purchases, each one dependent on the other. This is the "chain" situation which we deal with below.

In Butler to Burton, James the trainee assistant of Messrs. Rime attended on Mr. Black of Messrs. Makepiece with the purchaser's part of the contract and the cheque for the deposit. This might happen in a small town like Barset and has the merit of avoiding the vagaries of the postal service. But today it is rare. Solicitors are not frequently in such close proximity and exchange is nearly always through the post or by telephone. In these circumstances, as will be appreciated, there must be no doubt about the moment at which the contract becomes binding. This will depend on the circumstances and will be looked at in connection with linked transactions.

It will be apparent from our case that much of the investigation will have been done before exchange. No buyer's solicitor should commit his client in this way until he has had sufficient information on the seller's position and ownership to make him feel that the seller will be capable of completing the sale.

In Butler to Burton we notice the position regarding the risk on the property upon exchange of contracts. In contrast to the general law position, where risk passes to the buyer upon exchange of contracts, under a standard condition 5.1.1 the risk of physical damage passes at the date of completion not at the date of contract. Whilst the seller is not obliged to insure (5.1.3) he may be advised to maintain his insurance so as to be able to meet any damages claimed for breach of the s.5.1.1 obligations. Additionally standard condition 5.1.2 provides that the buyer may rescind the contract if at any time before completion the physical state of the property makes it unusable for its purpose at the date of the contract. In such circumstances the seller may only rescind if he could not reasonably have insured or it is not legally possible for him to make good the damage (for example planning permission was not available). Standard condition 5 is not well drafted and makes the buyer's solicitor nervous that a claim for damages by their client will be worthless against a seller with no insurance or inadequate insurance. Thus double insurance may result, with both parties to a transaction insuring a house from exchange of contracts.

REQUISITIONS ON TITLE

Traditionally in unregistered title conveyancing the buyer's solicitor has known little or nothing about the seller's title other than the brief reference to the root of title in the contract. The full details of the title were disclosed in the abstract of title delivered by his solicitor after exchange. Requisitions were then made up largely of questions prompted by examination of the abstract: technical questions concerned with the correctness or otherwise of the work of earlier conveyancers along the line from the transaction that created the root of title. Obviously, faults had to be corrected before completion could take place. Where, on the other hand, the replies to requisitions were satisfactory, the buyer's solicitor knew that provided there was no discrepancy between the abstract and what he found when he examined the deeds the title could safely be accepted.

Nowadays, registration of title makes a big difference in the way title is proved. Inspection of a copy of the entries in the register may be all that is required. This, as we see, is done before exchange of contracts. And in unregistered conveyancing, the facility of photocopying has made it convenient to provide copies of the deeds at the outset so that here also the buyer's solicitor can resolve difficulties on the title before contracts are exchanged. Consequently, there is often little left to enquire about on the title after exchange. Hence in these days the traditional stage of requisitions on title has lost much of its original purpose, namely to resolve title defects and doubts discovered after exchange. Today, the main use of requisitions is to clear up any outstanding practical points including the arrangements for completion. The reader will also notice the question whether the answers to Enquiries before Contract would be the same now that contracts are exchanged. To some extent then "Requisitions on Title" is a misleading heading.

It is common nowadays to use a printed form such as the one set out above (p. 130) and to alter or add to it as the case required. The form used in Butler to Burton is the short form for use where Enquiries before Contract have been replied to. A longer form is available where this is not so.

Careful attention is needed to the time limits for raising requisitions laid down in the Standard Conditions as these limits are "of the essence" and cannot, as of right, be extended (see note on Contract above, p. 153).

LAND REGISTRY SEARCH

Prior to completion, the buyer's solicitor will check the up-to-date state of the Land Register by means of a Land Registry Search in Form 94A in the case above: 94B where part only of the land is being transferred. It will be noticed that when he made out his form 94A for an official search of the Land Register, Miss Burton's solicitor gave as the date from which the search was required the date of issue of the office copy entries. The office copy can be implicitly relied on to represent the state of the register at that date and it is only possible changes in the intervening period that the certificate needs to cover. The certificate is normally dispatched within two days of the receipt of the application. Where the application is sent by first class post, the certificate will be returned first class. There are facilities for search by telephone or telex in case of urgency. The certificate will show not only new entries in the register, but also pending applications which will result in registration.

It will also be noticed that the certificate set out above gives the date of expiry of the "priority." This refers to the protection afforded to the buyer from the rights òf any other person whose application to register a transfer or other dealing in the property is received at any time before the thirtieth working day from the date of the certificate. This makes it important to make the search close enough to the date of completion to ensure that the period of protection will extend not just to the date of completion but for a sufficient time after that to enable the solicitor to submit his application for the registration of the transfer to his client. The procedure under which the priority period could be extended on application no longer operates. Even whilst it was available it seems that it was little used, although in the majority of cases the registration application was lodged outside the priority period.

It is still possible for a buyer's solicitor to make a fresh search, and this can be repeated as often as necessary. However, there is bound to be a gap of a day or more in which any application on behalf of a third party could obtain priority. The danger cannot be disregarded, as we can see just by looking at the contingency of bankruptcy. If in the meantime the seller has become bankrupt, his property will have vested in the Official Receiver and the complications from such an eventuality can readily be imagined.

COMPLETION

As envisaged in requisition 2(c) of the standard Requisitions on Title (Form Con 28B) the seller's solicitor, a week or so before completion date, sends to the buyer's solicitor a financial statement showing the amount to be paid over on completion and how it is made up. In a simple case, where there are no deductions or additions to be made from or to the contract price as in Butler to Burton, this can be dispensed with, the figures being confirmed in reply to requisition 2(c).

Generally speaking there will be found some matters requiring financial adjustment. Thus, the water rates may need to be apportioned to the date of completion: rates are mostly levied half yearly and payment is due at the commencement of the six-month period. Nowadays, however, when many householders take advantage of the instalments facility it is more usual to arrange the apportionment direct with the rating authorities so that the seller receives a refund and the buyer is billed from his occupation. Similar arrangements apply regarding the community charge or council tax. This was the course adopted in Butler to Burton.

Other adjustments may be required, *e.g.* on the sale of "investment properties" (*i.e.* properties occupied by lessees or tenants and bought for the sake of the rents) the rents must be apportioned to completion date. So must ground rents where a leasehold house or property is sold. The buyer may have to pay for the balance of a stock of fuel oil or coal left on the premises.

With the completion statement in hand and found to be in order the buyer's solicitor is able to arrange with the bank to draw the money on completion day. He bespeaks a banker's draft, as this is like a cheque drawn on a bank, rather than a particular account at the bank and once delivered is incapable of being stopped. It has the advantages of cash without the inconvenience and dangers of carrying about a bag of notes. It is the form universally accepted by solicitors where completion is conducted in person and is recommended by the Law Society.

The person attending completion is well advised, particularly when acting for the buyer, to make out an agenda. This ensures that each necessary detail is dealt with in proper sequence: beginning with the deeds and documents to be examined and checked against copies supplied, signatures to be checked, drafts of documents to be made up, documents not handed over to be marked, entries in abstracts to be marked as examined, documents due to be handed over to be safely received and checked for completeness and finally, money to be handed over.

For a completion in person, the buyer's solicitor always attends on the seller's solicitor. This may be at his office or that of the solicitor for the seller's mortgagee if the property is mortgaged and the mortgagee will not release the deeds to the seller's solicitor. The latter situation often occurs where the seller's solicitor is not on the panel of a particular building society and in the case of local authority mortgagees. If so, split banker's drafts may be required—one in favour of the mortgagee's solicitor for the amount outstanding on the mortgage and one in favour of the seller's solicitor representing the balance of the purchase monies.

The Standard Conditions contract provides that the time for completion on the day of completion is to be 2.00 p.m., assuming that the seller is selling the vacant possession and actually vacates by that time. Failure to comply with this time stipulation results in a deemed late completion on the next working day.

Where completion in person is not convenient, say, for a buyer's solicitor whose office is in another town, there are two possibilities:

1. An agency completion: this involves appointing a local firm of solicitors to act as agent and furnishing them with all the instructions and documentation they will need to carry out the completion in person. The agent may be sent a banker's draft for the completion money with the other instructions or alternatively the money could be telegraphed to him and he could then obtain a banker's draft from his own bank. The buyer's solicitor may even decide to telegraph the money direct to the seller's solicitor on his undertaking not to release the money to his client—though this might be considered to be somewhat risky.

    In any event, the agent will of course charge a fee for his services but this may still be cheaper than the buyer's solicitor travelling to effect a completion personally.

2. Completion by post: this needs to be agreed by the solicitors on both sides, but is very common in practice nowadays. However, balanced against its obvious convenience is the drawback that it is not entirely satisfactory for the protection of the buyer's interests since the seller's solicitor will undertake the duties of an agent for the buyer's solicitors, who will send him the banker's draft to hold on his behalf pending completion and forwarding of the title documentation. There is now in existence the Law Society's Code for Completion by Post which the solicitors may agree to use. Under the code the buyer's solicitor sends full instructions and the money to complete and the seller's solicitor acts as the buyer's agent to effect the completion. In addition the code asks the seller's solicitor to confirm that he has the seller's authority to receive the money and that he is the duly authorised agent of the proprietor of any charge to receive the part of the money paid to him which is needed to discharge such charge.

    One further point to consider is the method of payment which as with the agency completion discussed above may be by banker's draft or increasingly by bank telegraphic transfer (otherwise called credit transfer). The procedure for the latter method on a postal completion is for the seller's solicitor to provide the buyer's solicitor in advance of completion with details of his bank and his client account number with the bank. On completion day the buyer's solicitor asks his own bank to transfer the completion money from his client account to the seller's solicitor's client account. The process generally only takes an hour or two and the receiving bank can be asked to notify the seller's solicitor as soon as the funds are received.

Following completion, a different form of completion statement is required, that between the solicitor and his client, which will include in addition to the resolution of all financial accounting and adjustments a statement of the solicitor's fees.

POSSESSION

In domestic conveyancing—the transfer of residential properties for owner occupation—legal possession is tantamount to physical occupation. In the selling and buying of business premises it is possible to talk of the "legal possession" of premises, meaning the management of the property including the collection of rents and perhaps service charges. The sellers of business premises may have very good reason to arrange to transfer the management prior to completion. If they give legal possession in this way, their solicitors make sure it is on terms by which they will not be prejudiced if the sale "goes off."

The position of a house purchaser seeking physical possession before completion is not dissimilar: the seller's solicitor will want to be sure the buyer does not acquire legal rights by virtue of his occupation which will create any difficulties in recovering possession if the completion should not take place. Even with the most carefully drawn reservations, it can cause embarrassment to require a buyer to leave and in fact it is unusual to let the buyer into occupation before completion. It is more common for the seller to agree to the buyer having access, but the purchaser enters at his own risk if the sale is not completed.

STAMPING THE DEEDS

For nearly two centuries the transfer of ownership of land has attracted—the quaint phrase that is used—stamp duty. Every document of title (or "assurance"), subject to the exceptions, must carry an impressed stamp showing that the appropriate duty has been paid. This applies for instance to conveyances on sale, transfers on sale, and assignments on sale of a lease. The duty is "*ad valorem,*" *i.e.* it is on a sliding scale. This is varied periodically to reflect changes in property values, and provides a minimum figure below which no duty is payable. The scale effective from April 6, 1985 is as follows:

£		£	%
0	—	30,000	nil
30,001	—	any value	1

However, to obtain the nil rate an appropriate certificate of value must be included in the deed. Further, where more than one assurance is executed in connection with the same transaction, the duty must be calculated on the total consideration (*i.e.* the money or money's worth passing). Note that stamp duty was suspended for deeds executed between December 20, 1991 and August 19, 1992 where the consideration does not exceed £250,000.

In the case of leases *ad valorem* duty is payable on the premium/consideration as above and additional duty is payable on the rent reserved depending on the term of the lease. Mortgages have been exempt from duty since 1971. Many of the 50p fixed duty cases such as on powers of attorney and deeds of appointment of new trustees have recently been abolished.

When attending at the stamp office for stamping, the first step is to present the document at the counter where an Inland Revenue official looks through the document and marks in pencil the amount of the duty.

An improperly stamped or unstamped document (including one without a P.D. Stamp—as to which see below) is not only a breach of the Stamp Acts, but also it cannot be used in evidence in court until the omission is made good and this may involve the payment of a penalty as well as the duty. This liability continues for as long as the stamping defect remains and is the responsibility of whosoever is the owner for the time being of the property and the document in question.

The day-to-day work of administration of stamp duty in England and Wales is carried out by the Controller of Stamps. The head office is in London at Bush House, Strand. There are provincial offices in various cities which deal with straightforward stamping, for example of conveyances on sale, both over the counter and by post. There is an adjudication section in Worthing which deals only with specialist matters. In Butler to Burton, James attended personally at the Stamp Office in Barchester. As indicated above, Barchester would in fact have to be quite a big city to have a Stamp Office.

Messrs. Rime are "registered customers," which enables them to send their clerk with a cheque and have the document stamped immediately. If they were not registered, it would be necessary to leave the document for the cheque to be cleared and collect it later. Alternatively, payment can be made by banker's draft, or cash.

For the majority of solicitors application has to be made by post in which case, Form Stamps 61 must accompany the application. When using the post instruments should be sent to the correct local office to avoid delay.

All assurances of land, whether liable to duty or not, must also be impressed with the Inland Revenue Particulars Delivered stamp, shortly referred to as the PD Stamp. This is the means by which an official record is maintained in Government Valuation Offices of all land transactions. To obtain the PD Stamp, Form STAMPS L(A) 451 must be completed, as in the case of The Limes. Only after the document has been duly marked by the clerk receiving the form can it be presented at the stamping counter where, on payment of the duty, the *ad valorem* and PD stamps will be impressed. Documents sent for stamping through the post must be accompanied by the form L(A) 451.

Thirty days from the date of execution of the deed are allowed for bringing or sending a document to the Inland Revenue office for stamping. Beyond this period an explanation will be called for, coupled with an assurance that there is no intention to evade the payment of any duty. If the delay is not too long a reasonable explanation will be accepted but in other circumstances a penalty may be exacted. Under a new procedure in 1986 if a deed needs to be produced for a PD Stamp only because the consideration does not exceed £30,000 and the deed contains a certificate of value to that effect, the PD Stamp will be impressed at the appropriate District Land Registry, on either first registration or registration of the dealing.

In some legal matters a deed must be engrossed in duplicate. When the transaction is complete each party holds one copy. In some matters all parties sign both deeds, so that they are true duplicates when signed. In others the deeds are signed individually by the respective parties and exchanged on completion. In this case they are original and counterpart. A lease is prepared in this way.

Where the case attracts *ad valorem* duty of 50p or less, both are stamped at the appropriate value. If the duty is more, only one is stamped *ad valorem*, the other is stamped 50p. However, it is necessary to show on the deed stamped 50p that the *ad valorem* duty has been paid. This is the function of the blue denoting stamp, bearing the legend: "Duplicate or Counterpart—original fully and properly stamped."

To obtain the denoting stamp, both copies of the deed must be produced to the stamp office to be forwarded to the Controller of Stamps for stamping. The Counterpart lease executed by the lessee is an exception: this can be stamped 50p on its own without the denoting stamp.

Not all deeds fall precisely under a particular *ad valorem* scale and in exceptional or complicated transactions, the solicitor may be left in doubt as to what the correct duty is. He should not leave this to chance, because the fact that a document has been stamped is not conclusive proof that it has been correctly stamped. To provide for such circumstances the liability to stamp duty may be adjudicated by the Inland Revenue Commissioners. The deed must be submitted to The Controller of Stamps, Adjudication Section, Inland Revenue (D), West Block, Barrington Road, Worthing, Sussex, BN12 4SF. It must be accompanied by a plain copy or an accurate and complete abstract in usual conveyancing form. When the duty has been assessed a notice of provisional assessment is sent to the applicant. If the assessment is accepted the duty is paid. If not, representations can be made and, if desired, an interview can be arranged. Ultimately, a final assessment is issued. Deeds that have been adjudicated bear an adjudication stamp as well as the *ad valorem* stamp.

Until May 1, 1987 a voluntary disposition (*i.e.* deed of gift) had in any event to be submitted for adjudication. This is no longer the case and no duty, *ad valorem* or fixed, is payable. The deed should, however, contain an appropriate exempt instrument certificate.

As has been explained, the proof of an unregistered title depends on the production of deeds showing whatever changes of ownership have taken place for at least the last 15 years. In so far as any documents in the chain of ownership attracted stamp duty, their value as evidence is nil if the stamp duty is unpaid, because such documents cannot be used in evidence before a court until they have been duly stamped. Likewise where a PD stamp has not been obtained. Therefore, in examining an unregistered title the inspection of the stamps on deeds abstracted is an essential part of the investigation. If a deed proves to have been unstamped or improperly stamped the buyer's solicitor must require the seller to have the document stamped, paying whatever penalty may be exacted, before the title can be accepted.

LINKED SALE AND PURCHASE

Butler to Burton presented the uncommon combination of a seller who was not buying a property to move to and a buyer with no property to sell. This made it possible to present the basic sequence of steps both on the part of the buyer's solicitor and that of the seller in the simplest possible way. In practice the position is usually more complicated. The buyer with no property to sell is not altogether uncommon. The "first time buyer," usually a young couple starting life together and buying with the aid of an advance from a building society, is an everyday occurrence. The seller who is not also purchasing a property elsewhere is not so common.

We now look at the more normal situation where one party is involved in the dual transaction of buying and selling. We will not repeat the steps already gone over in detail in Butler to Burton, but will proceed by noting the additional points that arise.

Example

Butler instead of moving North to live with his daughter is using the proceeds of the sale of The Limes to buy a bungalow on the South coast. Acting for him as a purchaser, Messrs. Makepiece are dealing with a firm of solicitors in that area whom we shall call Messrs. Deeds or shortly, Deeds. Post and telephone must be relied on exclusively for communication with Deeds and if possible a trip to the South coast to complete the purchase will be avoided.

As part of his pre-contract enquiries on the bungalow, Mr. Black asks Deeds whether the seller is buying another property and if so the stage reached; if a mortgage advance is required, whether a formal offer has been received from the lenders or when it is expected. He learns in reply that the seller is buying another property, that no mortgage advance is required and that Deeds are ready to exchange contracts in that purchase. A tentative completion date is suggested 28 days from exchange of contracts. Mr.

Black, having completed his local searches and enquiries, agrees the contract for the purchase of the bungalow. He now knows there should be no hitch in exchanging contracts with Deeds.

On Miss Burton's purchase he in due course reaches the same point in the pre-contract arrangements and as Miss Burton is not selling a property he knows that Messrs. Rime do not have to deal on her behalf with another solicitor. Messrs. Rime have insisted that Standard Condition 2.2.2 shall not apply to the Burton to Butler contract and a special condition to this effect has been inserted in both parts of the contract ensuring that Miss Burton's deposit monies are held by Makepiece and Streiff as stakeholders.

Mr. Black asks Mr. Butler to come in to sign the two contracts and bring in his cheque for the deposit on the bungalow. The cheque having been cleared, Mr. Black sends the signed contract and the firm's cheque for the deposit by post to Deeds with a letter.

MAKEPIECE & STREIFF
Solicitors

Clement Amity
Anthony Adverse

Bank Chambers
Barset

Our Ref: CA/JB/Butler
Your Ref: ND/

Tel: 00765 4321
25th January, 1993

Messrs. Deeds, Solicitors
The Esplanade
Pebbles
Dear Sirs,

Beach View, Windyridge, Pebbles

I enclose the buyer's part of the Contract signed by the buyer together with our cheque for the deposit of £2,560.

As arranged, you undertake to hold these to our order pending exchange. It is proposed to complete on 24th February if this is convenient to your client.

I will telephone you as soon as I am in a position to exchange.

Yours faithfully,
(C. Amity)

Makepiece & Streiff

The next day he calls Mr. Reason who confirms that exchange can take place at once and that completion on February 24 will suit his client. He dates the buyer's part of the contract January 26 and inserts the completion date. Mr. Black does the same in the seller's part contract and they confirm to each other that this has been done. Mr. Reason arranges to send James around with the signed contract and cheque right away. On arrival James is shown into Mr. Black's office when, after exchanging a word of greeting, he sits at the desk and takes the contract and cheque out of his briefcase.

Mr. Black now telephones Deeds to exchange on the purchase

and speaks to Mr. Deed. They agree that this is to be a telephonic exchange. Mr. Deed inserts this day's date, January 26, and the completion date February 24 in both parts of the contract and confirms that he has done so. Mr. Black releases the purchaser's part contract and cheque from the condition under which it is held to Messrs. Makepiece's order. It is mutually acknowledged that exchange has now taken place. Mr. Deed confirms that he now holds the seller's part of the contract to the order of Messrs. Makepiece and will despatch it by first class mail by the next post.

Mr. Black is now ready to exchange with James and contracts are exchanged across the desk, and are examined on receipt by the respective representatives. Mr. Black also receives and examines the cheque.

Mr. Black then takes the precaution of writing to Deeds in confirmation of the arrangements made on the telephone.

The two matters now proceed normally towards completion. In the sale of The Limes, Mr. Black requests Mr. Reason to provide one banker's draft payable to Messrs. Makepiece.

Because Messrs. Deeds are some hundreds of miles from Barset, Mr. Black wishes to arrange to complete through the post with telegraphic transfer of the completion monies. Telegraphic transfer is particularly convenient in linked and chain transactions. Accordingly he adapts question 7 of the requisitions on title, to indicate that an answer is required to question 7B namely:

"We should like to remit the completion monies direct to your bank account. If you agree, please give the name and branch of your bank, its sorting code number, and the title and number of the account to be credited."

He will also add the following additional requisition:
(a) "Please confirm that you are willing to complete through the post adopting the Law Society's code for completion by post."
(b) "Will you act as our agents on completion?"

In his covering letter he tells Deeds that Messrs. Makepiece maintain accounts with three banks which he names. This enables Deeds to reply giving the number of an account in one of the banks named where they have an account. They also acknowledge their willingness to act as the agents of Messrs. Makepiece in completing through the post in accordance with the Code.

As February 24 approaches, Mr. Black arranges an appointment for completion of the sale of The Limes at 10.30 a.m. Following this completion, the completion monies are banked immediately by Joan who takes with her to the bank a signed letter of request and authority to the bank to telegraph the completion money for Beach View to Deeds at the Pebbles branch of the same bank. On her return, Mr. Black telephones Deeds to report that this has been done and that afternoon Deeds ring to report that the Pebbles branch bank has confirmed receipt and that completion has taken place. The deeds will be posted to Messrs. Makepiece by first-class recorded delivery mail the same day. They are duly received.

"SIMULTANEOUS" EXCHANGE

The dual transaction of sale/purchase is the daily experience of the domestic property conveyancer. And in this, the most critical moment is that of the exchange of contracts. It is common to refer to the correlation of the two exchanges as a "simultaneous exchange." Of course, this cannot in practice be so. If it were possible for one solicitor to act for both parties and it was so arranged, he could control the exchange completely. However, solicitors are not permitted by the Law Society to act for both parties, except in the rather exceptional circumstances mentioned earlier. Or if two owners contract to swap houses it is possible for the two solicitors acting to meet and exchange simultaneously. In the real world, a solicitor conducting a sale/purchase transaction for a client deals with two other solicitors. Even if the three were to meet to carry out the exchange, it probably would not help, because the two solicitors he is dealing with would themselves be likely to be conducting dual transactions with other solicitors. It is not uncommon for the line of sales/purchases to extend to four or five transactions on each side making up the familiar "chain." In these circumstances simultaneous exchange is not a realistic possibility. Absolute security for one client means some risk for the two other parties. If solicitor A insists on retaining both the contracts signed by his client until the two exchange parts are in his hands, Solicitors B & C can only exchange simultaneously on behalf of their clients if they are prepared to do so without immediate physical possession of the parts signed by A and if they trust A's solicitor to send them on.

Thus the conclusion must be, that in chain transactions in particular the conventional/traditional methods of exchange are not satisfactory. The physical exchange is impracticable as indicated above and exchange by post involving a number of solicitors will clearly be protracted with the inevitable danger, that before all contracts are exchanged the chain collapses by one party withdrawing—this is quite apart from the normal problems associated with any postal exchange, namely that of delay or loss of a contract in the post and that of being sure precisely when the contract is concluded (though normally it would be when the second part of the contract was posted in accordance with general contract law, this could be varied by the terms of a solicitor's accompanying letter). Accordingly the method of exchange adopted in our case is the telephone exchange based on a formula recommended by the Law Society in the light of the decision of the Court of Appeal in *Domb* v. *Isoz* [1980] 1 Ch. 548. In that case the Court acknowledged the impracticability of a physical exchange of contracts simultaneously where three or more solicitors are acting in the sale/purchase of two or more houses. The use of the telephone coupled with mutual agreement on the mode and moment of exchange, as they said, "substantially reduces the danger that any client will lose a bargain or be left without a home." The facts of the case were that the client was having difficulties in his purchase transaction. His solicitor had carried out the exchange on the sale on the telephone and was committed to post the part contract signed by his client but had not posted it when the client instructed him to withdraw from the sale. The court held that he could not do so: once he had been put in possession of his client's signed part (not before signing) his solicitor had implicit (*i.e.* ostensible) authority to commit his client to exchange and to use the telephone to do so.

The exchange was therefore effective from the moment of the agreement of the two solicitors on the phone.

Whilst approving the method of telephone exchange, the court acknowledged that a high level of professional care is required in using the method. In his judgment, Templeman L.J. suggested that the undertaking given on the telephone should be given by a partner or sole practitioner. It would seem realistic in practice that authority may be delegated to other responsible conveyancers. In any event, whoever conducts exchange of contracts by whatever method, should have the express authority of the partners to do so.

As indicated by Templeman L.J. identical attendance notes should be made to avoid evidential difficulties and to this end the Law Society produced their Formulae for Exchanging Contracts by Telephone/ Telex. Formulae A and B are the current ones. A formula C has been introduced but is little used.

In the example given above, Mr. Black was able to conduct what was virtually an exchange within an exchange: he kept James waiting whilst he telephoned Messrs. Deeds and exchanged with them in effect using Formula A since both parts of the contract were in the possession of one solicitor. This gave him the maximum control of the situation. Even so, exchange on the purchase of Windyridge preceded that on the sale of "The Limes." Equally, where both exchanges are effected on the telephone, one must follow the other. In this case, each exchange normally involves at least two calls: the first to make sure that everything is ready and that the terms of the exchange are agreed, the second, to bring the exchange into effect. Between the two, a call to the solicitors acting in the linked transaction ensures that that can also be the subject of an immediate exchange. In the end, the success of the system of conveyancing in interlocked transactions depends largely on the mutual confidence developed between firms of solicitors and their senior staffs. Clearly there is an element of risk in the telephone exchange but in chain transactions this would seem to be outweighed by the practical advantages of its use to speed matters along.

The alternative form of telephonic exchange (using Formula B) is sometimes adopted where the two parts of the contract signed respectively by the seller and the buyer remain in the hands of their own solicitors. This would be less usual than Formula A. Most recently a Formula C has been published by the Law Society as an addition to the latest versions of Formulae A and B and is specially designed for cases of linked/chain transactions.

Compared with the complexities of the exchange, the dovetailing of the completion arrangements for a dual transaction is fairly straight-forward. A seller/buyer will usually want to complete his sale first so that the money (or the balance of it after paying off the mortgage) is available to use for the purchase. The seller's solicitor, however, will not want completion to take place too late on the same day if he has himself a purchase to complete. If not, he may still reasonably wish to bank the proceeds before the bank shuts. Thus, the first completion is likely to be not later than midday by which time the removal vans should be fully loaded and the keys can be handed over. The later completion will usually be concluded by 2.00 p.m.

Where there is a chain of transactions it will extend to the point where on the one side there is a buyer who is not selling and vice versa on the other side. This extended chain produces great difficulty both in the solicitors' offices and for the clients themselves. Cases have been known where half a dozen clients have been held powerless for a week or more whilst one legal or practical snag is being sorted out. The frustrations and inconvenience to solicitors, clients and removal firms, to mention only the main participants, can be imagined. In these circumstances any expedients which may save a transaction at the expense of exposing a client to risk must plainly be resisted.

MORTGAGES

THE MORTGAGE ADVANCE

Nearly all purchases for owner-occupation are made with the aid of an advance on mortgage from a building society or possibly from a bank, finance company or local authority. Local authorities are particularly able to make advances for the purchase of the older houses on which building societies are less willing to lend. There is a great need to help purchasers in this way in the inner parts of the larger and older towns and conurbations, where the incidence of owner-occupation is much lower than in the newer and smaller towns and the outer urban suburbs. Funds for this local authority service are provided by central government and the rates of interest may be slightly different from those of the building societies. However, the amount of money that can be devoted to loans is dependent directly on government policy and when the local quota is exhausted, prospective borrowers may have to wait until the commencement of a new financial year before receiving an offer.

Banks are increasingly offering loans to buyers and a few insurance offices have funds to lend. However the number of cases is still small compared with the total of building society and local authority mortgages. An individual buyer may find a private lender but the opportunities for this are very scanty.

Solicitors are not generally concerned with the introduction of buyers to a building society. Normally, application has already been made at the time when instructions are received. If estate agents have negotiated the sale, their particulars of sale invariably give information on this. In acting for a buyer who is obtaining a mortgage advance, the solicitor is concerned to see that no binding contract will be entered into until the society's formal offer of mortgage has been accepted by the purchaser. Usually the solicitor will ensure that he sees this before exchange.

At the outset the solicitor will wish to ascertain who is to act for the building society or other lender who may be involved. As the property being purchased is the essential guarantee of the safety of the building society's money—its security—the society is as much concerned as is the buyer to see that a good title to the property is conveyed. Therefore, whatever investigation is normally carried out for the buyer must also be carried out for the building society. Occasionally this is done independently by a separate firm of solicitors. However, although restrictions are imposed on the same solicitor acting for both seller and buyer in a transaction (see p. 154 above) no similar restrictions apply in the case of a mortgage to an institutional lender. Indeed, as the buyer and the society have parallel interests in securing a good title to the property there is no reason why the same solicitor should not act and normally he does so.

Building societies for the most part maintain lists or "panels" of solicitors who act for them. A firm of solicitors which undertakes any volume of conveyancing work will expect to be on the list of all the national societies and those of any local societies there may be in the area.

Similarly, where a mortgaged property is sold there is nothing to prevent the seller's solicitor from acting for the building society on the redemption of the existing mortgage. Occasionally, but not often, a society may decide to appoint a separate solicitor to act for this purpose.

Whilst a solicitor may not frequently be called on to advise on the kind of mortgage a client should obtain, he is nonetheless involved at a later stage in giving effect to the terms of the advance and he needs to be familiar with the various bases for mortgage advances. We are not here referring to the form of the mortgage deed, a matter we shall advert to later, but to the financial details of the loan.

The amount a society will make available for a particular transaction will depend, of course, on the financial circumstances of the borrower, but there is in all cases a ceiling related to value and purchase price. No lenders will advance money without having a valuation carried out by a qualified valuer on their behalf. The borrower from a building society therefore pays a survey fee at the outset of his discussions with the society. The latter makes it clear that the purpose of the valuation is to inform the society of the reliability of the property as security for the loan. The valuer will therefore be considering and reporting on the market value of the property. Given the purpose of his commission, he is likely to be cautious and to give what he thinks is a safe estimate—a figure that can be realised in most market conditions. The report goes straight to the society and is not usually seen by the borrower, although some societies have reversed this rule and will let the borrower have a copy of the report.

Further, some societies are now prepared to offer a choice of surveys (obviously at varying costs) to a prospective borrower. These may range from the ordinary market value survey indicated above to a valuation, plus a mini-survey or even to a valuation plus a full structural survey. It would appear that the middle option is becoming quite popular but its limitations should be pointed out to the client and, for example, it in no way guarantees that the house is structurally sound.

It has been indicated by the courts (most notably in *Yianni* v. *Evans* [1982] Q.B. 438) that a surveyor who negligently prepares a report for a lender may be liable not only to the lender but also to a purchaser up to the amount of the agreed advance if it can be said that the purchaser reasonably relied on it. Furthermore even more recent case law has indicated that any exclusion clause imposed by a surveyor or a society is likely to be deemed unreasonable under the Unfair Contract Terms Act 1977. There is also the possibility that the client may be able to sue his own solicitor in negligence if the solicitor failed to advise the client about the importance of having an independent survey done. Clearly such advice should be given where no mortgage is being obtained and is arguably equally appropriate where the one by the mortgagee is not a comprehensive report including the structure.

Provided the income of the borrower justifies it, the offer of advance will be a percentage, perhaps up to 80 per cent., or even more, of the value of purchase price, whichever is the less.

In the past, building societies preferred to lend to the husband rather than to his wife. Sex discrimination legislation now requires lenders to lend to women on the same basis as they lend to men. Increasingly, young couples purchase together and hold the property in their joint names. The lender must when considering an advance to couples give full consideration to the wife's income if she is the main breadwinner.

REPAYMENT SCHEMES

The most popular form of building society mortgage is the repayment mortgage. Here the borrower undertakes to make equal monthly payments over the full term of the mortgage which may be 15, 20, or 25 years. The proportion of interest and capital in the monthly payments will change over the years. To start with the interest will take up the greater part of payments and only a little will be allocated to capital repayment. As the period proceeds and more and more capital is paid off, the balance is gradually reversed until in the final years the interest payments are very light and capital payments correspondingly high.

Building societies are often prepared on a repayment mortgage to go beyond the normal limit of their lending to meet the needs of their borrower if the latter pays for an indemnity policy at a single premium. This will guarantee to the society that, in the event of a borrower's default, the insurance will cover the loss up to a limit related to the excess borrowing to which they have agreed.

The other main basis for a building society loan is the endowment policy mortgage. Here the borrower, in addition to the mortgage, takes out a policy for the full amount of the loan, maturing either on death or after 15, 20, or 25 years, *i.e.* the term of the policy will be the same as the term of the mortgage. The endowment policy is then assigned to the building society and the borrower covenants to maintain premium payments in accordance with its terms. A medical examination may be required. The borrower pays interest only to the building society and of course is entitled to tax relief as in the case of the repayment mortgage. He can however no longer claim relief on his endowment policy premiums. Which of the two kinds of mortgage is most advantageous depends on the total circumstances of the borrower and a solicitor should give careful thought before he recommends either a type of repayment mortgage or an endowment mortgage, and in some cases the need to call in an independent specialist financial advisor might be appropriate. Various "low cost" endowment schemes and "with profits" schemes are available. Sometimes, however, a slightly higher rate of interest may be charged for an endowment mortgage.

Interest payments (but not repayments of principal) on a loan for the purchase of property which is the only or main residence of the borrower qualify for mortgage interest tax relief—save that there is no relief for interest on the excess of any loan over £30,000. Since April 1983 the MIRAS scheme (Mortgage Interest Relief at Source) has operated whereby the borrower pays his instalment to the mortgagee net of basic rate tax on the interest element. Any extra tax relief applicable to a borrower who pays higher rate tax is given through tax codings or notice of assessment. MIRAS applies equally to endowment mortgages where of course only interest is being repaid.

A hybrid arrangement between the repayment and the life endowment mortgage is found in the repayment mortgage coupled with a mortgage protection policy. Here payments are made under the mortgage in the ordinary way, but a separate life policy is taken out entirely at the option of the borrower. The cover extends to paying off the capital balance outstanding on the borrower's death. The risk to the insurers is obviously a diminishing one and this is reflected in the premium.

A relatively new type of mortgage, principally for the self-employed, is the pension mortgage. Under such an arrangement the borrower would pay only interest to the lender and at the same time make contributions to a pension plan. He will get tax relief on the pension contributions (up to a limit) at his highest rate of tax. At the retirement date under the plan, the borrower receives a pension, part of which can be converted into a tax-free lump sum to pay off the principal under the mortgage.

Example

We now change the Butler scenario slightly in that he is retired prematurely on pension because of ill health whilst "The Limes" is still in mortgage to the Barchester Building Society and he will require an advance to purchase "Beach View," an old seaside villa which he hopes to run as a modest guest house. Messrs. Deeds act for the seller.

In the course of receiving instructions on the sale from Mr. Butler, Mr. Black learns of the mortgage. Messrs. Makepiece are on the panel of the Society and he writes to request the deeds and giving the standard form of undertaking:

MAKEPIECE & STREIFF
Solicitors

Clement Amity   Bank Chambers
Anthony Adverse   Barset

                                          Tel: 00765 4321
Our Ref: CA/JB/Butler   25th January, 1993
Your Ref: ND/

Barchester Building Society
Barchester

Dear Sirs,

Roll No. 75,000
Mortgagor: Bernard Oliver Butler
Property: The Limes, Barset

We act for the above-named and have been instructed in connection with the sale of the property. We wish therefore to give notice of intention to redeem the mortgage.

To enable us to proceed with the sale, we would be glad if you could send us the deeds of the property on our undertaking to hold them on behalf of the Society pending completion and to return them to you on demand if requested. Subject to this, the deeds will be retained until the monies due on redemption are received.

Contracts have not yet been exchanged, but we will notify you of the date and request the figure for the redemption in due course.

Yours faithfully,
(C. Amity)

Makepiece & Streiff

The deeds come to hand and a little later Messrs. Makepiece receive from the local manager of the same Society formal Instructions to Solicitors. This states that the Society's offer of advance to Mr. Butler on the purchase of "Beach View" has been accepted.

Messrs. Makepiece are asked to act for the Society, to investigate the title and, subject to this, to prepare the mortgage deed. Details of the purchase price, loan interest rate and monthly repayments are all set out. Mr. Black notes the Society's case number which he will include in all further correspondence. Special conditions stipulate:

— that vacant possession will be given on completion;
— the premises to be insured through the Society with a nominated insurance office to a specified figure;
— the solicitor to confirm that there is no outstanding improvement grant;
— to confirm that the property is not affected by redevelopment or road improvement proposals;
— the existing mortgage, to be redeemed on or before completion.

The instructions are accompanied by:

1. The surveyor's identification plan;
2. A form of Report on Title for completion by Messrs. Makepiece;
3. Mortgage engrossment and two copies;
4. The Society's booklet of mortgage conditions;
5. A form on which to report to the Society the completion of the advance.

Mr. Black checks the details against his instructions and puts the documents on file pending exchange of contracts on both transactions.

Following exchange of contracts he writes to the Society to inform them of the completion date and request a figure for the redemption of the mortgage on "The Limes" on that date. The reply gives the redemption on the assumption that monthly payments are maintained as indicated and gives also a daily figure of interest applicable for the remainder of the month, in case completion should be delayed. The title to "Beach View" being registered, he is able at the same time to report to the Society on the form provided, that the title is satisfactory and that there are no onerous obligations or covenants affecting the property. The completion date is stated for the information of the Society's office dealing with the advance. Some eight days before the completion date Messrs. Makepiece receive a pro forma from the Society confirming acceptance of the report on title and enclosing the Society's cheque for the new advance. They instruct that the cheque must not be paid in until just before completion, allowing time only for clearance and if completion does not take place within 14 days of receipt, it must be returned for re-dating. Breach of this stipulation could result in a charge of interest against the firm. The pro forma also notifies the roll number by which the new advance is to be identified in the mortgage deed and in the Society's records and file. Mr. Black completes the mortgage deed (p. 176) and obtains Mr. Butler's signature in readiness for completion. Three days before the completion date, the advance cheque is paid in and is credited to the client's account from which the completion monies are to be drawn.

On the completion of the sale of "The Limes," at the offices of Messrs. Makepiece, Mr. Black receives from Messrs. Rime one banker's draft for the whole amount payable to his firm. The title being registered, the Charge Certificate is handed over on completion. In this, the mortgage is bound up. This deed must be "vacated," *i.e.* a formal receipt must be sealed by the Society acknowledging payment of all that is due under the mortgage. In this case, the receipt is given on Land Registry Form 53. As this cannot be sealed before completion, Mr. Black gives an undertaking in the Law Society recommended form to Messrs. Rime as follows:

MAKEPIECE & STREIFF
Solicitors

Clement Amity
Anthony Adverse

Bank Chambers
Barset

Our Ref: CA/JB/Butler
Your Ref: CR/JT

Tel: 00765 4321
24th February, 1993

Messrs. Rime & Reason, Solicitors
Invicta House
Market Square
Barset

Dear Sirs,

Butler to Burton
"The Limes," Lemon Terrace, Barset

In consideration to your today completing the purchase of this property by your client we undertake on behalf of our client forthwith to pay over the money required to redeem the mortgage and to secure the sealing of Form 53 by the Barchester Building Society and to forward the sealed form to you as soon as it is received.

Yours faithfully,
(C. Amity)

Makepiece & Streiff

To the extent that it is required for the redemption of the mortgage, the money received on completion of the sale of "The Limes" is the property of the Building Society, the balance only belongs to the seller. The banker's draft received is banked immediately in the firm's clients' account and the completion moneys required on the purchase of "Beach View" are drawn and telegraphed to Messrs. Deeds, as arranged with them. This leaves sufficient in the clients' account to redeem the mortgage and to meet the outgoings of stamp duty and registration fees and also to cover the firm's bill. Confirmation of the completions is sent in the usual way to Mr. Butler. At the

BARCHESTER BUILDING SOCIETY

MORTGAGE DEED dated   Twenty fourth February 1993

A Parties The Borrower: BERNARD OLIVER BUTLER of THE LIMES LEMON TERRACE
                               BARSET in the County of BARSETSHIRE

           The Surety (if any):

           The Society: BARCHESTER BUILDING SOCIETY BARCHESTER HOUSE
                               BARCHESTER

B

Original Advance £16,500 (receipt acknowledged)	Interest Rate 13% (variable)	Monthly payment £190 (variable)
Provisional Balance £ (on completion of works)	Original Term 15 yrs	Payment Date Twentyfourth day of the month

C The Property   Beach View, Windyridge, Pebbles

LAND REGISTRY   BARCHESTER DISTRICT REGISTRY
County or London   BARSETSHIRE   Title Number
      Borough   BT10001

Particulars of the lease (if any) under which the property is held

DATE	PARTIES	TERM	GROUND RENT

D The Borrower charges the Property by way of legal mortgage with the payment of all monies payable to the Society by the Borrower under the Mortgage.

E This Mortgage incorporates the Mortgage Clauses overleaf and the Rules of the Society.

F This Mortgage is made for securing further advances (see Mortgage Clause 3) but does not oblige the Society to make them.

G Mortgage Clause 7(k) contains an application to the Land Registry to register a restriction.

Signed as a Deed
by the Borrower in the presence of
J. Black
Invicta House
Market Square
Barset

Legal Executive

same time notification of the advance is given to the Society on the form supplied. (Though in fact some Societies no longer require this formal notification where completion has proceeded as arranged.) The firm's cheque for the redemption monies for "The Limes" and the form 53 for sealing by the Society are sent off under their appropriate reference number separately to the Society. The sealed form 53 is duly received and sent on to Messrs. Rime with a request that they acknowledge receipt and confirm that this releases them from their undertaking. This is received in due course.

When lodging the documents of title of "Beach View" with the Land Registry for registration of the transfer, Mr. Black includes the original mortgage and a certified copy.

Six weeks later, the Charge Certificate is received from the Land Registry. It has the original mortgage deed bound up in it. The Proprietorship Register (see p. 119) contains a restriction registered under clause 7(k) of the mortgage clauses, as referred to in clause G of the mortgage deed:

"RESTRICTION registered on 5th April 1989: Except under an Order of the Registrar no disposition by the proprietor of the land is to be registered without the consent of the proprietor for the time being of Charge No. 1."

On receipt of the Charge Certificate from the Land Registry all the title documents and papers are scheduled on a pro forma supplied by the Society in triplicate and sent off by recorded delivery post to the deeds registry of the Society. A receipted copy of the schedule is returned by the Society in due course.

So long as the mortgage subsists the Charge Certificate takes the place of the Land Certificate. In the case of unregistered land, the mortgagee takes all the deeds of the property as well as the mortgage deed.

THE MORTGAGE DEED

The mortgage, whether of land or chattels, is one of the oldest devices known to law, its history going right back to the ancient world. We are here concerned only with land.

The common lawyers wrestled for long with the problem of developing a legal form that would safeguard the lender's right to repayment of the loan whilst leaving the borrower in possession and enjoyment of his land so long as he kept to the terms of the loan, a form that would also give the borrower the unimpeded right to terminate the mortgage on repayment. One of the achievements of the Law of Property Act 1925 (the Act) was to provide a legal framework which makes the mortgage one of the simplest legal documents. Two forms of mortgage are now possible:

1. By demise. Under this the mortgagor, if a freeholder, grants to

the mortgagee a lease of 3,000 years. If he is a leaseholder he grants a sub-lease of 10 days or so less than the full term of his lease. Hence the original legal estate whether freehold or leasehold, remains with the mortgagor.

2. By legal charge. Here the mortgagor simply charges his property, whether freehold or leasehold, "by way of legal mortgage."

The Act contains standard terms and covenants largely regulating the rights and obligations of each party. These can be varied by the terms of the mortgage deed. As there is no practical difference between the mortgage by demise and the legal charge and as the legal charge applies to leaseholds as well as to freeholds, most mortgages today, particularly building society mortgages, are in the simple form of a legal charge. The Barchester Building Society mortgage above is an example. It will be seen that the mortgage clauses giving the respective rights of the parties are set out on the inside pages of the printed form (not reproduced). The back sheet contains the form of vacating receipt which, when the mortgage is redeemed, requires the seal of the society. In the case of registered land this, as we have seen, is given separately on Land Registry Form 53.

The matters dealt with in the mortgage clauses will be likely to include the following:

1. Redemption date. In the traditional form of mortgage the borrower undertakes to repay the whole loan shortly after the date of the mortgage, often six months after. This legal/contractual date for redemption is of largely historical significance since equity came to recognise the right to repay late, *i.e.* the borrower's equitable right to redeem at any time after the six month (or other) legal date and on payment of all monies due. This equitable right to redeem is jealously guarded. It arises only when the legal date has passed and, equity will not allow a "clog" or "bar" to be placed on it. For example, equity will not permit an undue postponement of the legal date for redemption thereby profiting redemption for an unreasonable period of years. However, what is an acceptable postponement period depends on the circumstances and in particular whether the mortgage as a whole is oppressive.

The power of sale given by the Act cannot be exercised (as to which see 9(iv) below) until the legal redemption date has passed.

2. In an instalment mortgage the borrower undertakes to pay the monthly sums due until the whole capital has been repayed and all interest payments discharged; to pay any other sums due under the mortgage clause, *e.g.* insurance premiums if the society insures on behalf of the borrower; in the event of the sale of the property following the borrower's default, if the sale proceeds do not cover the debt, to make good the deficit.

3. Detailed provisions as to how interest is to be reckoned from year to year with power for the society to change the rate.

4. Covenants for title. Here or in the deed itself (see Barchester Building Society Mortgage) the borrower "as beneficial owner" charges the property by way of legal mortgage, thereby bringing into operation covenants for title that apply to a conveyance of the legal estate by the beneficial owner.

5. The mortgage is to extend to cover all monies owed by the borrower, including further advances.

6. The Society may insure at the borrower's expense. This will avoid possible lapse of the policy due to the borrower's default. The Society may be given the option of having the insurance money used to make good damage or to pay off the mortgage debt.

7. The borrower is not to let, mortgage or part with possession of the property without the Society's consent. This excludes the power of leasing allowed by the Act.

8. The capital and interest to become immediately payable if the borrower defaults or in certain other circumstances. This could apply to:

    (i) default in payments for a specified number of days;
    (ii) breach of covenants;
    (iii) bankruptcy of borrower;
    (iv) death of borrower;
    (v) compulsory purchase order on the property;
    (vi) failure to repay on notice.

9. Mortgagee's remedies for default:

    (i) to take possession of the property;
    (ii) to appoint a receiver: useful only where there are tenants under the mortgagor from whom rents can be collected to offset arrears of interest, etc.
    (iii) foreclosure: this is the common law remedy of taking over all the mortgagor's rights and thereby depriving him of the property for good. It is rarely exercised.
    (iv) to sell. A power of sale is provided by the Act, but this is subject to restrictions:
        (i) notice requiring repayment must have been served and the borrower must have defaulted for three months after the notice; or
        (ii) some interest must have been in arrears and unpaid for at least two months; or
        (iii) there must have been a breach of some provision of the mortgage or the Act.

10. The borrower covenants to keep the property in repair; to observe the requirements of statutory authorities; to make no structural alterations without consent; to pay any legal or administrative costs incurred by the Society in connection with the mortgage.

11. The society reserves a right of entry to inspect, similar to that reserved by the landlord in a lease.

The building society will be slow to exercise its power of sale if there is any way round it. If obliged to do so it will want to obtain possession first in order to sell with vacant possession. The sale may be by private treaty, by tender or by auction but whichever method is chosen proper care should be taken since building societies have a statutory duty to obtain the best possible price and of course must account to the mortgagor for any balance after their costs and expenses and the mortgage debt have been discharged.

No mortgagee of a dwelling house can obtain possession of the property without an order of the court. In proceedings for possession the defendant mortgagor can apply to the court to postpone or adjourn the order or to adjourn the proceedings (Administration of Justice Acts 1970, s.36, and 1973, s.8(1)). This may bring about a settlement under which the mortgagor undertakes to discharge the arrears over a period.

SALE BY MORTGAGEE

Where this does take place the buyer from the legal mortgagee must check that the power of sale has arisen, *i.e.* the mortgage monies have become due by the passing of the legal date for redemption. However, the buyer is statutorily protected against any improper or irregular exercise of the power and thus need make no enquiries as to the precise nature of the borrower's default. If in fact the power is not exerciseable the buyer will still get a good title, and the aggrieved borrower could claim damages from the mortgagee.

SECOND AND SUBSEQUENT MORTGAGES

Second mortgages are often obtained by house purchasers to supplement the maximum loan the building society is prepared to offer. The rate of interest will usually be one or two per cent. higher than the building society rate. The second mortgage will invariably be by deed. A building society cannot advance money on second mortgage unless the prior mortgage was with that Society.

Where the original mortgage is by demise the second and any subsequent mortgages will be by demises each one day longer than the previous mortgage. Where the original mortgage is by charge the subsequent mortgages will be by similar deeds called second charge, third charge and so on.

A second mortgagee cannot, of course, hold the charge certificate or the deeds. His interest must therefore be protected in other ways. Any legal mortgage not being a mortgage protected by the deposit of the documents of title of the legal estate affected is known as a *puisne* mortgage. Where the land is unregistered the mortgagee in this case protects his position by registering a land charge, Class C(i). Where the land is registered, the second and subsequent mortgages are entered on the registered title and rank in the order in which they are registered.

Immediately, on completing an advance by *puisne* mortgage the mortgagee must give notice to all prior mortgagees. This ensures that the title deeds are not handed over to the borrower whilst a mortgage of which notice has been given is outstanding.

UNREGISTERED LAND

It is not within the scope of this chapter to expound the rules of the devolution of title at common law. Devolution refers to the passing of title from one owner to another. Each parcel of land ownership has its unique history. Changes in its ownership are only partly accounted for by sales and purchases. Bequests, intestacies, gifts *inter vivos* (*i.e.* between living persons), are all grist to the conveyancer's mill. Ownership may also pass "by operation of law" which means that one owner is divested of his land which then vests in another automatically. The land of a bankrupt vests in the trustee in bankruptcy. The court may order the transfer of ownership of land from one party to another. Or an owner may be obliged to convey land against his will, as where it is compulsorily purchased by a local or public authority. The conveyancer must know in every case how one person is divested of his ownership and how another acquires it, the instrument or formalities required and how the changes are proved for future reference.

If the land is unregistered, the proof in most cases depends on the production of the document by which the change in ownership is recorded. The vendor must be able to produce, or at least know the whereabouts of, all the documents he needs to prove the title.

The ownership of land is continuous through the centuries. An unbroken succession of owners has existed at least from the time the land was first taken into use for human purposes. One cannot be asked to go back to the beginning of history. Previously, the chain of transactions had to be proved over at least 30 years. This has been reduced to 15 years. However, the seller's solicitor needs to go one step further back than the 15 years, because the first transaction to be proved must be in the period before the 15 years commenced. Moreover, the particular transaction used as the starting point must on the face of it be a genuine bargain or transaction in the normal course of business or events, containing nothing to cast doubt on the ability and intention of the one party to transfer ownership or of the capacity of the transferee to receive it. Ideally the lawyer will choose a conveyance on sale because for this the buyer must in his own interests have fully investigated the title. A deed of gift is accepted; or a bequest by a testator who died before 1926, but only if it is a specific devise, that is where the bequest is of the particular property by name and not "all my freehold and leasehold property," or words to that effect. The transaction chosen to commence the proof in this way is referred to as a root of title. From the root of title on to the present, then, each step in the succession must be demonstrated by dependable evidence. Whilst a buyer cannot go back beyond the root of title it is sometimes necessary to abstract an earlier deed, for instance where land is described by reference to a plan in an earlier deed or where land is sold subject to covenants created by an earlier deed.

In a sale of house property and other cases where the whole of the land is conveyed, the deeds are passed to the new owner who will in turn pass them on to the next owner. If only a part of the land owned is sold or otherwise changes ownership the person conveying will naturally wish to keep the deeds in his own possession. A buyer, though, will need to be able to produce the original deeds if he ever needs to prove title. This position is met by giving to the buyer in the conveyance an acknowledgment for production and usually a complimentary undertaking for safe custody of the relevant deeds, which are often set out in a schedule to the conveyance, and the right to the supply of copies. One other safeguard is required: the previous conveyance or transfer document must be endorsed with a memorandum. For example: "By a Conveyance dated 29th day of March 1989 made between X and Y the land herein referred to known as ... was conveyed to Y for an estate in fee simple." On completion the buyer's solicitor will have either an abstract (see below) or more likely today a photocopy of the deeds the seller must retain and he will make up the copy or abstract as follows:

> "Examined with the original Conveyance in the offices of Messrs. Makepiece and Streiff, Bank Chambers, Barset, on the 29th March 1993. Rime and Reason, Solicitors, Invicta House, Market Street, Barset."

The production of the deeds and the handing over of those to be handed over are part of the formalities of the completion. To enable the buyer's solicitor to satisfy himself of what he will discover at the time of completing the transaction when he carefully inspects the original deeds, he is given copies in one of two forms. The traditional form is the abstract of title. This is prepared on brief-sized paper and contains sufficient of the contents of each deed to enable the buyer's solicitor to know all he will be looking for when he examines the original deeds. The abstract reads oddly to a non-conveyancer, because over the long years when the abstract was the only method of deducing title, a system of contractions was evolved for all the terms normally found in a deed. The abstract will, of course, reproduce any endorsements and one very important piece of information is the stamp duty on every deed that at the time of execution attracted such duty. Without this, the deed is worthless as evidence—the very purpose for which it is to be handed over—because no unstamped deed can be used as evidence in court if ever the title should be called in question. The buyer's solicitor is therefore careful to scrutinize every stamp (or the abstracted detail). He will check what was the rate of duty at the time the deed was entered into and if he finds that the right duty was not paid he will reject the title until the seller has repaired the omission. This involves making a special application to Inland Revenue Stamp Duty Office to be allowed to stamp the document out of time on payment of any penalty that may be imposed.

The alternative way of deducing title, now virtually the standard method, is to provide photocopies of all the deeds and documents constituting the proof of title and to send with them an epitome of the title, which is really no more than a schedule of the deeds, etc., of which copies are supplied. This has the great merits of speed and accuracy. The labour of preparing an abstract of title is considerable and unless both the solicitor or legal executive and his typist are thoroughly familiar with the art of abstracting it is not possible to produce an acceptable abstract in the time that can be devoted to it. There is, moreover, a residual doubt as to whether an abstract can be relied on 100 per cent. However, the conventions of the abstract of title cannot be discarded completely at present because a conveyancer will be likely to meet a case where an essential deed is not available for production, but the seller's solicitor is able to produce an examined abstract in which it is contained, *i.e.* an abstract in which each deed is marked by a firm of solicitors in the manner quoted above to show when and where the original was produced. This will be accepted as tantamount to the production of the deed.

There is one other possibility of proving a link in the chain of ownership where a deed is not available. Examination of one or two deeds will serve to show the old practice of setting out immediately after the names, etc., of the parties an account of how the ownership had devolved on the then present owner, each clause being introduced by "Whereas. . . ." It is in effect a very brief epitome of the latest links in the chain: there is no need to go over the last 15 years because it is in no sense a deduction of title. However, these recitals as they are called, sometimes have practical value in supplying a missing link, because provided the deed containing a recital is at least 20 years old (not 15, be it noted) it is accepted as proof of the facts recited in it (L.P.A. 1925, s.45(6)). Today, the inclusion of recitals in a deed is not so common.

It will be appreciated from what is said above that abstracting is a rapidly dying art. Students are unlikely to be called on to prepare an abstract. However, many titles still require the examination of an abstract in the course of title investigation and will continue to do so for many years. This applies particularly where a document forming a link in the title is not available for inspection and reliance must be placed on an examined abstract. It therefore continues to be of practical value to be able to read an abstract and to learn how it is made up. The specimen set out on pp. 184–186 deserves study from this point of view. Readers should note the way the several parts of a deed are set out from no fewer than five left margin positions. From a careful read of the specimen the standard abbreviations can also be assimilated.

We will now look briefly at an unregistered land sale/purchase and observe the main variations from the registered title transactions.

Example

The freehold title to "The Limes," which Mr. Butler is selling to Miss Burton is unregistered. The area of course, has now become a compulsory registration area and following completion of the purchase, the buyer must apply for the first registration of title. On receiving instructions from Miss Burton, Mr. Reason makes an Index Map Search in the district land registry. The registry has particulars of street numbers and names from the local authority and no plan is necessary for identification purposes where the boundaries of the property are already established. The search certificate satisfies him not only that the title is not yet registered, but also that

SPECIMEN ABSTRACT (WITH MARKING)

[NOTE.—For your information, the facts briefly are as follows:—

In 1884 William Smith sold to John Brown a piece of land in County
Lane, Badstone, in the County of Buntingdon. John Brown built two
houses on the land, sold one and mortgaged the other to a building society.
The mortgage was repaid by him. John Brown died in 1928 and by his will
gave his daughter Katie Lucky the house. Katie sold it to Samuel Lover
and his sweetheart; they had a building society mortgage, subsequently
married and repaid the mortgage. They are now selling.]

*   *   *   *   *

ABSTRACT OF THE TITLE
— of —
MR. & MRS. SAMUEL LOVER to fhld
prems site & kn as Barlan Villa, 45
North Rd, Badstone, Bunts.

5 Apr 1884
Stp 5/-

Exd with orig
at John Smith
& Co. Badstone.

Clever Dick &
Co.
Badstone
20.2.62.

BY INDRE of Convce so dtd BTN WM SMITH of Badstone Bunts Gent (Vdr)
of 1 pt & JOHN BROWN of Netton Bunts Builder (Pchr) of or pt
    RECTG Vdr was seised in f.s. in posson free fm incumbs of ppty
thnar descd & agt for sale
WITNED in psce of sd agt & in conson of £35 pd &c (rcpt &c) Vdr as B.O.
convd to Pchr

> ALL THAT pce or pcl of land or ground site
> in Badstone afsd bdd E by County Lane to
> wh it had a frontage of 30 ft or thbts on N
> by or land of Vdr & on S by land then
> recently sold by Vdr to Thos. Davies contg
> in whole an area of 378 sq yds or thbts as
> same was more parlarly deltd & descd in
> plan drawn on abstg presents & thrn dist by
> col pink wh sd pce or pcl of land thby convd
> was pt of a pce or pcl of land contg 1a. 39p.
> or thbts wh was convd to Vdr by Indre of
> 15.3.1883 mde btn John Simpkins & John
> Field of 1 pt & Vdr of or pt

To HOLD sd pce or pcl of land Unto & to use of Pchr
in f.s.

& VDR thby acknd rt of Pchr to prodn of befe mentd indre of 15.3.1883 &
to dely of copies thof & thby undertook for safe custody thof.
    DULY EXTED by both pties & atted.
MEMO endd of sale of villa erected on S pt of thr within descd pcl of land to
A. N. Other & of his rt to prodn and dely of copies of that deed.

29 Jun 1912
Stp 1/3

Orig prodd &
Exd as befe.
C.D. & Co.

BY INDRE of Mtge so dtd BTN sd J. BROWN (Mtgor) of 1 pt &
CLEREBOROUGH MUTUAL BUILDING SOCY Regd Office Market Place
Clereborough (duly certified &c) (Socy) of or pt
    RECTG seisin of Mtgor as befe abstd & agt for loan
WITNED in conson of £50 advanced &c rcpt &c) Mtgor covtd for rept
& ALSO WITNED for conson afsd Mtgor as B.O. thby convd unto Socy
    ALL hrdts in schdle thrto
    To HOLD same unto & to use of Socy in f.s.
PROVISO for vacatg on rept
DECLN Mtgor cld retain posson on repts bg mntnd & for Socy to have
posson on default
DECLN varying provons contd in Conveyancing & LPA 1881 relatg to
powers of sale & appt of Recr
DECLN agst leasing
COVTS to repair & insure (£150 at least—MF Insce Co Ltd)
PROVISO powers thby conferred addl to all or powers
DEFINITION clause.

SCHDLE

ALL THAT pce or pcl of land site in
Badstone Bunts bdd E by a rd fmly kn as
County Lane then as North Rd & to wh it
had a frontage of 15 ft on N by land then or
late of W. Smith on S by prems sold by
Mtgor to A. N. Other & contg in whole 192
sq yds or thbts & wh sd pce or pcl of land
fmd N portion of a pce or pcl of land contg
378 sq yds pchd by Mtgor of Wm Smith &
wh was more parlarly deltd in plan drawn
upon Convce thof to Mtgor (befe abstd)
TOGR with messe or tenements & or bldgs
erected thron kn as Barlan Villa North Rd
afsd then in occpn of Walter Smith
DULY EXTED by Mtgor & atted.

1 Jul 1926.
Exd C.D. &
Co.

BY RCPT endd CLEREBOROUGH MUTUAL B.S. acknd to have recd all moys
intdd to be secd by thr w/w Deed, paymt having bn made by sd J. Brown.

DULY s. & sgd by 2 members of Board &
Sec.

16 Sept 1928.

Sd J. BROWN died at Batstone.

19 Oct 1928.
Grant prodd
& Exd as
befe.
C.D. & Co.

PBTE of Will of sd. J. BROWN granted out of Neterton Dist Pbte Regy to
WILLIAM JAMES nephew of decd one of Exors named in Will Power
reserved to or Exor.
MEMO endd of next abstd Assent.

12 Dec 1928.
Orig prodd
& Exd as
befe.
C.D. & Co.

BY ASSENT so dtd sd WM JAMES (exor of sd Will proved &c as befe abstd)
as P.R. of sd J. BROWN assented to vestg in KATIE LUCKY of 1 Hope St
Lincash Tilts of

ALL lastly abstd prems
FOR an este in f.s.
& THBY acknd her rt to prodn of sd Pbte & to dely of copies thof.
DULY SGD & WITNED.

23 Oct 1947.

H.M. Land Charges Sch Certe agst sd K. LUCKY revlg no entries.

4 Nov 1947
Stps £9 &
Produced Stp.
Orig prodd &
Exd as befe.
C.D. & Co.

BY CONVCE so dtd BTN sd K. LUCKY (Vdr) of 1 pt & SAMUEL LOVER of 5
Russel St Klintborough Maltster & FELICITY SWEET of 6 Russell St
Klintborough Typist (Pchrs) of or pt
RECTG seisin of Vdr as befe abstd & agt for sale

WITNED
1. In psce of sd agt & in conson of £875 pd &c (rcpt &c) Vdr as B.O.
convd unto Pchrs

ALL THAT pce or pcl of land site in & havg a
frontage on E of 15 ft or thbts to North Rd
Badstone afsd (incl N half of overbuilt
passage way btn messes kn as Nos. 45 & 47
North Rd afsd) & bg in depth thfm 118 ft or
thbts on N side & contg 192 sq yds or thbts
bdd on N by ppty then or late of Wm Smith
on S by ppty then or late of A. N. Other
TOGR with messe or dwhse & prems erected
thon or on some pt thof kn as Barlan Villa
No. 45 North Rd Badstone afsd &
TOGR with existing rt of way over & along S
half of sd passage way

To HOLD same unto Pchrs in f.s. as jt tnts SUBJ to mntng house wall dividing messe thby convd fm adjg messe on S side bg No. 47 North Rd Badstone afsd as a pty wall & SUBJ to existing rt of way over & along N half of sd passage way thby convd in favour of owner or occupier of sd adjg messe on S

2. & 3. Jt Pchr clauses (Jt tnts beneficially)

4. Certe of value (£1,500).

DULY EXTED by all parties & atted.

5 Dec 1947
Stp £1.10.0
Orig prodd &
Exd as befe.
C.L. & Co.

BY LEGAL CHARGE so dtd BTN sd S. LOVER & F. SWEET (Mtgors) of 1 pt & sd CLEREBOROUGH MUTUAL B.S. (duly certified &c) (Socy) of or pt IN CONSON of £525 adv &c (rcpt &c) WITNED as followed:—

1. Mtgors jtly & sevly covtd for rept
2. Mtgors as B.O. thby chgd by way of legal Mtge

ALL & SINGULAR ppty comprised in schdle with payment to Socy &c

3. AGT & DEGLN as to excise of powers of sale & appt of Recr
4. Jt & sev covt to repair & to observe & perfm rules of Socy
5. To insure
6. Rate of int 4% or such or rate as fixed
7. Restron on rt to consolidation not to apply
8. No regn under Land Regn Act 1925 witht consent of Socy
9. Decln agst leasing (not exceeding 3 yrs witht consent)
10. Socy not answerable for loss
11. Attornment clause

SCHDLE

LASTLY abstd prems.

DULY EXTED by Mtgors & atted.

11 Feb 1948.
M/C prodd &
Exd as befe.
C.D. & Co.

Sd. F. SWEET intermarried with & became wife of sd S. LOVER at Psh Ch of All Sts. Badstone, Bunts.

5 Jun 1960.
Exd.
C.D. & Co.

BY RCPT endd on befe abstd Legal Charge CLEREBOROUGH MUTUAL B.S. acknd to have recd all moys intdd to be secd by thr w/w Legal Charge incl all int & costs Sd moys were pd by sd S. Lover & F. Lover (nee Sweet)

DULY s. by Socy & sgd by Director & Sec.

[NOTE.—An abstract of a mortgage or legal charge which has been repaid could be further abbreviated by saying "Clauses [3 to 11]—other usual clauses common in building society mortgages," unless it is a root of title and the mortgagees are selling under their power of sale.]

no caution against the first registration has been entered against the site.

In preparing the draft contract with the deeds before him, Mr. Amity has no authentic resumé of all the essentials of the property, its title, description, etc., such as are set out in the land certificate. He must extract the description carefully from a deed and if the property is identified by reference to a plan this must be reproduced or at least referred to in the contract. All appurtenant rights and obligations, whenever they may have arisen in the course of preceding ownerships, must be faithfully reproduced.

If there is any weakness in the title—it will only be an incidental defect in the chain of evidence, a major defect means that the title, must be rejected—he will carefully draw attention to it in the contract and say that this must be accepted by the purchaser without question. The draft will therefore be rather longer than most contracts in registered land sales.

Past generations of solicitors would tender the draft contract, leaving the abstract of epitome of title to be delivered after exchange, as the general conditions of contract provide. Today, it is more usual to deduce the title at the outset, just in the same way as the copy entries in the register are delivered.

The Standard Conditions of Sale (1992) provide at general condition 3.1.1 that the seller will sell free from incumbrances other than any adverse interest existing when the contract is made and any matter mentioned in the agreement itself. Adverse interests are defined at general condition 3.1.2 but the definition does not include covenants and conditions affecting the property. Thus if the Standard Conditions of Sale (1992) are used, covenants and conditions must be disclosed at the section of the contract form headed "Burdens" and details of them supplied to the buyer's solicitor. The disclosure, together with Special Condition 2 of the Standard Conditions Contract which bars out post contract requisitions on disclosed burdens, protects the seller and means that the covenants and conditions will be deduced to the buyer at the outset where this contract form is used.

In this case, Mr. Amity finds that the property has been in the Butler family since 1907 when Mr. Butler's grandfather purchased the land on which "The Limes" and the adjoining houses were built shortly after. His parents and grandparents are deceased. Having looked through the deeds and documents, Mr. Amity finds that on the death of his father the properties passed to his widowed mother who was the father's sole executrix. As all the father's property had been left to his widow, the latter in due course signed a document in her capacity as executrix vesting the property in herself beneficially. This is known as an assent and is effective to pass the ownership of real property although it is a signed document but not a deed. Many years later, the mother made a Deed of Gift to Mr. Butler of "The Limes," in which he was by then living, retaining the remainder of the property she had inherited for herself.

As the assent had been made well over 15 years ago, Mr. Amity relies on it as the root of title. He therefore writes in the draft contract:

"The title shall commence with an assent made by Ellen Emma Butler on the 26th March 1942."

Obligingly, he supplies the buyer's solicitor, Mr. Reason, with a copy of the assent and Deed of Gift, which was made in 1976.

On examining the assent, Mr. Reason will be aware that as it is over 15 years old it can sometimes be accepted, but like any root of title document it should satisfy the accepted common law definition of a "good root." This is an instrument which deals with the whole legal and equitable interest to be sold, contains an adequate description of the property, and contains nothing to cast any doubt on the title of the disposing party. Here Mr. Reason sees that the operative clause states that Mrs. Butler assented to the vesting in herself of the property "for all the estate vested in the said Oliver Butler at the date of his death." This is clearly defective in two respects, namely, the property is not described and there is no indication of what interest in the property the testator had. Mr. Reason therefore rejects it and requires an earlier root of title.

Mr. Amity now examines the earlier deeds and finds that no transaction suitable as root of title can be found later than the conveyance on sale in 1907 by which the property came into the family. The subsequent devolutions until the assent resulted directly from the death of the owner. By the 1907 conveyance the property of which the site of "The Limes" forms part was clearly identified and was conveyed for valuable consideration to Mr. Butler's grandfather. He therefore abstracts the conveyance and the subsequent probates which Mr. Reason is happy to accept.

Thereafter, the transaction proceeds normally: Mr. Reason finds that the assent is endorsed with a memorandum of the Deed of Gift, so that he is satisfied that the assent cannot be used in any future conveyancing transaction without the buyer being aware of the sale of "The Limes." He drafts the conveyance which is agreed with Mr. Amity and the engrossment supplied by Messrs. Rime is signed as a deed by Mr. Butler (pp. 189–191).

In the week before the completion, Mr. Reason searches in the Land Charges Register against the names of Mr. Butler, his mother, father and his grandfather, all of whom held the property in turn. The search certificate shows that there are no entries against these names.

At the completion Mr. Reason inspects the conveyance of 1907, the probates, the assent and the Deed of Gift. Of these only the Deed of Gift is to be taken over as it is the only deed that relates exclusively to "The Limes." He makes up his copies of all the other documents as having been examined with the originals.

Following completion, Mr. Reason has two months to lodge the deeds in the District Land Registry with the application for first registration. The requirements are more exacting than for the registration of a transfer of a registered title. The Chief Land Registrar must examine the title independently, although he will accept copies of deeds, etc., marked as examined with the original by a solicitor, without calling for the production of the originals. All the replies to

<u>THIS CONVEYANCE</u> is made the twenty ninth day of March One Thousand Nine Hundred and ninety three BETWEEN <u>BERNARD OLIVER BUTLER</u> of THE LIMES LEMON TERRACE, BARSET in the COUNTY OF BARSETSHIRE Retired (hereinafter called the vendor) of the one part and <u>MOLLY BURTON</u> of THE ROYAL HOTEL MARKET SQUARE BARSET aforesaid (hereinafter called the purchaser) of the other part

<u>WHEREAS</u>

(1)   OLIVER JOHN BUTLER late of Glebelands, Barchester Road, Barset in the County of Barsetshire Farmer died on the 14th day of March 1921 having by his will dated the 16th day of July 1918 appointed his son Oliver Butler late of Glebelands aforesaid his sole executor thereof who proved the same on the 20th Day of May 1921 in the Principal Probate Registry

(2)   The said Oliver John Butler being at the date of his death seised of the property described in the Schedule hereto (hereinafter referred to as "the property") for an estate in fee simple in possession free from incumbrance devised and bequeathed all his real estate to the said Oliver Butler for an estate in fee simple

(3)   The said Oliver Butler died on the 5th day of July 1941 without having made any assent conveyance or other disposition of the property having by his will dated the 30th day of May 1940 appointed Ellen Emma Butler of Glebelands aforesaid his widow the sole executrix thereof who proved the same on the 20th day of October 1941 in the Principal Probate Registry

(4)   By an assent dated the 26th March 1942 the said Ellen Emma Butler assented to the vesting in herself of the property for all the estate vested in the said Oliver Butler at the date of his death

(5)   By a deed of gift made the 26th day of October 1976 the said Ellen Emma Butler conveyed the property to the vendor her son to hold the same to the vendor in fee simple

(6)   The vendor has agreed with the purchaser for the sale to her of the property for an estate in fee simple in possession free from incumbrance at the price of forty-nine thousand pounds (49,000)

NOW THIS DEED WITNESSETH as follows:

1.   In consideration of the sum of forty-nine thousand pounds (49,000) paid by the purchaser to the vendor (the receipt whereof the vendor hereby acknowledges) the vendor as beneficial owner hereby conveys unto the purchaser ALL THAT THE PROPERTY to hold the same unto the purchaser in fee simple subject to the restrictions and conditions contained in the Schedule to a conveyance dated the 20th June 1907 and made between Niven Horation Fairfax Moresby Kerr of the one part and the said Oliver John Butler of the other part

2.   The purchaser hereby covenants with the vendor to perform and observe the said restrictions and conditions and indemnify the vendor and his estate against all actions claims and liability in respect thereof so far as the vendor and his estate remain liable thereupon after the date hereof

IN WITNESS whereof the said BERNARD OLIVER BUTLER has hereunto set his hand and seal the day and year first before written

THE SCHEDULE

ALL THAT piece or parcel of land situate lying and being in the
Parish of Barset in the County of Barsetshire and having a frontage of
twenty-one feet or thereabouts to and a depth of two hundred and twenty
feet or thereabouts from Lemon Terrace
Together with the dwellinghouse erected thereon or on some part thereof
and known as THE LIMES Barset aforesaid as the same are for the
purpose of identification only shown on the plan annexed hereto and
thereon edged in yellow

Signed as a deed
by the said BERNARD OLIVER BUTLER
in the presence of

    J Black
    Invicta House
    Market Square
    Barset

    Legal Executive

enquiries and certificates of search must, however, be produced. The application is prepared by Mr. Reason on Form 1B and is accompanied by a schedule of the title deeds, including the conveyance to the buyer, and the other papers submitted in support of the application. This is prepared in triplicate on Form A13 and the District Registry return one copy stamped in acknowledgment of due receipt. Messrs. Rime in due course receive the land certificate which they put into their strong room for safe custody on behalf of Miss Burton.

LAND CHARGES REGISTERS SEARCHES

A land charges search is an essential step in preparing for the completion of a purchase of unregistered land. Registration of a registrable matter is deemed to be actual notice of the interest registered to all persons and for all purposes connected with the land affected. Non-registration makes a registrable charge void against a purchaser of the legal estate.

There are in fact five registers, of which the register of land charges proper is the most important for conveyancers. Of the others, the registers of pending actions, writs and orders and deeds of arrangement are likely to be of importance mainly in connection with the possible bankruptcy of a buyer. A solicitor acting for a building society in connection with an advance on house purchase must search to check on the solvency of the buyer. If the land is unregistered the information will be obtained by adding the buyer's name to the general search against the previous owners of the land. Whilst no general search has to be made where the title to the land being purchased is registered, a separate "bankruptcy only" search is necessary against the buyer's name.

The land charges register classifies the charges registered into six classes, A–F with sub-divisions. Those most often met in conveyancing transactions are:

Class C(I): *puisne* mortgage, *i.e.* a mortgage not protected by the mortgagee having possession of the deeds.
Class C(IV): an estate contract. This phrase covers any contract under which a legal estate in land is to be created (*e.g.* by a new lease) or transferred. In normal house purchase transactions registration is not considered necessary, at least unless the period to completion is to be very prolonged. An option to purchase or to renew a lease, on the other hand, may be outstanding for years and should be registered. No registration is ever necessary in the case of a registered title, as the interest of the person entitled can be protected by an entry in the land register.
Class D(II) Restrictive covenants affecting the freehold and created after 1925.
Class F. Spouse's right of occupation of the matrimonial home under the Matrimonial Homes Act 1983. Here again, in the case of a

registered title, the spouse's interest is protected by an entry on the register.

The land charges register is at Burrington Way, Plymouth, Devon, PL5 3LP. Searches can be made in person, by post, by telephone or by telex. Personal searches are not often undertaken because of impracticability and the searcher does not have the benefit of the protection of the official certificate of search mentioned below.

The fee, now 50p per name, can be paid by cash (on a personal search), postal order, cheque or authorised credit account. Telephone and telex searches can only be made by persons with a credit account but this will include most firms of solicitors.

The registers, the system of searching and the issue of certificates are computerised. If possible the registry completes the search and issues the certificate on the date of receipt and the certificate date is one working day earlier. The certificate covers all entries to that date. To facilitate the recovery of firms' names and addresses from the computer's memory store, a key number is allocated to each firm, which should be quoted in the application.

By far the majority of searches are by way of the written postal application followed by issue of the official search as explained above. Where a search is made by giving the Land Charges Department the necessary information by telephone, then if there are less than five potentially relevant entries these will be read out. In any event the official search certificate is then posted to confirm the result of the search. With a telex application no return telex will be made but rather a search certificate posted in the normal way.

Charges are registered against the name of the estate owner whose property is subject to the charge and the entries are divided into local authority districts so that the application for search must specify the name and the district. It must also specify a period for each name, which will be the period during which the person named owned the land. The buyer's solicitor will search against the present owner(s) and the names of all previous owners who have held the land in the period from the root of title or the commencement of registration in 1926, whichever is the later. However, if satisfactory searches against previous estate owners have been made on previous transactions and the seller abstracts these then the present buyer's solicitor may rely on them without repeating the searches.

Searches are made on form K15 for the full search or K16 for the bankruptcy only search. Care must be exercised over both the name and the district. If an entry is revealed and its significance is not obvious, application can be made for an office copy of the registration in addition to raising a requisition with the seller's solicitor as to its significance.

In a computerised system, the computer can cope with a certain number of variant ways of presenting a name, but the use of initials for forenames, hyphenated surnames, the omission of second forenames and the reversal of forenames all present practical problems. The advice given by the Registry in their guide for Solicitors is therefore important:

(1) *Completing the form*

Names must be set out correctly on the form. Forenames must be entered on the first line of a box, followed by the surname on the next line, as follows:

		NAMES TO BE SEARCHED	From	To
		Please use block letters		
	Forename(s)	JOHN WILLIAM		
	Surname	SMITH		
	Forename(s)			
	Surname			

It is essential that the forename(s) and the surname should be correctly inserted on the designated lines because some forenames and surnames are capable of being reversed without it being apparent that a name has been specified incorrectly, for example, BARRY JAMES or JAMES BARRY.

(2) *Full names*

Each name of an individual, that is the full forenames and surname, will be searched exactly as it reads. It will also be searched (i) in the surname alone and (ii) in the initials of the forenames combined with the surname.

Searches will not be made against some only of the forenames or against a mixture of forenames and initials coupled with the surname unless these combinations are set out as separate names to be searched. The following example indicates the searches which are, and those which are not, undertaken for an application in respect of "JOHN WILLIAM SMITH":

Are included	*Are* not *included*
JOHN WILLIAM SMITH	JOHN SMITH
J. W. SMITH	J. SMITH
SMITH	JOHN W. SMITH
	J. WILLIAM SMITH
	WILLIAM SMITH
	W. SMITH

(3) *Initials of forenames*

	Surname			
	Forename(s)	JOHN W.		
	Surname	SMITH		

If an applicant provides only the initial letter of the forenames, the search will be made against the initials combined with the surname and also against the surname alone. The search will not cover the surname combined with any forename which happens to bear the stated initial. The following examples illustrate this point:

Example 1
Search: JOHN W. SMITH

Are included	*Are* not *included*
JOHN W. SMITH	JOHN SMITH
J. W. SMITH	J. SMITH
SMITH	W. SMITH
	Any forename beginning with "w"

Example 2
Search J. W. SMITH

Are included	*Are* not *included*
J. W. SMITH	J. SMITH
SMITH	W. SMITH
	Any forenames bearing the initials "J. W."

(4) *Abbreviated forenames*

Abbreviations of forenames such as JAS, THOS, HY, will be searched exactly as they are written, they will not be converted into a full name.

(5) *Multiple surnames*

Extreme care must be taken to ensure that the surname is entered on the appropriate line of the application form. This is especially important in the case of hyphenated names (WILSON-SMITH), prefixed names (DE LA CRUZ) and double or multiple barrelled names (HAMILTON SMITH). Although the computer system has been designed to overcome, as far as possible, inconsistencies in the use of hyphens, spacing and punctuation in surnames, the staff of the Land Charges Department have no possible way of knowing when part of a surname has been erroneously entered on the form as a forename. Therefore they cannot accept any responsibility for any errors arising therefrom. Whenever the applicant is in doubt as to which portions of a name are the proper surname, it is essential that he should apply for two or more distinct searches, thus:

Forename(s)	JOHN HAMILTON			
Surname	SMITH			
Forename(s)	JOHN			
Surname	HAMILTON SMITH			

(6) *Former or alternative names*

If a person is commonly known by an alternative name, or if a name has been changed by deed poll, or on marriage, each name to be searched must be entered in a separate box on the application form. Thus, for instance, the phrases ALICE SMITH neé JONES or ALICE SMITH (formerly JONES) or ALICE otherwise ALICIA SMITH should never be used.

(7) *Titles*

Words such as "Lord," "Duke," "Princess," or even "Sir" sometimes exist as forenames. Therefore it is essential that a person's titles should not be confused with his names. Subject to what is stated below, if genuine titles are quoted in the name box of an application they must be distinguished by being placed in brackets, thus:

	Forename(s)	(SIR) JOHN		
	Surname	SMITH		
	Forename(s)	(THE HON) JOHN HENRY		
	Surname	CARRUTHERS		

The words in brackets in the above two examples will not be fed into the computer and so cannot be reproduced on the certificate of the result of the search.

When the name of a titled person or a corporation sole (such as a bishop) contains a reference to a territorial designation, the whole name box in the application should be used for the name and the words "Forename(s)" and "Surname" should be deleted. There is then no need to use brackets. The following are examples:

		Please use block letters		
	Forename(s)	CHARLES JAMES HENRY VAUGHAN		
	Surname	7TH EARL OF BARCHESTER		
	Forename(s)	LORD CHARLES WILLIAM FREDERICK		
	Surname	MONTAGUE SMITH OF BROADOAKS		
	Forename(s)	THE RIGHT REVEREND JOHN HERBERT		
	Surname	WALPOLE THE LORD BISHOP OF CHELLS		
	Forename(s)	THE INCUMBENT FOR THE TIME BEING OF THE		
	Surname	BENEFICE OF EAST WESTLEIGH, BARSETSHIRE		

An applicant should always consider whether a registration may have been effected simply against a person's forenames and surname alone, devoid of any reference to his title or a territorial designation and, consequently, whether that name should also be separately searched. This situation is often found when a titled person has retained his surname as part of his title.

The correct designation of the district is equally important. It will be remembered that under the reorganisation of local government that took place on April 1, 1974 in some parts of the country districts were transferred from one county to another, county boroughs were abolished and new counties and district councils, in many cases with entirely new names and areas, were set up. It is essential when searching in respect of land in an area affected by name or boundary changes, that the old and the new names should both be given.

The changes in boundaries and names is clearly important where the period searched includes April 1, 1974. However, one category of charges is searched without reference to period, namely bankruptcy. It seems advisable, therefore, in all cases to include both the old and new district names.

A search on behalf of a client, who is acquiring an interest in the land, should be made within 15 working days of the actual completion. Provided completion takes place within this period, the client takes free of any charge not revealed by the search, but which may have been registered within the 15 working day period. This presents a practical difficulty in some cases:

Example

D, an estate developer of unregistered freehold land, has decided to impose restrictive covenants for the benefit of the estate. As new restrictive covenants, these must be registered as a class D(ii) land charge. Buyer P is buying his plot with an advance from building society S. The mortgage will be entered into on completion of the purchase. S's solicitor searches within 15 working days before completion and secures protection against any land charge registered within that period. D cannot register a D(ii) land charge until the covenants are entered into by the conveyance. But the mortgage is also completed at this time, with the benefit of a clear search certificate. Therefore, unless D's position can be protected by other means, S will take clear of the covenants and if at any time S exercises its power of sale, a buyer from it could take clear of the covenants.

The special means which D can take advantage of is the priority notice system. At least 15 days before completion of the sale, his solicitor completes and submits to the Land Charges Department form K6: Application for Registration of a Priority Notice. If the class D(ii) charge is registered within 30 working days thereafter, it takes effect at the time of creation of the charge.

Whilst mainly used for the imposition of new restrictive covenants the priority procedure is available for other classes of charge.

It should be appreciated that in some cases other searches may be appropriate before completion. Most notable is the Companies Register search where the present seller or a previous estate owner is a company. This is usually done through a firm of company agents and may reveal pre-1970 fixed charges (post 1970 they require registration at the Land Charges department), floating charges or winding up proceedings. Unlike the Land charges search there is no priority period given and no compensation provisions for errors.

LEASEHOLD LAND

The lease is no doubt the most versatile form of land ownership that the lawyer commands. It can be moulded to meet any conceivable economic or financial need. It provides for domestic needs as well as businesses. The rents charged can range from a peppercorn to rack rents of many thousands of pounds. It can be used to divide up the physical entity of a factory or complex office block into a score of individual holdings, the divisions being vertical or horizontal or both. It can endure for a year or a thousand years and one can metaphorically pile leaseholder on leaseholder in the succession of head lease, underlease, sub-underlease and still further subordinate holdings.

The relationship of lessor and lessee or, what is the same thing, landlord and tenant, can be and often is on the landlord's part purely an economic matter, an investment. The auctioneer's billboard advertising the sale of a terrace of tenanted houses as "investment properties" is familiar enough. To the tenant or lessee then, the lease, whether of business or residential property, may be a business asset that he may sub-let to recover what is called a profit rental. But equally the lease may provide the location of his livelihood or his home.

The versatility of the lease comes partly from this ability to divide land and buildings into any number and shape of leasehold holdings, but also from the fact that the terms of the agreement between the lessor and the lessee are whatever may suit the convenience and economic circumstances of the respective parties. The lease must set out in complete detail how the normal responsibilities of an owner for the use, care and management of his property are to be divided between the parties in relation to the property comprised in it.

The parties have in effect a dual relationship. On the one hand the lease grants a legal estate in land which enables the lessee to present himself to the world as a landowner. On the other hand the covenants and conditions of the lease place the two parties in a contractual relationship with each other. This duality permeates the law of leaseholds.

The student's introduction to leasehold is likely to be in the domestic context. In the past, much housing development has been on long term leases at a ground rent. Ninety-nine years is a common term. This is less attractive today because of two things: (a) inflation constantly reduces the real value of the rent reserved whilst the administrative costs of collection of the rent are always rising. Long leases granted today are usually on a rising rent with steps perhaps at 25 year intervals, (b) the owner-occupier's right to enfranchise the land, *i.e.* to require the lessor to sell him the freehold, makes it a less attractive proposition to the freehold developer. (See below p. 215).

However, in one section of the market, leasehold is firmly entrenched and will no doubt stay for the forseeable future at least. This is in the sale of flats and maisonettes, whether in purpose built blocks or formed by the conversion of older houses. Here, the needs of the individual lessee are to an extent the needs of all. They all want to see that the roof does not leak. And they will want to be assured that their neighbours will not conduct themselves so as to reduce their own security and quiet enjoyment. The lease caters for such common matters. The individual lessees may expect to contribute *pro rata* to the costs of maintenance of the structure and common parts of the building, but subject to this the landlord usually accepts responsibility for the maintenance involved. He will also impose stipulations for ensuring the reasonable and considerate conduct of the lessees towards each other.

Unfortunately, landlords die and landlord companies can be wound up. To safeguard the permanence of the management arrangements, the lessees themselves may join together to form a management company in order to buy the freehold and so become the complete controllers of the building as a whole. Other forms of ownership for the owner-occupation of a divided building have been tried. It is legally possible for each flat holder to have a freehold—the "flying freehold"—but to find an effective substitute for the unifying authority of the landlord has taxed the ingenuity of lawyers. Recently (July 1987) the Aldridge Working Group on Freehold Flats and Freehold Ownership of Other Interdependent Buildings has proposed a more sophisticated form of flying freeholds. Under the Commonhold proposals, as they are known, owners of flats within a Commonhold scheme would be spared the disadvantages of leasehold tenure not least of which is the very real problem indicated above of being locked into a property because the lease has become too short to be mortgaged. The Aldridge report contains detailed proposals for implementation of Commonholds but it remains to be seen whether they, or a similar scheme, are implemented by the government.

Returning to the granting of leases, to the prospective buyer of a leasehold property at a ground rent, assuming the lease has, say, 40 or more years to run, the transaction may seem no different from buying the freehold. His valuer will arrive at a figure for the purchase price which takes into account the rent and the lessee's covenants and obligations under the lease. The negotiations through the estate agent will follow the same pattern and the contract drawn up by the solicitors will have substantially the same general conditions. There will be the usual 10 per cent. deposit.

The buyer's solicitor must closely examine the lease to satisfy himself that there is no restriction on the sale of the lease or to note that the consent of the landlord has to be obtained, where this is necessary. This is not often to be found in a long lease at a ground rent, where the value is expressed in the purchase price rather than in the rent. His solicitor will check to see that the covenants and conditions are fair and reasonable and that they will give the buyer proper protection of his possession and ensure that when he comes to sell there can be no objection taken to the form of the lease. He will report on these matters to the client before exchange because, of course, he is buying not merely a property, but a property to which detailed rights and obligations are attached. Once they are fixed on the grant of the lease, the terms invariably remain unchanged during the whole term. Before contracts are exchanged, the buyer's solicitor must enquire whether the seller and any previous leaseholders have faithfully performed the covenants of the lease.

As in the case of the sale of a freehold, the buyer's solicitor will expect the seller to sell as beneficial owner and, as we have seen, this implies the covenants for title given by the Law of Property Act 1925, section 76. Where a lease is being sold, two additional covenants are implied by the section. Firstly, the seller covenants that the lease is valid and subsisting. The buyer's solicitor, however, may not rely exclusively on this covenant but may demand to examine the superior title out of which the lease was granted. If the Standard Conditions of Sale (2nd Edition) 1992 are used, Condition 8 provides that on the grant of a new lease for a period exceeding 21 years the seller is to deduce such title as will enable the buyer to register the lease with title absolute. This will oblige the seller to supply the superior title.

The second additional covenant implied by section 76 is that the rent is paid and that the other obligations under the lease have been performed up to the time of the sale. The buyer's solicitor always requires the seller's solicitor to produce the latest receipt for rent and the buyer is required to accept this evidence that the covenants have been performed to-date, unless there is evidence to the contrary. However, the seller invariably takes the view that it is the responsibility of the buyer to examine the state and condition of the property and to satisfy himself that the covenants for maintenance repair and decoration have been duly performed. Therefore, a clause is usually inserted by his solicitor in the contract as follows:

> "The parties hereto agree and declare that the covenants which are implied by section 24(1)(a) of the Land Registration Act 1925/LPA 1925, section 76(1)(A) by reason of the seller transferring or assigning as beneficial owner shall not imply that any covenant on the part of the lessee for repairing painting or decorating the property has been performed or observed up to the date hereof."

Following exchange of contracts, the transaction proceeds normally as for the sale/purchase of a freehold property. Following completion, the buyer's solicitor will give formal notice of the assignment and of the mortgage where there is one to the landlord or his solicitor.

THE GRANT OF A NEW LEASE

Here the negotiation of the terms of the lease is a major part of the conveyancing work, although the developers of a housing estate or a block of flats will naturally insist on the acceptance of a standard form of lease. The case set out below illustrates the position where a newly converted flat is sold under a contract providing for the grant of a long lease at a ground rent. For leases of shorter duration at a rack rent, *i.e.* where the full letting value of a property is covered by the rent, and there is consequently no purchase price there may be no contract. The solicitors merely negotiate the terms of a lease and the parties are not bound until the exchange of lease and counterpart takes place.

In the development of a housing estate, the developer may offer a building lease. This is a lease coupled with an agreement to build the property. Here the term of the lease will commence when the property is ready for occupation. This enables the builder to secure buyers at an early stage of his investment in the building works and gives him the economic security he needs to proceed with the development. From the buyer's point of view, the construction agreement is a vital part of the arrangements, as it will be his only guarantee of the standards of construction and conformity to the plans. The buyer's solicitors will therefore wish to ensure that the agreement is linked to a clear specification for the building works. In particular, the buyer's solicitor must advise the buyer to insist that he has the protection of the National House Building Council Scheme (see p. 219) and that all planning and building consents have been obtained.

We will now look at a case of the granting of a long lease of a flat in a newly converted house.

Example

Luxury Flats Limited to Burton

Luxury Flats Limited has purchased the freehold of 60 Church Walk, Barset to convert into three self-contained flats with fitted kitchens, bathrooms, etc., for disposal on 99 year leases. Their architects' scheme is being carried into effect by a building firm with which the company is connected. Bridging finance to enable the company to meet the builder's costs pending the sales has been advanced by the Northern Bank Limited and notice of intended deposit of the Land Certificate has been given to the Barchester District Land Registry in which the freehold title is registered. A note of the bank's interest is noted in the charges register and the certificate is held by the Bank. Under standing arrangements with the company for such developments, the bank issues a letter of consent for each sale and a formal release of the charge on the building is given when sufficient purchase money is in hand to cover their loan on the particular property.

Messrs. Makepiece have acted for Luxury Flats Limited in the purchase and will act in the granting of the leases. They have the title details they require and when they learn that the flats, now nearing completion, have been placed on the market through Messrs. Sellars, Wright, Quick (here referred to shortly as Sellars), Mr. Amity applies to the Land Registry for two sets of office copy entries of the freehold title for use in the first sales.

The asking price is £58,000 and there is a ground rent of £100 p.a. Notification of sale of the ground floor flat to Miss Burton, whose offer of £57,500 subject to contract, has been accepted by the Company, is sent by Sellars to the parties and their solicitors. She has paid them a preliminary deposit of £250.

Mr. Amity drafts the contract. The draft is a fully prepared typescript, the Standard Conditions of Sale (2nd Edition) 1992 being incorporated by reference. He also drafts the lease which will, when approved in this case, be the standard form of lease for all the flats in the property.

Having received a copy of the Notification from Sellars, Mr. Reason of Messrs. Rime writes to Messrs. Makepiece to confirm that the firm are acting for Miss Burton and to request a draft contract. He despatches his local search form (LLC 1) to the local authority with the enquiries of local authorities form (Conveyancing 29). He directs his search and enquiries to the whole property: it is in any event unlikely that any local authority action would affect less than the whole building or perhaps the area in which it is situated.

In reply to Mr. Reason's letter, Mr. Amity sends him the draft contract and lease, with carbon copies in each case. He encloses a set of office copy entries in the land register and the filed plan, also a copy of the planning permission for the conversion of the building into three flats subject to conditions:
1.   to pave the front garden area to provide off-street parking
2.   to build brick-sided enclosures for the refuse bins of the three flats.

At the same time, to help the buyer's solicitor and save time, he encloses the standard form of Enquiries before Contract with the replies which he has previously agreed with the company (not here reproduced, but see p. 122).

The draft lease is at the same time sent to the company for approval. He asks them to prepare two plans on linen for incorporation in the engrossments of the lease.

On receiving the papers from Mr. Amity, Mr. Reason makes amendments to the lease in red ink, making up the carbon copy lease to agree. He writes to Messrs. Makepiece, thanking them for the courtesy of the additional copies of the drafts. He says the contract is agreed and returns one copy of the amended draft lease for approval. He states that the replies to enquiries are accepted subject to the further enquiries which he poses on a separate typed sheet.

On receiving the contract, draft lease and supplementary enquiries, Mr. Amity further amends the draft lease in green ink. He returns it to Messrs. Rime with replies to the supplementary enquiries (p. 203).

Having received the re-amended draft lease and the replies, Mr. Reason writes accepting the further amendments to the lease. He writes to Miss Burton asking her to come in to sign the contract and to bring in her cheque for the deposit. When she comes in he runs through the clauses of the lease, explaining briefly the significance of the covenants and provisions. He also takes her through the replies to the standard form enquiries (Conveyancing 29) and to the supplementary enquiries. Miss Burton accepts that an undertaking to comply with the conditions to the local planning authority's development consent (question 4) within three months is reasonable, because the paving of the forecourt cannot be started until the internal structural work is complete. She will follow up her complaint of defects in the flat with

SUPPLEMENTARY ENQUIRIES
FLAT 1, 60 CHURCH WALK, BARSET
LUXURY FLATS LTD to BURTON

1.   Please supply copy of the insurance policy

    1.   Herewith

2.   Please confirm that the consent of the Northern Bank plc to the sale will be given and that the land certificate will be lodged at the Land Registry on or before completion and the deposit number notified

    2.   Confirmed

3.   We understand that the conditions imposed by the local authority remain to be carried out. Please confirm that these will be done before the lease is granted

    3.   The Sellers cannot complete this work immediately but will give an undertaking to complete it within 3 months

4.   The buyer has drawn the seller's attention to the defects shown in the enclosed list. These must be rectified before completion

    4.   The list is being passed to the Sellers for their attention

(signed)

R & R

Rime and Reason
Purchaser's Solicitors
5 January 1993

(signed)

M & S

Makepiece and Streiff
Vendors' Solicitors
11 January 1993

the contractors on the site. As Miss Burton is not tied to a particular date for her removal and the lessor company will be pleased with the earliest completion date that can be obtained, he says that he will arrange the completion date as "on or before 28 days from the date of contract" with intention that the remaining stages will proceed as quickly as may be and that the completion date will be arranged accordingly. This is agreed on the telephone with Mr. Amity. Mr. Reason sends off to Messrs. Makepiece the buyer's part of the contract, signed by Miss Burton and his firm's cheque for the deposit.

THIS AGREEMENT is made   the day of   1993
BETWEEN LUXURY FLATS LIMITED whose registered office is at High Cross Barchester in the County of Barsetshire (Hereinafter called "the Lessors") of the one part and Molly Burton of The Royal Hotel Barset in the County of Barsetshire Nurse (Hereinafter called "the Lessee") of the other part.
WHEREBY IT IS AGREED as follows:

1.   IN consideration of the payment of £57,500 the Lessors shall grant and the Lessee shall accept a Lease of ALL THAT ground floor flat known as 60A Church Walk Barset aforesaid as the same is more particularly described in the draft lease (hereinafter called "the Lease") which has been approved by the solicitors to the parties hereto and a copy whereof is annexed to this contract.
2.   THE Lessee will on the signing hereof pay 10 per cent. of the purchase price as a deposit to the Lessors' solicitors which they will hold as stakeholders pending completion when the Lessee will pay the balance of the purchase price by banker's draft drawn on a London clearing bank in favour of the Lessor's solicitors who shall be at liberty to invest the said deposit with a Building Society or Bank in the joint names of the partners of such solicitors.
3.   THE Lease shall be granted and taken up on or before 28 days from the date hereof at the offices of Messrs. Makepiece & Streiff, Bank Chambers, Barset, at which time and place the Lessee shall pay the balance of the said sum of £57,500 credit being given for the said deposit and the Lessee shall thereupon be given vacant possession of the said property.
4.   THE Lessors' title to the said property is registered at H M Land Registry with Freehold Title Absolute and such title shall be deduced in accordance with section 110 of the Land Registration Act 1925.
5.   THE Lessee shall pay the Lessors the sum of £30 as a contribution towards the cost of preparing and engrossing the said Lease and counterpart thereof.
6.   THE Standard Conditions of Sale (1st Edition) shall be deemed to be incorporated in this Agreement so far as the same are applicable to a sale by private treaty and are not inconsistent with the foregoing conditions and the prescribed rate of interest shall be 4 per cent. above the Northern Bank Limited basic lending rate.
7.   THE Lessors hereby affirm and undertake that any leases of flats in No. 60 Church Walk already granted or to be granted before or after the grant of the Lease contain or will contain a covenant by the Lessees to observe covenants stipulations and restrictions in the same terms as the covenants stipulations and restrictions contained in the Lease.
     AS WITNESS the hands of the parties.

H. M. Land Registry

LAND REGISTRATION ACTS 1925–1986

COUNTY: BARSETSHIRE
PARISH OR PLACE: BARSET
TITLE NO: BT 100001

THE PARTIES

THIS LEASE is made the   day of   1993 BETWEEN LUXURY FLATS Ltd. whose registered office is situated at High Cross Barchester in the County of Barsetshire (hereinafter called the Lessor which expression where the context so admits includes the owner or owners for the time being of the reversion expectant hereon) of the one part and MOLLY BURTON of the Royal Hotel Barset in the County of Barsetshire (hereinafter called the Lessee) which expression shall where the context so admits includes her successors in title) of the other part WHEREAS the

RECITAL

Lessor is the owner in fee simple in possession of the property numbered 60 Church Walk Barset aforesaid (hereinafter called the building) now divided into three flats the postal addresses of which are respectively 60A, 60B and 60C Church Walk Barset and has agreed to grant to the Lessee a lease of No. 60A Church Walk aforesaid _____

NOW THIS DEED WITNESSETH as follows:

TESTATUM

1. IN consideration of the sum of FIFTY SEVEN THOUSAND FIVE HUNDRED POUNDS (57,500.00) paid by the Lessee to the Lessor (the receipt whereof the Lessor hereby acknowledges) and of the rents and covenants hereinafter reserved and contained the Lessor demises unto the

PARCELS

Lessee ALL THAT flat known as 60A Church Walk aforesaid and for the purposes of identification only shown edged red on the plan annexed hereto being part of the ground floor of the building and including one half in depth of the joints between the ceilings of the said flat and the floors of that part of the building above it and one half in depth of the joists between the floor of the said flat and that part of the building beneath it ALL WHICH premises are hereinafter referred to as "The Flat" and forms part of the land comprised in the Title registered at HM Land Registry above referred to TOGETHER with the easements rights and privileges set out in the first schedule hereto but EXCEPT and RESERVED the matters set out in the second schedule

HABENDUM

hereto TO HOLD the same unto the Lessee for term of ninety-nine years from the 29th day of September One thousand nine hundred and ninety two PAYING there-

REDDENDUM

fore yearly during the said term the rent of ONE HUNDRED POUNDS (£100) payable in advance by equal half-yearly payments on the 25th day of March and the 29th day of September in each year free of all deductions the first payment thereof being a proportionate part of the said yearly sum calculated from and payable on the execution hereof to the next rent day thereafter AND ALSO PAYING by way of additional rent on demand such sum as shall from time to time be equal to one third of the amount the Lessor may expend annually in effecting or maintaining the insurance of the building under the covenant set out in clause 4(b) hereof _____

LESSEE'S MUTUAL COVENANTS

2. THE Lessee HEREBY COVENANTS with the Lessor and with and for the benefit of the lessees and occupiers from time to time of the other flats comprised in the building (hereinafter called the upper flats) that the Lessee will at all times hereafter observe the restrictions set forth in the First Schedule hereto _____

LESSEE'S COVENANTS

3. THE Lessee <u>HEREBY COVENANTS</u> with the Lessor as follows:

To pay rent

(a) TO pay the said rents at the times and in manner aforesaid _____

To pay outgoings

(b) TO pay all rates taxes assessments charges and outgoings which may at any time during the said term be assessed charged or imposed upon the demised premises or the owner or occupier in respect thereof and one third of any such as may be assessed or charged on the building _____

To repair

(c) TO keep The Flat and all walls drains pipes cables wires and appurtenances thereto other than any such as are included in the covenant of the Lessor under clause 4(e) hereof and the Lessor's fixtures therein in good and tenantable repair and condition and in particular (but without prejudice to the generality of the foregoing) so as to support shelter and protect the parts of the building other than The Flat _____

To contribute to cost of repair of common parts

(d) AT all times during the said term when requested by the Lessor to contribute one third of the expense of maintaining repairing and (so far as the same or any of them are now painted and decorated) painting and decorating the external walls of the building and the foundations of the buildings below the mid depth level of the ground floor joists the roof chimney stacks gutters and drain pipes the drive edged brown on the said plan the gas and water pipes drains and electric cables and wires in under or upon the building and enjoyed by the Lessee in common with the occupiers of the upper flats the main entrance front door hallway stairs and landings of the building and the dustbin housing area shown edged purple on the said plan _____

To decorate interior

(e) IN the year 1999 and in every subsequent seventh year during the said term to paint with two coats of good quality paint and paper all the inside woodwork and other inside parts of The Flat previously painted or papered _____

To permit entry for inspection

(f) TO permit the Lessor and his surveyors or agents with or without workmen and others at all reasonable times on notice to enter into and upon The Flat or any part thereof to view and examine the state and condition thereof and thereupon the Lessor may serve upon the Lessee notice in writing specifying any repairs necessary to be done by her under these covenants and requiring the Lessee to execute the same and if the Lessee shall not within three months after service of such notice proceed diligently with the execution of such repairs then to permit the Lessor to enter upon The Flat and execute such repairs and the cost thereof shall be a debt due to the Lessor from the Lessee and shall be forthwith recoverable by action _____

Not to make alterations

(g) NOT to make any structural alterations or structural additions to The Flat nor to erect any new buildings thereon or remove any of the Lessor's fixtures without the previous consent in writing of the Lessor _____

To pay costs of notices

(h) TO pay all costs charges and expenses (including solicitors' costs and surveyors' fees) incurred by the Lessor for the purpose of or incidental to the preparation and service of any notice under The Law of Property Act 1925 arising out of any breach of covenant on the part of the Lessee herein contained notwithstanding that forfeiture may be avoided otherwise than by relief granted by the court _____

To deliver notices to lessor

(i) FORTHWITH after service upon the Lessee of any notice affecting the demised premises served by any person body or authority (other than the Lessor) to deliver a true copy thereof to the Lessor and if so required by the Lessor to join with the Lessor in making such representations to any such person body or authority concerning any proposals affecting The Flat as the Lessor may consider desirable and to join with the Lessor in any such appeal against any order or direction affecting The Flat as the Lessor may consider desirable _____

To notify transfers   (j) WITHIN one calendar month after such document or instrument as is hereinafter mentioned shall be executed or shall operate or take effect or purport to operate or take effect to give notice to the Lessors or their solicitors of every transfer of this Lease or mortgage or legal charge of this Lease and also every underlease of The Flat for substantially the whole of the unexpired term and every assignment of such underlease and also every probate letters of administration order of court or other instrument effecting or evidencing a devolution of title as regard the said term or any such underlease as aforesaid for the purpose of registration and for such registration to pay to the Lessor or their solicitors a fee of five pounds in respect of each such document or instrument _____

Consent to assignment in last 7 years   (k) DURING the last seven years of the said term not to assign underlet or part with the possession of The Flat or any part thereof or the said fixtures (if any) without the previous consent in writing of the Lessor such consent not to be unreasonably withheld _____

To permit lessor to enter to do repairs   (l) AT all reasonable times during the said term on notice to permit the Lessor and his lessees of the upper flats with workmen and others to enter into and upon the demised premises or any part thereof for the purpose of repairing any adjoining or contiguous premises and for the purpose of making repairing maintaining rebuilding cleansing lighting and keeping in order and good condition all sewers drains pipes cables watercourses gutters wires party structure or other conveniences belonging to serving or used for the same and also for the purpose of laying down maintaining repairing and testing drainage gas and water pipes and electric wires and cables and for similar purposes the Lessor or his lessees (as the case may be) making good all damage occasioned thereby to The Flat _____

To render up in repair   (m) AT the expiration or sooner determination of the said term peaceably to surrender and yield up to the Lessor The Flat together with all additions thereto and all landlords fixtures and fittings (if any) in good tenantable repair and condition _____

LESSOR'S COVENANTS   4. THE Lessor HEREBY COVENANTS with the Lessee as follows:

Quiet enjoyment   (a) THAT the Lessee paying the rents hereby reserved and performing and observing the several covenants conditions and agreements herein contained and on the Lessee's part to be performed and observed shall and may peaceably and quietly hold and enjoy The Flat during the said term without any lawful interruption or disturbance from or by the Lessor or any person or persons rightfully claiming under or in trust for them _____

To insure   (b) THAT the Lessor will at all times during the said term (unless such insurance shall be vitiated by any act or default of the Lessee) insure and keep insured the building against loss or damage by fire storm aircraft flood subsidence and such other risks (if any) as are normally covered by a property owner's comprehensive household policy to the full rebuilding value thereof in some insurance office of repute and whenever required produce to the Lessee the policy or policies of such insurance and the receipt for the last premium for the same and will in the event of the building or any part thereof being damaged or destroyed by any of the risks against which the Lessor shall have insured or is liable to insure hereunder as soon as reasonably practicable lay out the insurance moneys in the repair rebuilding or reinstatement of the building and in case the money received in respect of the said insurance shall be insufficient for this purpose to make good the deficiency out of the Lessor's own money _____

To all lessees to have same restrictions and covenants

(c)   THAT the Lessor will require every person to whom he may hereafter transfer or grant a lease of any flat comprised in the building to covenant to observe the restrictions set forth in the First Schedule hereto and to covenant in terms similar mutatis mutandis to these contained in clause 3 hereof _____

To enforce covenants against other lessees

(d)   THAT (if so required by the Lessee) the Lessor will enforce the covenants similar to those contained in Clause 3 hereof which have been or may be entered into by lessees of the upper flats or either of them on the Lessee indemnifying the Lessor against all costs and expenses in respect of such enforcement and providing such security in respect of costs and expenses as the Lessor may reasonably require _____

To repair common parts

(e)   THAT subject to the payment by the Lessee of the contribution hereinbeforeprovided the Lessor will maintain repair and cleanse those parts of the building and its curtilage and the pipes and other appurtenances referred to in clause 3(d) hereof and (so far as the same are now painted and decorated) not less than once every seven years of the said term to paint and decorate the same in a good and substantial manner _____

PROVISO FOR RE-ENTRY

5.   PROVIDED ALWAYS and it is hereby agreed that if the rents hereby reserved or any part thereof shall be unpaid for twenty one days after becoming payable (whether formally demanded or not) or if any covenant on the part of the Lessee herein contained shall not be performed or observed then and in any such case it shall be lawful for the Lessor at any time thereafter to re-enter upon the demised premises or any part thereof in the name of the whole and thereupon this demise shall absolutely determine but without prejudice to any right or action or remedy of either party in respect of any antecedent breach of any of the covenants on the part of the other or the conditions herein contained _____

CERTIFICATE OF VALUE

6.   IT IS HEREBY CERTIFIED that the transaction hereby effected does not form part of a larger transaction or of a series of transactions in respect of which the amount or value or the aggregate amount or value of the consideration other than rent exceeds the sum of Thirty thousand pounds

TESTIMONIUM

IN WITNESS, etc.

SCHEDULES: LESSEE'S RESTRICTIONS

THE FIRST SCHEDULE above referred to Restrictions to be observed by Lessees

To use as private dwelling only

1.   NOT to use the Flat nor permit the same to be used for any purpose whatsoever other than as a private dwelling house in the occupation of one family nor for any purpose nor in any manner from which a nuisance or annoyance can arise to the occupiers of the upper flats or the neighbourhood nor for any illegal or immoral purpose _____

Not to render insurance void

2.   NOT to do or permit to be done any act or thing which may render void or voidable any policy of insurance on the building or may cause an increased premium to be payable in respect thereof _____

Not to throw out dirt etc.

3.   NOT to throw dirt rubbish rags or other refuse or permit the same to be thrown into the sinks baths lavatories cisterns or waste or soil pipes in The Flat or otherwise cause or permit any obstruction thereto _____

Restriction on
mechanical
reproduction and
music

4. NO piano gramophone wireless loudspeaker or mechanical or other musical instrument of any kind shall be played or used nor shall any singing be practised in The Flat so as to cause annoyance to the occupiers of the upper flats or so as to be audible outside The Flat between the hours of 11 p.m. and 7 a.m. _____

No signboards on
exterior

5. NO name writing drawing signboard plate or placard of any kind shall be put on or in any window on the exterior of The Flat or so as to be visible from outside The Flat _____

No annoyance from
pets

6. NO bird dog or other animal which may cause annoyance to any occupier of the upper flats shall be kept in The Flat _____

EASEMENTS ETC.
GRANTED

Support

THE SECOND SCHEDULE above referred to
Easements rights and privileges included in the Lease

1. THE right of support shelter and protection from other parts of the building _____

Passage of service
supplies

2. THE free and uninterrupted passage of water and soil gas and electricity from and to The Flat through the sewers drains and watercourses cables pipes and wires which now are or may at any time thereafter be in under over or passing through the building or any part thereof _____

Right of entry in other
parts to repair mains,
etc.

3. THE right for the Lessee with servants workmen and others at all reasonable times on notice (except in the case of emergency) to enter into and upon other parts of the building for the purpose of repairing cleansing maintaining or renewing any such sewers drains and watercourses cables pipes and wires causing as little disturbance as possible and making good any damage caused thereby _____

Right of entry in other
parts to repair structure

4. THE right for the Lessee with servants workmen and others at all reasonable times on notice (except in the case of emergency) to enter into and upon other parts of the building for the purpose of repairing maintaining renewing altering or rebuilding The Flat or any part of the building giving subjacent or lateral support shelter or protection to The Flat

Benefit of restrictions
on other lessees

5. THE benefit of the restrictions contained in any transfer and leases to be granted of the upper flats _____

To contribute to cost of
repairs, etc.

6. ALL the above easements rights and privileges are subject to and conditional upon the Lessee contributing and paying as provided in Clause 3 (d) of this Lease _____

Right of way over
entrance and passages

7. FULL right and liberty at all times by day or by night and for all purposes to go pass and repass over and along the drive shown edged brown on the said plan on foot only over the entrance hall stairs and landings of the building _____

Right to use dustbin
area

8. THE right to use the space allocated for the purpose and shown edged purple on the said plan for keeping a dustbin _____

Right to park motor

9. THE right to park one motor car in the drive in the space allocated by the Lessor from time to time _____

EASEMENTS, ETC.
EXCEPTED

Reciprocal to
easements, etc.,
granted

THE THIRD SCHEDULE above referred to
Exceptions and Reservations

There are excepted and reserved to the Lessor and the owners and occupiers of other parts of the building capable of benefiting therefrom and all others authorised by them easements rights and privileges over along and through The Flat equivalent to those set forth in clauses 2, 3 and 4 of the Second Schedule to this Lease.

ATTESTATION

[Not set out in draft documents]

Mr. Amity throughout maintains contact with the managing director of the Company on the revisions in the draft lease and the

outstanding works. He secures the signature of the managing director to the contract and receives with the signed contract the two
plans on linen he has requested for the lease. He now receives in the
post the contract signed by Miss Burton and Messrs. Rime's cheque
for the deposit. The letter requests that the interest of the buyer be
noted on the insurance policy and that confirmation of this be given.
As the contract does not incorporate a receipt for the deposit, it also
requests a separate receipt. In sending on the contract signed by the
managing director, Mr. Amity confirms that the insurance company
have been notified on the telephone to note the interest of the buyer
and will write to confirm. He acknowledges receipt of the contract
and encloses the seller's part by way of exchange and the deposit
receipt. At the same time he sends the approved draft lease and
plans to a firm of law stationers to engross the lease and counterpart.
They are asked to make and supply a carbon copy of each. Mr.
Amity writes to the company to confirm exchange and as a matter of
courtesy writes similarly to Sellars. He writes to inform the bank and
to request the letter consenting to the lease and to ask to have the
land certificate for lodging at the Land Registry. Mr. Reason, on
receipt of the contract, prepares and despatches his requisitions on
title.

Mr. Amity receives the engrossments, one of which is marked
"counterpart." This is sent on to Messrs. Rime for the lessee's
execution, with the replies to requisitions and a completion statement. The replies propose completion by post. At the same time the
engrossment of lease is sent to the company for their seal to be
affixed thereto and to the plan.

Mr. Reason receives the replies to requisitions and the counterpart lease. He writes asking Miss Burton to come in again to execute
the counterpart lease and sign the plan. He requests her to bring in
her cheque for the balance of the purchase money and a sum to cover
the additional amounts included in the completion statement in
respect of ground rent. His letter contains a financial statement with
the figures in Messrs. Makepiece's completion statement, adding a
sum to cover the stamp duty and Land Registry fees and the £30
contribution to the costs of preparing the lease. Miss Burton calls to
report that the faults in the builders' work to the flat have been put
right.

At this time Mr. Reason sends off his application for search in the
Land Register against the flat, using form 94B (search against part of
land in a title) and enclosing a photocopy of the lease plan to identify
the part. Following his interview with Miss Burton, the certificate of
search being satisfactory, he checks on clearance of Miss Burton's
cheque. This enables him to send to Messrs. Makepiece the sealed
counterpart lease which, in his covering letter, he states is delivered
"in escrow." This means that it is not in law delivered as an operative
deed, but is to be held in suspense pending the despatch of the lease
by Messrs. Makepiece. With the counterpart lease he sends his
firm's letter of authority to Sellars to release the deposit.

A banker's draft is enclosed for the purchase money. As this is
capable of being endorsed over to a third party, for safety in transit it

is endorsed "account payee only." The letter also reminds Messrs. Makepiece that Messrs. Rime will require the authority to the Land Registry from the Northern Bank releasing the flat from the notice of intended deposit and the undertaking to comply with the local authority's conditions.

Having received the letter and enclosures, Mr. Amity is able to complete. Both parts of the lease are accordingly dated this day. Having in hand the Land Certificate from the bank, this he lodges through the post by recorded delivery to the Barchester District Land Registry, using cover A15 (documents placed on deposit to await a registration). In a short letter to Sellars he says completion is taking place this day and they are to release the keys to the purchaser. He encloses Messrs. Rime's letter releasing the deposit. He writes to Messrs. Rime acknowledging receipt of their letter and enclosures and sends the lease. He confirms that he has authorised the release of the keys, that he has lodged the Land Certificate with the Land Registry and will notify the deposit number when it is received. He encloses the Bank's letter authorising release of the flat from the notice of intended deposit and Messrs. Makepiece's undertaking "on behalf of our clients" to comply with the local authority's conditions.

As arranged with the bank, the completion money is banked to the credit of the company's account and the bank is asked by letter to acknowledge that this discharges Messrs. Makepiece's undertaking. They report completion to the company, giving the figure of apportioned ground rent included in the completion money. They remind the company that the balance of the agent's account remains to be met after crediting the deposit of £250.

On receipt of the lease Mr. Reason contacts Miss Burton so that she can collect the keys and begin to move in. He writes to confirm the completion of the matter and sends her a copy of the lease and insurance policy for retention. Subject to any wish she may express, he says he will retain the original lease in his strongroom.

The formalities of stamping and registration follow and are similar to those already described in the case of Butler to Burton.

THE LEASE: ENGROSSING AND STAMPING

It has been seen that, whereas on the conveyance, assignment or transfer of the freehold or a lease, the deed of conveyance, etc., is prepared and engrossed by the buyer's solicitor, a new lease is engrossed by the seller's solicitor, who must in any case prepare it. In the above case, Miss Burton agreed to pay a contribution of £30 towards the cost of preparing the document. Where no premium is paid, it is not unusual for the lessee to be required to pay the whole of the lessor's solicitor's costs. The engrossment is in duplicate, as we have seen, and the lease executed by the lessor is exchanged on completion for the counterpart executed by the lessee.

The lease itself is stamped "ad valorem," the assessment being twofold: on the purchase price and on the rent. Where a transaction is given effect to by legal documents in duplicate in this way, both require to be stamped. In many cases they must be produced together at the stamp office. One will be stamped with the appropriate level of duty and the other will have a blue denoting stamp indicating the value of the stamp on the other copy. The duplicate having the denoting stamp will be stamped as a duplicate with a stamp of 50p. In the case of a counterpart lease, however, a denoting stamp is not required. The counterpart may be left with the lessee's solicitors so that both can be stamped together or the counterpart may be submitted for stamping separately by the lessor's solicitor, which is the normal practice.

The Form and Content of the Lease

The following explains the names of the parts of the lease set alongside the clauses of the lease above.

(1) *The parties*

This is as in a conveyance or transfer. The widening of the definitions of lessor/landlord and lessee/tenant to include their respective successors makes it unnecessary to repeat these words in every covenant.

(2) *Recitals*

These are not often needed in a lease, but in an underlease there may be a recital that it is granted with the licence of the superior lessor.

(3) *Testatum*

The operative words, conferring the legal estate. The words "demises" and "leases" are interchangeable. Any capital sum or premium is stated here.

(4) *Parcels*

As in a conveyance, the description must be specific enough for identification. In a lease of a flat or part of a building it is necessary to define the dividing lines of walls and floors. In this case a plan is invariably supplied. Such a lease will also require easements over the non-demised parts of the building and corresponding reservations of easements in favour of other lessees in the building. Whilst the easements and reservations form part of the parcels, the details are usually contained in schedules.

(5) *Habendum*

As a lease is for a term of years, it must be of fixed or ascertainable duration. This does not prevent the fixed term being extended indefinitely so that a lease can be for a specified number of years "and thereafter from year to year." This enables either side to give notice of termination at the end of any year subsequent to the fixed term. The term may commence immediately or in the future (up to a limit of 21 years from the grant). It may be reckoned from a date past, but the liabilities of the parties then operate from the date of the grant.

(6) *Reddendum*

The rent. This must be fixed or ascertainable and nearly always is in money, although rent by services or even goods is possible. The traditional way of expressing a nil rent is a "peppercorn." The parties decide whether rent is payable in advance or arrear. If this is not specified, it is payable in arrear. An annual rent may be made payable half-yearly or in quarterly instalments.

(7) *Lessee's covenants*

In negotiations for a lease the heads of agreement may provide for "the usual covenants." These would certainly include lessee's covenants to pay rent, rates and taxes, to keep in repair and to permit the landlord to enter to inspect. The extent of the repair obligations varies from nothing to everything. In a very short lease the lessor may accept full responsibility, the lessee being responsible only for damage beyond fair wear and tear. In the case of dwellings however the position is affected by statutory obligations on the part of the landlord. In a long lease at a ground rent, the lessee must expect to have the full financial responsibility for repairs and if need be for rebuilding the property. There will usually be covenants to make no structural alterations without consent and to use the premises only for a specified purpose (*e.g.* "as a single dwelling house only"). The lease set out above serves to show how the lessee's obligations can be further extended in a long lease at a ground rent.

(8) *Lessor's covenants*

The covenants of the lessor are fewer. In his case the "usual covenants" would include a covenant for quiet enjoyment which ensures that the lessee's occupation and enjoyment will not be interfered with by the lessor or anyone claiming under him. Unless there is a positive covenant by the lessee to insure, the lessor will covenant to do so. The party who is to insure must, if the other party is to be fully protected, covenant to rebuild if the property is destroyed and to make good any deficit in the insurance money out of his own pocket. In a lease of a flat, as the above case shows, the lessor will undertake that other leases in the building will be to the like effect and with the same lessees' covenants. He will undertake to enforce the lessees' covenants on behalf of another lessee if called on to do so, but at the other lessee's expense.

(9) *Forfeiture*

Leases usually provide for the forfeiture of the lease for non-payment of rent or breach of other covenants. If a landlord seeks to terminate a lease on any ground other than non-payment of rent, he must first serve a notice on the lessee under section 146 of the Law of Property Act 1925 giving notice of the breach complained of and requiring the tenant to make good the breach or pay compensation. The lessee then has the option to comply with the notice in a reasonable time or to apply to the court for relief against forfeiture. The court has a wide discretion to grant relief on such terms as appear reasonable having regard to the circumstances of the parties and the case.

A forfeiture clause may extend to forfeiture in case of bankruptcy and this is particularly necessary to protect the lessor's position in the case of a business premises lease. In a long lease of a dwelling at a ground rent, the clause is not appropriate and a building society will not normally advance money on a property held under a lease containing such a clause. This is because there are restrictions on the mortgagees right to relief against forfeiture and hence the security may be jeopardised.

(10) *Certificate of value*

This is included in all leases granted in return for a capital sum or premium where the amount is less than the sum on which the maximum rate of stamp duty is charged.

(11) *Testimonium*

This clause establishes the character of the document as a deed. It describes the formalities of signing. The formula varies, depending on whether the party executing is an individual or a corporation. If the party executing is a company or other corporation aggregate, the execution is valid if the seal is affixed in the presence of, or attested by, the secretary and a director of the company or member of the governing body of the corporation. If the deed is signed by someone under a power of attorney this will be explained here.

(12) *Attestation*

This is the point at which the parties will sign the Lease and Counterpart as a deed. It is expressly provided in the Law of Property Act 1925 that a mark is sufficient in place of signature. Here also the witnesses add their signatures, names and addresses. If the witness's signature is not easy to read his name should be printed alongside. A transfer of registered land must by law be attested by at least one witness.

ENFRANCHISEMENT

As we have seen, 99 years is the common length of term for a leasehold house or flat where the rent reserved is a ground rent. Many leases are for less, other for longer commonly 999 years. A problem arose in the post-war years when so many of the leases created in the last century expired or "fell in." The owners who or whose families had occupied the property for many years, perhaps for several generations, had no rights comparable with those of a protected tenant under the Rent Acts and were obliged to obtain other accommodation. However, protection similar to that enjoyed by occupiers under weekly, etc., tenancies under the Rent Acts now extends to lessees who are in occupation on the expiry of long leases at a low rent (Landlord and Tenant Act 1954, Part I). More significantly, under the Leasehold Reform Act 1967, such residents may have the right to acquire the freehold of the property: to "enfranchise" the land.

The 1967 Act applies to houses (not generally to flats) and to take advantage of its provisions the leaseholder must have been in residence for upwards of three years. To be within the scope of the Act, the lease must have been of more than 21 years be at a low rent and the rateable value must be within certain prescribed limits.

The requirements relating to rateable values create problems where the relevant rateable value was that on or after April 1, 1990 when domestic rateable values were abolished. Alternative criteria were introduced by the References to Rating (Housing) Regulations 1990 which amend the 1967 Act. For tenancies entered into on or after April 1, 1990 and are as follows:

(1) a "low rent" means not more than £1,000 per annum if the property is in Greater London and £250 per annum if the property is elsewhere;

(2) the term "within certain rateable value limits" is replaced by hypothetical market rent figures which are reached by applying a complex formula incorporating any premium paid and based on the length of the term.

The old rateable values are still the applicable criteria for tenancies entered into before April 1, 1990. The rent under the lease must be a "low rent" which normally means a rent of not more than two thirds of the rateable value. If all these prerequisites apply at the date when the tenant commences his procedure under the Act, the tenant has two rights:

(i) to have a new lease for a term of 50 years plus the unexpired residue of the existing lease on advantageous terms; *or*

(ii) to enfranchise the land, *i.e.* to buy the freehold. The price payable to the landlord depends upon which of the two methods of calculation set out in the 1967 Act is applied:

    (a) Firstly, the price will be the amount which at the date of the notice the property might be expected to realise if sold on the open market by a willing seller with the tenant living there (but not buying or seeking to buy) and assuming that this sale is subject to the tenant's lease, including the 50 years extension he is entitled to.

    (b) Secondly, if the rateable value is above £500, or £1,000 in Greater London or, (where applicable, *i.e.* for tenancies entered into after April 1, 1990) the hypothetical market rent exceeds a certain figure under the formula mentioned on p. 215, different assumptions will apply, *e.g.* the 50 year extension is ignored.

If there is no agreement on price, then one can be determined by the Leasehold Valuation Tribunal with a further appeal possible to the Lands Tribunal. Note that the tenant pays the landlord's legal and surveyor's costs on any enfranchisement.

In either case the leaseholder serves a notice in the prescribed form on the landlord and the latter has two months in which to reply stating whether he is prepared to grant the request. Refusal is possible only in two cases: where he establishes that he intends to demolish the property and redevelop the land and where he requires the property for the occupation of himself or his family.

Where the leaseholder applies for enfranchisement, the landlord may give notice requiring a small deposit of three times the amount of the annual ground rent or £25, whichever is the greater and this sum has to be paid within 14 days of the notice. The landlord may require that the tenant should deduce his title to the lease and may call for evidence by statutory declaration of the tenant's entitlement to exercise the rights conferred by the Act.

The Act regulates the conveyancing procedures necessary for the conveyance of the landlord's estate in the land. There are also provisions to cover the circumstances where the landlord owns adjoining land and reasonably desires to impose restrictions to preserve the amenities of the occupiers of that land.

The procedures on the granting of an extended lease are comparable with those for enfranchisement. Clearly no price is payable other than the rent due under the lease. That rent is calculated initially as a ground rent representing the letting value of the site (excluding any buildings on it) at the commencement of the new lease. In practice most tenants will enfranchise rather than claim an extended lease.

LEASES OF BUSINESS PROPERTY

Leases of factories, shops and other commercial premises are often for relatively short terms of up to 21 years. The rent in these cases will invariably be at the full letting value of the property and there may be no capital sum paid as purchase price. (In the case of leasehold, the purchase price may be referred to as a premium or a fine).

In these circumstances there may be less call to have a contract. The parties and their surveyors negotiate a rent and "heads of agreement" setting out in simple terms the division of responsibility between lessor and lessee for the maintenance, repair and decoration of the building, because of course these responsibilities directly affect the level of the economic rent. Where the lease is for more than seven to 10 years it is likely to be a "full repairing lease," *i.e.* one in which the total burden of maintenance falls on the tenant.

Invariably these days there will be a rent review clause under which the lessor is entitled to re-negotiate the rent during the course of the term, often at five or seven year intervals but possibly even every three years. Somewhat different in its practical effect is the break clause entitling either party to decide to terminate the lease during its term, perhaps at the same points. A break clause may on the other hand give the option to lessor or lessee or to both. Unless the lessor undertakes all the obligations of maintenance and repair, the lessee must at the end of the term leave the premises in a proper state of repair, etc., in conformity with the covenants. After that time the landlord will inspect the property or have it surveyed and draft a schedule of defects which constitute breaches of the lessee's covenants. This is the schedule of dilapidations. The landlord can recover from his former lessee the cost of having the defect remedied. However, the landlord may not profit out of the situation, so he cannot for instance claim dilapidations if he is about to pull the premises down or if for any other reason the restoration of its state is unnecessary. A schedule of dilapidations may be served during the continuance of a term, but this is unusual and there is statutory protection for the lessee against the unreasonable exercise of this power (Leasehold Property (Repairs) Act 1938).

On the other hand a lessee of business premises who carries out improvements during the term which increase the letting value can claim compensation at the end of the lease. To ground a claim he must either have obtained the landlord's concurrence to the proposed works or have obtained a certificate of the court that the improvement is a proper one. This is additional to the statutory compensation referred to below which a lessee may be able to claim when the landlord refuses to grant a renewal of a lease of business premises.

When letting property for business use the lessor must have in mind the lessee's right to claim a new lease at the end of the term. Before this right was conferred by the Landlord and Tenant Act 1954, Part II, the lessee who had worked up substantial goodwill and for whom no alternative location was available could be forced to pay more than the market rental only to preserve what he had created. Even when other suitable and convenient premises could be found, the outlay on removal and adaptation would make the choice between moving and paying an excessive rent a difficult one. Now, when the term of a lease of business premises expires the lessee can stay on, as the lease does not come to an end until the statutory system of notice, counternotice and application to court has been followed through.

The protection applies to any lease or tenancy occupied by the tenant wholly or partly for business purposes other than certain excluded categories (*e.g.* agricultural tenancies, which have their own code of protection). However a fixed term tenancy not exceeding six months is excluded from protection. If the lease period is to be longer a tenant can contract out of his statutory rights, but only if, on a joint application by the parties before the tenancy is granted, the approval of the court is obtained. An order giving approval must be endorsed on the lease or tenancy agreement.

A landlord wishing to terminate a tenancy within the Act's protection must serve what is called a Section 25 Notice on the tenant not less than six or more than 12 months before the expiry of the term or the date on which, according to its terms, it can be terminated. The notice must state whether the landlord is willing to grant a new lease. If he is not, the notice must also state on which of the statutory grounds he relies for his refusal. The tenant has two months to serve a counter-notice claiming a new lease and he must follow this up, on the expiry of the two months but before the expiry of four months from the service of the landlord's notice, by applying to the court for a new lease. If the landlord does not take the initiative in serving notice to terminate the lease, the tenant may himself serve a notice requesting a new lease within the same period as applies to a Section 25 Notice. It is then for the landlord to serve the counter-notice and the tenant must apply to the court more than two months but not more than four months from the landlord's notice.

If a new tenancy is ordered then the court must, in the absence of agreement between the parties, determine its terms. The new lease to be granted by the court will be for not more than 14 years (and often it is for the same duration as the old lease) at the normal market rent, disregarding the special position of the tenant, the goodwill of the business and any improvements carried out by him. The other terms, in the absence of agreement, will normally closely follow the terms of the old lease. Applications can be made by either party to the court to fix an interim rent pending the court's determination. The vital point for a solicitor acting for the tenant in obtaining a new lease is that the notices to be served by him and the application to be made to the court must be served and made within the prescribed periods as there is no provision for extension and failure means loss of the tenant's rights.

If a new lease is not granted the tenant may in certain circumstances where no fault is attached to him be entitled to disturbance compensation of the rateable value of the premises, or twice the rateable value of the premises if the same business has been carried on there for more than 14 years by him and his predecessors in title. The Reader will remember that as from April 1, 1990 there has been a re-rating of commercial property. The Landlord and Tenant Act 1954 (Appropriate Multiplier) Order 1990 contains transitional provisions which will last for 10 years until April, 2000. A tenant eligible for compensation can take either compensation based upon the new rateable value lists or compensation based on the old rateable value lists, this being multiplied by eight. Tenants should be advised of this choice and obviously would be concerned to take the higher figure.

THE NATIONAL HOUSE BUILDING COUNCIL'S SCHEME

The pre-war and post-war decades have seen an almost continuous boom in house building. In the twenties owner-occupation accounted for only a tiny proportion of family houses, but this now covers the majority. Only in the late seventies did the curtailment of capital investment severely reduce the production of new homes for sale. This trend has now been in part reversed and still the building societies mop up a considerable part of national savings and channel them into purchases by newly weds and others with banks and other institutions playing an increasingly active role in the mortgage market.

Amid the expansion of these decades it would be surprising if the building industry did not draw in some operators without either the skills or resources (or both) needed. The purchaser of a new house from a builder or developer has always been vulnerable. Buildings in course of construction have been left unfinished when the builder has absconded or gone bankrupt. Completed houses have developed structural faults not detectable when the house was just occupied.

Parliament took a hand in the early seventies when a law was introduced requiring builders to build dwellings in a workmanlike manner, using proper materials and to ensure that the completed dwelling was fit for habitation (Defective Premises Act 1972). However, there was still the problem of the builder who went bankrupt or disappeared.

After the war the building industry itself, concerned for the good name and standing of the majority of its members, took the initiative in setting up a body able to provide effective remedies for the defenceless purchasers against both bad builders and bad building. The body they set up is now called the National House Building Council and it has upwards of 20,000 builders in registered membership. It is an independent non-profit making body having on the Council representatives from all the national bodies concerned with the product of the industry: the building societies, architects, and surveyors organisations, building firms and trade unions. The building societies will not advance money on mortgage on a new property unless the builder is registered as a member of the Council or the construction is supervised by an architect. The scheme extends to houses, purpose-built flats and maisonettes, and there are separate schemes for other situations such as for flats created by the conversion of existing buildings.

The method by which the benefits are conferred on purchasers has changed somewhat and we shall look at the position as it affects purchasers at the present time under the Buildmark scheme. This scheme is an improved version of the previous NHBC 10 year warranty and applies to all homes registered with the Council after April 1, 1988.

It should first be pointed out that the builder warrants to the purchaser that the home has been built or will be built in accordance with the NHBC's requirements and in an efficient and workmanlike manner and of proper materials and so as to be fit for habitation. The purchaser's rights for breach of these warranties (whether contractual or otherwise under common law or statute) are in addition to any other rights he may have under the Buildmark.

The Buildmark protection is essentially in three stages: Firstly, when the home is being built it provides insurance up to £10,000 to safeguard deposits lost through the Builder's insolvency, or to put right defects which prevent the issue of the 10 year notice. (This notice states that the home appears to have been designed and constructed substantially in accordance with the NHBC's requirements.) Secondly, in the first two years after construction, the Buildmark requires the builder to put right, at his own expense, any defects which arise as a result of his not keeping to NHBC's standards for materials and workmanship. If the builder does not repair the defects, the Buildmark gives the purchaser a right to arbitration and to compensation if the builder is insolvent. Thirdly, in the third to tenth years after construction, the Buildmark insures the purchaser against major damage due to any defect in the load bearing structure. It does not insure ordinary repairs or defects which do not cause major damage.

It is to be noted that under the new scheme, if the first purchaser(s) sells the home before the Buildmark cover ends then the second and subsequent purchasers are insured against new defects which appear for the first time after they bought the home.

The procedure to follow and the documentation involved are different under the new Buildmark. The changes in procedure, etc., can be summarised as follows. The member (who is the developer or house-builder registered with NHBC) sends to NHBC application form HB3 to register the home for inspection and insurance. The NHBC then sends to the member an Offer of Cover Form (BM1), an Acceptance Form (BM2) and the Buildmark Booklet (BM3) in which the member is referred to as the builder. All these documents should be sent by the member to his solicitor (or licensed conveyancer or other authorised person) for onward transmission to the purchaser's solicitor on entering into contracts. After this the purchaser, through his solicitor, should sign the Acceptance Form (BM2) and send it to the NHBC. Receipt of this form will be acknowledged by the issue of the 10 Year Notice (BM4) which will be sent to the purchaser's solicitor in duplicate when the home has been completed. The top copy of the BM4 Notice should be sent to the purchaser to be retained by him along with the Buildmark information booklet. The duplicate copy is to be kept with the title deeds and this will normally involve it being sent to the purchaser's building society or other lending agency. The NHBC will send to the member confirmation that the 10 Year Notice has been issued. Where building control has been carried out by NHBC's wholly owned subsidiary, the NHBC Building Control Services Ltd., the 10 Year Notice is confirmed with the Statutory Final Certificate (BM4/BC) and a separate Final Certificate is sent to the relevant local authority (BM4/LA).

It will be observed that under this new scheme the member/builder has nothing to sign or exchange and there is no house purchaser's agreement as exists under the pre-April 1988 scheme. All the member has to do is send the NHBC documents to his solicitor for handover to the purchaser at exchange of contracts. One further document which may be encountered is the Common Parts Ten Year Notice (BM5) which will be issued in duplicate (and in the same way as the BM4 Notice) when the home is a flat or maisonette. All the documents the purchaser and mortgagee receive under the Scheme should be kept together and passed on to the respective subsequent purchasers and lenders.

LAND REGISTRY PRACTICE

The case examples above will have illustrated many of the more frequently met points in H.M. Land Registry practice. We now take a more general look at this. It will have been noticed that the owner of land with a registered title is called the registered proprietor. A conveyance is referred to as a transfer and a transaction in registered land is a dealing.

The land certificate entries set out in pages 119–121 are reproduced without their stiff covers. Readers who can ask to see an original land or charge certificate should do so. On the front cover will be found a certificate that the land referred to in the entries is registered against the stated title number, which is unique to that property. The certificate bears the impressed seal of the district land registry. The warning against unofficial alterations should be noted: any alterations other than those made by the registry are of no effect. The significance of the land certificate is that it is a certified copy of the entries in the register held at the district registry at a particular date. That date is set out on the inside front cover and is the date on which the certificate was last compared with the register. This is the date from which searches must be made, unless an office copy of the entries of more recent date is in hand.

THE ENTRIES IN THE REGISTER

Turning to the copy entries, we see that the certificate is divided into three separate registers:

A. Property Register

B. Proprietorship Register

C. Charges Register

This makes the use of the word "register" ambiguous, because "the entries in the register" clearly refers to all three component registers. It is also possible to refer to "the land register," meaning the contents of all the separate title registers held in the registry.

It will be noticed that the entries are liberally marked with the registry seal or stamp as a means of authentication.

The property register (A) opens with a description of the land. Essential to the description is the reference to the filed plan. This brings us to the kernel of the land registration system, because it is based on the Ordnance Survey maps, which are possibly unrivalled for their accuracy and completeness. A plan is prepared for each title and the site of the title is edged red. A copy is bound up with the certificate and this makes it possible to reduce the verbal description to the minimum, often the postal street name and number and the address with a reference to the plan.

The property register also contains particulars of any easements, rights or privileges of which the land has the benefit, or to which it is subject. Where the adjoining owner or owners are subject to restrictive covenants for the benefit of the land in the title, a note may be found here to this effect. However, this is not entered automatically but only on specific application. There may also be a reference to the ownership of mines and minerals under the land—other than those that cannot be privately owned. There is no guarantee if the minerals are not referred to that they are included in the title.

In the case of a leasehold title, there will be a note of the parties, term and rent of the lease, exceptions and reservations therefrom and the lessor's title number, if registered. In the register of the lessor's title also there will be a note of the leasehold title. Any provision prohibiting assignment or sub-letting will also appear in the lessee's property register.

The proprietorship register (B) is headed by the category or grade of the title, which varies as between freehold and leasehold. Freehold titles are:

(i) *Title absolute*: equivalent to fee simple absolute and subject only to registered encumbrances and overriding interests, such as unregistered rights of way over the land or other easements. A person who acquires a registered title as a gift, or otherwise without giving value, may also be subject to minor interests. These are mentioned below.

(ii) *Possessory Title*: this does not guarantee the registered proprietor against the possible existence of other valid claims to rights over the land, existing from before registration. A possessory freehold title can be converted to an absolute title by the Registrar, if satisfied as to the title, or if the land has been registered for at least 12 years and the Registrar is satisfied as to the registered proprietor's unchallenged possession for that period (possession includes receipt of rent and profits).

(iii) *Qualified Title*: this is rarely met and is granted when the chief land registrar specifies particular rights to which the land may be subject. Again it can be upgraded in due course.

Leasehold titles are:

(i) *Absolute Leasehold*: equivalent to absolute freehold, available where the freehold and any other superior titles have been deduced or are registered.

(ii) *Good Leasehold*: this is granted where the superior titles are not registered and have not been investigated. It is therefore subject to the rights of the owners of those titles.

(iii) *Possessory Leasehold*: similar to possessory freehold. Application to convert to good leasehold may be made and the Registrar must affect this if satisfied as above with freehold possessory title.

Indeed, apart from the specific examples above, the provisions for upgrading have in general been improved by the Land Registration Act 1986, section 1. This has substituted a new section 77 into the 1925 Act containing the new and simpler rules for conversion. It is now more straightforward to upgrade any of the lower grade categories when change in circumstances justifies this, *e.g.* good leasehold can be converted to absolute leasehold when the superior titles are registered.

The first entry in the proprietorship register is the name, address and date of registration of the proprietor(s). His trade or occupation will be mentioned where this has been given, but this is inessential and is often omitted today. The chief land registrar addresses all notices affecting the title and interests therein to the registered address. This makes it important, particularly when a client is buying for owner-occupation, to complete the box at the top of page 4 of the application cover with his new address at the property. The name and address can be updated at any time after registration if the registered proprietor does not live at the property or ceases to do so, on production of the certificate to the registry.

The price paid is no longer included in the entry, except on request. Previously, when it was inserted automatically, conveyancers sending copy entries to a purchaser's solicitor would snip this out and pass over the snippet on exchange of contracts—a rather unbecoming practice.

Following the personal particulars there follow any entries required to record the interests of third parties that may affect future dealings with the property: cautions, restrictions and inhibitions. These are explained below.

The charges register (C) sets out all incumbrances and their proprietors. The principal example is a mortgage and where there is one, as we have seen, the whole certificate becomes a charge certificate and is issued to the mortgagee. The charges register also details any restrictive covenants to which the land is subject. If extensive, they may be just referred to here and set out on a separate sheet as a schedule.

APPLICATIONS

The land or charge certificate must be lodged at the district registry whenever there is a dealing with the land comprised in a title or any part of it. In addition to normal sales and purchases, grants of new leases and so on, this would cover gifts and transmissions on death or bankruptcy. The certificate is required at the registry for the entry of a restriction or inhibition but not, as we shall see, for the entry of a caution.

When a certificate is lost, application may be made by letter for a new certificate, supported by a statutory declaration explaining the loss. Notice has to be given in the London Gazette and the chief land registrar may require other advertisements. The full cost must be met by the applicant.

The registration of a transaction is, as previously mentioned, either a first registration or a dealing. Fees are paid on a sliding scale relating to the value of the transaction.

The whole of England and Wales is now a compulsory registration area but first registration is not obligatory until a "specified transaction" takes place. By Land Registration Act 1925, section 123 as amended the specified transactions are:

1. The sale of the freehold.

2. The grant of a registrable lease for a term of more than 21 years.

3. The assignment on sale of a registrable lease having more than 21 years to run at the date of the assignment.

It will be appreciated that gifts of land and transmissions on death do not have to be submitted for first registration. Neither do mortgages granted independently of any sale.

Two months are allowed following the completion of a specified transaction for the submission of the application for first registration. Failure to apply within the time renders the deed conveying or transferring the title void as regards the passing of the legal estate. However, the chief land registrar will extend the time, on application with an explanation of the delay and registration will then rectify the position.

The documents for registration, as we have seen, are submitted inside the sheets of the application cover. Three forms of application for first registration of land are published for use by solicitors—namely Form 1B for freehold, 2B for leasehold land on behalf of other than an original lessee and 3B for leasehold land on behalf of an original lessee. The application cover where the purchaser is a company contains a certificate that the company has the necessary power to own the land and that no debentures or debenture stock have been created.

The first registration application is accompanied by:

(i)   the conveyance, lease or other document of title;

(ii) a certified copy;

(iii) all searches, title deeds, abstracts and other documents required to prove the title;

(iv) a schedule in triplicate;

(v)   where a mortgage is granted, the mortgage deed;

(vi) a certified copy;

(vii) the fee.

The application cover contains a certificate for signature by the solicitor certifying that the title has been investigated in the usual way and all proper searches have been made, and that he knows nothing by which the title could be called in question.

As indicated above there are numerous versions of the first registration application form, each of which requires the applicant's solicitor to answer the relevant questions and give the relevant information. It is important, therefore, to use the correct form. Not only is it easier to complete a form that exactly fits the circumstances, but it avoids the delay and needless expense involved when the chief land registrar is obliged to call for additional information.

It is also important on first registration to ensure the accuracy of any plan used on the deed by which the title is transferred. It must be borne in mind that the land registry have to reconcile this plan with the Ordnance Survey map and with the filed plans of any contiguous registered titles. If possible such plans should be to the scale used by the land registry, namely 1:1250.

It is to be emphasised that Land Registration Act 1925, section 123 referred to above only provides machinery for the first registration of hitherto unregistered titles. Once the title has been registered, all subsequent dealings authorised by the Act must be registered whether the transaction constitutes a sale or not—and the legal estate only passes to the buyer or donee once he is registered in place of the seller or donor. Application Form A4 should be used for a transfer of whole, Form A5 for a transfer of part.

The complex position regarding leases was improved by the Land Registration Act 1986 with its concentration on 21 years as the cornerstone in deciding the issue of whether first registration is or is not required. No lease for 21 years or less can be registered. The 1986 Act also permitted the registration of a lease with an absolute prohibition against assignment. However a number of complexities do remain. Firstly, where the lessor's freehold title is registered a new lease of more than 21 years must be registered within the priority period conferred by the buyer's Land Registry Search (30 working days). There is no two months time limit applicable for registration. In addition, the lease should be noted on the Charges register of the title to the reversion. Secondly, if the lessor's freehold title is not registered then a lessee taking a grant of a term of more than 21 years must register that lease. A lessee can ascertain whether his lessor's title is registered from a search of the Public Index Map.

A conveyance of a freehold or grant of a lease pursuant to the right to buy provisions of the Housing Act 1985 is also compulsorily registrable.

RIGHTS OF THIRD PARTIES

The principal exception to the property rights compulsorily registrable is overriding rights. These might be typified by the description used by an authority about one of them as "a jumble of rights." The list (contained principally within the Land Registration Act 1925, section 70(1)) is long and many are so rarely encountered as to be of no practical importance. The following deserve mention:

(i) Legal easements over the land. Examination of a few land certificates will show that often these are found in the property register. Where they appear on the register they are of course protected and are no longer overriding interests. It is nonetheless important when buying land in a registered title to make the necessary inquiries of the vendor and to inspect carefully for signs of any rights there may be, because the absence of a note on the register is no guarantee that such rights do not exist.

(ii) Leases for terms not exceeding 21 years. As we have seen, these are not registrable.

(iii) Rights of persons in actual occupation of the land (or receipt of rents and profits). These include, *e.g.* rights of spouses or others living on the land whose names are not on the legal title but who have acquired an equitable interest by contributing to the purchase price. Such rights will bind future purchasers or mortgagees save in so far as any right or interest is denied on inquiry. Great care must be taken to ensure this does not happen by requiring those persons to join in the transaction or to release their rights. It should be further emphasised that occupation in itself is not an overriding interest but rather is a form of notice of any right which may exist. The right to be protected as overriding must essentially be proprietary in nature and, for example, a non-owing spouse's personal right of occupation under the Matrimonial Homes Act 1983, is not capable of being an overriding interest—but see below under minor interests.

(iv) Rights being acquired by prescription. One example of such rights is the case of the squatter who, when the period within which the owner can bring proceedings for eviction expires without any opposition to his occupation, can assert ownership of the land.

(v) Rights under local land charges unless or until registered or protected on the Register in the prescribed manner.

(vi) In the case of possessory, qualified or good leasehold title, all estates, rights, interests and powers excepted from the effect of registration. This underlines the limited guarantee given by titles which are less than absolute.

Rights of third parties, other than registered incumbrances and overriding rights are minor interests and can be protected by an appropriate note in the register. They do not depend for their existence on registration. Registration, on the other hand, directly affects their enforceability against subsequent registered proprietors. They are often equitable interests but not exclusively so. A purchaser for value takes clear of all minor interests whether or not he has notice of them, unless they are noted on the register. One who receives the title as a gift (a donee) on the other hand takes subject to all minor interests of which he has notice. The note can take one of several forms: notice, caution, inhibition or restriction. Except the caution, all these entries require the return of the land or charge certificate to the district registry and the entries will be amended accordingly. The caution, on the other hand, does not require the co-operation of the registered proprietor or mortgagee and can imply a contentious situation. We now look at these forms of entry.

(1) *Notice*

The registration of a notice is appropriate for any matter which, if the title were not registered, would be protected by the registration of a land charge, *e.g.* an estate contract or restrictive covenant. The entry is made in the charges register and gives notice to all taking the land of its existence. Therefore the transferee takes subject to the matter revealed.

It is also used to note the deposit of the land certificate with another person, usually as security for a loan. In the case of unregistered land, a bank or other lender will advance money against the deposit of the deeds on which they thereby acquire a lien until the money is repaid. In the case of registered land, the deposit of the land certificate is not adequate protection. The lender must ensure that a notice is entered in the charges register.

The statutory charge, protecting rights of occupation under the Matrimonial Homes Act 1983, can no longer be protected by way of a caution, but rather has to be protected by way of a notice. Obviously this means that the rule that a notice will not be accepted unless the Land Certificate is available to the Registrar does not apply to a notice lodged for this purpose.

(2) *Caution*

A notice refers to an established interest. A caution only gives notice of the existence of a claim. The interest may be any such as could be protected by notice on the register. The application does not require the co-operation of the registered proprietor in depositing the land or charge certificate. The application must be supported by a statutory declaration showing that a valid claim or right exists justifying the entry. The effect of registering a caution is that when the registry receives an application to register a dealing with the land, the chief land registrar gives notice to the cautioner allowing a period of up to 14 days in which he must show cause why the dealing should not be registered. An oral hearing may be arranged. If the caution is not disallowed, an appropriate note is entered in the register.

(3) *Restriction*

Unless there is anything on the register to the contrary, anyone dealing with a registered proprietor can assume his powers of disposition are unlimited. This may in fact not be the case and the appropriate way to record this is to enter a restriction. This specifies by its terms the circumstances in which, or the conditions on which, a dealing may be made. For example, land owned by a charity may have a restriction:

"Restriction. No disposition or other dealing is to be registered without the consent of the Charity Commissioners."

The chief land registrar may register a restriction against any disposition before a specified date, where the title has been registered following the loss of the earlier deeds.

It is by means of a restriction that the equitable interests arising under a settlement or trust for sale are normally protected. For example, where two persons who are beneficial tenants in common apply for registration, the survivor will have no power on his own to deal with the property and an appropriate restriction can be entered to reflect this limitation on the power of disposition.

(4) *Inhibition*

This is another form of notice preventing any further dealings with the land until the inhibition is removed. It may be imposed by the chief land registrar or by the court. The only occasion on which an inhibition is likely to be met in practice is where a receiving order is made against a bankrupt. The inhibition then puts a stop on any applications affecting the title until a trustee in bankruptcy is appointed.

THE NATIONAL CONVEYANCING PROTOCOL

The Protocol was introduced during the boom conveyancing time in the late 1980s and its objective was to streamline conveyancing procedures, thus making the buying and selling of houses quicker and easier for clients to understand. The Protocol is not compulsory, but if a solicitor wishes to use the Protocol in a domestic conveyancing transaction, he should at the beginning of the transaction confirm to the other side that he is proposing to proceed under the Protocol, be it in full or in part. Once the solicitor has indicated that the Protocol has been used, then if the solicitor feels it necessary to depart from any standard Protocol procedures, then he must notify the other side of this.

The Protocol is based upon the seller's solicitor obtaining as much information about the property as possible from the title deeds provided, from searches, and from his client. When a buyer is found, the seller's solicitor will send a set "package" to the buyer's solicitor. This package will contain:

(i) A draft contract—it is intended that the Standard Conditions of Sale (Second Edition) 1992 be used. This set of conditions was drafted with the Protocol in mind and is written in plain language which should be easier for a lay client to understand.

(ii) Office copy entries (or photocopies of the land/charge certificate if these are not yet available) where the land is registered. If dealing in unregistered land then a full epitome of title must be supplied.

(iii) A local land charges search and additional enquiries with the local authority together with any usual pre-contract searches for that particular area, *e.g.* a Coal Board search or a Commons registration search. If dealing in unregistered conveyancing, then a Central Land Charges Search against the names of all sellers should be provided.

(iv) An answered Property Information Form. The seller's solicitor should be able to complete this form with the aid of a Protocol questionnaire which will have been filled in by his client.

(v) A completed fixture, fittings and contents form. The solicitor should have given this to the seller initially to complete. This form will then form part of the contract, confirming which items have never existed, will be left at the property or which will be removed upon completion.

(vi) If the property is leasehold, then a copy of the lease is to be provided together with details of insurance, maintenance charges, observance of covenants, etc.

(vii) The seller's anticipated completion date.

(viii) The buyer's solicitor will be asked initially if a 10 per cent deposit is to be paid.

Initially the seller was liable to pay the cost of all searches, but as from October 1, 1990 the protocol has been amended to allow the seller to do the searches but also allowing the seller to charge the buyer for them later. The scheme anticipated the problem of an out of date local search and provides for a search validation scheme, backed by insurance, which will extend the "life" of a search for up to six months. This insurance costs £10 for cover up to £250,000 and £20 for cover up to £500,000 and covers the local land charges search and replies to additional enquiries. Either the seller or the buyer can apply for the insurance.

The Property Information Form is intended to replace the Conveyancing 29 Preliminary Inquiries Form and is set out in non-legal language which it is hoped a lay client will be able to understand. There is no restriction on users of the Protocol raising relevant additional enquiries, in particular those arising out of the office copies or epitome of title which will be supplied. It is intended that title should be investigated prior to exchange of contracts and special condition 2 of the Standards Condition (Second Edition) 1992 provides that the burdens (*i.e.* covenants and conditions, etc.) have been disclosed to the buyer and the buyer will not raise any requisitions upon them after exchange of contracts.

There is no change to the methods of exchanging contracts which may be used. The most appropriate method will be picked by the solicitors concerned. The conveyancing procedure between exchange of contracts and completion is unaffected by the Protocol. If completion is to be by post then the Law Society's Code for Completion will be used, unless the parties agree otherwise.

The Protocol has met with varying degrees of success throughout England and Wales and is by no means universally adopted by solicitors.

Self-Testing Questions

1. What is the difference between a freehold property and a leasehold property?
2. State the nature and advantages of registration of title to land.
3. What is a local land charges search and why is it made?
4. What are enquiries before contract and why are they made?
5. What is meant by exchange of contracts? When can this be done by telephone?
6. What are the requisitions on title and when are they made?
7. What will a mortgage usually contain?
8. What does a conveyance usually contain?
9. How are third party rights in registered land protected?
10. State the usual terms and conditions to be found in a long lease of a house or flat

SPECIMEN INSTRUCTIONS and FILE DATA FORMS

1. SOLICITOR ACTING FOR SELLER

Date:

CLIENT, Full names (including spouse, if co-owner):
        Address:
        Client's Bank: Name: Tel No: Home:
                 Branch: Business:
                 A/C No:

PROPERTY:
PURCHASER(S), Full names:
        Address:

PURCHASER'S SOLICITOR: Tel No:
           Address: Reference:
      ESTATE AGENTS: Tel No:
           Address: Reference:

CONTRACT PRICE (exclusive of Chattels)   £
        Preliminary deposit: £   paid to:
FURNISHINGS/CHATTELS: Price   £
        Description:
SALE: (2) WITH VACANT POSSESSION/SUBJECT TO
        TENANCY(IES)
        (2) AS BENEFICIAL OWNER/TRUSTEE/OTHER
        PARTICULARS OF TENANCY(IES)—if any:
        IF LEASEHOLD,
           Particulars of Lease,

        Term: Commencing: Expiring:
        Rent:
        Insurance; Office:
            Address:
            Policy No:

LOCAL AUTHORITY:
        Address:

Community Charge/Council Tax rate for   199.
WATER AUTHORITY:
        Address:

Water, etc. rate paid to: 198.

MORTGAGE REDEMPTION,
        Building Society/Other Mortgagee: Tel No:
        Branch:
        Roll No: Ref.:
        Amount outstanding:
TITLE DEEDS HELD BY:
        (If registered) Title No:
        District Land Registry:
SUGGESTED COMPLETION DATE:
CLIENT'S SPECIAL INSTRUCTION:

2. SOLICITOR ACTING FOR BUYER

Date:

CLIENT, Full names:
     Address:
     Client's Bank: Name: Tel No: Home:
              Branch: Business:
              A/C No:
     Full names of spouse or other co-purchaser:

PROPERTY:
SELLER(S), Name:
     Address:

SELLER'S SOLICITOR: Tel No:
          Address: Reference:
ESTATE AGENTS: Tel No:
          Address: Reference:

CONTRACT PRICE (exclusive of Chattels)   £
     Preliminary deposit: £   paid to:
FURNISHINGS/CHATTELS: Price   £
     Description:
PURCHASE WITH VACANT POSSESSION/SUBJECT TO TENANCY(IES)

IF LEASEHOLD,
     Particulars of Lease, Term: commencing: expiring:
                  Rent:

LOCAL AUTHORITY:
          Address: Community Charge/Council Tax for   199.

WATER AUTHORITY:
          Address: Water, etc. rate paid to: 199.

MORTGAGE ADVANCE
     Building Society/Lender:
     Branch: Tel No:
                           Reference:

     Survey Report obtained: YES/NO
     Structural Survey: RECEIVED/TO BE OBTAINED/NOT REQUIRED
     Formal Offer Accepted: YES/NO
     Advance: £

     Mortgage by REPAYMENT/ENDOWMENT POLICY/OTHER

     INSURANCE:
          Arrangements to be made on exchange
              Insurance Office:
                   Address:

     SUGGESTED COMPLETION DATE:
     CLIENT'S SPECIAL INSTRUCTIONS:

CHAPTER 6

CRIMINAL PROCEDURE

INTRODUCTION

Criminal and civil procedures now have relatively little in common. The principal differences are:

1. Because the government institutions of law making and enforcement ("the state") are involved, and often the liberty of the subject, matters are arranged so that criminal procedure is very much swifter than civil;

2. Apart from the summons, charge or indictment in which the offence alleged is set out, there is nothing corresponding to the pleadings in a civil case;

3. Laymen (magistrates and jurymen) play an important role in criminal trials. There is no lay participation in the civil process except in the very few remaining cases where a civil jury is used;

4. The rules of evidence regulating what it is proper to bring before the court, are more stringent for criminal proceedings;

5. There are other procedural features whose purpose is to give a special protection to a person accused of a crime.

These differences arise because of the difference of objectives between criminal law and civil law. Civil laws (*e.g.* tort and contract) exist to define rights and wrongs between individuals so that rights may be enforced and wrongs compensated. The state provides the institutions which can decide civil disputes (the civil courts) and these courts have of course been given powers not merely to judge such disputes, but also to enforce their judgments. Most civil cases are brought by individuals to obtain monetary compensation (damages) for wrongs done, although there are other remedies which the courts can employ, for example injunctions, declarations or decrees of specific performance. The state may also pass legislation to regulate the purely civil rights of individuals, and these Acts are usually passed to clarify (or overrule) case-law precedents. There are relatively few such Acts in the fields of tort and contract, where the rights of the parties are mainly determined by case-law.

The main function of the state in the civil field is thus to provide the institutions to decide disputes between parties, and these institutions themselves to a large extent provide the law which defines rights and wrongs in a civil context. Apart from this, however, the organs of law enforcement are entirely passive. They are not concerned with whether individuals commit torts against each other or break their contracts. If I libel you but you do not choose to sue me that is the end of the matter. If I injure you by negligent driving, I can be convicted of driving without due care and attention and can also be sued by you for the tort of negligence. The possibilities of recovering compensation through the criminal courts are very limited and would not be available at all in such a case. Therefore, if you do not yourself sue me in separate civil proceedings the state will do nothing to compensate you for the injury, however serious. Indeed, even if the state imposes a financial penalty on me in the criminal trial, that fine goes to the state and not to you.

Moreover, even where the civil courts make an award of damages in a case, the courts remain passive in that they do not themselves take any steps to enforce the award until the plaintiff himself institutes further procedures for this purpose.

The nature of the criminal law is that it forbids conduct which is anti-social or harmful. Since it is generally impossible to prevent human misconduct in advance, the only machinery available to the state is to punish wrongdoing after the event in the hope that this will be a deterrent to those who might otherwise have embarked upon similar wrongdoing. The effectiveness of this deterrent is increased by the state providing a police force to ensure the more successful detection of crimes, apprehension of offenders, and preparation of successful prosecutions before the courts. The extent to which severity of punishment may also act as a deterrent to wrongdoing is a matter of debate beyond the scope of this chapter, but the criminal law may generally be said to rely for its effectiveness on these two factors operating on the mind of a potential wrongdoer: namely the likelihood of detection and apprehension, and the probability of unpleasant consequences.

The state therefore has an active role in criminal proceedings. As a general rule a victim of crime has little say in whether or not police proceedings are brought against the wrongdoer. Criminal proceedings are usually initiated by the police (see later for notes on commencement of proceedings). The police are given more extensive powers in many respects than private citizens enjoy and consequently, when an individual falls under suspicion of having committed a crime, he may feel that he has the full powers of the state ranged against him in the manpower, technical resources, special powers, and finances of the police. To counterbalance this apparent disadvantage, the law provides a number of substantive rights and procedural features to improve the position of the accused. The most important of these, which will be amplified and illustrated later, include:

1. The fairly generous provision of legal aid to persons lacking means who are accused of offences of any real seriousness;

2. The fact that the prosecution must prove its case "beyond reasonable doubt," *i.e.* to a very demanding standard;

3. The need for the prosecution in a serious case to convince a large majority of a jury of laymen so that at least 10 out of 12 jurors must agree on the accused's guilt;

4. The accused's right not to reply to police questioning and to remain silent throughout criminal proceedings;

5. There is a number of rules designed to exclude, (*i.e.* to prevent the prosecution using) certain kinds of evidence which may unfairly prejudice the trial of the accused. For example, generally evidence of an accused's previous criminal record is not permitted until he has been convicted; this is because it is thought that the laymen (magistrates or jury) who try most criminal cases would not be able to put out of their mind their knowledge that an accused who was say, charged with burglary, had 10 previous convictions for the same offence. Another example, is that a confession statement may not be used unless the prosecution prove that it was obtained in circumstances so that it is entirely reliable (*i.e.* that it was not extracted from the accused by threats or promises); also hearsay statements, *i.e.* reports of statements made by persons not giving evidence before the court—are not permitted;

6. A number of rules designed to protect the accused's position whilst he is in police hands, such as requirements that the police caution him at certain times during questioning; a general right to contact a solicitor and (in principle) to have him present during questioning; rules regulating the conduct of identity parades and so on;

7. The accused having much more extensive rights of appeal than the prosecution.

The impact of these rules of procedure varies with the relative importance of the rule in question. Some rules are so crucial that if there is a breach of them the consequences for the prosecution are fatal. Thus if for example the judge wrongly permits evidence of an accused's criminal record to be given, any conviction will be quashed (and since there is no *general* power to order a re-trial the accused will be released and cannot be charged again with that offence); similarly if the prosecution have improperly obtained a confession statement (*e.g.* by promising an accused bail if he will make a statement) then the statement cannot be used at all. Other rules are less vital so that the consequences of a breach of them are left to the discretion of a judge trying a case. So, if, for example, there has been a breach by the police of the procedural rules relating to the questioning of suspects, it is up to the judge to weigh the importance and to use his discretion as to whether to rule out completely any evidence obtained in breach of the rules or merely to reprimand the police and leave the matter to the jury. To give a concrete example, as we shall see subsequently, an identity parade ought to have eight people as well as the suspect in the line which the witness walks along in an attempt to identify the suspect. If for some reason the police organised such a parade with only seven people in the line, there could be little doubt that the judge would merely reprimand the police. If there were only five people he might leave the matter to the jury, but in directing the jury point out that there were features of the identity parade which made the identification evidence possibly unreliable, but if there were only two others in the parade the judge would almost certainly rule out the identification evidence entirely.

Who may Prosecute?

The general rule is that a prosecution can be commenced by anyone. However there are many exceptions to this rule so that in certain circumstances prosecutions can only be brought by a specified person or body, such as the Attorney General, or a local authority or government department. Because the police now concern themselves with all serious crime, private prosecutions are usually only instituted where the police refuse to become involved, *e.g.* cases of trivial assaults in disputes between neighbours or spouses. Thus in the overwhelming majority of cases prosecutions are commenced by the police. Until 1985 most police forces had a prosecuting solicitor's department which operated on a local basis with a number of local variations in practice. However in 1985 the Prosecution of Offences Act set up the Crown Prosecution Service. This is a national service and is quite independent of the police in funding and organisation. Although the police commence prosecutions, it is always for the Crown Prosecution Service to consider whether it is appropriate to continue with the prosecution once commenced. In this they exercise independent judgment. Thus, if a Crown Prosecutor in charge of actually presenting a case in court concluded that there was little chance of conviction, or that the offence was too trivial to proceed with, or that it was being pursued for improper reasons by the police officer concerned, he could discontinue the prosecution.

Reference Books and Authorities

There is no reference book for criminal procedure with quite the same kind of authority that the Supreme Court Practice and the County Court Practice have in the civil courts. In the magistrates' court the work most in use is Stones' *Justices Manual*, which runs at present to three large volumes and 9,000 pages. This book has an enormous amount of material covering the range of magistrates' jurisdiction, which, apart from criminal cases, extends to matrimonial, licensing, rating and many miscellaneous matters. The book is not very systematically arranged however, and on a practical level an inexperienced practitioner who wanted to know, for instance, in a given situation, what to do next, where to get certain forms, how to complete them, and so on, would have to look elsewhere for assistance.

In the Crown Court the book most often used is Archbold, *Criminal Pleading Evidence and Practice*, presently running to three weighty volumes and more than 3,000 pages and a work of both academic reputation and practical usefulness.

Archbold, which has been the bible of the criminal practitioner for decades is now rivalled by a relatively new publication Blackstone's Criminal Practice which although less weighty in terms of amount of material is an excellent practitioners' manual.

POLICE POWERS AND THE DETECTION OF CRIME

It is obvious that in a civilised society the prevention and detection of crime must have considerable importance. So that these objectives may be achieved it is vital to have an efficient police force and so that that police force can be efficient, it is vital that individual police officers should have greater powers than are available to the rest of the citizens. They must have certain powers of arrest, entry of premises, etc. The problem of defining what powers it is proper for police to have is a very difficult one. It is always vital to attempt to balance the need to give the police certain powers over their fellow citizens, with the rights of those fellow citizens who are law abiding to go about their business without being subjected to what may appear as harassment. We shall now consider some aspects of the powers of the police in connection with the prevention and detection of crime.

Unless the perpetrator of a crime either remains at the scene of the crime, is personally known to the victim or any eye-witness, or gives himself up, then generally some work of detection by the police is called for. Such detective work may involve fingerprinting, blood—or tissue—typing, the tracing and questioning of witnesses, examination of documents, reference to police records, and many other methods. Once the police have some idea as to who may have been responsible for the crime, they may proceed in a number of ways. Experience indicates that the most useful and conclusive kind of information is usually obtained from suspected persons by questioning them away from their home in the unfamiliar surroundings of a police station. Therefore, unless there is so much other evidence that a statement from the suspect is superfluous (and even then the police may wish to question him about other unsolved crimes) the police will generally wish the suspect to come to the police station for questioning.

ARREST

The police have no broad general power to *make* just anyone answer questions *or* attend at a police station. A person who is *required* to "assist police enquiries" cannot be detained for that purpose only. Consequently, if a policeman wishes a suspect to come to a police station he must either persuade him to do so voluntarily, or arrest him under one of the specific powers now to be described.

First, an arrest may be made with the authority of a warrant of arrest issued by a magistrate. The warrant is of course usually obtained by the police themselves on presentation of a written statement of the particulars of the offence alleged, called an "information." A police officer will swear to his belief in the truth of it on oath before a magistrate who will then sign the warrant. The police obtain a warrant from a magistrate either at court or out of court hours at his home. It can be applied for only in the case of an indictable offence (for explanation see later) or an offence punishable by imprisonment, or where the person to be arrested has no settled address.

Secondly, arrest may be made for certain offences without a warrant. This is indeed by far the most common method of arrest now because the police have such wide powers to arrest without a warrant anyway that it is usually superfluous to obtain a warrant. For the purpose of defining powers of arrest, criminal offences are divided into *arrestable* offences and *non-arrestable* offences. An arrestable offence is an offence, or attempt to commit an offence, for which the penalty is fixed by law, (*e.g.* murder, for which the penalty is life imprisonment) or for which the maximum sentence on a first conviction is five years imprisonment or more. In addition, certain other relatively serious offences for which the maximum penalty is less than five years have been màde arrestable offences by the section of the Police and Criminal Evidence Act 1984 which deals with powers of arrest, that is section 24. We shall refer to this Act so frequently hereafter, that it will just be called "the 1984 Act."

In other words, all offences of any seriousness are arrestable. So for example theft is an arrestable offence because the maximum penalty for it is imprisonment for 10 years. This means that *any* instance of theft is arrestable so it is irrelevant that a trivial amount might be involved in any case so that in the end a much smaller penalty than 10 years imprisonment will be imposed by the court. Thus, shoplifting a tube of toothpaste is an arrestable offence despite the fact there is no possibility whatsoever of the person doing it being sentenced to 10 years in prison.

The police have the power to arrest without warrant any person they reasonably suspect of committing, having committed or being about to commit an arrestable offence. (The 1984 Act s.24).

In the cases of offences which are not "arrestable" that is ones for which there is a lower penalty there is normally no power of arrest. Most motoring offences come within this category; however a constable does have a conditional power of arrest in cases if and only if:

   (i) the person refuses to give his name and address

  (ii) he fails to give a satisfactory address for service of a summons

 (iii) the officer has reasonable grounds for believing that arrest is necessary in order to protect a child or other vulnerable person, or to prevent physical injury, loss of or damage to property; or an offence against public decency or unlawful obstruction of the highway.

It is obvious why the police have the power of arrest in such situations. If a person they suspected of a motoring offence simply attempted to get away naturally the police ought to have powers to prevent this (if they would have no other means of tracing the person) even though the eventual charge is not likely to be a very serious one.

Private citizens also have some of the rights of arrest referred to above. Since in the overwhelming majority of cases arrests are made and prosecutions initiated by the police, no attempt will be made to outline differences between the rights of the police and those of private citizens.

PROCEDURE ON ARREST

On arrest a person must be cautioned in the following words: "You do not have to say anything unless you wish to do so but what you say may be given in evidence." In addition, an arrest is unlawful unless at the time, or as soon as is practical thereafter the person is informed of the ground for the arrest and this applies whether or not it is obvious what the ground for the arrest is anyway. This does not mean that a suspect must be told in technical language what the offence is, nor of course does the policeman have to tell the arrested person exactly what section of which statute is the one under which he may eventually be charged, but the circumstances which constitute the offence must be clearly indicated to the person arrested.

For this purpose the kind of cryptic language that one often hears in police TV series (*e.g.* "you're nicked for the Bermondsey blag") would no doubt be sufficient.

AFTER ARREST

Once a person has been arrested the policeman must take him to a "designated police station" as soon as practicable. A "designated police station" means one which has the facilities for the purpose of detaining arrested persons.

AT THE POLICE STATION

On arrival the suspect is handed over to the *custody officer*. A custody officer is a police officer of at least sergeant rank who has various responsibilities at the "designated police station." He must in particular keep a *custody record* which records details of the course of a suspect's detention and interrogation and he is also the person who is formally in charge of arrested persons and has the duty of supervising the detention and interrogation of such persons. The custody officer will if necessary have the right to refuse officers of higher rank a request, *e.g.* where they wish to interview a suspect at excessive length. A custody officer has every incentive to keep a meticulous custody record and to ensure that the law and Codes of Practice relevant to the detention of suspects are scrupulously observed, because if these matters are contested during a criminal trial it is the custody officer who will be called to account for himself.

When the person is brought to the police station after arrest, the custody officer will at that stage decide whether there is sufficient evidence to charge him with the offence for which he was arrested. If there is then he will be charged forthwith. He may then be released on bail or kept in custody until his first appearance before the court and we shall consider this topic shortly.

If there is not sufficient evidence to charge him at this stage then it is likely that the police involved in the case will want to detain the person for questioning or further inquiries. We are now going to consider the powers of the police in relation to the suspect.

SEARCH

(1) *Search of the accused*

A custody officer may order the search of an arrested person if he considers it necessary to ascertain or record property that that person has in his possession when he is brought to the station. The custody officer may order a personal search if he considers it necessary to effect this purpose, so that if he is not satisfied that everything will be found by ordering the suspect to turn out his pockets he may order a strip search. This may be done with reasonable force if the suspect does not co-operate. Intimate body searches however may only be carried out on the authority of an officer of the rank of superintendent or above.

(2) *Search of premises*

Search of premises can be made only by the authority of one of the two following procedures:

   (i) the police may apply to a magistrate for a search warrant and if the magistrate is satisfied that there are reasonable grounds for believing that a "serious arrestable offence" (we shall define this shortly) has been committed and that the evidence in question would be admissible at a trial for that offence and is of substantial value to the investigation and that if an attempt is made to obtain the evidence by consent of the person in whose possession it is without a warrant it will disappear, he may grant a search warrant (1984 Act s.8).

  (ii) Under s.17 of the 1984 Act a constable may without a warrant enter and search any premises for the purpose of arresting a person. When the suspect is actually under arrest, then by s.18 of the 1984 Act a constable may, with the written authority of an officer of inspector rank or above, search the premises for evidence relevant either to that offence or to some other arrestable offence which is connected with or similar to the offence in question. If the arrest has taken place on the premises so that the suspect has not yet been taken to the police station and there is some urgency about the search a constable may search the premises without this prior written authority provided that he reports the matter to an officer of inspector rank or above as soon as practicable after the search.

Where during any lawful search of premises the police seize any articles which they reasonably believe to be evidence of an offence, such articles may be retained provided the police reasonably believe that seizure is necessary to prevent the article's disappearance. Thus, the evidence in question does not have to relate to the specific offence in respect of which they search the premises so long as they act in good faith.

SERIOUS ARRESTABLE OFFENCES

We have already considered that for the purpose of the law of arrest offences fall into two categories namely "arrestable" and 'non-arrestable." However for other purposes, particularly the power of search as we have seen and also for matters relevant to the treatment of suspects during questioning, there is a further sub category of arrestable offences namely "serious arrestable offences." These are prescribed by the 1984 Act, s.116 and fall into two categories:

(i) arrestable offences that are *always* "serious." These include murder, rape, serious sexual offences against children etc.

(ii) arrestable offences that may *sometimes* be "serious." Other arrestable offences are only serious if the offence in question is committed in such a way that it involves certain consequences in particular:

  (a) Serious harm to the security of the state or to public order or
  (b) serious interference with the administration of justice or the investigation of offences or
  (c) the death of or serious injury to any person or
  (d) substantial financial gain or serious financial loss to any person.

In connection with this last category the Act goes on to say that the word "serious" means "serious for the person who suffers it." Accordingly the theft of say £10 from an old age pensioner might well amount to a serious arrestable offence notwithstanding that the amount involved is not great.

TREATMENT OF SUSPECTS DURING DETENTION AND INTERROGATION

We have already noted that if the custody officer thinks there is sufficient ground for charging a person he should be charged straight away. The custody officer will then have to consider whether the person should be released on bail or detained until his first appearance before a court which will usually be the next day. We are going to return to the subject of bail below. We are now however concerned with the situation where the custody officer did not think there was sufficient evidence for a person to be charged and therefore the police will want to detain that person. They may detain him whilst they make other enquiries elsewhere (*e.g.* try to find the stolen goods and see if his fingerprints are on them, or question witnesses), or they may wish to interrogate the suspect. We are now going to consider their powers in relation to detention and interrogation.

There is clearly an imbalance which will exist between a professional interrogator and a suspect. An ordinary individual in the power of the police is in a strange and possibly frightening environment. This imbalance may clearly be greater or lesser pending upon the individual's intelligence, age, personal anxieties, experience of the police and so on. The police questioner, if he believes that he has a person who has committed a crime before him, will hope to hear a confession of guilt. In questioning, the policeman must above all avoid doing anything which improperly induces a confession. For example, he must not threaten the accused with violence, promise that he will give him bail, promise that he will leave the suspect's wife out of enquiries, etc. Moreover the circumstances surrounding the questioning must not be oppressive, *e.g.* the questioning must not be unduly lengthy or persistent without permitting reasonable rest. If the prosecution fail to prove that the confession is "reliable" that it was not obtained improperly, then it must be excluded by the judge and therefore will be of no use to the police. Where a confession is unreliable the judge has no discretion; he must exclude it.

The Police and Criminal Evidence Act 1984 and the Codes issued with that Act now lay down the law on the questioning and treatment of suspects. Where there is a breach of the Act or of these Codes of Practice by the police and a confession has been obtained, it does not *always* follow that the confession will be automatically excluded by the judge. Everything will depend upon whether what was done improperly has affected the *reliability* of the confession. Evidence of serious breaches of the Codes or the statute will however generally lead the court to conclude that the confession may be unreliable.

The most relevant provisions of the 1984 Act and codes of practice as to the treatment of persons in police custody are as follows:

1. Where a person has been arrested and is being held in custody he should be entitled if he so requests to have one person notified of his whereabouts unless in the case of a serious arrestable offence, the police have reason to believe that such notification will lead to interference with evidence, the alerting of other persons suspected, or will hinder the recovery of property concerned (Police and Criminal Evidence Act 1984, s.56).

2. A person held in custody in a police station shall be entitled privately to consult with a solicitor at any time unless there is good reason to refuse it in similar circumstances to those

referred to immediately above. (Police and Criminal Evidence Act 1984, s.58).

3. As soon as a police officer has grounds to believe that a person has committed an offence and in any event when arresting him, he must caution him in the following words:
    "You do not have to say anything unless you wish to do so but what you say may be given in evidence." Such a caution must also be given or repeated at the beginning of each interview.

4. Full records must be kept of all interrogations. Where an interrogation takes place at a designated police station it is now invariably tape recorded. A copy of the full tape must be kept and supplied to the suspect or his legal adviser at the appropriate time. If for any reason an interview has taken place away from the police station, *e.g.* when police call at premises where an offence has just been committed, or perhaps during a conversation in a police car taking a suspect to the police station, a full note must be made of anything relevant said at the time.

5. There must be reasonable provision for rest, food and exercise during interrogation.

6. As soon as the police have enough evidence to charge a suspect they should do so as soon as possible and caution him again and thereafter they should not question him any further except to clarify any ambiguity or to prevent or minimise harm or loss to some other person or where it is in the interests of justice that the person should have the opportunity to comment on further information which has come to light since the charge. Where such questions are to be put, a further caution should also be administered.

PERIODS OF DETENTION

As we have seen, this is subject to the supervision of the custody officer. There is an overriding duty on the police to charge an individual as soon as there is sufficient evidence to justify a charge. Accordingly the custody officer will enquire into this matter frequently. There is of course more than one custody officer at any given police station so that there is always one on duty.

Basically no person may be detained for more than 24 hours from the time at which the arrested person was brought to the police station save where the offence being investigated is a "serious arrestable offence." In the case of "serious arrestable offences" the police have greater powers than they have in the case of other offences. In such cases the total period may only be up to 36 hours however, with the authority of an officer of at least superintendent rank who has reasonable grounds for believing that it is necessary to detain that person without charge, in order to secure or preserve evidence or to obtain such evidence by questioning him. Moreover the investigation must be conducted diligently and expeditiously. If the police then require to detain a person beyond 36 hours, an application must be made to the court on oath for a "warrant of further detention." The magistrates are supposed to enquire properly into this matter and not "rubber stamp" police applications. At such a hearing the person must be presented and has the right to be legally represented. Detention may then be authorised until a total period of 96 hours from the time at which the person first came to the police station.

Reviews must be made of the person's detention. These must occur not later than six hours after the detention was first authorised by the custody officer and thereafter every nine hours to ensure that the reasons which justified detention still apply. The *review officer* is an officer of inspector rank who must not have been directly involved in the investigation (where the arrested person has not been charged) or the custody officer if the person has been charged. If the review officer concludes there is no further proper ground for continued detention then the arrested person must be released.

FINGERPRINTING

A person's fingerprints may be taken only with his consent or if:

1. An officer of at least the rank of superintendent authorises them to be taken, and this officer has reasonable grounds for suspecting the involvement of the person whose fingerprints are to be taken in a criminal offence and for believing that his fingerprints will tend to confirm or disprove his involvement.

2. He has been charged with a recordable offence or informed that he will be reported for such an offence and he has not had his fingerprints taken in the course of the investigation of the offence by the police.

3. He has been convicted of a recordable offence.

(Police and Criminal Evidence Act 1984, s.61.) Reasonable force may be used if necessary.

IDENTIFICATION

The courts now treat evidence of identification very cautiously following a number of well reported cases which focused attention on miscarriages of justice caused by mistaken identification. The most suspect kind of identification evidence is that where a witness briefly glimpses the face of the criminal at the scene of the crime (unless the criminal has been previously known to the witness). Such identification is no longer generally sufficient to secure a conviction unless the prosecution can also bring other evidence to support it. The former practice of showing to a witness police photographs from criminal records of suspects and later simply asking the witness to identify the man in the dock during the trial is now disapproved.

Under section 66 of the Police and Criminal Evidence Act 1984 a Code of Practice for the conduct of identification parades has been issued. Failure to carry out the terms of the Code may not mean that all the evidence of identification will be ruled inadmissible but may lead to the judge warning the jury at the end of the case of the risk that the identification evidence is unreliable. The object of an identification parade is to test the ability of a witness who saw the criminal at the scene of the crime to pick out the person concerned from a group. A suspect cannot be forced to take part in such a parade but if he refuses then at a subsequent trial the judge or magistrates may be told that he refused and of course the witness may then identify the accused in the dock. It is, of course, obviously easier for a witness to do this than to pick one man out of several at an identity parade.

The rules for the conduct of the parade include the provision that the suspect may have a lawyer or friend present; that there should be at least eight other people of similar appearance in the parade; the parade should be conducted by a police officer who is not concerned with the case; the suspect should be able to pick his own position in the line; the witness must be warned that the person concerned may not be in the line at all.

THE CRIMINAL COURTS

The courts which try criminal offences are the magistrates' courts and the Crown Court. The magistrates' courts have lesser powers of punishment and try the less serious offences. They also conduct the preparatory stage of the more serious cases—the committal.

Magistrates, also called justices of the peace, are, for the most part, unpaid laymen, appointed by the Lord Chancellor on the advice of a local committee of magistrates. A magistrate is appointed to act within a particular commission area, usually a county or borough. The magistrates in a particular locality are collectively referred to as "the bench" and this term is also used in referring to the magistrates who are hearing a particular case.

In London and other very large towns the work of the lay bench is partly taken over by professional magistrates called stipendiary magistrates, appointed from among practising barristers and solicitors of experience. The administrative work of the magistrates' court is carried out by the clerk to the justices and his staff. The clerk to the justices is invariably a barrister or solicitor and he and his senior colleagues who sit in court during sessions have a role in advising the lay bench on the law.

The jurisdiction of magistrates is generally limited to the area for which they are commissioned. They will, therefore, issue summonses and try summary offences in respect of crimes committed within the area. There are also special rules in respect of crimes in which several persons are implicated. In the case of indictable offences, they are able to deal with all offenders who are present in the area and appear before them, regardless of where the offence was committed.

Magistrates have a variety of functions of which the trial of summary offences is the principal one. Sitting to try offenders, magistrates sit in benches of two or more. In fact, they usually sit in threes, so that there is never an evenly divided vote. Stipendiary magistrates, on the other hand, sit alone to hear cases.

Magistrates can sit singly to deal with ancillary matters, including remanding a defendant on bail or in custody, issuing a warrant of arrest and acting as examining magistrates in committing a defendant for trial before a jury at the Crown Court (see below).

The magistrates also have jurisdiction in civil matters, particularly in matrimonial matters (to be dealt with in Volume 2), and in various semi-administrative subjects such as licensing and rating.

More than 98 per cent. of all criminal cases are dealt with by the magistrates and in the remaining two per cent. the defendant appears before them to be sent for trial at the Crown Court.

The Crown Court deals with more serious crime and exercises powers of punishment limited only by the law relating to particular offences. In the Crown Court professional judges of three different kinds, Recorder, Circuit Judges, and High Court Judges sit to try cases with a jury of 12 laymen.

COMMENCEMENT OF PROCEEDINGS

In a case where the accused has not been arrested, that is straight-forward motoring offences, etc., the police lay an information before the court. An information is a statement, verbal or in writing which states that on a certain date and at a certain time X committed the offence of which details are given. For summary offences the informa-tion is verbal, but when coupled with an application for a warrant of arrest it must be in writing and verified on oath. When it is in writing a separate information is required for each offence alleged.

The information is laid when it is presented before a justice of the peace or a clerk to the justices. It may not be presented to a sub-ordinate officer of the court. An information may be laid by a police officer or by any other person authorised by the prosecutor.

Unless the accused has already been arrested, the information is laid in his absence and it may be before he has any knowledge that he is to be taken to court. The court must first secure the attendance of the person named to answer the allegation. This is effected by issuing process to call the defendant before the court at a particular date and time. Process consists of either a summons or a warrant of arrest. Warrants have already been dealt with above (p. 237). The summons is used where there is no reason to suppose that the defendant will fail to appear before the court and is the appropriate method for the majority of the less serious offences. The police officer or other person laying an information will usually have the summons ready prepared for the magistrate's signature when he lays it. This usually takes place in court at the start of the day's session, but if need be it can be done in private. Summonses are served by post or sometimes personally on the defendant by the police. When served by post the letter is sent by recorded delivery. A summons delivered at the defendant's usual or last known abode may be left there for him with some other person. Only one offence may be included in a summons. If an accused has been arrested and charged, the charge is read out to him and his response noted. The charge sheet is then passed to the court and becomes the information. The charge sheet will specify the date upon which the person is to appear before the court. If the accused has been kept in custody this is likely to be the next day after the charge. If he has been released on bail it may be some time in the future as in the case of a summons.

In most summary offences the information must be laid within six months of the discovery of the defence (Magistrates' Courts Act 1980, s.127). In certain road traffic offences (including careless driving and speeding), unless the defendant is warned at the time that he may be prosecuted, he must be served with either a summons or a notice of prosecution within 14 days.

We shall now consider a simple prosecution for theft in the magistrates' court.

A PROSECUTION FOR THEFT

Police v. Arthur Brown

A Mr. Arthur Brown has telephoned for an appointment with Messrs. Makepiece, having asked to see someone for advice about a "court case" but declining to be more specific about the nature of the case when fixing the appointment. As his reticence suggests a criminal case, the appointment is made with Mr. White who generally prepares the defence of clients charged with crime.

Arthur Brown proves to be a former client, a young man of 24 who is unemployed. He tells Mr. White that he has been charged at the Barset Police Station with theft of a bicycle and bailed on condition that he appears at the magistrates' court at 10 a.m. on October 26, 1992. He admits taking the bicycle away late in the evening when he had no other way of getting home, but wishes to have legal advice and representation because he has been in trouble with the police before and is afraid of being sent to prison. Before proceeding further to discuss the case itself, Mr. White asks if he needs legal aid. A brief discussion shows that Mr. Brown has about £450 savings and receives £40.00 per week in unemployment benefits. Mr. White therefore completes the Green Form (G.F.I.—see Legal Aid, p. 76) to cover the fees for the initial interview and advice and any preliminary inquiries. As an unmarried man Mr. Brown is not eligible to offset any allowances for dependants against his capital or income. However, both his disposable capital and disposable income are below the lowest figures at which a contribution would be payable. Mr. White is happy to tell him that no money is required of him at this stage and that application will be made to the magistrates' court for legal aid for his defence. For this purpose he completes form LA1, the formal application, and another form, Form 5 giving details of his means. He gives as much detail about his criminal record as he can remember.

The questions on the legal aid form do not all have to be answered by the applicant but the more information he can give the easier it will be for the court to assess whether he should receive legal aid. There is a lengthy questionnaire in the form (not reproduced) which calls for details of the applicable income, capital and expenses. Expenses include the maintenance of dependants, rent, mortgage, other payments for accommodation and expenses in connection with the applicant's employment such as travel to work. Arthur Brown has very little in the way of income as we have seen and only £450 savings and so his answers to the questions are mainly negative. He discloses that he contributes £10 per week to his parents for his keep and he has a few months to pay in respect of a credit payment for stereo equipment. There is no doubt at all in Mr. White's mind that Mr. Brown will qualify on the means test without having to pay any contribution. In order to ensure that the court takes proper notice of the risk of a custodial penalty to Mr. Brown in the light of his past record Mr. White asks Joan, who is assisting him, to get out the old file of papers from when the firm last represented Mr. Brown. She does so and they look through it to extract a full account of Mr. Brown's criminal record. They find that this is not quite as he recalled it in that certain dates are wrong and he has overlooked a shoplifting offence for which he was convicted two years before. Mr. White notes the details accurately, the most important one being that on February 21, 1992 Mr. Brown was convicted by the Barset magistrates' court of the theft of records to the value of £32 and sentenced to three months imprisonment suspended for two years.

Mr. White accordingly completes at the relevant point in the legal aid application form details of this penalty hanging over Mr. Brown's head and also mentions his other previous convictions. The form is then signed by Mr. Brown.

Mr. White then takes a statement from Mr. Brown in longhand:

"Arthur Brown of 23 Railway Cuttings, Barset, born May 3, 1967, is charged with the theft of a bicycle of the value of £80 from James Morrison on September 29, 1992, and is to appear before the Barset Magistrates' Court on October 26, 1992. He states:

On September 29 I had been out in the evening to the 'Newt's Head' a pub in Lambsbury. I had gone there with my friend Robbie Krieger in his old car. The pub is about six miles out of Barset. We were in the pub from 6 p.m. till 10 p.m. and had about two pints to drink each. We then had an argument as a result of which Robbie left the pub and drove off leaving me there. I cannot now remember what the argument was about. I was stranded there because the last bus past the 'Newt's Head' goes at 9.45 p.m., so I faced a long walk home. I had no money for a taxi and it had begun to rain heavily. I had just recovered from a very bad cold and I had no raincoat with

OYEZ Form 1 of the Legal Aid in Criminal and Care Proceedings (General) Regulations 1989

Application for Legal Aid in Criminal Proceedings
Magistrates or Crown Court
(Regulations 11 & 18)

I apply for Legal Aid—

*Cross out whichever does not apply

For the purpose of proceedings before | the | Crown/Magistrates/Juvenile Court*

1. Personal Details (Please use BLOCK letters and BLACK ink)

| (1) Surname. | BROWN | (5) Date of birth. | 3.5.1967. |

(2) Forenames. | ARTHUR

(3) Permanent address. | 23 Railway Cuttings, Barset BB71 9LD

(4) Present address (if different from above).

2. Case Details

(1) Describe briefly what it is you are accused of doing, e.g. "stealing £50 from my employer", "kicking a door causing £50 damage." | Steading a bicycle worth £80

(2) The following other person(s) is/are charged in this case. | N/A

(3) Give reasons why you and the other persons charged in this case, if any, should not be represented by the same solicitor. | N/A

3. Court Proceedings (Complete section 1 or 2 whichever applies)

*Cross out whichever does not apply

(1) I am due to appear before .... | the BARSET | Magistrates/Juvenile Court*
| on October 26 | 19 2 at 10 am/pm*

or

(2) I appeared before.................... | the | Magistrates/Juvenile Court*
| on | 19 at am/pm*

and ☐ I was committed for trial to the Crown Court

(tick whichever applies) ☐ I was convicted and committed for sentence to the Crown Court

☐ I was convicted and/or sentenced and I wish to appeal against | conviction and/or sentence*

[P.T.O.

4. Outstanding Matters

(1) If there are any other outstanding criminal charges or cases against you give details including the court where you are due to appear (only those cases that are not yet concluded)

N/A

5. Your Financial Position *(Tick the box which applies)*

(1) [/] I attach a statement of my means in these proceedings *(details of your income and expenditure)*

(2) [ ] I have already given a statement of my means to the _____ Magistrates Court

and there has been no change in my financial position *(A new statement is required if there has been any change).*

(3) [ ] I am under 16 and attach a statement of my parent's means. If you are unable to provide a statement of their means give their name and address

6. Legal Representation

Note: 1. *If you do not give the name of a solicitor the court will select a solicitor for you.*
2. *You must tell the solicitor that you have named him, unless he has helped you complete this form.*
3. *If you have been charged together with another person or persons, the court may assign a solicitor other than the solicitor of your choice.*

(1) The Solicitor I wish to act for me is.

C Amity

(2) Give the firm's name and address (if known).

Makepiece and Streiff
Bank Chambers
BARSET

7. Signature

I understand that the court may order me to make a contribution to the costs of legal aid, or to pay the whole costs if it considers that I can afford to do so and if I am under 16, may make a similar order with respect to my parents.

Signed [*A. Drum*]   Dated 19 oct 92

8. Reasons for wanting legal aid

* To avoid the possibility of your application being delayed or legal aid being refused because the court does not have enough information about the case, you must complete the rest of this form.
* When deciding whether to grant you legal aid, the court will need to know the reasons why it is in the interests of justice for you to be represented.
* If you need help completing the form, and especially if you have previous convictions, you should see a solicitor. He may be able to advise you free of charge or at a reduced fee.

Please complete pages 3 & 4

Reasons for wanting Legal Aid

Note: If you plead NOT GUILTY neither the information in this form nor in your statement of means will be made available to the members of the court trying your case unless you are convicted or you otherwise consent. If you are acquitted, only the financial information you have given in your statement of means will be given to the court.

(Tick any boxes which apply and give brief details or reasons in the space provided.)

		For court use only
1. I am in real danger of a custodial sentence for the following reasons: *(You should consider seeing a solicitor before answering this question)*	☑ Bad criminal record; apart from the suspended sentence I have other convictions for dishonesty offences.	
2. I am subject to a: suspended or partly suspended prison sentence ☑ conditional discharge .... supervision order .... probation order .... deferment of sentence .... community service order...... care order........................ *(Give details as far as you are able including the nature of offence and when the order was made)*	On February 21 1992 I was sentenced to 3 months imprisonment suspended for 2 years for theft.	
3. I am in real danger of losing my job because: ☐		
4. I am in real danger of suffering serious damage to my reputation because: ☐		
5. I have been advised by a solicitor that a substantial question of law is involved. *(You will need the help of a solicitor to answer this question)* ☐		
6. Witnesses have to be traced and interviewed on my behalf. *(State circumstances)* ☐		

[P.T.O.

Reasons (Continued) *(Tick any boxes which apply and give brief details or reasons in the space provided.)*

		For court use only
7. I shall be unable to follow the court proceedings because: (a) My understanding of English is inadequate. ☐ (b) I suffer from a disability. ☐ *(Give full details)*		
8. The case involves expert cross examination of a prosecution witness. ☐ *(Give brief details)*		
9. The case is a very complex one, for example, mistaken identity. *(You may need the help of a solicitor to answer this question)* ☐		
Any other reasons: ☐ *(Give full particulars)*		

Reasons for Refusal

This section must be completed by the Justices' Clerk if the application is refused because:
(a) It does not appear desirable in the interests of justice, and
(b) The applicant is entitled to apply for legal aid to the area committee.
State briefly the reasons for that decision.

Signed   Justices' Clerk

Date

For court use only

OYEZ The Solicitors' Law Stationery Society Ltd., Oyez House, 7 Spa Road, London SE16 3QQ   6.91 F20187

Criminal 1   5072105
★ ★ ★ ★ ★

me, so I was very worried about my health. On leaving the pub I noticed a bicycle by the side wall had no padlock and chain on. I took it on the spur of the moment and rode it home. I still got soaked. When I got home I was tired and wet and just put the bike in our shed out of the rain and went in to get dry and go to bed. Unfortunately, I forgot all about the bike. I had intended to take it back the next day, I never intended to keep it. A couple of weeks later I remembered the bike being in the shed and got it out. I decided to take it back to the pub and leave it there and I was on my way when I was stopped by P.C. Densmore who knows me from a time before when I was in trouble. It was last Monday, October 12, I was stopped in Springsteen Street. He questioned me about whose the bike was and I told him I had borrowed it from a mate. I was then taken to the Police Station and questioned again. I did not make a written statement. I then admitted it was not my mate's. I told them I had taken it on September 29 from the pub but that I was going to take it back. My account of the events of that evening was as I have told it to you. I was then charged with theft.

I went to Barset Comprehensive School, where I got three 'O' levels. After leaving school in 1983 I worked as a trainee mechanic at Barset Motor Co., and subsequently in two other garages around Barset. I was only out of work twice between jobs, once for two months in 1986 and again for just a week in 1988. In 1988 I got a job in Dylan's Warehouse driving a forklift truck. I worked there for just three years until the first week in August 1992 when the factory and the warehouse closed down making everyone who worked there redundant. I have been looking for work since and have just had an interview. If I get the job I start on November 2nd as a mechanic.

I am an only child and live with my parents. I am engaged to Miss Janis Joplin of 11 Railway Cuttings, Barset. She is a shop assistant and we hope to get married next summer. She knows about this charge and will stand by me.

I have been in trouble before. About three years ago I was convicted of stealing a car with two friends. I got fined. After that I was convicted of the same thing about six months later—I was fined again. I never had a solicitor. About six months ago I was charged with theft of some records after a party. It was all a mistake. I thought my friend had left them behind and was taking them home to look after them. I was represented by Mr. Amity. They did not believe me and I got a suspended sentence of three months. I am very worried about this sentence."

19–10–92

On hearing Mr. Brown's story Mr. White tells him that if he is telling the truth he need not plead guilty to theft. If he honestly intended only to borrow and return the bicycle he is not guilty because he would not have had the necessary intention to permanently deprive its owner of it. He could have been charged with an alternative offence of taking the bicycle without the owner's consent, but he has not been charged with this and therefore the magistrates cannot deal with this alternative possibility, but must convict or acquit him on the charge of theft alone.

Mr. White questions Mr. Brown closely about his story, pointing out that it is not very convincing that he kept the bicycle for two weeks. Mr. Brown insists that he had forgotten about it and was actually taking it back when he was arrested. Mr. White also points out that Springsteen Street where he was arrested is to the South of Barset and the Newt's Head at Lambsbury is in the opposite direction. Mr. Brown says he had to call in at his aunt's house to deliver a message and was then going to cycle to the pub to leave the bicycle outside and catch the bus back. In reply to Mr. White's question, he says his aunt is Mrs. Sophie Brown, a widow, of 49 Springsteen Street. Asked why he was visiting her he said his mother was authorised to draw her pension as she is housebound and he was taking the money to her. Mr. Brown now insists he wishes to plead not guilty. Mr. White questions him further to try to get him to amplify his statement but Mr. Brown's recollection is vague. He says his friend Krieger will not come to court to give evidence, and he insists that he had had only two pints in the four hours and that drink played no part in the offence. Mr. White advises him that he may be more severely dealt with after an unsuccessful not guilty plea than if he had pleaded guilty and shown contrition; and also advises him of his right to a jury trial. Mr. Brown is adamant that he will plead not guilty and wishes to have the magistrates' court deal with the case.

Mr. White therefore forwards the completed Legal Aid Forms LA 1 and 5 (not illustrated) to the Barset Magistrates' Court with a short covering letter. He also writes to Miss Joplin saying he understands that she is willing to come to court to give evidence on behalf of Mr. Brown and requesting her to confirm this.

Mr. White then telephones the police who are prepared to discuss the case informally. They tell him that the evidence will prove Brown's presence in the pub on the night of the theft, his admission that he had taken the bicycle on that night and his possession of it two weeks later. They confirm that Mr. Brown did not make a written statement. (Had he done so they would have had to supply a copy to the defence solicitor). They also confirm that Mr. Brown has no other convictions since the most recent one known to Mr. White. They say that their witnesses will be available for the first hearing on October 26 and that the case can proceed on that day. They are agreeable to summary trial. The prosecution agree to post to Mr. White that day copies of the statements of their witnesses.

On October 21, the magistrates' clerk telephones Mr. White to tell him that legal aid has been granted and that a legal aid order will be sent out to Messrs. Makepiece in the evening post. Mr. White tells the clerk that there will be no application for an adjournment and that the case can proceed on October 26.

Mr. White writes to Mr. Brown telling him that legal aid has been granted and asking him to call in on October 23, to go through his statement. He attends accordingly, and the partner, Mr. Amity, who will represent him in court comes into the room to exchange a word before meeting him at the court. As Miss Joplin has not replied to the letter, Mr. Amity asked whether he is sure she will attend. He replies that she has arranged time off and will come. Mr. Amity also questions his client generally on the allegations, in order to make as sure as he can that Mr. Brown will not create difficulties by changing his plea at the last moment. He learns that Mr. Brown starts work on November 1.

On the morning of October 26, Mr. Brown and Miss Joplin are met by Mr. Amity in the waiting area of the court just before 10 a.m. Mr. Amity goes through Mr. Brown's statement with him and questions Miss Joplin to ascertain the kind of answers he may expect to receive from her when she is in the witness box. He tells her that as she is not a witness in relation to the alleged offence, but only if necessary on the question of mitigation, she may be present in court to hear the case.

Mr. Amity asks Mr. Brown to think carefully about whether he ought to give evidence or not. Mr. Brown has the right not to give evidence if he wishes. Mr. Brown decides that he does wish to testify.

THE HEARING

The case is called after an hour's wait. The charge is read out, but Mr. Brown does not plead at that stage. The prosecution is presented by the Crown Prosecutor, Mr. Hendrix, who tells the bench that the prosecution and the defence consider summary trial appropriate. After very briefly conferring the magistrates agree to deal with the case. Nonetheless the magistrates' chairman still proceeds to explain to the accused his right to trial at the Crown Court and reminds him of the magistrates' powers to commit him to the Crown Court for sentence if they eventually convict him and after obtaining information about his record and character conclude that greater punishment should be imposed than they have the power to order. Brown replies that he consents to summary trial. The charge is repeated and he pleads not guilty.

The Prosecutor then outlines the case to the bench and calls his first witness, James Morrison. Mr. Morrison, called by a policeman, comes into the courtroom, enters the witness box and takes the oath. In evidence he tells the court, in reply to Mr. Hendrix's questions, that he is the owner of the bicycle in question and his unlocked cycle was taken from outside the "Newt's Head" on the evening of September 29, 1992. He arrived at the pub at 8.30 p.m. and went out for his bicycle at 10.00 p.m. He has now had it returned by the police and it is undamaged, although very dirty, giving the impression of considerable use whilst it was missing. He says he does not know Brown by name but has seen him at the "Newt's Head" on many occasions. He was in the pub on the night of September 29 and had already left when he left the bar to get his bike. He confirms that he gave no one permission to take the cycle.

Mr. Amity now has the opportunity to cross-examine Mr. Morrison. The purpose of cross-examination is to shake the credibility of witnesses by pointing to inconsistency or unlikely matters in their evidence, or to obtain admissions of facts helpful to the person represented by the cross-examiner. Here there is nothing in what Mr.

Morrison has said that can possibly be disputed except the inference from the dirty state of the bicycle that it had been in constant use. If this impression is not removed from the magistrates' minds it will obviously be fatal to the claim that Mr. Brown genuinely forgot about the bicycle for two weeks while it was in his shed. So Mr. Amity, politely and in a friendly tone puts the following questions:

Amity:	Mr. Morrison, you say the bicycle was dirty when you got it back?
Morrison:	Yes, very dirty.
Amity:	When had you last cleaned it before it was taken?
Morrison:	I am not sure—perhaps a week before.
Amity:	So it might not have been clean when you lost it?
Morrison:	No—not completely—but certainly not in the state it was when I got it back.
Amity:	And I am sure you remember that on the night it was taken there was very heavy rain?
Morrison:	Yes—I remember—although I only live 200 yards from the pub I got drenched running home after the police had been.
Amity:	And I am sure you would agree that the state of the road surface between Lambsbury and Barset leaves something to be desired?
Morrison:	It certainly does—it's full of potholes and the lorries from Lambsbury quarry are always leaving mud and filth all over the road.
Amity:	So anyone cycling on a night like September 29 from Lamsbury to Barset might well have got a bicycle very dirty indeed?
Morrison:	I would not be surprised . . . yes I suppose so.
Amity:	Thank you.

Mr. Amity has got as much favourable response from Mr. Morrison as it was possible to get, and there was no point in asking anything else.

The next witness is P.C. Densmore. He tells the court that he had been involved in answering the call to the "Newt's Head" on the night of the theft when he took particulars of the incident and the bike from Mr. Morrison. A fortnight later on October 12, he had seen the accused riding a bicycle answering to the description given by Mr. Morrison on Springsteen Street and had stopped him. (In truth, as Mr. Amity well knows, P.C. Densmore also stopped Mr. Brown partly because he knew him to have a previous criminal record but the policeman is not allowed to tell the magistrates this as they are not allowed to hear any evidence which might tend to show that he was known to the police and therefore had a criminal record).

The P.C. says that after first saying the bicycle was his mate's, Mr. Brown admitted taking it as alleged to get home with. He said "I am sorry—I meant to take it back. In fact, I am on my way there now." He did not believe his story, because Springsteen Street is not on the way to Lambsbury from his home in Railway Cuttings. He was arrested, refused to make a written statement, and was then charged and released on bail.

Mr. Amity must, if he can, show that his client's story that he was on an errand to his aunt before making for the "Newt's Head" could be true. He therefore rises to cross-examine the witness:

Amity:	Constable, you have stated that as soon as you questioned the defendant he said it was his intention to take the bicycle back to where he had taken it from.
Densmore:	Yes.
Amity:	Did you question him about this?
Densmore:	No.
Amity:	Why?
Densmore:	If he had really been going to Lambsbury, he would not have been in Springsteen Street.
Amity:	Did you know he has an aunt who lives at 49 Springsteen Street?
Densmore:	No.
Amity:	But when you stopped him he was cycling towards that house.
Densmore:	Yes.
Amity:	Would you be surprised to know that the defendant was in the act of delivering pension monies to his aunt Mrs. Sophie Brown at 49 Springsteen Street, for his mother?
Densmore:	I suppose it is possible.
Amity:	Do you not think you should have discovered this for yourself?
Densmore:	No doubt I could have asked but it would not have changed my view that he was not intending to go to Lambsbury on that day.
Amity:	To put it at its lowest there is no evidence to contradict that he had intention.
Densmore:	Well, he had already had the bike a fortnight.

Mr. Hendrix then tells the magistrates that the prosecution case is closed.

Mr. Amity rises and tells the magistrates that he wishes to make a submission that there is no case to answer. This is made when the defence contend that the accused should be acquitted without having to risk calling evidence himself because either,

(1) The evidence for the prosecution is so weak or has been so shaken by cross-examination that no reasonable man could convict, or

(2) The prosecution have failed to establish some essential ingredient of the offence alleged.

Here Mr. Amity submits that the prosecution have failed to prove an intention permanently to deprive the owner of the bicycle of it and contends that no evidence has been brought of any such intention, merely of the fact of possession by Mr. Brown.

Mr. Hendrix has a right to reply to this submission and says to the magistrate that since actual intention is a matter known only to the accused the court is entitled to act on a reasonable inference as to what this intention might be, drawn from the obvious facts, and that this is sufficient evidence of intention.

The magistrates retire to their room to deliberate, and return to say that they reject the submission. They are not obliged to give reasons and they do not do so. Mr. Amity opens the defence by calling Mr. Brown. He appears unconvincing. When cross-examined by the prosecuting solicitor he gives no convincing explanation of the two weeks between the taking of the bicycle and his arrest. At the end of the evidence Mr. Amity is entitled to a closing speech and again submits that as there must be reasonable doubt that Brown had the intention to steal, such doubt must be resolved in favour of the accused, and that the prosecution have failed to prove the case beyond reasonable doubt.

The magistrates retire and call their clerk in to advise them briefly on the law as to intention in theft. He returns to court whilst they consider their verdict. Shortly after they return and announce that they find the case proved. Mr. Brown's criminal record is then read out to the magistrates by the prosecution and Mr. Amity is invited to address them.

His main anxiety is to keep his client out of prison. He asks the bench to take a lenient view, to see the offence as spur of the moment foolishness rather than premeditated dishonesty; to take account of his good work record; his having just obtained a job; his recent engagement which ought to be a stablising factor. He calls Miss Joplin to give evidence that she will stand by him.

The magistrates retire again to consider sentence. They return after some minutes and announce that they propose not to implement the suspended sentence because the property was recovered undamaged, and to give Brown one last chance. They fine him £150 and order him to pay a contribution of £25 towards the costs of the prosecution. Mr. Amity briefly discusses this with him and advises him to make a reasonable offer to pay this sum weekly. Mr. Brown says that he could pay £10 per week, with some difficulty, from next week when he starts work.

Mr. Amity applies on his client's behalf for time to pay the total of £175 and offers £10 per week. The magistrates accept this and order him to pay at that rate. They also remind him that the original suspended sentence remains in effect until the two-year period has expired.

Outside Mr. Amity advises his client more fully concerning the former suspended sentence. Mr. Brown asks him whether it is possible to appeal. Mr. Amity tells him that appeal to the Crown Court is possible, against either conviction or sentence, or both. Mr. Amity also tells him that an appeal to the High Court is sometimes possible but only on a point of law, and that no point of law arises in the present case.

An appeal to the Crown Court, however, can be put in motion by giving written notice of appeal, within 21 days of sentence being passed, to both prosecution and the magistrates' court. The appeal would then be a complete re-hearing of the evidence before a Crown Court judge (sitting without a jury in this case).

Mr. Amity advises strongly against an appeal however. He has formed the impression that his client is an unconvincing witness—and he warns him of the risk of a heavier sentence including the possibility of immediate imprisonment and a greatly increased order that he contribute to the costs of his legal aid. He insists that Mr. Brown goes away to think things over for at least a week and then makes an appointment with him to discuss it further if he wishes to consider appeal.

On return to the office Mr. Amity makes an immediate file note of the time spent at court including travelling time, waiting time, time spent on interviews and discussions with the prosecution; hearing time in court; and time spent on advising Mr. Brown about appeal afterwards. He then passes the file back to Mr. White to complete the Legal Aid form on which a claim for costs is made.

Mr. White fills in the legal aid claim form with details of the time spent on the case and forwards it in duplicate with a copy of the Legal Aid Order and a copy of Mr. Brown's statement to the Legal Aid area office. Payment is claimed for on the basis of time spent with a certain hourly rate being appropriate for time spent in advocacy in court and a slightly lower rate for time spent interviewing with a lower rate still for time spent travelling to court or waiting. A set rate of payment is also prescribed for letter writing and telephone calls. He also completes the reverse of the "Green Form" with his claim for the costs before full Legal Aid was granted and forwards this to the Area Office along with several other Green Forms from other matters. Costs are claimed on a time basis as in full Legal Aid.

THE CLASSIFICATION OF CRIME

The Magistrates' Court Act 1980, amending the Criminal Law Act 1977, classifies crime for procedural purposes into three categories:

1. There are those triable only *summarily, i.e.* before the magistrates' court, basically because their relatively trivial nature would not merit the time and expense of a jury trial. These include most driving offences, minor assaults on policemen and offences of criminal damage where the value of the damage is less than £2,000 (as specified in Schedule 2 to the Act).

2. There are those triable only on *indictment*, that is, only by the Crown Court. These include all serious offences such as murder, rape and robbery.

3. There are offences triable *"either way," i.e.* either summarily or on indictment. These include offences which may be either more or less serious depending on the amount of property involved, the degree of violence, or other surrounding circumstances. They include such offences as theft, bigamy, certain burglaries, certain forgeries, and certain sexual offences. These are contained in Schedule 1 of the Act, although unfortunately not all such offences are included there because some offences have been made specifically triable "either way" by the Act creating them.

MODE OF TRIAL

Where a case which is triable *only summarily* or *only on indictment* comes before magistrates there is no difficulty. In the former case the magistrates will proceed to try the case, and in the latter they will hold a preliminary hearing (called a *committal,* see later). Where however the offence is one triable "either way" there must first be an investigation and decision as to the mode of trial. The practice of the courts varies as to when this may take place. It sometimes happens at the very first appearance of the accused before the court but more commonly will happen at an adjourned hearing. The defendant is entitled to a considerable amount of knowledge about the substance of the prosecution's case before this hearing. The 1985 Magistrates' Courts (Advance Information) Rules provide that before the mode of the trial hearing the defendant may request that the prosecution furnishes him with advance information consisting of a copy or summary of every written statement which contains information as to facts and matters which the prosecution wish to adduce in evidence. In other words, the defendant is entitled to have sight of the witness statements for the prosecution or a summary of those statements. This will assist him in deciding how he wishes to conduct his case. The court must ascertain before proceeding with the mode of trial hearing that the defendant has been given this information. As we saw in *Police* v. *Brown* the mode of trial hearing was dealt with very shortly because it was a relatively trivial offence and there was prior agreement between the prosecution and the accused. The procedure has two stages. After the court has satisfied itself that the advance disclosure rules have been complied with, the charge is read out to the defendant, who is not required to plead guilty or not guilty at that stage. Then, both prosecution and defence are invited in turn to make representations as to which mode of trial they prefer. The magistrates then make an initial decision as to the more suitable mode of trial having regard to the nature of the case, its seriousness, their sentencing power and any other relevant circumstances.

One thing that the magistrates cannot take into account is the past record of the accused, indeed they do not know this at this stage. If they decide that he must be sent for trial by the Crown Court, that decision is final. They will then, either straightaway or at some later date, go on with committal proceedings.

If, however, they feel that trial before themselves is more appropriate, *e.g.* if the amount stolen is small, or an assault is relatively trivial, they then announce that decision, but there is a further stage. The chairman of the magistrates, after telling the accused of the decision, must ask if he consents to summary trial and caution him as to his rights by explaining in simple language that he may refuse to be tried by magistrates and can opt for jury trial, and that, if he does consent to magistrates' court trial and is found guilty, the magistrates may still send him to the Crown Court for *sentence* if after obtaining information about his character (*i.e.* his criminal record) the magistrates consider that he should receive greater punishment than they have power to inflict.

It may be wondered why then, if the accused has, as it were, the right to overrule the magistrates' decision and choose jury trial, does the preliminary stage exist? The answer is that this procedure was designed to make an accused think seriously about the consequences of choosing jury trial. Before 1977 there was no preliminary stage at which the magistrates could express their own opinion as to the most suitable mode of trial in the case of offences triable either way, or "hybrid offences," as they were then known. Now, if the accused overrules a magistrates' decision and insists on a jury trial, say in a trivial shoplifting case, causing a great deal of the higher court's time to be spent and a lot of extra legal expense, then if at the end of the case he is convicted the Crown Court may well make an order for costs against him that reflects its opinion of the waste of time and money.

It should finally be noted that where a prosecution for an offence triable either way is begun by the Attorney-General or the Director of Public Prosecutions they may insist on trial before the Crown Court and the magistrates have no say in the matter.

SUMMARY TRIAL—THE PLEA OF GUILTY

Except where mode of trial inquiry is held or the accused is in custody, summary trial usually comes about after the service of a summons on the accused either personally, or by post to, or delivery to someone at, his usual or last known place of abode.

The defendant having entered the box provided for the accused, the clerk reads the charge out to him and he is asked how he pleads. To be accepted, a plea of guilty must be unequivocal. If there is any doubt as to what the plea is, the court must enter it as a plea of not guilty. If, for example in the case of the *Police* v. *Brown* above, Arthur Brown had not been legally represented and had attended court, pleaded guilty, but when asked if he had anything to say before sentence had said that he had intended to return the bicycle, then because that is not just a mitigating circumstance, but would, if believed, be a complete defence to a charge of theft (as Mr. White in fact advised him) the court should have refused the plea of guilty and entered a not guilty plea.

If the defendant pleads guilty, the prosecution read a short statement of the facts of the offence and the court then invites the defendant or, if he is represented, his advocate to address the court in mitigation. A plea in mitigation, as before briefly mentioned, is an attempt to persuade the court to view the offence itself as less serious than it may appear, or to treat the offender more leniently because of some personal circumstances which either contributed to his having committed the offence, or which may indicate that he has the potential to reform, or has reformed, since the offence. No list of such factors could be exhaustive, but matters which frequently recur in pleas in mitigation are an account of the defendant's home background, good character, service record, details of any particular temporary stress which may have led to the offence, such as illness or unemployment, hardship to any third party, *e.g.* to a child if its mother is imprisoned, other non-judicial penalty already imposed—*e.g.* dismissal from work, and so on.

On consideration of the plea in mitigation the court hears any evidence which the defence wish to give, for which purpose it may adjourn the case, sometimes for some weeks. If, for example, the court itself wishes to obtain more information about the defendant it may ask the probation service to prepare a report, called a Social Enquiry Report, on the defendant. The court will then pass sentence.

PLEADING GUILTY BY POST

The Magistrates' Court Act 1980 (s.12) provides that where a summary offence is involved which is punishable with not more than three months' imprisonment, the prosecution may serve upon the defendant a statement of facts alleged and of the procedure for dealing with the case in his absence. The defendant may notify his plea of guilty by post and set out either in letter form, or on the form provided, anything he wishes to say in mitigation. The court will at the hearing only permit the prosecution to read out the same statement of facts which was served on the defendant, and will then consider what the defendant has written, before sentencing him in his absence. This procedure is appropriate only in the case of minor crime such as the less serious driving offences. If the court wishes to disqualify the defendant or sentence him to imprisonment then he must be brought before it at an adjourned hearing. A defendant may change his mind and attend court and plead not guilty even where he has written in notifying a guilty plea. This procedure is only available to a defendant if it is offered by the prosecution. A defendant may not insist on this procedure.

TRIAL OF A NOT GUILTY PLEA

The Crown Prosecutor—or in a private prosecution usually the victim of the alleged offence, or his solicitor—will make an opening speech, outlining the facts, legal matters—for example describing the ingredients of the offence alleged—and also referring to the evidence by which he hopes to prove the facts.

All witnesses remain outside court until they give evidence in a criminal case. The prosecutor then calls his witnesses, that is those witnesses whose evidence he hopes will be helpful to his case, and they give that evidence on oath. Each witness is examined by him in chief, that is, he presents his evidence, which the advocate expects will be in accordance with his statement to the police. Knowing the answers he may expect, the advocate is in danger of putting a question in a way that suggests and invites that answer. This is to ask a *leading question* and is not allowed. There are, however, two circumstances in which this rule is relaxed: (i) In matters which are not in dispute, to save the time of the court, it may be agreed between the respective advocates that the witness may be "led"; (ii) When a witness is difficult and obstructive, the court may agree that he be dealt with as a *hostile* witness, and then leading questions may be put.

There is another important rule: the Crown prosecutor must not refer to any discrepancy between what the witness says on oath in the witness box and what he has down in his statement. The statement itself is not put before the court. If the witness does not say what is in his statement (*i.e.* he cannot remember or is unintelligent), it is said that the witness does not "come up to proof," *i.e.* answer consistently with his proof of evidence. In such a case where the prosecutor (and the same rule applies to the defence lawyer) is faced with an unhelpful witness there is very little that can be done about it.

At the close of the examination in chief, the witness is cross-examined by the defendant or his advocate. Cross-examination is intended either to elicit further information helpful to the defendant or to shake the credibility of the witness. This can be done by showing that he is untruthful, mistaken, confused, forgetful, or that what he says is inconsistent with other things he has said or with what other witnesses have said or with some established fact. The rule on leading questions does not apply to cross examination.

In particular the person cross-examining is obliged to put to a witness any different version of the facts which the witnesses to be called by the cross-examiner will give, so that the witness may have the opportunity of commenting on them.

After cross-examination the prosecutor may re-examine, that is to ask further questions of the witness, but only to clarify matters arising in cross-examination, and not so as to introduce new matters. Each prosecution witness is thus called in turn and when the last has been called the prosecution case closes.

The defence can then, as we saw in the case of *Police* v. *Brown*, make a submission that there is no case to answer if the evidence is weak or has been so shaken by cross-examination as to lack credibility, or if the prosecution have failed to prove some crucial element in the offence. As the submission that there is no case to answer raises a matter of law, the prosecutor has the right to reply. If this submission is not made, or if it is rejected, it is then for the defence to present their case.

The defence will call the defendant and any other witnesses. It must be remembered that the defendant is not obliged to give evidence at all. The defendant, if he gives evidence, and any other witnesses are then in turn subjected to cross-examination by the prosecution and may be re-examined by the defence. At the close of the defence evidence, on rare occasions the prosecution, having been met with evidence it could not have anticipated, asks the leave of the court to call a witness to give evidence in rebuttal.

When all the evidence has been presented the defence advocate addresses the court. At this time he wants to persuade the bench that the evidence against his client is insufficient to justify conviction. Or he may argue that the prosecution have not proved all the ingredients of the offence in law. In the latter event, the prosecution advocate will reply to the points of law raised. Subject to this, the prosecution in the magistrates' court do not have the right to make a closing speech. The order of speeches in a Crown Court case is rather different, as we shall see.

The bench then give judgment. For this purpose, they may or may not retire to deliberate. If they retire, their clerk stays in court as he can only be called in to advise if a question of law arises. The decision is by a majority and if there are only two magistrates and they are evenly divided a new trial must be ordered before different magistrates.

If the court decides that the defendant is not guilty there will then usually be an application by the defence in relation to costs, either that they be paid by the prosecution or from Central Funds. Where the defendant has received legal aid the contribution which he will have to pay the costs of his representation will have been fixed at the outset. In a case where he has been acquitted the magistrates will then usually order that he should have his contribution remitted to him so that he does not bear any financial liability in respect of the case. If the defendant is found guilty they will call for details of his criminal record and then hear what his advocate has to say in mitigation. They will then, usually, again consult their clerk as to any matter of law arising in connection with sentence, and will then announce sentence. After sentence they will then consider any defence application for time to pay a fine or application by the prosecutor for costs.

Where the defence announce an intention to appeal, they may ask that the defendant be given bail pending appeal if he has been sentenced to imprisonment, or that he should be permitted to keep his driving licence pending appeal if they have disqualified him from driving.

Under the Powers of Criminal Courts Act 1973, s.35, a court may order a person to pay compensation for personal injury, loss or damage to the victim. The defendant's conviction may, therefore, be followed by an application for compensation. However even if no application is made by the victim the court now has a duty to consider compensation.

A CASE TRIABLE EITHER WAY

Regina v. *Black*

Mr. Amity is consulted by Mrs. Penny Black, the wife of Peter Black, M.A., J.P., headmaster of Barchester School, who is an established client of the firm. She has been charged with the theft of a sweater from Harridges Ltd., a department store in Barchester. Mr. Amity prepares an attendance note:

MAKEPIECE & STREIFF

Attendance Note

INTERVIEW   DATE: Jan 29, 1993
WITH: Mr. and Mrs. P. Black   OF: 20 Meadow Close
                                                        Barset.
TAKEN BY: C.A.   TIME: 10.45–12.15

Mrs. Black says she was in Harridges store, Barchester, Jan 28, in the course of a shopping expedition. Nothing particular in mind. Window shopping. About 11.30 a.m. Looking around the ladies' clothes she saw a red sweater. Decided to look at it, possibly try it on. She had the money to buy. Also had bank, etc. cards. As she picked it up to look at the pattern and ticket her attention was taken by the wail of a siren. She looked up to see the flashing light of a police car passing the shop. She walked over to the shop entrance and looked out. There was a small knot of people up the street. Possibly 100 yards up. Left. Had given no more thought to the sweater. Left the shop intending to have a look and walked in direction of crowd. Had not walked many yards when she was tapped on shoulder by a woman who pointed to the sweater in her shopping bag. Were other goods in bag. Bag was open at top. Sweater was lying on top. The person who stopped her said she was the store detective. Mrs. Black felt awful and "just crumpled." She felt her knees give. Store detective helped her back to store. Given a chair and tea. Taken to office. There she was spoken to by the detective and a man. Understood he was the store manager.

Mrs. Black says she was too upset to give a coherent explanation. Asked several times to be allowed to speak to her husband. This was not allowed. The detective rang the police. She had to wait until a policewoman arrived. The detective told the policewoman she had seen Mrs. Black acting in a suspicious way. This was not true. The detective said Mrs. Black had put the sweater in the basket very quickly and walked briskly to the door and went out. Mrs. Black insists she did nothing in a hasty way. She heard the police car and walked over to the entrance where she paused to look. Only went out to see what had happened.

Has no witnesses. Was on her own. Does not know what the incident in the street was.

She was so upset she cannot remember much of what she told the manager and detective. She does not recall mentioning the police car.

"Mrs. Black was taken to the police station where she was asked to make a statement. Declined saying she wanted her husband to be called. Charged with theft. Bailed without condition to appear at Barchester magistrates' court Feb 2. Telephoned Mr. Black, who called and took her home."

As a magistrate himself, Mr. Black had been able to explain the procedure in cases that can be tried either by the magistrates or the Crown Court. Both Mr. & Mrs. Black are conscious of the damage to the standing of both of them that the prosecution will entail. The most vital thing is to establish Mrs. Black's innocence. Nothing should be left to chance. Mr. Black is also conscious of the embarrassment to him if the case is tried by the Barchester magistrates, the very bench on which he sits. Mr. Amity points to the greater time, expense and publicity involved in a trial by jury at the Crown Court, but feels this in the circumstances is the safer course. This is endorsed by Mr. Black and accepted by Mrs. Black.

Mr. Amity says he will try to find out about the incident outside the store. He does not remember reading anything in the Barchester Chronicle that morning and this is confirmed by the Blacks.

When the clients leave, Mr. Amity writes to the local police stating that it is important for his client to know the nature of the incident to which apparently the police had been called outside Harridges on Thursday morning and asks to be supplied with details.

Mr. Amity also telephones the prosecution to let them know his firm is representing Mrs. Black and that she is to plead not guilty. He says he is inclined to advise her to elect for jury trial and asks what the prosecution view is. The prosecution clerk says that although he feels there are no special factors in favour of the Crown Court, he has no strong feelings. He agrees to send Mr. Amity summaries of the prosecution evidence under the rules relating to advance disclosure.

Mr. Amity, conscious that not all clients are frank with their own solicitors about their previous convictions asks the clerk to confirm that there are none against Mrs. Black. He confirms this.

Mr. White then telephones the office of the clerk to the justices at the magistrates' court to confirm that he will be ready for the mode of trial hearing on Tuesday, to be followed by an adjournment.

On Tuesday morning Mr. Amity meets Mrs. Black at court, and learns that nothing has changed her mind about the way the defence should be conducted. He speaks to the Crown Prosecutor Mr. Allman, who agrees to the course proposed. He also exchanges a word with the court clerk to confirm his intention.

The case is called into court:

Clerk:	Is your name Penny Black?
Mrs. Black:	Yes.
Clerk:	Your worships, in this case Mr. Allman appears for the prosecution and Mr. Amity for the defence. I understand that Mr. Amity wishes to make an application.
Chairman:	Mr. Amity?
Mr. Amity:	Your worships, as your clerk informed you, I appear for Mrs. Black. This case concerns an allegation of theft. There will therefore need to be a preliminary enquiry as to mode of trial. I was only instructed some four days ago, and, whether the matter were to proceed as a summary trial or as a committal hearing, neither the prosecution nor myself are ready to proceed with the hearing today. There will, therefore be a joint application for an adjournment in any event. There is, however, no reason why the preliminary matter of mode of trial cannot proceed today, which may save a further adjournment. I have already had advance disclosure of the prosecution evidence in summary form.

Chairman:	That seems sensible—do you agree Mr. Allman?
Mr. Allman:	Yes, your worships.
Chairman:	Very well.
Clerk:	Mrs. Black—you are charged that you did on January 28, 1993 at The Parade, Barchester steal a red cashmere sweater the property of Harridges Ltd. of the value of £38.95 contrary to section 1 of the Theft Act 1968.
Mrs. Black:	Not guilty.
Clerk:	There is no need to plead at this stage Mrs. Black. Mr. Allman?
Mr. Allman:	While the prosecution has no strong feelings as to the mode of trial we have no information leading us to suppose that this is other than a straightforward shoplifting case of the kind with which this court frequently deals and we know of no special feature making the expense and delay of Crown Court trial more appropriate.
Clerk:	Thank you Mr. Amity?
Mr. Amity:	Whilst there is nothing in the amount involved or the nature of the case itself making this case particularly suitable for Crown Court trial, there is one particular matter which is relevant here. By section 19(3) of the Magistrates' Court Act 1980 you must have regard to "any other circumstances" and in my submission there are certain relevant circumstances in this case. The circumstances to which I refer are the embarrassment to my client and her husband, and indeed to the bench which might have to hear this case if it were to proceed as a summary trial. The embarrassment would be caused, your worships, because of course my client's husband is himself a member of the bench. In my submission this is a sufficient factor to make your worships direct trial to take place at the Crown Court.
Chairman:	(after discussion with colleagues): In view of what Mr. Amity says we are inclined to agree that this case is more suitable for trial by Crown Court.
Mr. Allman:	In that case your worships, so that papers can be prepared hopefully with a view to a Section 6(2) committal I would apply for an adjournment of three weeks.
Mr. Amity:	I agree with my friend's application and consider that it is very probable that the Defendant will be able to consent to a Section 6(2) committal.
Chairman:	Very well, the case will be adjourned to February 23 for committal proceedings. Now what about bail?
Mr. Allman:	There is of course no objection to bail being continued, Sir. There are no sureties or conditions.
Chairman:	Bail will continue until February 23 as at present.

Outside court Mr. Amity arranges an appointment with Mrs. Black for Mr. White to see her on February 15, by which time he hopes the committal papers will have arrived and he will have had a reply from the police to his enquiry.

Outside the court, Mr. Amity expresses to Mrs. Black his satisfaction that he was able to persuade the magistrates themselves to direct jury trial, so that if unhappily Mrs. Black is convicted, no blame can attach to her for choosing jury trial in a possibly trivial case and if prosecution costs are awarded against her, the order is unlikely to be inflated by any sense of annoyance that the time of the court has been wasted.

Shortly after, Messrs. Makepiece receive a letter from the police to say they have no record of an incident at 11.30 a.m. in the Parade Barchester, to which the police were called. Mr. Amity sends a copy of this to Mrs. Black and asks if she can give any details which will enable him to follow the matter up. She does not reply.

The following day a police officer delivers a bundle of papers to Messrs. Makepiece. These are the copies of statement by prosecution witnesses forming the committal papers:

BARSETSHIRE CONSTABULARY
STATION: BARCHESTER

STATEMENT OF: GRACE SLICK
AGE: OVER 21
OCCUPATION: STORE DETECTIVE
ADDRESS: 11, WHITE RABBIT ROAD, BARCHESTER

This statement consisting of 2 pages each signed by me is true to the best of my knowledge and belief and I make it knowing that if it is tendered in evidence I shall be liable to prosecution if I have wilfully stated in it anything which I know to be false or do not believe to be true.

Dated 28th day of January 1993
Signature G. Slick

I am a store detective and have been employed for the last four years by Harridges Ltd.

On 28th January I was on duty on the ground floor of the store in the Parade, Barchester. At about 11.30 a.m. I began observing a woman, who I now know to be Mrs. Penny Black. She seemed to be acting in a furtive manner. I saw her pick up a red sweater and hold it against herself in a mirror. She did this for some time, carefully examining the sweater, apparently looking for imperfections. She did this three times, each time returning the sweater to the rack and going to examine other clothes, but each time returning to the sweater.

The last time she did not even unfold the garment, but looked over towards the front of the shop to where the shop attendants were. At the same time she dropped the garment in her bag and walked briskly to the door, not looking about her, but straight ahead. I ran after her and caught up with her about 30 yards outside the store as she was hurrying along the pavement. I said "Excuse me, but may I look in your bag." She went white and seemed to be about to faint. I held her arm and escorted her back to the store. She was given a chair and when she seemed to have recovered I took her to the manager's office where I explained to him what I had seen. In her presence he took the sweater from her bag and asked me to telephone for the police which I did.

Signature G. Slick

BARSETSHIRE CONSTABULARY
STATION: BARCHESTER

STATEMENT OF:	PATRICIA BENATAR
AGE:	OVER 21
OCCUPATION:	WOMAN POLICE CONSTABLE
ADDRESS:	BARCHESTER POLICE STATION

This statement consisting of 1 page each signed by me is true to the best of my knowledge and belief and I make it knowing that if it is tendered in evidence I shall be liable to prosecution if I have wilfully stated in it anything which I know to be false or do not believe to be true.

Dated 28th day of January 1993
Signature P. Benatar

I am a police constable. On the morning of 28th January 1993 at 11.30 a.m. I was on foot patrol in the Parade, Barchester, when I received a radio message to go to the manager's office at Harridges Limited. When I arrived there I found a woman whom I now know to be Penny Black, together with the manager of the store Mr. Seger, and Miss Slick, a store detective. I checked her identity from her driving licence and then on the basis of what I was told I cautioned Mrs. Black and asked her if she had anything she wished to say. She replied "I didn't know I'd done it. I didn't mean to steal. Please let me go to my husband. He will know what to do." At that point Detective Constable Walsh arrived. In his presence I asked her to come to the police station and she agreed. Miss Slick accompanied us too. I later was present while Detective Constable Walsh questioned Mrs Black and she declined to make a written statement. He asked her how much money she had on her and she showed us her purse which I examined and found £74.50 in cash. She also had a cheque book, cheque card and Access card. Detective Constable Walsh then produced her to Police Sergeant Churchill the designated custody officer at Barchester police station who formally charged her with theft of a sweater worth £38.95. She said "I don't think I had better say anymore—my husband will know what to do."

Signature P. Benatar
J. Walsh

BARSETSHIRE CONSTABULARY
STATION: BARCHESTER

STATEMENT OF:	ROBERT SEGER
AGE:	OVER 21
OCCUPATION:	STORE MANAGER
ADDRESS:	23 NUTBUSH RD, BARCHESTER

This statement consisting of 1 page each signed by me is true to the best of my knowledge and belief and I make it knowing that if it is tendered in evidence I shall be liable to prosecution if I have wilfully stated in it anything which I know to be false or do not believe to be true.

Dated 28th day of January 1993
Signature R. Seger

I am the general manager of Harridges Ltd. of the Parade, Barchester. At about 11.35 a.m. on 28th January Miss Grace Slick, who is one of our full-time security staff, came to my office with a woman who later identified herself to me as Mrs. Penny Black. In the presence of Miss Slick I looked in Mrs. Black's canvas shopping bag and found a red cashmere sweater with our price tag attached—the price of the garment being £38.95. I asked Mrs. Black if she had paid for it and she said "There's been a terrible mistake—I don't know what I was doing." She then offered to pay for it there and then and said she had never done such a thing before. She begged me not to call the police. I asked Miss Slick to telephone the police and waited with Mrs. Black until the police came. When I further looked at the garment I found that the part of the price-tag which is removed when an article is sold was still attached. No-one had authority to take the sweater from the store without paying for it.

Signature R. Seger

BARSETSHIRE CONSTABULARY
STATION: BARCHESTER

STATEMENT OF:	JOSEPH WALSH
AGE:	OVER 21
OCCUPATION:	DETECTIVE CONSTABLE
ADDRESS:	BARCHESTER POLICE STATION

This statement consisting of 1 page each signed by me is true to the best of my knowledge and belief and I make it knowing that if it is tendered in evidence I shall be liable to prosecution if I have wilfully stated in it anything which I know to be false or do not believe to be true.

Dated 28th January 1993
Signature J. Walsh

I am a detective constable in the Barsetshire Constabulary stationed at Barchester. On 28th January I received a call to attend at Harridges Ltd. in the Parade. At 11.48 a.m. I arrived at the manager's office where I found a woman I now know to be Mrs. Penny Black being questioned by W.P.C. Benatar in the presence of the manager, Mr. Seger, and the store detective who had observed the incident, Miss Slick. W.P.C. Benatar asked Mrs. Black to come to Barchester police station to which she agreed. We walked there, a distance of 200 yards. I then asked Mrs. Black to make a statement in writing and she declined. I asked her how much money she had and she showed her purse to W.P.C. Benatar, who counted £74.50 and also found a cheque book, a cheque card and Access Card.

I then produced Mrs. Black to Police Sergeant Churchill, the designated custody officer at the police station, who formally charged her with theft of a sweater worth £38.95 the property of Harridges Ltd of the Parade, Barchester. She said "I don't think I had better say anymore—my husband will know what to do."

Signature J. Walsh
P. Benatar

Mr. Amity sends copies of these statements to Mrs. Black and asks her to note down any points she wishes to make on them, as to their accuracy and as to any matters omitted, in readiness for their meeting on February 15. On that day she calls at Messrs. Makepiece for the interview and Mr. Amity takes her through the statements. He then takes a full statement from her in the form of a proof of evidence. She denies Miss Slick's statement that she had handled the sweater three times or that she held it against herself looking in a mirror. She agrees that the time she did take it up she did not unfold the garment. There was not time to do so when her attention was distracted. She admits she was confused when she was confronted with possession of the sweater in her bag. She says she was very insistent on seeing her husband because she felt sure he would understand how it could happen to her and would know how to handle the situation. She agrees with the statement of the store manager that she offered to pay for it and begged them not to call the police. She was desperate and wanted, above all, to protect her husband from any slur on the family's reputation. She did not do it because she was guilty.

Mr. Amity points out that it will be difficult to use her evidence about the police car and the possible incident in the absence of a supporting report from the police. He will ask counsel to make what he can of this in cross-examining M/s Slick but it would not be wise to use it in an endeavour to discredit the prosecution case completely and as the basis of a submission that there is no case to answer. This being so, there is no possibility of avoiding a trial and therefore there is no point in disputing the prosecution evidence at the committal proceedings.

He explains that by agreeing to a section 6(2) committal the proceedings in the magistrates' court would be reduced to a formality, involving only the submission of the written statements of the prosecution witnesses—which would not be read out—and a formal consent by Mr. Amity on Mrs. Black's behalf to the committal.

On February 23 Mrs. Black meets Mr. Amity as previously arranged. He takes the opportunity to discuss her statement with her. He points out that she will be subject to severe cross-examination at the trial on her version of how she came to put the sweater in the bag. He attempts to probe her account of the incident involving the police car. He asks if she is sure she saw a crowd of pedestrians. He tells her frankly that whilst she is of course entitled to put her case before a jury he is not optimistic. Nonetheless Mrs. Black insists on maintaining her plea of not guilty.

The case is called in court. Mrs. Black goes into the dock again and is asked her name. The clerk asks Mr. Allman what form the committal will take and is told it will be a section 6(2) committal. He then hands in the four statements served previously on Messrs. Makepiece. The clerk then turns to Mr. Amity and asks if his client consents to a section 6(2) committal. Mr. Amity rises and assents. He says he wishes for full attendance orders, *i.e.* orders requiring the attendance of all four of the prosecution witnesses.

The clerk asks if there are any other matters Mr. Amity wishes to raise. Had Mrs. Black been eligible for legal aid, Mr. Amity would have made the application at this point, but clearly not in this case. Bail must, however, be applied for and he requests that this be continued till trial. The prosecution does not object and the magistrates grant bail accordingly, without conditions.

The defendant is then warned by the clerk that if she wishes to rely on an alibi at the trial she must give particulars of it either there and then or within seven days to the Crown Prosecution Service. A written notice to this effect is handed to her, containing also the name and address of Mr. Allman. Mr. Amity tells the court that there is no alibi in the present case.

This concludes the proceedings.

"Going for Trial"

The offence of theft being one triable either way, Mrs. Black had the option to be committed for trial before a jury at the Crown Court—to "go for trial." In her case the option was exercised and the case was sent for trial.

Factors in Favour of One or Other Court Where the Defendant has a Choice

1. Despite inconclusive statistical evidence on rates of acquittal, most practising lawyers tend to believe that there is a greater chance of acquittal on certain types of offence before a jury. Magistrates are thought to become "case hardened" by the sheer number of similar cases they see. Shoplifting in particular is one such type of case. The jury are thought to be more open minded (or perhaps more naive!) and more likely to believe a defendant, *e.g.* one who says that he walked past the check out having forgotten to pay.

2. Some advantage may be gained by the defence in a Crown Court hearing if there is a question of admissibility of evidence. In the Crown Court the legal argument as to admissibility is heard by the judge in the absence of a jury. There may be less point in objecting to the admissibility of evidence in the magistrates' court where the magistrates are present throughout and therefore have to hear the evidence first and, even if they rule it inadmissible, may be unable to put it from their minds.

3. In some cases, the opportunity that the committal process affords to examine the prosecution evidence may give the defence an opportunity of having the case dismissed at that stage.

4. In favour of the magistrates' court however is the relative speed of the procedures. The case will be over in a few weeks at most, whereas in the case of trial by jury there will be a wait of several months. If the defendant is bearing his own costs he must think seriously about the additional expense of having counsel in the Crown Court and the danger that if the prosecution are awarded costs following conviction these too will be much greater. In addition the speed may be better for someone who is already in custody pending trial, or of a nervous disposition. The ordeal is much less in a magistrates' court which is considerably less formal than the Crown Court.

5. There is also the question of publicity. Very little is allowed to be published about committal proceedings since obviously the members

of the jury whoever they might turn out to be might be prejudiced by what they could read in the press before the trial. However, the press interest in the eventual Crown Court hearing may be much greater than in the magistrates' court case. This point is more significant in large cities where press coverage in the magistrates' court is much less complete. However, in Barchester or other small towns and especially those with local newspapers and especially in the case of respected local personages like the wife of a headmaster, publicity is unfortunately inevitable wherever the trial might take place.

COMMITTAL

The committal stage is designed to be a filtering-out process at which the prosecution must produce enough evidence to show that the defendant has a case to answer. If the prosecution are unable to do this then the case will be dismissed there and then. If they do show that there is a case to answer the defendant will be committed for trial at the Crown Court.

Until the coming into force of the Criminal Justice Act 1967 these committal proceedings were invariably in the same form. Prosecution witnesses had to give sworn evidence to the magistrates; they could be cross-examined by the defendant or his advocate if he wishes, in an attempt to shake this evidence; and every word the witness said had to be copied down in longhand and at the end this statement was signed by the witness. The defendant could also give evidence and call witnesses if he wished, although this was rarely done.

Although this was a useful filter in some cases, and it sometimes proved possible so to shake prosecution witnesses that the case might be dismissed there and then, it was an enormously time-consuming and therefore expensive procedure because:

1. it had to be gone through even if the defendant was going to plead guilty;

2. it had to be gone through even if there was clearly a case to answer;

3. as a matter of tactics, however much the defendant might hope to shake the prosecution witnesses, he preferred to reserve his weapons until trial rather than to cross-examine the witnesses strenuously at the committal, thus giving warning of the line of attack in advance of the trial.

This kind of committal, known as a "full committal" (or sometimes an "old-style" or "old-fashioned" committal) still exists and the accused may always elect to have it if he wishes to attempt to show that the prosecution case should be dismissed at that stage. If he does wish to do so the matter proceeds as above outlined and the magistrates must decide if there is a case to answer at the end of the hearing.

What is now far more common however, is a committal under section 6(2) of the Magistrates' Courts Act 1980, originally known as a "section 1" committal because it was introduced by section 1 of the Criminal Justice Act 1967, of which we have just seen an example in *Regina* v. *Black*. It is also known as a "formal" or "paper" committal. Under section 6(2), which can only be used where the defendant is legally represented, the prosecution serve copies of witness statements on the defendant who, if after reading through them agrees that they disclose a case to answer, can consent to the case being committed for trial without the magistrates having to consider the evidence.

It will be noted that in either case the defendant has the chance to examine the prosecution evidence in advance of the trial proper. There is of course no comparable provision for the defendant to have to give advance notice of his defence except in the case of an alibi defence.

<h2 style="text-align:center">ALIBI</h2>

An alibi is evidence tending to show that the defendant could not have been in the area where the offence is alleged to have been committed at the time it was committed, because he was elsewhere at that time. A defendant is required to give particulars of this defence to the prosecution either at the committal hearing or within seven days afterwards (Criminal Justice Act 1967, s.11). This is to enable the defendant's claim to be checked by the police, who will usually interview the witnesses who say they saw the defendant. This avoids the need for an adjournment, if the prosecution were taken by surprise by this defence at the trial. This is the only *general* case of a defendant having to give the prosecution details of his defence before trial. Moreover it applies only in trials in the Crown Court so that in the magistrates' court there is no obligation to give prior warning of an alibi.

<h2 style="text-align:center">*ADJOURNMENTS*</h2>

In *Regina* v. *Black*, the magistrates agreed to an adjournment of the proceedings after deciding on the mode of trial. The magistrates have a general power to adjourn proceedings at any time either before or during the hearing. Such adjournments may be made either on the application of one of the parties to the proceedings or of the court's own motion. Cases rarely proceed to a conclusion at the first hearing unless a simple guilty plea to a trivial offence is involved. Common reasons for adjournments are:

1. unpreparedness of either side due to inadequate time (*e.g.* where a defendant first contacts a solicitor only the day before trial);

2. illness or holidays of witnesses;

3. adjournment because the trial cannot conveniently be completed on that day. (Note that in such a case, as magistrates are

unpaid laymen who sit by rota, the adjournment may not be to the following day but may be for some weeks—until the three magistrates are next due to sit);

4. adjournment after conviction but before sentence, to allow reports (medical or social enquiry reports) to be prepared;

5. absence of the defendant. Adjournment while warrant of arrest is issued and executed.

Adjournments are normally to a fixed date, but may be indefinite— the date to be fixed subject to some future event—*e.g.* the arrest of the defendant.

BAIL

In neither of the cases which we have considered was there any difficulty with bail. In both cases, the persons concerned had a settled address and although Arthur Brown had a criminal record, the offence with which he was charged was relatively trivial. In the case of Mrs. Black there was of course no risk of her absconding. However, the question of bail must always be considered. As we have seen, the police have substantial powers to detain persons pending enquiries. If the decision not to proceed with a prosecution is taken the person will be released. If there is sufficient evidence upon which to charge, the person will be charged and this is one of the duties of the custody officer, namely to keep the state of the evidence under review. Once the charge is brought it is for the police to consider bail. Under section 43 of the Magistrates' Court Act 1980, the police have to decide whether to release a person from custody until he is due to attend court or whether they will keep him in custody until his first appearance before a magistrates' court (which in these circumstances would normally be the next day). In the case of *police bail*, indeed it is also possible for the police to give bail even though they have *not* charged a suspect. For example they may decide that they will organise an identity parade in a few days' time or they may need some delay to establish the ownership of some allegedly stolen property. In such a case they may give bail under section 43 of the Magistrates' Court Act 1980, to the person suspected, on condition that he returns to the police station at some fixed future date. What happens then will depend upon either the outcome of the identity parade or whether the police feel they have sufficient grounds to prosecute. If so they will either question further and/or charge him and if not they will tell him that their inquiries are concluded.

When a person is arrested by warrant issued by a magistrate the warrant may be "backed for bail," *i.e.* it may contain an instruction to the police to release the arrested person on bail to attend the court. If the warrant contains such a condition the police must obey it.

From the moment of first appearance before the court the police lose their powers to grant bail, which it now falls to the court to decide. The courts may grant bail as follows:

1. The magistrates' court may grant bail at any time when a case is adjourned; or after conviction; or after sentence if a notice of appeal is given.

2. A Crown Court judge may grant bail at any time after it has been refused by a Magistrates' Court. Application may be made to the Crown Court judge in chambers. A Crown Court judge may also grant bail at any time after committal to the Crown Court for trial or sentence or at any stage during Crown Court proceedings or after sentence pending appeal.

3. A High Court judge may grant bail at any time pending trial by magistrates after an application has been refused by magistrates.

4. The Court of Appeal may grant bail pending appeal to it, and pending further appeal to the House of Lords.

Until the Bail Act 1976 bail was usually granted on the defendant's own "recognisance" of a certain sum of money. That is, if the defendant failed to surrender to his bail he forfeited this sum (and was of course arrested and would be unlikely to obtain bail again). Since 1976 this method of attempting to ensure the defendant's appearance has been replaced by simply making it a specific offence for a person to fail to surrender to his bail (Bail Act 1976, s.6).

The court still has the power to ask for "sureties" however, which are persons who are prepared to guarantee the appearance of the defendant at court or forfeit the amount of the surety. (The offence under section 6 of the Act would of course also be committed by the absconding defendant). Bail may be granted conditionally upon sureties being obtained later if they are not present in the court when it is granted. The defendant is released when they come forward and give the requisite undertakings. The policy underlying the law is that defendants shall be granted bail until they are convicted. The main exceptions are where there are substantial grounds for believing that the defendant if released would:

1. fail to surrender to his bail; *or*,

2. commit further offences; *or*,

3. interfere with witnesses or otherwise obstruct the course of justice; *or*,

4. should be kept in custody for his own protection.

The court must normally consider bail on each occasion when the accused appears before it save that, where there has already been a full application refused by a magistrates' court, magistrates dealing with the same case subsequently need only hear a full application if there is some new factor which changes the circumstances (Criminal Justice Act 1988, s.154).

The matters to be considered by the court when considering grounds 1–3 above are:

1. the nature and seriousness of the charge or default (default

means failure to comply with some previous court order, *e.g.* probation or community service order)

2. the character, antecedents, associations and community ties of the defendant

3. the-defendant's previous behaviour when granted bail

4. the strength of the prosecution case (clearly there are only limited opportunities to investigate this at the preliminary stage)

5. any other relevant matter (Bail Act 1976, Sched. 1, para. 9).

So in considering bail the obligation is clearly put on the prosecution to establish why a defendant should *not* have it rather than on a defendant to establish why he should. Moreover, because of this it will be rare indeed for a defendant who has once obtained bail, and abided by any conditions connected with it, to be refused bail subsequently, unless there is a drastic change in circumstances. An exception to this is that on a charge of a serious nature being dealt with at the Crown Court it is usual for the accused to be kept in custody once the jury have retired—no doubt because the accused is likely to be in an excitable state of mind at that stage and the temptation to abscond may be too great—especially after an adverse summing up by the Judge. Where an offence is not normally punishable with imprisonment, it is only in very exceptional circumstances that a defendant may be refused bail—chiefly if there has been a previous failure to surrender to bail.

The court has a duty to record all decisions relating to bail and must state its reasons for refusing it or varying its conditions.

CONDITIONS OF BAIL

The court releasing a defendant on bail has the power to attach conditions to it, for example by requiring the defendant to give up his passport, or report to a police station every day, or not to contact witnesses.

LEGAL AID IN CRIMINAL PROCEEDINGS

An outline of the legal aid system, in both civil and criminal matters has already been given (Chapter 4, above). An example of the form required for the application to the magistrates' court is set out in *The Police* v. *Arthur Brown* (p. 249). It will be noticed that a part of the form is devoted to the answer to the question "Circumstances justifying the grant of legal aid," and this is usually completed in only a few words. Nor is it necessary to indicate whether the plea will be guilty or not guilty. Legal Aid is available for a plea in mitigation on a guilty plea as well as for contested hearings.

The court in dealing with an application must consider two things: the nature of the charge and the means of the applicant. Where any doubt exists, it must be resolved in favour of the applicant. The financial limits for qualifying are mentioned in Chapter 4.

Provided the applicant's means are not such as to exclude him from the scheme then legal aid ought normally to be granted in the following cases:

1. where the charge is serious, in that there is a risk of loss of liberty, livelihood, and/or damage to reputation;

2. where there is a substantial point of law involved;

3. where professional skills are necessary, *e.g.* for tracing witnesses or cross-examination;

4. where the defendant is handicapped in some way, *e.g.* by illiteracy or poor grasp of English. (Legal Aid Act 1988, s.22.)

The application of these criteria means that in almost every case of dishonesty or violence or sexual cases, legal aid is granted to those whose means qualify and this is obviously especially so in cases reaching the Crown Court.

The application forms are considered by the court, sometimes at the start of a stage of the proceedings, but more often are sent in to the court by post or by hand and are considered in the absence of the defendant. Although each individual case ought to be considered on its merits, relative percentage for grants and refusal of applications varies markedly from area to area and from court to court within a particular area as we have previously remarked.

After the application is dealt with by the magistrates a legal aid order, if granted, is sent out to the applicant's solicitor together with a form on which to claim fees subsequently (Form Crim. 5). Fees are paid at certain prescribed rates as mentioned at the conclusion of the section on the case against Arthur Brown. At the end of the case the form claiming fees is sent to the area office for the area of the court concerned, and after any queries have been raised by him and dealt with payment is eventually made by the Legal Aid Board. The legal aid order will cover all work done from the grant of the certificate up to advice to the defendant about appeal. As we saw in *The Police* v. *Brown*, work done before the certificate is granted can be covered by the Green Form scheme.

A court will when it grants legal aid also makes a contribution order unless the disposable income and capital of the accused are below a certain level. That level and the size of the contribution to be made by a person whose resources are above the level is fixed in regulations. The court has a discretion as to the period over which the contribution must be paid and will usually order this by instalments. If the legally aided person fails without good reason to make the payment the court will be able to revoke the legal aid order. At the conclusion of the case the court will have power to remit any payments under the contribution order which are outstanding. This would happen if for example the accused were sentenced to a custodial sentence. If a legally aided person is acquitted the court may order repayment of the sums already paid.

It should be noted that a magistrates' court has power to grant legal aid for proceedings in the Crown Court where it commits a defendant there for trial or sentence. And the Crown Court has power to grant legal aid for proceedings before it on a written application in a similar form to that in use in the magistrates' court. The Court of Appeal itself grants legal aid as does the House of Lords.

Finally, it should be noted that criminal legal aid is not available for an appeal to a High Court judge against a refusal of bail by magistrates. Application can, however, be made under the civil scheme and merits must therefore be shown as normally under the civil system. Such applications are in any event only rarely granted.

DUTY SOLICITOR SCHEMES

A client who is kept in custody is quite likely to have first seen a duty solicitor. Duty solicitor schemes were instituted under the Legal Aid Act 1982. They provide that persons are entitled to free legal advice up to an initial limit of £90 in the police station. Under the police station scheme, solicitors who are volunteers in ordinary private practice with experience of criminal cases who participate on a rota basis are available for periods of 24 hours. They may be called out by telephone to either go to police stations or to give telephone advice to persons in custody. The necessity for this latter provision is obvious particularly in view, in large conurbations or rural areas, of the sheer number of police stations which a duty solicitor would have to cover whilst on duty. There is also a court duty solicitor who will see persons who are unrepresented, especially while they are in the cells before court starts. On that occasion the duty solicitor's main task will be to obtain bail for the person concerned though much depends on the practice of local courts. In some courts only bail is dealt with at the first hearing. Because of the time pressure in interviewing all those in custody between arrival at court early in the morning and the start of the session at 10 a.m., solicitors may well require the assistance of legal executives in this work. For the latter this is an opportunity to gain valuable experience.

PROCEDURES AFTER CONVICTION

After conviction, the court may proceed immediately to the question of sentence. Indeed this would be the norm in the magistrates' court for routine offences. However, there may be intervening steps between conviction and sentence. The court will of course want to hear from the police about the offender's criminal record which will not have been known to them before this stage. In addition they may find it appropriate, either of their own motion or on the application of the defence solicitor, to order social inquiry reports or psychiatric or medical reports on the offender. In certain circumstances the court must obtain a report before sentencing (Criminal Justice Act 1991 s.3). A social inquiry report is carried out by a member of the probation service who usually visits the offender, preferably in his home environment, on one or more occasions to see what there may be in that environment which contributed to the offence and to see whether anything could be recommended to improve the situation. If there is to be a social inquiry report there will inevitably be an adjournment usually of three to four weeks. As indicated, it is preferable if this report is carried out whilst the offender is in his home environment and therefore ideally the magistrates should release the convicted person on bail pending this report. This is not of course always appropriate depending on the nature of the offence for which he has been convicted and the risk of his absconding.

Whether the court proceeds to sentence then and there, or whether there is an adjournment, the defence lawyer will then have an opportunity to address the court in mitigation. Mitigation is an attempt to persuade the court to treat the offender leniently. It is a very important part of the criminal advocate's task. He should be fully informed about his client's background and personal circumstances so as to make the best possible plea on behalf of the client. A plea in mitigation usually deals with the following matters:

(1) *The offence itself*

If there is anything about the offence which makes it less serious than it might appear this should be put forward. For example, in the case of an assault where the offender has been subject to considerable provocation this would clearly be a mitigating factor. Likewise, courts are always more willing to be lenient in the case of impulsive acts than cunning or deliberately planned ones. So for example, a person who stole £100 on impulse when he saw it unattended on a table might well be thought less blameworthy than someone who had set about getting the same amount of money by a cunning plan.

(2) *The offender himself*

The plea in mitigation should deal with the personal circumstances of the offender pointing to anything which may have contributed to the crime. In particular, any stresses or financial pressures or illnesses suffered by the offender at about the time of the crime should be put forward. In addition, anything creditable in the offender's past record for example community service of some kind as a councillor or charity worker and so on. Of course in this connection the best possible mitigation is that it is the offender's first offence, *i.e.* that he has no criminal record.

(3) *Conduct in relation to the prosecution*

It is always good mitigation to show that the offender co-operated fully with the police at an early point. Thus a full confession and a guilty plea, especially if the offender also assisted in recovering the stolen goods undamaged, etc., will have a considerable effect in reducing the eventual sentence. Similarly, the point that a good deal of court time and costs have been saved by a prompt plea of guilty will also be of benefit to the accused.

(4) *Capacity for reform*

Here, it will be important to point out to the court anything which indicates that the offender will not return to criminal ways. Anything which tends in this direction will be useful. It may be possible to put something forward in this connection, even on behalf of someone with an apparently bad criminal record. If one can point to the fact that say after lengthy unemployment the accused has just obtained a job or has an interview for a job, or is about to change his lifestyle in some dramatic way which bodes well for the future, *e.g.* by taking on new responsibility such as getting married or having a child then it may be possible to persuade the court to be more lenient. A strong plea under this heading may well be combined with the suggestion to the court that sentence should be deferred (as to which see below).

The above are general principles relevant to mitigation. Of course in borderline cases the main object in mitigation is usually to try and ensure that the client does not receive a prison sentence. The decision to be made by a court as to whether to impose a prison sentence is now affected by Part I of the Criminal Justice Act 1991. In general terms this Act provides that an offender should be sentenced on the basis of the seriousness of the offence of which he has been convicted and that undue weight should not be given to his criminal record. It is now always imperative that a court should only pass a custodial sentence on an offender if it is of the opinion that the offence in question was so serious that only a custodial sentence is justified or, where the offence is one of violence or a sexual offence that only a custodial sentence would be adequate to protect the public from serious harm from the convicted person. In all other cases the court should consider a "community sentence" under section 6 of the 1991 Act.

After the plea in mitigation has been made, the court will then turn its mind to the question of sentence. The judge, or magistrates, may sentence immediately or may retire briefly to consider the matter or may even adjourn until the next day for such consideration.

SENTENCING

The power of magistrates' courts to sentence offenders is subject to set limits. They can fine up to £5,000 and imprison for not more than six months on any one charge or, where they are dealing with more than one either way offence, a cumulative total of not more than 12 months. For many offences the maximum penalty is laid down by the statute creating the offence. This may be more or less than the general maxima just mentioned. If the maximum for the individual offence is less, the court is bound by that also.

Some statutes prescribe specific penalties that must be imposed unless there are special reasons, *e.g.* endorsements of driving licence for some motoring offences and disqualification for others. Subject to the general limits quoted above and any special provisions for individual offences, the court has complete discretion in the penalty it imposes.

If after considering all the facts of the offence the magistrates consider that their own sentencing powers are inadequate to deal with an offender they may commit him to the Crown Court for sentence, the Crown Court's sentencing powers being limited only by the maximum sentence prescribed for the offence in question.

Before considering sentence as such it is convenient to deal with two other matters.

(a) *Taking other offences into consideration.* Where a defendant is convicted of an offence he may ask the court for other offences which he is then prepared to admit to, to be "taken into consideration." This is an opportunity for him to clear any other crimes which he has committed out of the way. It thus "wipes the slate clean" and effectively precludes future prosecution for those offences. Since admitting other offences (sometimes very numerous ones) shows some degree of honesty and contrition, often a court will not markedly increase sentence as compared with what the court would have awarded for the actual offence charged.

(b) *Deferred Sentence.* The magistrates' court may be section 1 of the Powers of Criminal Courts Act 1973 defer passing sentence for a period of up to six months after conviction. The consent of the convicted person is required. The purpose of this is to give the offender the opportunity to show an intention to reform before sentence is passed (*e.g.* by getting employment, staying out of trouble, or perhaps voluntarily compensating a victim).

We now pass on to consider some of the various sentences which the magistrates' court can impose.

(1) *Absolute Discharge*

This is imposed for a trivial or technical offence and is not strictly speaking a penalty at all: it means instant release from the court and exemption from punishment.

(2) *Conditional Discharge*

A court may discharge an offender on condition he does not commit any other offence for a specified period, up to a maximum of three years. If he does commit another offence then he is sentenced for both the new offence and the original one in respect of which he was conditionally discharged.

(3) *Fine*

A magistrates' court may impose a fine up to £5,000 or to the maximum in the statute creating the offence. This is the most usual form of penalty and is appropriate for most kinds of offences, but especially for driving offences, alone or in addition to other penalties. An offender must be given time to pay the fine unless he has the means to pay it forthwith or there are some other special factors, *e.g.* that he is a tourist here only briefly.

Of course one of the problems with fines is the problem of fairness as between offenders. Thus a fine of £250 to a poor person may be a dreadful burden whereas the same amount to a wealthy man is of no consequence. In order to, at least partially, address this problem of unfairness section 18 of the Criminal Justice Act 1991 provides the power for a Magistrates' Court to impose a fine which is linked to the offender's weekly income.

(4) *Probation*

With the agreement of the offender the court may impose a probation order of up to three years. This involves the offender being supervised by a probation officer whilst otherwise remaining in the community. It is strictly speaking not a *sentence*, but an alternative to a sentence. It is most used in the case of fairly young adults to give assistance to them in establishing themselves in the community properly, especially where something in their present lifestyle or home circumstances shows that the assistance of a sympathetic trained social worker would be beneficial.

(5) *Community Service Order*

With his agreement the offender may be ordered to do a certain number of hours (up to a maximum of 240) work for the benefit of the community, typically decorating or gardening, under supervision. Community Service Orders may now be linked with probation under section 11 of the Criminal Justice Act 1991.

(6) *Curfew Orders*

Under section 12 of the Criminal Justice Act 1991 a person of 16 years or over may with his consent be ordered to remain for periods specified in the order at any place so specified. The nature of this order is to ensure that an offender remains at home within certain hours, typically over the hours of darkness. The court will make someone responsible for monitoring the offender's movements and this may in some cases be done by electronic "tagging."

(7) *Disqualification from driving and endorsement of licence*

In the case of many driving offences the court may order endorsement of the offender's licence. "Penalty points" are attached to offences for which endorsement is ordered. The number (specified in the Road Traffic Offenders Act 1988 Schedule 2 (as amended by section 26 of the Road Traffic Act 1991)) varies from one (carrying a motor cycle passenger unlawfully) to 11, (*e.g.* motor racing on public highway and drink related offences).

There are also a number of offences for which disqualification from driving must be ordered (again unless there are special reasons for not doing so) even if there are no previous endorsements. To examine the precise powers and duties of magistrates in respect of sentencing for driving offences reference would have to be made to Stone's *Justices' Manual* or to the specialist book in this field, Wilkinson's *Road Traffic Offences*.

(8) *Imprisonment*

Generally up to the maximum of six months in the case of one charge or up to a total maximum for more than one either way offence of 12 months, but subject to any lower maximum prescribed in the statute creating the offence in question.

(9) *Suspended Sentence of Imprisonment*

Actual imprisonment (especially for the first time) is likely to have a serious effect on an offender, leading usually to loss of job and sometimes to loss of hope and break-up of family. It is therefore something of a weapon of last resort in the magistrates' armoury. The concept of suspended sentence is intended to indicate quite clearly to an offender that this is really his "last chance" and that in the event of a further offence being committed during the period of suspension he will not only be punished for the new offence but the sentence which has been suspended will also be imposed. The magistrates may suspend the sentence which they impose for a period of up to two years (Powers of Criminal Courts Act 1973, s.22).

(10) *Compensation Orders*

In addition to a penalty as such a court may order an offender to pay a specified sum in compensation for personal injury loss or damage resulting from the offence (Powers of Criminal Courts Act 1973, s.35).

Magistrates may order this up to a maximum of £5,000. They may also order the restoration of stolen goods to their true owner. If they decline to make a compensation order they must state their reasons (Criminal Justice Act 1988, s.104).

(11) *Forfeiture*

Where property (*e.g.* a car or burglary implements) was used in the commission of an offence it may be ordered to be forfeited (1973 Act, s.43).

(12) *Deportation*

In certain cases of offences committed by non-citizens deportation may be ordered by the Home Secretary. The court has power to recommend such an order.

THE CROWN COURT

The Crown Court which in the early seventies took over the work of the assizes and quarter sessions, is part of the Supreme Court, in which only barristers at present have a general right of audience. It has jurisdiction over offences committed anywhere in England and Wales and deals with all cases committed to it by magistrates for sentence or for jury trial and also with appeals against conviction or sentence by magistrates' courts. There is also a relatively small civil jurisdiction, including some local government and licensing matters.

The country is divided into circuits, each of which is presided over by a High Court judge, and on each circuit there will be a number of Crown Courts. Three sorts of judge sit in the Crown Court on criminal business, namely:

1. High Court judges;

2. circuit judges, who also deal with civil cases in the county court;

3. recorders: barristers or solicitors who are in practice but sit as judges for a certain number of days each year in the Crown Court.

This number may also be supplemented by deputy circuit judges appointed from practising barristers or solicitors for short periods to relieve backlogs (or to give experience to those being considered for full judicial office).

Offences are divided into four classes for the purpose of deciding which kind of judge will try them. Naturally, in each case the judge of the Crown Court, whatever his status, will have the same powers, *i.e.* limited only by the statute creating the offence.

Class 1   offences can only be tried by a High Court judge. These include murder, and genocide.

Class 2   offences *should* be tried by a High Court judge but may be released by the presiding judge of each circuit to a circuit judge. These include rape, piracy, manslaughter, certain offences of incest.

Class 3   offences may be tried by any category of judge. These include most other offences triable *only* on indictment.

Class 4   offences may be tried by any category of judge but will normally be tried by a circuit judge or recorder. These include all offences triable "either way" as well as a number only triable on indictment such as robbery and causing grievous bodily harm with intent under section 18 of the Offences Against the Person Act 1861.

The question of which kind of judge ought to hear a case is dealt with by magistrates when committing for trial. High Court judges sit only in the Crown Courts of larger towns, *e.g.* Manchester, Birmingham, and in smaller towns only circuit judges sit. If, for example, magistrates dealing with a theft case (which may be tried by any class of judge) feel that because of some factor, say the amount involved, the case ought to be dealt with by a High Court judge, they will commit the defendant for trial to a court where a High Court judge sits.

RIGHTS OF AUDIENCE IN THE CROWN COURT

Barristers of course have a right of audience in any proceedings in the Crown Court as elsewhere. Solicitors at present have certain limited rights of audience also by virtue of two practice directions of the Law Chancellor. The first of these relates only to certain named courts (*e.g.* Bodmin Crown Court), but the second is of more general application and provides that a solicitor may conduct

1. An appeal against sentence only if the solicitor (or his partner or assistant solicitor) appeared in the magistrates' court whose sentence is appealed against.

2. Certain civil cases involving an appeal against a magistrates' court decision.

It will be observed that these rights are very limited and certainly do not cover trial on indictment, the staple fare of the Crown Court. Under the Courts and Legal Services Act 1990, ss.27–33, there are detailed provisions relating to the grant of rights of audience. It is proposed that rights of audience in the higher court shall eventually be granted to solicitors and, possibly, others. At the time of writing detailed consultation about these proposals is still under way but it is conceivable within the reasonably early future that some extension will be made to solicitors' rights of audience at least in Crown Court trials.

TRIAL AT THE CROWN COURT

The basis for the trial of an accused person committed for trial at the Crown Court is the indictment. This is a short document, prepared by the prosecution or an officer of the court setting out (i) the offence charged, with a reference to the relevant statute, and (ii) particulars of the offence, including the personal particulars of the defendant and the basic facts. These must disclose that the defendant's action included all the elements of intention, etc., comprising the offence. More than one offence can be included in a single indictment, each one being called a count.

Before the trial can take place, a jury must be empanelled. The summons to jury service is by random selection from the register of electors. Some categories of persons, including practising lawyers and others connected with the administration of justice, are exempt. Others who have served terms of imprisonment are disqualified and it is always possible for a person summoned to ask to be excused on health or other personal grounds.

Sufficient persons to form a panel from which the jury can be selected are summoned to attend court. They remain outside until the defendant has pleaded to the charge, which of course is the opening stage of his trial. For this purpose the indictment is read over to him by the clerk and he is asked whether he is guilty or not guilty to each count in turn.

After he has pleaded guilty to one or more of the counts in the indictment the panel is brought into court and the clerk selects 12 by ballot. It is then possible for counsel on either side to challenge individual jury members though now a challenge may only be made for good cause, such as bias or ineligibility.

The trial commences by an opening speech from the prosecuting counsel relating the facts of the case and explaining what he must prove in law to establish the defendant's guilt.

As we have seen, witnesses may be summoned by full attendance orders or they may be subject to conditional attendance orders. The latter attend only if notice has been served by the defence requiring this. If they are not required to attend, their evidence is in effect accepted by the defence and their statements will be read out by the clerk. The defence will have received, in the meantime, not only the statements of witnesses which were presented at the committal, but also statements of any further witnesses the prosecution may decide to call.

The examination of witnesses, in chief, by cross-examination and re-examination proceeds as in a trial in the magistrates' court. The salient difference here affects the cross-examination by the defence counsel. Having the prosecution witnesses' statements before him, he is able to winkle out inconsistencies between the two accounts. Knowing the version of the events the defendant and his witnesses will give, the defence must also carefully cross-examine the prosecution's witnesses on all points where the defence evidence differs.

As in committal proceedings and, indeed, in the trial of summary offences, at the close of the prosecution case, counsel for the defendant may submit that there is no case to answer. This will be ruled on by the judge after hearing argument from counsel on both sides.

Counsel for the defence then opens his case. Provided he proposes to call one or more witnesses to the facts in addition to the defendant, he is entitled to make an opening statement. He then calls his witnesses who are examined by him and are then subject to cross-examination and re-examination.

At the conclusion of the defence case, both counsel address the jury, the prosecution counsel speaking first.

The final stage before the jury retires is the judge's summing up. The judge in the course of his summing up explains to the jury their function as sole judges of the facts and credibility of witnesses. He explains to them the nature of the burden and standard of proof resting on the prosecution, *i.e.* to prove the facts beyond reasonable doubt so that they are sure of the defendant's guilt. He reminds them of salient points of the evidence and gives them directions on matters of law. In addition he may suggest by comment and explanation how they should approach individual items of evidence and what tests they might apply in deciding whether they believe or disbelieve any individual witness. For example the judge may in describing a witness's evidence comment on obvious inconsistencies or implausibilities in what the witness has said. The judge must deal with each count of the indictment separately and instruct the jury to give a separate verdict on each count and, if there is more than one defendant deal with each defendant separately also. Finally the judge reminds the jury that it is their duty to endeavour to reach a unanimous verdict.

In due course, provided that the jury have spent at least two hours and 10 minutes deliberating (or longer in a complex or difficult case) the judge may indicate to the jury that it is permissible for him to accept a majority verdict but only where he is satisfied that there is no possibility of obtaining a unanimous verdict. By majority verdict is meant that at least 10 out of 12 jurors must agree on the verdict. If by illness of jurors or jurors withdrawing for any other reason the number on the jury has fallen below 12 to 11 or 10, the judge must only accept a verdict on which nine of the jurors agree.

YOUNG OFFENDERS

There are special rules dealing with the criminal liability of children under the age of 14. There are also special courts which deal with offenders who are under 17 years of age. These are known as youth courts, and the categories of young persons with which they deal are divided into "children," *i.e.* those aged between 10 and 13, and "young persons," *i.e.* those aged 14 to 16 inclusive.

These courts have the same status as magistrates' courts and cases are dealt with by magistrates who are specially experienced in dealing with children and young persons. As one might expect there are various procedural measures which are intended, in so far as it is feasible, to put the child or young person at his ease and to protect him. Thus, there are rules that the three magistrates must not all be of the same sex, that the general public are excluded from the proceedings, that whilst newspaper reporters may report the case they may not publish anything that will lead to identification of the juvenile concerned. The child or young person is not asked to plead guilty or not guilty, a conviction is referred to as a "finding of guilt" and the form of the oath is a "promise to tell the truth."

As well as the conduct of the proceedings themselves there are other differences in the way persons in these age groups are treated. Thus there are rules to ensure that the parents can be present whilst the police are questioning the young suspect. Children and young persons must also be held separately from adult offenders when in custody; most importantly of all, after a "finding of guilty" the range and nature of the penalties which may be imposed are very different from those which apply to adults. The chief of these are as follows:

(1) *Fines.* There are limits on the amount of fines which may be imposed; moreover in the case of a child the court *must*, and in the case of a young person it *may*, order the parents to pay the fine unless the court is satisfied that the parents attempted to exercise proper control over the child.

(2) *Supervision Order.* This is similar to probation in the case of an adult, in that a social worker keeps contact with the offender for a fixed period to attempt to assist him to become a responsible member of society. Conditions may be attached to such orders (*e.g.* as to where the offender resides). Unlike probation, the offender's consent to the order is not required.

(3) *Care Orders.* A detailed consideration of care proceedings is beyond the scope of this text but in the purely criminal context, it involves a court, following a finding of guilt, coming to the conclusion that there is something so wrong with the child or young person's environment that he is unlikely to receive proper care and control. If they do come to this conclusion they will commit the offender to the care of the local authority social services department who will then take over parental functions in respect of the child.

(4) *Detention in a young offender institution.* If a court concludes that a custodial sentence is appropriate the sentence will be served in a young offender institution. In fact offenders in the age group 17 to 21 also serve their sentences in such specialised institutions. The young offender must have legal representation

and in almost all circumstances a social inquiry report should be obtained. Moreover the young offender should only be sent to a young offender institution where the court is satisfied that he has a history of failure to respond to non-custodial penalties, or that only a custodial sentence would be adequate to protect the public, or that the offence of which he has been convicted was so serious that a non-custodial sentence can be justified. The maximum term of youth custody for a 15 or 16 year old is 12 months but for someone between 17 and 21 it is the maximum term of custody that could be imposed for the offence concerned. The usual sentencing restrictions on magistrates' powers of course apply however, and therefore if the magistrates have in mind a more severe sentence than six months for any one offence they must commit the case to the Crown Court.

Finally, it should be noted that the police may caution young persons who admit guilt for crimes without bringing them to court at all.

In conclusion, despite what is set out above, it is possible for persons under 16 to be tried by the ordinary magistrates' court, where they are jointly charged with an adult offender. The exact procedural requirements are complex and depend upon the plea, amongst other things. Moreover, normally after conviction a child or young person must be sentenced by the youth court, to which his case is then remitted.

APPEALS

It is obviously a necessary part of a civilised system of justice that there should be the possibility of appeals, whereby higher courts may review the decisions of inferior courts. In the criminal system of appeals there are various possibilities depending upon whether the appeal is primarily to challenge a finding of fact, or a decision on a matter of law, or the sentence passed. As mentioned in the introduction, the prosecution have very limited rights of appeal.

APPEAL TO THE CROWN COURT

An accused who is convicted after pleading not guilty can appeal *as of right* (*i.e.* there is no screening mechanism to sieve out unmeritorious or hopeless appeals). The appeal may be on a matter of fact or law, or both. The procedure is simple and involves sending a written notice of appeal to the clerk of the magistrates who convicted, and to the prosecution, within 21 days of sentence being passed. The notice is usually very brief and need not set out detailed grounds—it is usual in an appeal against conviction for the notice merely to say that the magistrates were in error in fact and/or in law. There may also be an appeal against sentence by the same procedure, and again the notice is usually brief stating only that the sentence was excessive.

Example:

Notice of Appeal to Crown Court

To: The Clerk to the Justices, Barchester Magistrates Court and
To: The Crown Prosecution Service
Take Notice that John Smith of 1 The Cuttings, Barset intends to appeal
against his conviction at the Barchester Magistrates' Court on the 1st
April 1993 for theft and against the sentence of three months' imprison-
ment passed on him on the grounds that:

(1) Their worships erred in fact and in law when convicting him and
(2) That the sentence was excessive in all the circumstances
Dated 5th April 1993

Rime and Reason,
Solicitors for the Appellant,
Barset.

Appeals to the Crown Court take the form of a complete new
hearing at which it is possible to call new witnesses who did not give
evidence in the lower court and raise new legal arguments.

Appeals are heard by a Crown Court judge sitting without a jury but
usually with two or more magistrates. At the conclusion of the hearing
the Crown Court may acquit, dismiss the appeal and, even if the appeal
was against conviction only, vary the sentence imposed below to any
other which the magistrates' court might have been able to impose;
there is thus a risk of an *increased* sentence although this is rare in
practice. The prosecution have no right of appeal to the Crown Court.

APPEAL TO THE HIGH COURT

Where the appeal is on a point of law alone there is an alternative
method of appeal. This is open to both prosecution and defence. This
form of appeal is by "case stated" to the Divisional Court of the
Queen's Bench Division in London.

The procedure is as follows:

(1) The party wishing to appeal must formulate the point of law
involved, *e.g.* the interpretation of a statute governing the case.

(2) Within 21 days of sentence the appellant must ask the magistrate to "state a case"—that is, to prepare a statement of matters
relevant to the point under appeal. This statement contains:
  (a) the charge.
  (b) findings of fact (these cannot be challenged).
  (c) points of law raised and authorities cited.
  (d) their decision on the point of law.
  (e) the question for decision by the Divisional Court.

The case (after an opportunity has been given to the parties to approve the way in which it has been prepared and to make representations) is then sent to the appellant who must lodge it with a notice of appeal at the Crown Office in London.

The case will then come into the list for hearing by the Divisional Court, consisting of three Queen's Bench Division judges. After purely legal argument they may quash the conviction, confirm it, or if the appeal is by the prosecutor confirm the acquittal or send the case back to the magistrates with a direction to convict.

It should be noted that after an appeal from the magistrates' court to the Crown Court there is a further appeal on a point of law only from the Crown Court to the High Court by the case stated procedure.

Apart from the forms of appeal outlined above, the decisions of magistrates may also be called into question by application to the Queen's Bench Divisional Court for a judicial review and the issue of an order of certiorari. This is granted on the same grounds as those applying in the other instances where it is used—for example where the magistrates are guilty of a failure to observe the rules of natural justice, or bias, or gross irregularity, etc.

The procedure is as follows:

(1) An *ex parte* application for leave to apply for judicial review must be made within three months by a statement of grounds and affidavit in support being lodged. The case is listed for a hearing and counsel may be heard to amplify the matters in the grounds and affidavit.

(2) If leave is given, the applicant must then serve notice of motion and affidavit on all parties including the magistrates whose order is the subject of the application for judicial review.

(3) There may be affidavits in reply, and other procedures appropriate to civil cases apply, *e.g.* discovery or interrogatories— although these are not usually relevant in this kind of case.

(4) The case is heard with all interested parties being represented and the order sought is granted, or refused.

The procedural requirements on appeals to the Crown Court are contained in the Crown Court Rules. For cases stated to the High Court they are in RSC, O. 56 and for Judicial Review, RSC, O. 53.

After trial in the Crown Court appeal may in certain cases be made by the defendant only to the Criminal Division of the Court Appeal. This topic is outside the scope of this text.

Self-Testing Questions

1. Explain the powers of arrest of the police.
2. Explain the functions and duties of the custody officer.
3. Explain the procedure for carrying out identity parades and obtaining fingerprints.
4. What factors are important when a court decides whether or not to grant legal aid?
5. What is a mode of trial hearing and what form does it follow?
6. What is a submission of no case to answer?

7. How are crimes classified for procedural purposes?
8. When can a defendant plead guilty by post?
9. What are the forms of committal proceedings?
10. What are the relevant factors which would help one in deciding whether to choose magistrates' court or Crown Court trial where the choice exists?
11. Explain the procedure for the rights of appeal in relation to decisions of magistrates' courts.
12. What factors do the magistrates take into account when deciding whether to grant bail?
13. What powers does the court have to grant adjournments?
14. Explain the powers of search of the police.
15. How are proceedings commenced in the magistrates' court?

CHAPTER 7

PROCEEDINGS IN THE COUNTY COURT

THE COURT

There are some 300 county courts and county court districts, into which the whole of England and Wales is divided. The court in the City of London, which is a separate district, retains its old name of The Mayor's and City of London Court. The judges who sit in the county court are circuit judges and are addressed as "Your Honour."

Each district has its own court and court premises under a district judge. A district judge is appointed by the Lord Chancellor from among solicitors and he is responsible for the business of his court. The larger courts in big urban areas (Manchester, Birmingham, etc.) have more than one district judge, indeed sometimes as many as five or six. These are then known as "joint district judges." Sometimes deputy district judges are appointed from the ranks of practising solicitors to sit temporarily as district judge at times to assist in clearing backlogs of work or during holidays. In some areas courts are collected together in a small group which only has one district judge between them. The district judge, then, is the most important person in the county court. He has judicial functions as well as administrative ones. He decides most of the questions of procedure which arise in the stages between the starting of an action and the actual trial where the circuit judge will sit to decide the matter in open court. The district judge himself will act as a judge in a range of minor cases. He is assisted by clerical staff under a chief clerk. They hold and issue the stock of forms, issue summonses, keep the court diaries, keep the court records, receive fees and generally administer the court's service on behalf of the district judge.

All correspondence with the court should be addressed to "the chief clerk" who is in charge of the administrative functions under the district judge.

Finally, in dealing with the personnel of the court one should mention the court bailiffs. They form a separate department and they are court officers responsible for the personal service of summonses and other documents when required and for the practical steps in enforcing judgments by what is known as "a warrant of execution" to which we shall return later.

Every court office, or if a court has more than one office then at least one of those offices, is open every day except Saturdays and Sundays, Bank Holidays, Good Friday and the afternoon before Good Friday, the Tuesday after the Spring Holiday and two additional working days at Christmas. The office opening hours are usually 10.00am to 4.00pm although in the months of August and September the court office may close earlier in the afternoon. In August and September the number of sittings of the judge in the county court is greatly reduced.

The County Courts Act 1984 is the main Act which governs proceedings in the county court. It consolidates all previous statutes relating to the powers of the court. It must, however, now be read in the light of the High Court and County Courts Jurisdiction Order 1991 which substantially expands the powers of the county court giving it a wider jurisdiction than it had before that Order came into effect in July 1991.

THE RULES

As one can imagine in earlier times in the civil courts the litigants came with their witnesses before the judge, said what they had to say, called the evidence if necessary and then received judgment immediately. In the modern world such a system of litigation would be quite impossible. The complexity of modern life and of the substantive law leads to regulation. It would be quite unfair as a means of getting at the truth of the matter for the parties simply to attend and argue matters out then and there. The primary objectives of the County Court Rules (C.C.R.) like those of the Rules of the Supreme Court which apply in the High Court (R.S.C.) are:

1. to ensure that the matters in dispute are accurately and succinctly set down so as to be plainly understood by the other parties and the court;

2. to clarify any matters of fact which may assist the court in coming to its decisions;

3. to ensure so far as practicable fairness between the parties and avoid any party being taken by surprise where he ought reasonably to have been informed;

4. to save the time of all concerned and thereby minimise costs.

Accordingly the various rules of procedure, which often seem elaborate and even pointless to the uninitiated, have come about. They are there to make litigation fairer and more efficient and not to unnecessarily hamper the parties with rules and regulations. A solicitor or legal executive who knows how to make best use of the rules and when to take certain steps and by what method will be able to conduct litigation in his client's best interests. Someone who is not properly experienced in the use of the rules will inevitably be disadvantaged and so will his client. This does not imply that the experienced legal executive is obtaining any kind of unfair advantage. The whole point of employing lawyers after all is to obtain an expertise which the layman does not have. The greater this expertise is, the better the lawyer.

The reference book for the code is the County Court Practice, an annual publication (The Green Book). The rules are contained in a series of Orders covering the different stages and facets of proceedings. Each Order is divided into a number of rules detailing the requirements for every procedural step and regulating communications between the parties and with the court. Particular rules are cited, *e.g.* Ord.8, r.3. Whilst the student may not be expected to learn Order and rule numbers, they are included in the text so that the reader can consult the source of what can only be summarised here when applying the rules in practice. Students are well advised to make use of the Green Book in the course of their work in the office and to familiarise themselves with the layout of its various sections.

We shall mention one or two preliminary matters:

(1) *Time*

Naturally, time limits are imposed for each procedural step in the county court. These time limits can almost always be extended or abridged either by the consent of all the parties or with the leave of the court if one party will not agree. A party who wants an extension of time (and as we will see some of the time limits given for the various steps are quite short) invariably seeks his opponent's agreement to the extension in the first instance. One reasonable extension of a week or a fortnight is almost always given as a matter of professional courtesy between lawyers. Thereafter, if a further extension is necessary and is refused by one's opponent, application must be made to the court to extend the time. Generally anyway, time limits are less rigidly adhered to in the county court than they are in the High Court. Some time limits of general application are set out in a table for reference at the very end of this chapter.

(2) *The forms*

The County Court Rules prescribe a number of forms for use at various stages of proceedings. These are the formal documents by which applications to the court are made or applications between the parties. The form should be followed as closely as possible though must be varied to meet the circumstances of each case.

(3) *The Court file*

In the county court a file is kept in which almost all documents of any importance are retained. It follows, therefore, that important procedural stages usually (but not always) occur through the court so that a party wishing to take a certain step will send the necessary documents to the court, one of which the court will retain on the court file and the other which it will post on to the opposite party. It follows from this that almost all business can be done with the county court by pre-paid post. Communication should be addressed to the chief clerk of the court and any court fees, etc., must be paid with the relevant application. If a reply from the court is necessary to the party writing then a stamped addressed envelope is required. Personal attendance of the parties' solicitors or legal executives is required for certain kinds of hearing on procedural matters in the stages preparatory to trial as we shall see.

(4) *The cases*

The different forms of procedure will be illustrated by a number of fictitious cases. These will show the various important stages. We shall start by showing how judgment can be obtained in a simple debt case against a defendant who does not participate in the proceedings. This is called "judgment in default." After this case we shall consider some important matters to do with procedure generally.

RECOVERY OF A DEBT

William Dunbar and Co. v. *John Cowper*

William Dunbar and Co. are a firm of timber merchants. They are established clients of Messrs. Makepiece & Streiff and in particular they often instruct Messrs. Makepiece in connection with trade debts. This time, they send to the firm copy invoices for timber supplied together with a statement of account and a copy of a demand for payment. In this case the legal executive Mr. White, who has the conduct of this client's debt collecting business, supervises the preparation by the trainee legal executive Joan of the documents required to recover judgment for the debt and costs. It seems that William Dunbar & Co. have supplied a small local builder John Cowper with a considerable quantity of expensive teak wood.

Joan therefore sends a letter to John Cowper reminding him of the debt and how it arose and of the time it has been outstanding. The letter concludes "if payment is not made directly to ourselves within seven days from today that is to say by no later than January 14, 1993 proceedings will be commenced against you in the county court to recover the debt and costs." The writing of this letter is not a mere formality or courtesy. It is vital to ensure that the facts are as stated by the firm in their instructions and that there has been no misunderstanding on the part of the debtor, for example that he has been allowed credit, nor that he has any legitimate ground for refusing to pay. If proceedings had been commenced without the step of writing this letter, then even though it would not have affected the merits of the case if Cowper had paid at once, it is very likely that the court would have thought the plaintiffs unreasonable in commencing the action without giving the debtor this further chance to pay and would have not awarded the firm their legal costs.

After January 14th Joan allows a further two working days for possible postal delays and then prepares a default summons against the defendant. She also prepares particulars of claim to be served with the summons on the defendant, with a further copy of the particulars for the court and a further copy for her own file. The form of summons sent out to the defendant is illustrated below. As will be observed, the back of the summons contains information and instructions to the defendant as to how to deal with the matter. The form of particulars of claim annexed to the summons is also illustrated. The particulars of claim are drafted to claim not only the original debt which is due but also interest on this sum. In such cases interest can be claimed by virtue of section 69 of the County Courts Act 1984. The rate currently allowed by the court without any investigation is 15 per cent per annum and the plaintiff will be happy to settle for interest at this rate. If he had wished to claim a higher rate there would need to have been a court hearing to assess the rate and in fact it is most unlikely that the court would have allowed any higher rate. If the terms of any written contract between the plaintiff and the defendant had stipulated a rate of interest which would be paid on sums outstanding then that would be the applicable rate at which interest would be claimed and interest would be due pursuant to the contract rather than under s.69 of the Act. The particulars of claim must be drafted therefore not merely to claim the sum due but also the interest on the sum, and as there is no provision in the contract in this case interest is claimed at 15 per cent per annum under section 69 of the County Courts Act 1984. This must be shown as an exact figure quantified to the date of issue of the summons and at a daily rate thereafter, so this will allow the defendant to know precisely what his obligation is in respect of the debt plus interest on any given day.

RECOVERY OF A DEBT

William Dunbar & Co. v. J. Cowper

Mr. White has signed the completed Summons and the Particulars of Claim in the firm name, under the general authority vested in him by the partners. Joan takes the Summons and Particulars of Claim with one copy and the money to cover the plaint fee to the county court office. Joan hands over the relevant documents at the court counter. In small county courts it may be possible for the documentation to be dealt with then and there but in busier courts one has to leave the documentation for checking and later issue. In the present case, as Barset is a busy county court Joan has to leave the documents and three days later the court actually issue the summons. To do this the court staff allocate a case number to the case; they then attach to the summons and particulars of the claim a Form of Admission Defence and Counterclaim (form N9) which indicates that the defendant has various options upon receipt of the summons and particulars of claim. These are then posted by first class post to the defendant. At the same time a notice of issue of default summons in form 205A is sent out to the plaintiff's solicitors. This contains details of the case number and constitutes the official receipt for the court fee. It also has attached to it a form of request for judgment which we shall discuss below.

When the court sends out a summons and particulars of claim by post the defendant is deemed to have received them seven days after the date of the postmark. He then has a further 14 days in which to deal with the summons and particulars of claim received. To do this he has to complete form N9 indicating whether he admits the claim; whether

County Court Summons

Case Number	^{Always quote this} 93 0242

In the BARSET

County Court

The court office is open from 10 am to 4 pm Monday to Friday

(1) Plaintiff's full name address.

William Dumbar and James Dunbar
(trading as William Dunbar & Co)
1 High Street
Barset

Telephone:

(2) Address for service (and) payment.
(if not as above)
Ref/Tel no.

Makepiece and Streiff
Bank Chambers
Barset

Ref EW/90031   Tel 00765 4321

Seal

(3) Defendant's name address.

John Cowper
47 Elm Street
Barset

This summons is only valid if sealed by the court.
If it is not sealed it should be sent to the court.

What the plaintiff claims from you

Brief description of type of claim

The price of goods sold

Particulars of the Plaintiff's claim against you

See attached particulars of claim

Amount claimed	1256	22
Court fee	43	00
Solicitor's costs	59	00
Total amount	1358	22
Summons issued on	19.1.1993.	

What to do about this summons

You can

- dispute the claim
- make a claim against the Plaintiff
- admit the claim in full and offer to pay
- pay the total amount shown above
- admit only part of the claim

For information on what to do or if you need further advice, please turn over.

Signed

Plaintiff('s solicitor)
(or see enclosed particulars of claim)

N1 Default summons (fixed amount) (Order 3, rule 3(2)(b))

Keep this summons, you may need to refer to it.

You have 21 days from the date of the postmark to reply to this summons

(A limited company served at its registered office has 16 days to reply.)

If you do nothing	**Judgment may be entered against you without further notice.**
If you dispute the claim	Complete the white defence form (N9B) and return it to the court office. The notes on the form explain what you should do.
If you want to make a claim against the plaintiff (counterclaim)	Complete boxes 5 and 6 on the white defence form (N9B) and return the form to the court office. The notes at box 5 explain what you should do.
If you admit all of the claim and you are asking for time to pay	Fill in the blue admission form (N9A). The notes on the form explain what you should do and where you should send the completed form.
If you admit all of the claim and you wish to pay now	**Take or send the money to the person named at box (2) on the front of the summons.** If there is no address in box (2), send the money to the address in box (1). Read How to Pay below.
If you admit only part of the claim	Fill in the white defence form (N9B) saying how much you admit, then **either:** Pay the amount admitted as explained in the box above; **or** Fill in the blue admission form (N9A) if you need time to pay.

Interest on Judgments

If judgment is entered against you and is for more than £5,000, the Plaintiff may be entitled to interest on the total amount.

Registration of Judgments

If the summons results in a judgment against you, your name and address may be entered in the Register of County Court Judgments. **This may make it difficult for you to get credit.** A leaflet giving further information can be obtained from the court.

Further Advice

You can get help to complete the reply forms and information about court procedures at any county court office or citizens' advice bureau. The address and telephone number of your local court is listed under "Courts" in the phone book. When corresponding with the court, please address forms or letters to the Chief Clerk. Always quote the whole of the case number which appears at the top right corner on the front of this form; the court is unable to trace your case without it.

How to pay	To be completed on the court copy only
• **PAYMENT(S) MUST BE MADE to the person named at the address for payment quoting their reference and the court case number.** • **DO NOT bring or send payments to the court. THEY WILL NOT BE ACCEPTED.** • You should allow **at least 4** days for your payments to reach the plaintiff or his representative. • Make sure that you keep records and can account for all payments made. Proof may be required if there is any disagreement. It is not safe to send cash unless you use registered post. • A leaflet giving further advice about payment can be obtained from the court. • If you need more information you should contact the plaintiff or his representative.	Served on By posting on Officer Marked "gone away" on

OYEZ The Solicitors' Law Stationery Society Ltd, Oyez House, 7 Spa Road, London SE16 3QQ

County Court N1

1991 Edition
3.92 F22118
5039008
* * * *

In the Barset County Court   Case No 930242

BETWEEN

William Dunbar and James Dunbar   Plaintiffs
(trading as William Dunbar and Co)
and
John Cowper   Defendant

Particulars of Claim

The Plaintiffs claim is for the price of goods sold and delivered by the
Plaintiffs to the Defendant at his request and for interest thereon
pursuant to s.69 County Courts Act 1984.

Particulars

23 September 1992:   12 lengths best teak   £1,200

And the plaintiffs claim
   (1) The said sum of £1,200
   (2) Interest pursuant to the said statute of the rate of 15% per
       annum on the sum of £1,200 from 23rd September 1992 to the
       date hereof equivalent to a sum of £56.22p.
   (3) Interest at the said rate equivalent to a daily rate of 49p from
       the date hereof until judgment or earlier payment.

Dated January 19, 1993

To: The Chief Clerk of the Court   Makepiece and Streiff
     and the Defendant   Bank Chambers Barset
                                         Solicitors for the Plaintiffs
                                         who will at that address
                                         accept
                                         service of proceedings.

he is able to pay at once or needs time to pay; or whether he disputes the claim entirely or in part. He is informed in the accompanying documents that he must return this form no later than 21 days after the date of the postmark on the summons. If on receipt of the form the defendant admits the claim in full and is able to pay the money all at once, then the form instructs him to send the money direct to the plaintiff. If the defendant does not respond to the summons at all within 14 days from the date on which he received it, or is deemed to have received it, then judgment can be entered. This happens "over the counter" at the court office and there is no hearing before a judge of any kind. Accordingly, in the present case, after the 14 day period has elapsed Mr. White asks Joan to prepare the form of Request for Judgment. This enables the plaintiff's solicitor to specify what order as to payment the court is asked to make. The plaintiff's solicitor may ask that the whole amount be payable immediately or may fix instalments over a period. Mr. White takes into account the fact that his client will want to recover the whole amount as soon as possible given that it has been outstanding for some months. Accordingly he tells Joan to allow seven days for payment of the whole amount. Joan then takes the request to the county court office and there is then a further check that no form of defence has been received by the court. She hands in the request and the chief clerk enters judgment for the plaintiff for the amount of the claim, together with interest up to the date when judgment is entered and for the amount of fixed costs. The chief clerk then sends to the defendant by post the judgment for the plaintiff. If the defendant fails within the seven days to discharge the debt by paying the whole amount into the court office, Mr. White will then consider what courses are open to him to enforce the judgment. We shall consider the options in relation to this below at page 361.

We have so far therefore, considered in outline a straightforward debt collecting case where no resistance was met from the debtor. Before going on to consider rather more complicated kinds of proceedings, and alternative possible outcomes to the case we have just introduced we shall consider a number of preliminary matters.

PRELIMINARY MATTERS

THE COUNTY COURT JURISDICTION

Until 1991 the general jurisdiction of the county court under the 1984 County Courts Act was limited, in most cases, to actions involving less than £5,000. The High Court and County Courts Jurisdiction Order 1991 dramatically increased the jurisdiction of the county court with the overall objective of transferring a large number of cases from the High Court, where previously they would have been dealt with, to the county court. The position now is as follows:

(1) *Personal injury cases*

Cases involving a claim for personal injury must now be commenced in the county court unless the plaintiff's solicitor can certify at the time when the action is commenced that the case involves a total sum of more than £50,000. Thus only personal injury cases of considerable severity can now be commenced in the High Court and all others must be commenced in the county court and this is so even if they present great difficulties of law or evidence. The only relevant criterion for choosing the court in which one must commence personal injury actions is the question of value of the case.

(2) *Cases other than personal injuries*

The county court now has no upper jurisdiction limit in mainstream actions in tort and contract. Such cases may therefore now be commenced in either the county court or the High Court which are the two civil courts of first instance. However, although one can commence such cases (with a few exceptions) in either court that is not to say that those cases will remain in the court in which they start right through until the end of the trial. The question of which is the appropriate court for *trial* will be reviewed at a later stage. When reviewing the question of which court is the appropriate one for trial then value of the case is one important criterion and, in principle, cases involving £25,000 or less are likely to be tried in the county court unless they raise grave difficulties of law, fact or evidence or questions of general public interest. Cases involving more than £50,000 are likely to be tried in the High Court; and cases within the bracket £25,000–£50,000 may be tried in either court depending on the complexity of the facts and issues, questions of general public interest, etc., mentioned above. Consequently, as a very broad rule of thumb, cases involving less than £25,000 will probably be started in the county court because that is likely to be the eventual court of trial anyway; and cases involving more than £50,000, even if they appear relatively straightforward cases, will usually be started in the High Court. It ought to be said that, although practitioners will now have considerable choice in respect of many kinds of action, there are often thought to be cogent features favouring the High Court over the county court in certain types of case even if quite modest sums are involved. Debt collecting cases of the kind we have just seen above are often thought particularly suitable for the High Court where the early procedures are somewhat faster and more efficient, and the enforcement methods available are similarly thought to be rather more effective. Detailed discussion of the features of High Court procedure which tend to be more advantageous in debt collecting actions are, however, beyond the scope of the present book and readers should consult *Introduction to Legal Practice* Volume II. Having said that the High Court is often thought to be more suitable for efficient disposal of debt collecting actions, it is unlikely that a case such as *Dunbar* v. *Cowper* above would have been commenced in the High Court having regard to the very modest amount claimed. However, it is fair to say that cases involving, perhaps, £5,000 or thereabouts would still very probably be commenced in the High Court if the plaintiffs hoped for an early resolution of them because the defendant had no real defence.

(3) *Exceptional cases*

There is a handful of exceptional cases where the plaintiff has no option as to choice of court but must issue proceedings in the county court however much is involved. This is because there are certain statutes which confer exclusive jurisdiction on the county court in relation to the kind of actions brought under those statutes. An example is the Consumer Credit Act 1974 and there are other examples relating to proceedings between landlord and tenant.

WHICH COUNTY COURT?

Until 1991 the plaintiff had to demonstrate some local connection with the action before he could issue in any given county court. Basically the plaintiff could only issue his summons in the court within whose district the cause of action arose or within which the defendant resided. Now, however, that restriction has been abolished and a plaintiff may commence a default action in any county court whatsoever. He will naturally therefore choose the county court most convenient either to him, or probably to his solicitor's office. However, what happens to the action thereafter depends upon whether it is an action for a liquidated sum such as a debt or a case where damages have to be assessed by the court. If the action is for damages then when the defendant files a defence, if he does so, he may apply in writing for the case to be transferred to another county court (*e.g.* the one where he lives or where his solicitor's office is). The district judge of the court will then give the plaintiff the opportunity to make representation before deciding where, on a balance of convenience, the case should continue. In a debt case, however, then once the defence is filed the proceedings are automatically transferred to the defendant's nearest court without his needing to make any specific application for this to happen. Thereafter it is up to the plaintiff to write to the district judge of that court requesting that the proceedings be transferred back to the court from which they were issued if he wishes.

In indicating above that the plaintiff's solicitors are usually keen to see that the action proceeds, if at all possible, in the county court nearest their offices this is not of course to say that they expect in any sense to receive "home town justice." It is simply a matter of convenience. If for appointments at the court a five-minute walk down the street is all that is necessary, this will be greatly to the firm's advantage and will save the client costs. If, on the other hand, proceedings have to be pursued in a county court an hour's drive away, someone will have to pay for the time spent making the drive there and unfortunately it is likely to be the client.

ACTIONS AND MATTERS

We have already used the terms "plaintiff" and "defendant" and these are appropriate for legal proceedings between parties in tort and contract. These are known as "actions." Most routine proceedings in the county court then are actions commenced by a summons issued by the court after being presented by the plaintiff. Other forms of proceedings are called "matters" and have separate rules specifying how they are commenced and conducted. For example, matrimonial cases which are within the jurisdiction of some county courts are commenced by lodging a petition and the parties are then referred to as "petitioner" and "respondent." Similarly, bankruptcy proceedings are a type of matter commenced by petition. In the rest of this text we shall only be considering ordinary actions between plaintiff and defendant.

LIMITATION OF ACTIONS

This phrase refers to the time limit within which a person whose legal rights have been infringed must bring an action to enforce those rights or to obtain compensation. In *criminal* cases, unless some statute provides otherwise there is no limitation. A serious offence can be prosecuted even decades after the crime if it takes that long for the criminal's culpability to come to light. In civil cases however there are limitation periods laid down by statutes in particular in the Limitation Act 1980. This is because memories fade and witnesses become hard to trace. Therefore persons who think they have a right of action are given a set period within which they must commence their proceedings so that a defendant does not have such possible actions hanging over his head indefinitely. The rules relating to limitation periods are complicated and cater for a variety of special circumstances. For example, suppose that there is a road accident and a person suffers a broken leg. The usual period within which an action must be commenced in such a situation is three years from the accident and this causes no basic difficulty. Three years is after all long enough for anybody to realise they have been badly injured and consult a lawyer who can commence proceedings in court within the time. What, however, if that person had been:

(a) only 8 years old or;

(b) had suffered head injuries and gone into a coma for 3 years or;

(c) did not know who had been the driver of the vehicle concerned and took 4 years to find this out?

There are a variety of rules catering for these and other more difficult situations. However, in straightforward cases the rules are that, in ordinary actions in contract and tort there is 6 years from the time when the cause of action arose until the writ must be issued; in personal injuries cases the period is basically 3 years subject to exceptions and to a general discretion in the court to extend the period for good reason; and in actions concerning land the limitation period is usually 12 years from the cause of action arising. It ought to be obvious from these periods, that so long as the client consults the solicitor or legal executive in time a lawyer who attends promptly to his client's matters is unlikely to be in danger of exceeding the period allowed by the law. This is however an important point at which to remind oneself of what appears earlier in this book in connection with the keeping of efficient diaries. If negotiations get under way with an insurance company in an attempt to settle a client's injury claim, clear warning dates should be put in the diary well ahead of the expiry of the 3 year limitation period so that if the negotiations prove unfruitful court proceedings can be issued in good time.

THE PARTIES

If it is a simple matter of one sane adult suing another there is usually no problem. However there may be more complicated situations and we shall now consider some of these:

(1) *Limited companies*

A limited company is a "legal person" and is able to sue and be sued in its own corporate name. It has all the rights and obligations of a natural person and can sue and be sued without needing to employ a solicitor in the county court.

(2) *Other corporations*

There are other corporate bodies such as local authorities, trade unions and "corporations sole," *e.g.* a public officer whose functions pass from one office holder to the next such as a mayor. All these persons may sue and be sued in their corporate name.

(3) *Partnerships*

We have seen from the form of proceedings that William Dunbar & Co. is a partnership. This is not like a limited company. A partnership can sue for debts owed to it and can be sued. Creditors of a partnership can enforce payment of debts not only against the partnership property but also against the individual personal property of the partners. A partnership sues as shown in the particulars of the claim illustrated earlier, that is usually by either naming the partners or by suing in the business name or both. It is common to add the words "suing as a firm."

(4) *Sole traders*

An individual trader who trades in his own name is in the same position as a private person and there is no problem. If he uses a business name, however, to conduct his business, for example a shop-keeper who calls his shop and business "Rainbow Aquarium Supplies," he must use his own personal name when he sues someone else. However, when someone wishes to sue him they may sue him either in his own name or in his business name.

If a business name is used in the title of proceedings, whether by a partnership or a sole trader, then any other party to those proceedings can request to be told the names and addresses of all the persons who are partners or the person who is the proprietor of the business at the time when the cause of action arose. If the firm concerned does not comply with this request, an application can be made to the court for an order compelling them to do so.

(5) *Unincorporated groups*

There are special rules with regard to clubs and charities when they bring proceedings or are sued in the county court. We shall not consider these further here because of their complexity.

(6) *Persons under a disability*

The term "person under a disability" does not mean someone who is suffering the consequences of an accident. It means someone who is under a *legal* disability, that is someone who is either a *minor* or *a mental patient*. Such persons cannot sue or be sued in their own names but must have a sane adult to protect their position. Such a person who wishes to sue someone sues by his "next friend." This is a relative or other person who takes on the burden of acting for the plaintiff in the proceedings. The name of the plaintiff is then entered in the proceedings as "AB (A minor) suing by DB his (mother and) next friend." The same rules apply to mental patients.

When minors or mental patients are sued they must also have an adult to represent them though in such a case the adult is known as a "*guardian-ad-litem*." Accordingly someone wishing to sue a person under a disability must see that a *guardian-ad-litem* comes forward or is appointed by the court. Exceptionally, if a minor is sued for a liquidated sum, (*i.e.* a debt) the court may on the application of the plaintiff direct that no appointment of a *guardian-ad-litem* is necessary.

The position of the person who appears in proceedings on behalf of minors and mental patients is that when acting for a plaintiff the next friend becomes personally liable for costs of the action. Accordingly, if the plaintiff loses then the next friend will have to pay the costs, although he may recover these if he can from the person under a disability. Accordingly, a next friend must give an undertaking to the court to pay any costs awarded against the person under a disability at the start of proceedings. He also of course has to meet the legal costs of the person under a disability himself to his own solicitor if any. In the case of the *guardian-ad-litem* however the position is not so grave.

Since in such a case the person under a disability had no say whether or not he was dragged into the proceedings, a *guardian-ad-litem* acting for such a person is only liable for costs if these are incurred due to his own misconduct or neglect.

JOINDER OF PARTIES AND ACTIONS

In the case where one individual or limited company wants to sue another there is clearly no complicating factor. What however if there is more than one cause of action or more than one person who wants to sue, or a plaintiff who wants to sue more than one defendant? Can these things all be done in the one set of proceedings with the object of saving time and costs? We shall now discuss this aspect.

(1) *Joinder of parties*

Where damage or loss arising out of a single transaction or series of transactions is caused by several persons either jointly or in the alternative then the person who has been affected can sue those other persons in the one set of proceedings *provided that* the same questions of law or fact apply as against all the defendants.

Example

Three vehicles collide at an unmarked junction and one of them spins off on to the pavement injuring a pedestrian P. It is unclear to P which of the drivers was to blame because he was not watching the junction. Possibly all three were to blame. Accordingly, he will sue all three in the same proceedings being virtually certain of success and leaving them to argue out their respective degrees of blameworthiness.

The same provision applies with a number of *plaintiffs*. Suppose that five persons are standing in a queue at a bus stop when a vehicle negligently driven by D swerves off the road and into the queue injuring all five. The five plaintiffs can sue in the same set of proceedings.

It should be noted that this rule is simply one that gives the persons affected a *possibility*. There is no compulsion on them to sue in the same proceedings and they can if they like sue separately. It would have been foolish for the plaintiff in the example given above to have sued each of the drivers separately because he had no way of knowing which of them was to blame. Suing all three together was a very convenient way of letting the court sort that problem out. Had he risked suing just one of them he might have chosen the one who was actually innocent in the collision. In the second example, however, each of the plaintiffs could if he wished have sued the driver in separate proceedings. In such a case this would normally be better because the rule is that where plaintiffs sue jointly they must use the same solicitors and counsel and all proceed in tandem. Often each plaintiff wants to use his own solicitor and proceed at different speeds. For example, someone in the bus queue who had suffered only a minor foot injury might be anxious to get a couple of hundred pounds very quickly whereas someone who had suffered much more major injuries might wish to delay matters until the medical position had stabilised. Although joint *plaintiffs* have to use the same solicitor, joint *defendants* do not, indeed often the essence of the case of joint defendants, as in the road accident example given above, is that they will all wish to blame each other and so must be separately represented.

(2) *Joinder of causes of action*

If one person wishes to sue another in respect of two different causes of action this is normally possible provided that each person sues or defends in the same capacity. In other words, one could not sue X in respect of two debts for one of which he is personally liable and for the other where he is liable as the executor of his aunt's estate. Separate actions would have to be commenced in respect of each debt. However, if both parties are in the same capacity then any number of actions can be joined. Suppose for example that A owes B a debt of £10,000. They meet to discuss terms for repayment and in the course of the discussion tempers become frayed and A punches B on the nose. A little while later A who is still very upset about the whole business describes B as "a crook and a swindler" to a neighbour. In this situation B can sue A for the debt, the battery and the defamation in the same proceedings if he chooses. Again the rules merely permit this if he wishes; they do not compel him to do so and it would arguably be bad tactics and complicate matters unduly to issue the one set of proceedings and better to sue separately for each.

(3) *Consolidation*

If a number of persons start proceedings separately against one defendant then it is possible to consolidate all the actions. For example, where damage or loss is caused in the same way, by a single person to several unconnected individuals, their causes can be consolidated and either heard all together or heard separately in succession by the judge who will reserve judgment until the last case.

Example

Barset District Council decides to obtain vacant possession of old houses to make way for redevelopment. All the tenants are resisting eviction. They claim that the development is an unjustified oppressive use of powers. The tenants all have identical interests and as they defend each action brought against them in turn all the actions are consolidated into one. The same would apply if the tenants had taken the initiative and found cause to sue the local authority, again the actions could have been consolidated.

STARTING THE ACTION

(1) *The necessary documents*

We have already considered in the case which we have briefly looked at, *William Dunbar & Co.* v. *John Cowper*, how an action is commenced. The document used was a *default summons*. There are in fact two forms of summons. A default summons is the standard procedure where all that is claimed is money, whether for a debt or some other specified amount which is known as a liquidated sum or for damages which the court itself will have to fix which is known as an "unliquidated sum." That case showed what happened in a simple case where the defendant made no response to the summons so that judgment was entered in default.

The other kind of summons is known as a *fixed date* summons. A fixed date summons is appropriate where the claim is for something which is not measurable in money terms. For example, for the return of goods which have been unlawfully obtained by the other party, or for an injunction or for the recovery of possession of land. In such a case the summons itself notifies the defendant of a fixed date on which a hearing is to take place. With a default summons, the summons does not mention any date. It merely instructs the defendant to respond to the summons by returning the form of Admission Defence and Counterclaim within 14 days. Fixed date summonses are briefly dealt with below at p.339.

In addition to the summons, a *particulars of claim* must be filed at court at the time of issuing the summons. In the particulars of claim the plaintiff specifies the legal basis of his claim, his "cause of action" and the relief or remedy which he is seeking and states briefly all the material facts on which he relies. The particulars of claim is known as a "pleading." It must be carefully drafted. If the action is to recover a simple debt and the particulars are short enough to conveniently be put into the summons itself this is normally allowed. However, if this is not done, then a copy of the particulars of claim must be filed at court for the court record and an additional copy provided for service on every defendant to be served. The plaintiff or his solicitor must sign the particulars of claim. In either case, an address for service must be given, that of the solicitor himself or if there is no solicitor the plaintiff personally.

In addition to the summons and the particulars of claim with sufficient copies, Joan would have had to pay a court fee at the county court when issuing proceedings. The rates of fees are prescribed in the County Court Fees Order 1982 as amended. It is vital to take a correct fee down to court at the time of issue. The County Court staff will accept a solicitor's cheque but ordinary individuals will have to provide a cheque supported by a banker's card, or cash. The cheque is made payable to "H.M. Paymaster General." If sending documents for issue to the court by post it is vital to ensure that the correct fee is provided otherwise delay and difficulty will be experienced.

(2) *What the court does*

Once the court has received the proper documents then the documents and court file will be prepared by the clerical and typing staff of the court. This may take a little time, perhaps a week or more in a busy urban county court. The court will then deal with service of the documents to which we shall come shortly. The documents to be delivered to the defendant are the summons, a copy of the particulars of claim with the court stamp on and, as we have discussed above (p.298), a form which the county court itself prepares (form N9) called an "Admission Defence and Counterclaim." This is a form of questionnaire to the defendant inviting him to respond to the summons and particulars of claim which he will have received. We shall consider the alternative responses in due course.

SERVICE OF PROCEEDINGS

Having commenced the action by the delivery of the correct documents to the county court we must now consider how the necessary documents, once issued are to be brought to the attention of the defendant. There is a variety of options and which one is to be adopted will depend amongst other things on speed and certainty. We will explain this a little more fully in due course.

So that no injustice is caused, it is obvious that care must be taken to bring the documents to the attention of the person to whom they are directed. The following methods are available for service of these documents, that is to say the default summons, the particulars of claim and the form of Admission Defence and Counterclaim. Service may be either by the court itself or by the solicitor for the plaintiff.

(1) *Service by the court*

(a) *By post.* In most cases, except perhaps in debt collecting cases where it is suspected that the defendant may attempt deliberately to evade service, service by post will be sufficient. If the plaintiff is happy for the court to serve the documents by post then he may so indicate and there is no charge for the court doing so. In the case of postal service the chief clerk will send a certificate of the date of service to the plaintiff. As we have seen, the summons is deemed to have come to the defendant's notice on the seventh day after posting where the defendant is an individual. If the defendant is a limited company there is a separate rule that the defendant is deemed to have received the documents on the second working day after posting.

(b) *By the court bailiff.* Service of documents by post is likely to be good enough where there is no reason to suppose that the defendant will be difficult or evasive or claim non-delivery. Accordingly, in say ordinary personal injuries litigation where the defendant will refer the summons immediately to his insurance company, and there is no great urgency, postal service will suffice. If, however, greater certainty is required, and a common instance of this is debt proceedings, especially where the defendant may have already failed to respond to a number of letters and reminders about the debt, application can be made to the court for service by the court bailiff. A further fee is payable for this. The bailiff will attend personally at the address given and hand the summons, etc., to the defendant. If he refuses to take the documents it will be sufficient for the bailiff to tell him what it is and to throw it down in his presence. Where this method of service is used the bailiff will report to the chief clerk and a certificate of service will again be sent to the plaintiff.

(2) *Service by the plaintiff's solicitors*

The plaintiff's solicitor may, instead of relying on the services of the court, ask for the documents back once they are issued by the court with a view to serving them himself. He is likely to want to do this by one of two methods.

(a) *Personal service.* If for any reason the plaintiff's solicitor doubts whether bailiff's service will be effective and there is some need for absolute certainty in service, as where the plaintiff suspects from the defendant's previous conduct in relation to the matter (particularly in a debt case) that he is likely to prove evasive, the plaintiff may prefer the greater certainty of arranging for service by a process server. Process servers are members of firms of inquiry agents (or private detectives as the layman often knows them) who specialise in serving court documents on individuals. They are very skilful at gaining access to persons' houses and they tend to arrive at times when they are likely to feel the people will be home, (*e.g.* late evening and very early morning—times when the court bailiff is not at work). A fee is of course payable by the solicitor to the process server for this service but in fact the fee may not be substantially higher than the fee payable to the court bailiff anyway. Where personal service is made by a process server then the process server has to prepare an affidavit of service. This is a document by the process server sworn on oath before a solicitor (though not the one who instructed him) or at the counter of the court before an officer of the court. Suppose that in the case that we have already considered of *William Dunbar & Co.* v. *John Cowper*, the plaintiff's solicitors have decided to opt for personal service by process server and had arranged for the documents to be returned from the court for that purpose. A copy of the affidavit of service in such a case appears by way of illustration at the end of this section.

(b) *Service on the defendant's solicitor.* If the defendant has already instructed solicitors who have already written to the plaintiff's solicitors, saying that they will accept service on the defendant's behalf when proceedings are issued, then the plaintiff's solicitors should arrange to get the documents back from the court and forward them to the defendant's solicitors by ordinary post. This will then be satisfactory service. It is important to note, however, that the defendant's solicitors must have specifically undertaken that they will accept service of documents in respect of this case. It is not good enough to serve documents on a firm of solicitors whom the plaintiffs know have acted for the defendant before in other matters, (*e.g.* a conveyancing transaction). There must have been a specific undertaking to accept service for the present case given in advance.

(3) *Time of service*

Where documents are served personally they must not be served on a Sunday, Christmas Day or Good Friday except in the case of urgency and with the prior permission of the court. Service on any other day, and indeed at any time of day, is permissible.

So far we have considered service of the summons by which the case is commenced. However, the formalities for service of all other documents are nowhere near as great. Subject to an exception to which we shall shortly come, all other documents in the course of the case may be served by post, either by the court or by the party who wishes to serve them at the address for service given by the parties concerned. The plaintiff when initiating the proceedings must give an address for service which will of course be the address of his solicitor if he has one. When the defendant files his form of Admission Defence and Counterclaim at court then he will also give an address for service, and henceforth there is no need for personal service of documents and postal service will almost always suffice.

The exception to this principle is that where some order is made by which a party is required to do something or to refrain from doing something on pain that non-compliance will amount to a contempt of court, personal service is again necessary. An example is an injunction say, to a defendant requiring him to pull down a wall which he has erected in breach of a right of way, or to refrain from making excessive noise at night time. In such a case the document must again be served personally by the court bailiff or by the plaintiff's solicitors employing a process server. Such kind of document which intimates to the person receiving it that he will be liable to be committed to prison for contempt of court if he does not comply has to be indorsed with what is called a "penal notice." This is in a form of words bringing home to the person affected the consequence of disobedience. The notice says:

"Take notice that unless you obey the directions contained in this order you will be guilty of contempt of court and will be liable to be committed to prison."

In the Barset County Court   Case No 93 0242

BETWEEN

William Dunbar and James Dunbar   *Plaintiffs*
(trading as William Dunbar and Co)
and
John Cowper   *Defendant*

Affidavit of Service of Summons

1. John Doe of 33 Acacia Avenue Barchester, process server make oath and say as follows:
    1. I am over 16 years of age and am a process server instructed by Makepiece and Streiff of Bank Chambers, Barset, solicitors for the above-named plaintiff.
    2. I did on 21st January 1993 serve the summons a true copy of which is annexed hereto and marked "JD1" on the defendant John Cowper by delivering the same personally to the defendant at 47 Elm Street Barset.

Sworn at the Court House ⎫
High Cross Barchester in the ⎪
County of Barsetshire this 22nd ⎬
of January 1993 ⎭

Before Me

Officer of the Court,
appointed
by the Judge to take affidavits.

DEFAULT SUMMONS: POSSIBLE OUTCOMES

In *William Dunbar & Co.* v. *John Cowper*, as we have seen, the defendant took no action at all. This is quite common in straight-forward debt cases. This left it open to the plaintiff, when the 14 days for the defendant's response have expired, to apply to the court by filing a request to have judgment entered for the debt, the accumulated interest, and the amount of fixed costs shown on the summons. We are now going to consider what alternatives there might have been. First it is necessary to say a word about the nature of the form of Admission Defence and Counterclaim.

This form as we have seen is a sort of questionnaire to the defendant inviting him to respond in one of various ways to the documents served upon him. Within 14 days of service of the summons on him (and as we have seen if the summons is served by post it is deemed to be served seven days after posting) the defendant must return the form of

Admission Defence and Counterclaim duly completed to the county court office. In fact, if the defendant instructs solicitors they will probably not use the court form of Admission Defence and Counterclaim. If solicitors are instructed by the defendant, a proper defence will be drafted responding to each paragraph of the plaintiff's particulars of claim with the defendant's case. A defendant acting in person, however, will probably use the court's form of Admission Defence and Counterclaim. In fact there is very little space on this form to set out a properly pleaded defence which is why it is mainly used by a layman. The form is, however, in a "user friendly" style indicating clearly where it is to be filled in by a litigant in person. We shall now consider the various alternatives such as might have been taken by Mr. Cowper in the action which we have considered.

ADMISSION

If the defendant wants to admit the whole of the amount of the plaintiff's claim and is able to pay the sum immediately, then the money must be taken or sent to the plaintiff or his solicitors direct. It must not be sent to the court. If the defendant admits all the claim but is asking for time to pay then he should fill in the admission part of the form (N9A). The notes on that form tell him what to do and how to put forward his offer of payment by instalments or his request for time to pay. The form should then be returned to the court who will make a photocopy of it and send it out to the plaintiff. The defendant in that position is also required to fill in some details of his income, capital and outgoings. Thus, say that in John Cowper's case he had admitted the whole claim and put forward an offer to pay it in two instalments, one in a month's time of, say £500 and the other in the following month for the whole of the balance, in that situation the court would have sent out a photocopy of the form when it was received direct to the plaintiff, and if the plaintiff had been happy with that proposal the plaintiff would simply send in a form (N225) to the court confirming that he accepted the offer.

Suppose, however, that some less acceptable method of payment had been proposed. In other words suppose that John Cowper had written into the court accepting liability for the debt but stating that he could only afford to pay at £10 per month and perhaps disclosing on the form that his circumstances had changed, for example, by his having to go out of business and that he has a number of other debts and dependants and outgoings but no capital or savings. Obviously the plaintiffs would be very disappointed in such a case because payment of the sum due to them at £10 per month would take many years to recover even if the instalment payments were kept up regularly. In that situation therefore the plaintiffs would be likely to fill in form 225 and send it to the court indicating that they did not accept the proposal and giving their reasons together with their counter proposals. In that case the court would proceed to a "disposal" of the action. Usually such disposals are carried out by the chief clerk and he would review the offer of payment, the background information, and what the plaintiff had to say in his response. He would then make a provisional determination of the rate at which the defendant should repay the sum owed. In other words, if he did not accept that John Cowper's position was as desperate as he claimed, he might order him to repay the sum at, say, £25 per week. Once the chief clerk has dealt with the disposal in this way, either party, if he is displeased with the outcome, can request a hearing and the disposal will then be dealt with by an oral hearing before the District Judge in Chambers. At that hearing the plaintiff will be able to cross-examine the defendant on his means and may insist on seeing documentation to prove what is claimed, *e.g.* pay slips, P45, bank accounts and so on.

ADMISSION OF PART OF THE CLAIM

What if the defendant only admits part of the claim? In such a case the defendant should either send the amount that he does admit direct to the plaintiff and complete form N9 indicating why he disputes the balance. If he does not have the money at present he should fill in the form N9A again requesting time to pay and giving details of income and outgoings. The plaintiff is then usually given an opportunity to say whether he accepts the partial admission or whether he wishes the case to proceed. If he wishes the case to proceed then a pre-trial review is fixed by the court at which both parties are called before the district judge to consider how the matter should proceed.

ADMISSIONS IN AN ACTION FOR AN UNLIQUIDATED SUM

So far we have been considering the action in a *Dunbar* v. *Cowper* type case for a simple trade debt. Suppose however the action had been of another kind, say for damages for personal injuries or for inconvenience and distress. In such a case, a defendant on his form of Admission Defence and Counterclaim may either admit liability, in which case the plaintiff may obtain judgment on liability with an order for damages to be assessed later, or may if he thinks fit actually offer a specific sum, in which case the plaintiff has the right to accept or refuse as in the case of offers related to liquidated demands discussed above.

DEFENCE

Suppose, however, that the defendant admits nothing. In such a case, if he is going to continue acting in person, he should complete the relevant section of the form within the time allowed and setting out what his case is in response to the plaintiff's claim. A copy of that defence will then be sent out to the plaintiff. If solicitors are to be instructed then usually they will prefer to draft a proper pleading in a formal way and they should then supply a further copy to the court for sending on to the plaintiff. Where solicitors are instructed, the address given on the form of defence will become the defendant's address for service of future documents by the court and the plaintiff.

The consequence of a defence being filed is that after the court has sent a copy of it to the plaintiff the case will then go in the way described below.

If the sum outstanding does not exceed £1,000 and a defence is filed, the proceedings will automatically be referred to arbitration and we shall consider the nature of this below.

COUNTERCLAIM

If the defendant wishes to make a counterclaim against the plaintiff then he is given the opportunity to do so in the same proceedings. Odd though it may seem, the nature of the counterclaim need have nothing to do with the plaintiff's claim against the defendant. Suppose for example that the plaintiff claims the defendant owes him a debt of £1,000. The defendant goes to the plaintiff's home to discuss the matter and after the discussion, as the defendant is leaving, he trips on some uneven flagstones in the plaintiff's drive and injures his leg. If the defendant believes he has a claim against the plaintiff under the Occupiers Liability Acts then he can if he wishes, when the plaintiff sues him for the debt, make a counterclaim in respect of his separate cause of action. Although the proceedings have nothing legally speaking to do with each other they can be brought to court at the same time so that the balance of liability between the parties can be considered in the light of their claims against each other.

SETTING ASIDE JUDGMENT IN DEFAULT

We have already seen what happened in the *John Cowper* case where he chose not to participate at all in the proceedings. Judgment was given. In that case the merits of the plaintiff's case were not tested in any way. The giving of judgment was an entirely administrative act at the court counter and no judge was called upon to investigate the case nor was there any evidence given on oath about the claim. There may however sometimes be good reason why a defendant does not deal with a summons in time and in view of this, if the defendant against whom judgment in default has been given can give a satisfactory explanation of his apparent inactivity and show that he has a defence to the claim, or a counterclaim which he wishes to bring against the plaintiff, the court has the power to set aside the judgment. In particular, the defendant will be entitled to have it set aside if he proves that the summons did not in fact come to his knowledge in time. As we have seen, postal service of a summons is quite permissible and is deemed to come to the defendant's notice on the seventh day after posting. The defendant then has a further 14 days in which to send his form of admission, defence, etc., to the court. Suppose that a defendant had, unknown to the plaintiff, actually gone away on a month's holiday the day before proceedings were posted to him. By the time he came back he would find that judgment in default had been given against him. In such a situation the defendant will apply to the court on a general form of application (illustrated at page 330) asking for judgment to be set aside. The defendant should of course apply immediately he comes back from his holiday because if there is any further substantial delay the court will be unlikely to permit judgment to be set aside. If nobody is at fault as in the example given, where the plaintiff bona fide believed the defendant would receive the documents and the defendant has in fact gone on a lengthy holiday, then the court will not make any order as to the costs thrown away by the application. If, however, some party is at fault, *e.g.* where the plaintiff did not really know the defendant's home address and merely had the documents posted to an address where it was believed the defendant might go from time to time, or on the other hand where the defendant did actually receive the documents but due to inefficiency or forgetfulness did not deal with them in time and later wants to have the judgment set aside, then in either of these two cases the court will order costs wasted to be borne by the party whose conduct led to them being incurred.

SUMMARY JUDGMENT WHERE NO REAL DEFENCE

So far we have considered what will happen where the defendant responds in one of various ways to the summons. Suppose, however, that a defendant sends in a defence which the plaintiff believes is totally unfounded. Suppose for example in the *Dunbar* v. *Cowper* case the defendant had filled in on his form of Admission, Defence and Counterclaim the following. "The teak was of very poor quality and warped immediately I used it. It caused me a lot of inconvenience as I had to take it out of the building into which I had put it and replace it and I do not intend to pay at all as it was totally useless."

Suppose that Messrs. Makepiece and Streiff had taken their client's instructions on this and had been told that this defence was totally fictitious. The teak had come from a much larger batch, all of which had proved to be of perfect quality when used by the firm or sold to other builders. They therefore did not believe it and think the defence is a "try on" used as a means of spinning the case out, probably because Cowper cannot afford to pay at the moment.

In such a case, where the defendant delivers to the court a document which purports to be a defence but which the plaintiff believes is totally unfounded, then so long as the sum at stake is not less than £1,000, the plaintiff in these circumstances can make an application to the court supported by an affidavit (that is a sworn statement by him) verifying the facts on which his claim is made and stating his belief that, despite the purported defence delivered, there is no proper defence to the claim. The advantage of doing this is that the plaintiff can obtain a hearing for his application for judgment before the district judge in chambers, probably at a very early date only a few weeks away. If he did not make this application, then unfortunately for him the case would take its normal progress at a somewhat leisurely rate towards a full trial before a judge in court which would be many months away and possibly longer than that. It should be carefully noted, however, that this form of application must only be made if the plaintiff is absolutely sure (and is prepared to say so on oath!) that there is no proper defence. If there is some defence on the facts which is at least arguable, even though the plaintiff does not accept it, then this procedure must not be used and to use it would in fact be an abuse of procedure by the plaintiff.

Where application is to be made for summary judgment in this way, the affidavit and an application must be delivered to the chief clerk who will then insert a date for the hearing of the application. A copy of the application and of the affidavit by the plaintiff must be served on the defendant not less than seven days before the hearing of the application. If, at the hearing the plaintiff's application is approved, that is, the district judge accepts that there is no arguable defence, the defence is then struck out and judgment entered for the plaintiff for the whole or part of the claim as the case may be. If the district judge, whilst not wishing to decide the case on the merits, believes that there may be something arguable in what the defendant has put forward then he will give the defendant leave to defend and the case will go on as normal. The district judge will then go on to give directions as to how the proceedings are to be conducted in the future. Alternatively, if the district judge, whilst not entirely convinced that there is an arguable defence, is hesitant to give judgment there and then he may give the defendant leave to defend on conditions. A common condition is that the defendant should pay the money in dispute into court funds for safekeeping pending the trial.

It should be noted in respect of this kind of application that simply because the district judge gives leave to defend, he is not in any way prejudging the outcome of the case. All he is saying is that there seems to be some argument which it is wrong for him to dispose of so quickly without the normal pre-trial procedures being gone through between the parties. Even if at the eventual trial the judge finds that the plaintiff wins hands down so to speak this does not mean that the district judge necessarily "got things wrong" in refusing the plaintiff's application for summary judgment. The issues in the two proceedings were different. The district judge only had to decide if there was some *arguable* defence, he did not have to decide who would win on the merits at a full trial.

PERIODS OF TIME

We have already considered the most important time period for any procedural step, that is the 14 days which a defendant has between service of the summons on him and the last date on which he must lodge his response at court. It is his duty to ensure that this is received at court within the 14-day period, so if he trusts to the post it is at his own risk. There are various other times at which certain steps must be taken. The most important of these are that for interlocutory applications (see below) two days' clear notice before the hearing date is required. In other words if in such a case a hearing date is obtained on say a Friday, notice of that hearing day must be given no later than the Tuesday preceding so as to leave the Wednesday and Thursday as clear days. In the two days, moreover, Saturday and Sunday must not feature so that if a hearing date is obtained for such an application on say a Tuesday then notice of that application must be served no later than the preceding Thursday, leaving the Friday and Monday as clear days and the weekend being left out of account.

Often the court itself will specify a period within which a certain action must be done. In such a situation the order of court should specify precisely what is meant. There are certain presumptions so that, *e.g.* if a step has to be taken not less than say 10 days *before* a specified date it must be done so that, counting from the day after the step is taken, the 10 days will elapse before the specified day is reached. Where a step has to be taken *within* 10 days *before* a specified date, the 10 days is counted back from the day before the specified date. Where a step has to be taken *within* 10 days *after* or *from* a specified date the days are counted from the day after the specified date. In computations in which the word "month" is used, that word always means a calendar month. Accordingly, to comply with a court order made on January 31 that a certain act be done within one month it must be completed by the last day of February. The word "forthwith" in court does not in fact mean absolutely immediately but nor does it mean "as soon as the other party gets around to it." It is interpreted to mean "as soon as is practicable."

A list of time limits of general application will be found at the end of this chapter. It must always be remembered that the parties may themselves agree to enlarge or shorten any time limit and if they are not in agreement, application may in any event be made to the court to extend the period concerned.

ADJOURNMENT

The court has a general power to adjourn (or to advance the date of) any hearing. In doing this, it may act on its own motion or on the application of one or both of the parties. The power can be exercised by the circuit judge or the district judge. Where application is made on the ground that a party is too ill to attend court and is supported by a medical certificate, the application is usually not refused. Notice of adjournment or advancement of date is given by the chief clerk to all parties and persons interested who are not present when the order is made. (C.C.R., Ord. 13, r. 3).

A hearing may be adjourned "generally" or "*sine die*," *i.e.* without a new date for the hearing being fixed. In this case any party can apply for a new date to be fixed. If 12 months elapses without a new date being fixed, the chief clerk may take steps to have the proceedings struck out (C.C.R., Ord. 13, r. 3).

Closely allied to the adjournment is the "stay of proceedings." This occurs, for instance, when several actions are brought before the same court against the same defendants. Where the actions arise out of the same facts and the court orders a selected action, subject to the defendant undertaking to be bound as against the other plaintiffs by the judgment in the selected case, the court will stay proceedings in all other cases pending the outcome of the selected action (see above, "Joinder" p. 308).

ARBITRATION AND SMALL CLAIMS

It is always possible for the parties to a dispute to refer their differences to the arbitration of another person and it is common for contracts and other documents (leases, for example) to provide that all disputes shall be referred to arbitration and to specify how the arbitrator is to be selected. Where a dispute is determined by the decision of an arbitrator, his award, as it is called, can be enforced through the courts as if it is the judgment of the court (C.C.A. 1984, s.64). The judge and district judge of the county court are available to act as arbitrators between the parties to an action and arbitration is now established as the normal method of dealing with disputed cases in which the sum claimed or the amount involved does not exceed £1,000. The rules provide that all such cases shall stand referred for arbitration by the district judge on receipt of a defence to the claim. Any party can apply to the district judge for an order referring the arbitration for hearing by the judge or an outside arbitrator (C.C.R., Ord. 19, r. 2(3)). However, the reference can be rescinded if a party satisfies the district judge on application that—

(a) a difficult question of law or a question of fact of exceptional complexity is involved; or

(b) a charge of fraud is in issue; or

(c) the parties agree that the case shall go to court; or

(d) arbitration would be an unreasonable course having regard to the subject-matter, the circumstances of the parties or the interests of other persons who may be affected by the award (C.C.R., Ord. 19, r. 2(4)).

Where arbitration takes place under the rules, the normal procedures are replaced by the following terms of reference:

"(1) The arbitrator shall appoint the date for the preliminary consideration of the dispute and ways of resolving it, unless the size or nature of the claim or other circumstances make such a course undesirable or unnecessary.

(2) At or after the preliminary appointment, if there is one, the arbitrator shall fix a date for the dispute to be heard (unless the parties consent to his deciding it on the statements and documents submitted to him) and shall give such directions regarding the steps to be taken before and at the hearing as may appear to him to be necessary or desirable. Where the district judge is the arbitrator, he shall have the same powers on the preliminary appointment as he has under Order 17 on a pre-trial review.

(3) Any hearing shall be informal and the strict rules of evidence shall not apply.

(4) At the hearing the arbitrator may adopt any method of procedure which he may consider to be convenient and to afford a fair and equal opportunity to each party to present his case.

(5) If any party does not appear at the arbitration, the arbitrator may make an award on hearing any other party to the proceedings who may be present.

(6) Where an award has been given in the absence of a party, the arbitrator shall have power, on that party's application, to set the award aside and to order a fresh hearing, as if the award were a judgment and the application were made pursuant to Order 37, rule 2.

(7) With the consent of the parties and at any time before giving his decision and either before or after the hearing, the arbitrator may consult any expert or call for an expert report on any matter in dispute or invite an expert to attend the hearing as assessor.

(8) Subject to the provisions of Order 19, rule 6, in respect of claims involving £1,000 or less, the costs of the action up to and including the entry judgment shall be in the discretion of the arbitrator to be exercised in the same manner as the discretion of the court under the provisions of the County Court Rules."

Rule 6 referred to in paragraph (8) provides that in such arbitrations no solicitors' costs shall be allowed except (a) the costs stated in the summons or which would have been stated in the summons if the claim had been for a liquidated sum; (b) the costs of enforcing the award; and (c) costs certified by the arbitrator to have been incurred through the unreasonable conduct of the opposite party. The result is that apart from these costs, the plaintiff may expect to receive only his expenses, such as the cost of obtaining the opinion of an expert or of securing the attendance of witnesses.

Automatic Directions, The Pre-Trial Review, and Interlocutory Applications

Until 1990, when the defendant filed a defence at court so that it became apparent to the court the case was going to go on as a contested action, the court would itself fix an appointment for what was called a "pre-trial review" and send out notice of this appointment to both the parties. Both parties would then attend before the district judge in chambers for a hearing, often quite a short one, at which the district judge would thoroughly review the state of the case so far and make procedural orders as to what each of the parties should do to ensure that the case was properly prepared for a trial which could take place as early as possible. These procedural orders made at this stage are known as "directions." It became apparent that in the vast majority of cases the self-same types of orders were always required and consequently the attendance of both parties at the pre-trial review was an unnecessary waste of legal time, and indeed of the district judge's time also. Consequently, with effect from 1990, in most cases there is no pre-trial review and the parties are required to comply with "automatic directions." The nature of these automatic directions is that no application to the court is necessary to find out what is required and the parties can refer to the rules of court which now stipulate precisely what they should do after the defence has been filed in order to get their cases ready. The result is that in routine cases after filing of the defence the parties carry out the "automatic directions" directly between themselves without the intervention of the court at all, and thus no hearings of any kind are necessary between the start of the action and the trial itself. The following are the main "automatic directions." For a full statement of the relevant rule regard should be had to C.C.R., Ord. 17, r. 11. These automatic directions take effect when the pleadings are deemed to be closed. Pleadings are deemed to be closed 14 days after a defence has been filed, of if the case is one which involved a counterclaim, 14 days after a defence to the counterclaim has been filed:

(i) There should be discovery of documents within 28 days and inspection of documents within seven days thereafter save that in a action for personal injuries arising out of a road accident discovery shall be limited to disclosure of any documents relating to the amount of damages.

(ii) Except where the court gives leave, or where all the parties agree even if the court does not give leave:—
(a) No expert evidence may be adduced at the trial unless the substance of that evidence has been disclosed to the other parties in the form of a written report within 10 weeks and
(b) the number of expert witnesses of any kind shall be limited to two except that in personal injury cases the number of expert witnesses shall be limited to two medical experts and only one expert of any other kind.

(iii) Photographs and sketch plans and, in an action for personal injuries, the contents of any police accident report book shall be receivable in evidence at the trial and shall be agreed if possible.

(iv) Unless the date for the trial has already been fixed the plaintiff shall within six months request the chief clerk to fix a day for the hearing and file a note (which shall if possible be agreed by all the parties) giving an estimate of the length of the trial and the number of witnesses to be called.

    (v) If no request for a date of hearing is made within 15 months of the day on which pleadings are deemed to be closed (or within nine months after the expiry of any other period fixed by the court for making such a request) the action be automatically struck out.

These then are the automatic directions and they are applicable in most mainstream cases. There are, however, many exceptional cases where they do not apply, for example in actions for rent, for the recovery of land, and in particular in cases where an admission of part of a claim is filed. In such a case, because the case is likely to prove a complex one it is thought better that there should be a pre-trial review. It must be carefully borne in mind that in other cases the parties will be expected to carry out automatic directions promptly and in accordance with the due time limits. However, the rules do stipulate that nothing in the automatic directions should prevent the court from giving, of its own motion, or where either party applies, any further or different directions as may in the circumstances be appropriate. Accordingly, if it seems to either plaintiff or defendant that the automatic directions do not provide everything that is required in the form of procedural orders in his/her actual case the party concerned can apply to the court to give further or different orders. Thus, for example if the action concerns a significant sum, say £40,000, and there are great complexities of expert evidence so that it seems appropriate to call more experts than the rules allow a party could apply to the court to vary the usual orders in automatic directions. If one party does wish to apply for further or different directions the district judge is likely to consider the case at large and see what possible ways he can suggest for cutting down the areas of dispute and highlighting what are the true differences between the parties.

    Applications to the court for procedural orders between the start of the action and the trial are known as "interlocutory applications." They would include applications for such things as an order relating to the number of expert witnesses to be called at trial, or relating to discovery of documents referred to above (which is explained more fully hereafter on p. 327).

THE PLEADINGS

As we have seen, the pleadings in the usual case constitute the particulars of a claim in which the plaintiff sets out all the factual matters on which he relies to prove his cause of action and the defence in which the defendant responds to each allegation answering it with his denial or counter allegation. The trial is said to be "on the pleadings," that is that the parties are only allowed to call evidence about the matters of which they have given full notice by properly drafted pleadings. As can be imagined it is a very skilled task to draft pleadings in a case of any complexity. One must be careful to set out all relevant facts but to set them out in a sufficiently general way so that one's hands are not tied unduly at trial. If one pleads a case too specifically then one can be greatly hampered at trial because one will not be able to go outside the pleadings whatever evidence comes to light subsequently.

Example

Suppose that in pleading a plaintiff's case in respect of a motor accident his lawyer had drafted the pleading simply saying that the defendant drove negligently by going into a junction at an excessive speed. Shortly before trial an eye witness is interviewed who says that not only was the speed possibly excessive but that he thinks the defendant was partly on the wrong side of the road and was distracted by looking round into the back seat of his car where his dog was jumping about. In this case, since the plaintiff has pleaded his case too specifically he may well be made to rely only on the allegation of excessive speed and not allowed to call evidence about these other matters which also of course go to establish negligence. Because of this problem it is common, particularly in accident cases to "throw the whole book" at a defendant in one's allegations alleging a whole series of breaches of the duty of care in driving so that at least one or two may stick at trial. For example, it is very common to plead of a defendant that he drove at excessive speed, failed to steer properly, failed to keep a proper look out, failed to take necessary steps to avoid a collision, etc., etc., thus leaving as wide a scope as possible for whatever evidence may come out at trial.

A consequence of this however is that pleadings when properly drafted are often so general or vague as not really to indicate to the opposite party precisely what is being said. Where a party considers that his opponent's pleading is in this category he can ask for further and better particulars to be delivered. "Further and better particulars" means that the party requesting them is making an attempt to cut down the area for manoeuvre in his opponent's pleading. To take an easy example suppose that a plaintiff, alleging that a defendant has caused a road accident by his negligence, alleged that "the defendant drove in breach of the Highway Code." Now, since the Highway Code is a very long document comprising numerous paragraphs it would be totally unclear to the defendant exactly what allegation was being made against him. Did the allegation mean that he was driving too fast, or left insufficient distance between himself or the vehicle in front or failed to have his lights on at dusk, etc., etc? Accordingly the defendant can quite properly ask for further and better particulars namely in this instance "specify which precise provision of the Highway Code it is alleged the defendant contravened."

The method of requesting further and better particulars is to do so first by letter to the defendant. With the letter is enclosed a formal document, set out like a pleading with the heading in the action, and asking the precise questions to which an answer is required by reference to the numbered paragraphs of the opponent's pleading of which one wants further particulars. For example, suppose that the above allegation had appeared in paragraph 4 of a particulars of claim, the defendant's request for further and better particulars would read (omitting the formal headings):

> "In paragraph 4 of the particulars of claim of the allegation that the defendant failed to observe the provisions of the Highway Code, state which precise provision of the Highway Code is it alleged the defendant contravened."

The plaintiff should then reply to this request giving details of the exact paragraph of the Highway Code to which he refers. If the plaintiff declines to do so then the defendant will apply to the court for an order that the plaintiff should. An appropriate time to apply for this order is of course the pre-trial review. Therefore, this is one of the matters which will be routinely considered namely whether either party is requesting further and better particulars of the opponent's pleading.

AMENDMENT OF PLEADINGS

One might think that by the time negotiations had broken down and the parties had brought their cases to court, that each would have sufficient information about his case to know precisely how it should be pleaded. This is however not always so. Fresh evidence often arises so that it becomes apparent that the pleading as drafted will not do. Sometimes it is even necessary to add a new party such as a further defendant, (*e.g.* another driver whom it is now thought may have contributed to the accident concerned) or to add a new cause of action, for example in the case of a factory accident where the accident concerned appears to be both a breach of statutory duty and an instance of the tort of negligence. The court has a wide discretion to correct errors in the pleadings and will allow such changes as are necessary to be made in order to ensure the true issues between the parties are brought to trial. Amendment will be liberally allowed.

A party who wishes to amend his summons and pleadings to add or substitute any other party, must make application to the court for an order permitting him to do so. In the case of any other kind of amendments to the particulars of claim or defence however, amendments can usually be made, without an order of the court, simply by filing a copy of the amended pleading at court with a copy for service on the opposing party. If the need for amendment arises only after the pre-trial review if there is one, an order of the court is necessary which is obtained by an application made on notice the procedure for which we shall consider below. However if both parties consent, no order of the court is necessary. Where the summons or particulars of claim is to be amended the original document is amended by showing the original wording struck through in red, but so as to leave it still legible in case any dispute arises later as to what was originally alleged. The new wording is then inserted in red. Usually the whole document will have to be retyped so as to leave space to insert new paragraphs. If any subsequent amendment is necessary the next amendment is made in green.

DISCOVERY AND INSPECTION OF DOCUMENTS

(1) *Discovery*

A party who has to make discovery is required to send his opponent a formal list in the format required by the County Court Rules. In fact list of documents forms can be purchased from Law Stationers or a precedent held on a word processor. This phrase, "making discovery," means the disclosure of papers or documents which have any relevance to the case by one party to the other. Each party is obliged, either under the automatic directions or in consequence of an order made at a pre-trial review, if there is one, to disclose to his opponent all the documents which are, or have ever been in his custody or possession or power which have any relevance to the matter in hand. Moreover, under this rule the party is obliged to disclose any documents which are relevant to the action even is they are actually harmful to his own case. Where discovery and inspection occur (and it will occur in every action save the very simplest where both parties confirm that there are no such relevant documents) the procedure takes place in two stages: In this list there are two schedules and the first of them is in two parts. Schedule 1, part 1 sets out the documents which the party has in his possession and is willing to produce for his opponent's inspection; Schedule 1 part 2 includes those which he has but is not willing to produce. The proper ground for refusing to produce documents is that a document is "privileged." The meaning of the word "privilege" involves a discussion of a difficult area of substantive law but basically it refers to a kind of document which is confidential according to the rules of evidence so that it need not be produced. The categories of documents which are "privileged" are wide but for our purposes the two most common categories are any correspondence between a solicitor and his client (because it is obvious that this should have the right of confidentiality at all stages) and in addition, in litigation cases, anything which the lawyer has obtained on his client's behalf (such as witness statements or advice from counsel, etc) made with reference to the litigation. Documents in these categories must still be listed in the Schedule. However it is usual to list them in a vague way so that, for example one does not list witness statements by reference to the witnesses' names because otherwise the opponent might be able to trace the witnesses concerned and interview them. It is usual simply to say "witness statements—various," and then to put the claim for privilege as illustrated in the document shown hereafter. Schedule 2 contains documents which the party once had in his possession but does no longer have. He must also include a statement of what has become of the documents concerned. For example if the document has been lost or destroyed or sent to some other person these facts must be given in the list.

After the list has been sent to one's opponent there follows the next stage.

(2) *Inspection of documents*

Where the existence of documents is disclosed by discovery the opposing party must be allowed to inspect and take or be sent copies of all those in Schedule 1 part 1, (he is not of course permitted to see those in Schedule 1 part 2). So a party who furnishes a list of documents must give notice of when and where they may be inspected. It is usual to provide at the end of the list of documents that any relevant documents may be inspected at the offices of the plaintiff's solicitors in normal working hours by arrangement.

More normally these days, unless the party concerned thinks there is something to be gained by the actual physical inspection of the document, *e.g.* where the very fabric of the document may reveal useful evidence, it is more normal to request that a photocopy of any relevant documents be sent to avoid the time and expense of attending at one's opponent's solicitors office for the purpose of carrying this out. As will be noted under the automatic directions, inspection of documents must be carried out within seven days after the exchange of lists of documents. If a party believes that his opponent has not carried out discovery honestly it is possible to apply to the court for a further order that that party swear an affidavit verifying the truth of his list. To swear such an affidavit falsely would be the crime of perjury and a very serious matter. After discovery and inspection has taken place usually the parties' solicitors agree which documents are useful and relevant for the trial and put them in so called "agreed bundles" so that they all appear neatly and in chronological order with page reference numbers. An identical bundle is therefore prepared for each party's barrister and for the judge so there is ease of reference at trial and the trial can proceed efficiently and expeditiously.

EXPERT EVIDENCE

In many kinds of action expert evidence is required. This may be expert evidence in personal injury cases, *e.g.* medical consultants to say what kinds of injuries were caused to the plaintiff and how long it may take him to recover; accountants, valuers, or consultant engineers. To be an expert witness one does not necessarily have to have a string of degrees or be professionally qualified in some way, it is sufficient if the person can show genuine expertise. Thus for example, if an issue concerned, say, repairs to a motor vehicle then a skilled motor mechanic, even one who had never taken any examinations in the subject would undoubtedly qualify as an expert witness about the matter in question. It used to be common for each party to call expert evidence at trial without disclosing what their experts were going to say in advance. Now however there is a strong likelihood that in order to attempt to cut down the area of dispute and perhaps shorten the trial, if a party wishes to call expert evidence he must supply a copy of the evidence of that expert in written form to his opponent substantially in advance of the trial. This is so that there is an opportunity for the opponent to consider whether he can agree with the experts' evidence thus avoiding the need for the expert to be called at trial for in that case his written report alone will be presented to the court. Let us take a personal injury case where the plaintiff and defendant's solicitors have each had the plaintiff medically examined by a consultant. The plaintiff's consultant says that the plaintiff has suffered a nasty injury and will undoubtedly not be able to go back to work for at least a further three months. The defendant's consultant says that medically the injury has already cleared up and that the plaintiff is in effect malingering and should have gone back to work by now. Obviously a good deal of money will depend on the resolution of the dispute between the experts. The experts' reports will be exchanged so that it can be seen what areas of agreement and disagreement there are. Of course in the case just mentioned, no agreement is likely to be possible because there is a radical difference of views. However in other cases it may be that the experts are saying substantially the same thing and therefore by exchanging their reports in advance of trial, agreement of the medical issues at least, subject to liability, can be achieved and a good deal of time and costs saved by putting forward the expert evidence in written form rather than calling the experts at trial and having to pay substantial fees for doing so. As will be noted, the automatic directions provide for pre-trial disclosure of expert evidence and also for the limiting of the number of witnesses in the interests of saving time and expense. If there should be a pre-trial review then the district judge, in all save the most exceptional cases, will certainly order that experts' reports be exchanged well in advance of trial and that the number of experts be similarly limited.

Obtaining a Date for Trial

As we have seen, under the automatic directions the basic procedure is for the plaintiff to apply for a date for trial when he is ready to do so, but in any event no later than 15 months after the pleadings are deemed to be closed. He does this by writing to the court (a letter will do), indicating that the parties are ready and giving an estimate of how long the trial is likely to last and how many witnesses are to be called. An attempt should be made with the defendant to agree these matters so that the court can be fully and accurately informed in the interests of fixing the right length of trial in order that, on the date when the case is to be called, a proper amount of judicial time is available for it. So that, if, for example, the plaintiff or defendant agree their case is going to take a whole day of court time, on the date of their case that and no other case, is listed. On the other hand, if they agreed that the case would only take 2 hours they would be likely to find that 2/3 other cases at least had been listed for the same day. The maximum use of judicial time is of the utmost importance and that is why it is vital to co-operate at this stage, no matter how bitterly the litigation is being contested otherwise, so as to give the court the most accurate information possible.

It should be noted that there is a very draconian sanction should the plaintiff not apply for a hearing date within 15 months of pleadings being deemed to be closed (or within nine months of any other time limit given by the court subsequently). The rules provide that the Chief Clerk will direct that the case be struck out automatically. The increasing computerisation of County Court records will facilitate the Chief Clerk seeing when the time limit has expired. No application by the defendant is necessary and the court will proceed automatically to strike out the plaintiff's claim. The plaintiff will in principle be liable for the defendant's costs. If the limitation period has meanwhile expired, the plaintiff will be unable to start a second action and he will have lost his right of action though, if the oversight has been due to his solicitor's negligence, he will have an apparently unanswerable case against those solicitors.

APPLICATIONS TO THE COURT

As we have seen above, most of the procedural orders necessary in routine litigation are provided for in the automatic directions. In most cases where there are no automatic directions there will be a pre-trial review at which the parties ought to ask for everything they need. Sometimes however applications need to be made which are not covered in automatic directions or perhaps arise after any pre-trial review has occurred. We have already seen one such, namely summary judgment where there was no real defence, described on p. 318. In cases where an interlocutory application needs to be made to the court it is made on a court form number N.244. This sets out the usual heading, that is the case number and parties and goes on to state

TAKE NOTICE that the Plaintiff intends to apply to the district judge of this court   at   on   day the   day of   199 at   o'clock for (and then the order that is sought).

The party who wishes to make the application completes the form leaving the hearing date blank and then takes down to the court two copies together with the original. The court will then enter in a date of hearing and note this in the district judge's diary, retaining one copy and returning the remaining forms enabling one to be sent to the other party. At least two days notice is required before the hearing of such applications. Service by ordinary post is sufficient on a party who is already on the record.

The procedure described above is what is called application "on notice" which enables the other party to attend at the hearing and be represented to oppose the application if the party so desires. Sometimes notice of application of the other party is not strictly necessary. For instance, if proceedings claiming damages are served on a defendant who does not reside or carry on business in the district of the court where an action has been commenced he may, after he has delivered his defence to the court office, apply *ex parte* in writing to that court for an order that the action be transferred to the court for the district where he does reside. The phrase "ex parte" means "by one side only." In this case the district judge may grant the application, though more usually he will adjourn it so the other side can be given an opportunity to make representations. There are relatively few applications which can be made *ex parte* and such as there are deal mainly with minor procedural matters. Usually the justice of a situation will require that both parties be permitted on notice to attend court to put their case about any matter of substance. In any event, where an application is made whether on notice or *ex parte*, either party who is aggrieved by the decision of the registrar can appeal as of right to a county court judge in chambers.

AN UNLIQUIDATED CLAIM

A Default Summons (Unliquidated Sum)

Robert Greene v. *Matchless Kitchens Ltd.*

Mr. Greene has had a fitted kitchen installed by Matchless Kitchens Limited, a London company with a branch in Barset, at a cost of some £5,000. This included the provision and installation of washing and dishwashing machines. The subsequent events are sufficiently related in the following letter sent by Messrs. Makepiece to the company:

MAKEPIECE & STREIFF
Solicitors

Clement Amity
Anthony Adverse

Bank Chambers,
Barset.
Tel: 00765 4321

Our ref: EW/90399

8th January, 1993.

The Manager,
Matchless Kitchens Ltd.,
The Broadway,
Barset.

Dear Sir,

Mr. R. Greene of 25 Poplar Row, Barset, has consulted us about the damage he has suffered as the result of defective workmanship and/or design in the installation of the kitchen fitments and machines in his home by your company.

As you have been informed, after the installation was completed, Mr. Greene noticed water on the floor of the kitchen and it became clear that flooding occurred as the result of using the machines and the sink basin. Your maintenance engineers have been back several times over the past two months, but have not yet found and dealt with the cause of the trouble. It seems likely that the whole of the plumbing will need to be changed and this will mean a major upheaval of my client's domestic arrangements for the second time.

Inspection of part of the flooring shows that the hardboard underlay has perished and this will need to be renewed together with the flooring itself. This can, of course, only be done when the work to cure the flooding has been carried out.

Our client has repeatedly asked you and your representative to take effective action to put the installation in proper working order and I must repeat the demand that you do so right away.

Mr. Greene is suffering great inconvenience, for which your company are liable in damages, and if the necessary work is not carried out in fourteen days, I have his instructions to commence proceedings against the company for the cost of the work and damages together with the costs of the proceedings.

I shall be glad to hear from you.

Yours faithfully,

(signed)

<u>Makepiece & Streiff</u>

The reply from the manager, dated January 14, 1993, and marked "without prejudice," states that it has become clear from inspection by his installation engineers that the trouble was caused by the way in which the waste pipe had originally been installed and this is not the company's responsibility. They would be prepared as a goodwill gesture to make the necessary changes which they estimate to cost £1,000 but they would look to Mr. Greene to meet 50 per cent. of the cost.

On reporting receipt of this letter with the offer to Mr. Greene Mr. White receives instructions from him to reject the offer. Mr. Greene is dissatisfied with Matchless Kitchens Ltd.'s workmanship and wants nothing more to do with them. He has himself obtained estimates for having the work correctly done and these are substantially larger than the figure mentioned by Matchless Kitchens Ltd. Accordingly, Mr. White is instructed to commence proceedings. He asks Joan to prepare the default summons. Mr. White himself prepares the particulars of claim (see overleaf). In the particulars of claim he pleads details of the contract and of the defective workmanship and of the problems caused to his client. When quantifying the amount that he wishes to claim for his client he claims the cost of an estimate that Mr. Greene has received to have the work put right and the cost of replacing the flooring which will have to be moved. Apart from these sums however, which are simply going to be reimbursement of monies Mr. Greene will have to pay out, Mr. White also claims general damages for inconvenience and discomfort caused so far and while the work is being done to the kitchen. Mr. White expects that the court will award a relatively modest figure for inconvenience and discomfort and he decides that probably about £1,000 will be awarded. It will also be noted that Mr. White claims interest pursuant to the County Courts Act 1984 section 69. However as he does not know the final total figure which the court will award he cannot work out the exact amount of interest due and therefore he leaves this for the court to assess when giving judgment. It will be remembered that in a case where only a liquidated sum is claimed it is usually for the plaintiff to work out the interest due at the rate of 15 per cent. and to provide exact figures for this.

Joan takes the prepared papers and the court fee to the court office and enters the action. The court assigns case No. 93 0353 to the case.

IN THE BARSET COUNTY COURT   Case No. 930353

BETWEEN

Robert Greene

Plaintiff

and

Matchless Kitchens Limited

Defendant

PARTICULARS OF CLAIM

1. On 19th September 1992 the Defendant contracted with the Plaintiff to supply kitchen fitments and equipment and to install the same at 25 Poplar Row, Barset, in accordance with a scheme prepared for the Defendant including installation of a washing machine and dishwashing machine.

2. The Plaintiff relied on the professional and technical skill of the Defendant in all matters arising under the contract.

3. By reason of negligent or incorrect installation of the said machines, the flooring of the Plaintiff's kitchen has been damaged beyond repair by water and will have to be replaced.

4. The Defendant has failed to carry out effective repairs and/or alterations to the installation to prevent a recurrence of the damage.

5. The Plaintiff has been put to expense and has suffered inconvenience and discomfort in consequence of the Defendant's neglect and/or failure.

6. The loss, inconvenience and discomfort suffered by the Plaintiff are caused by the failure of the Defendant to ensure the professional skill and expertise and/or to take the degree of care in the performance of the said contract to which the Plaintiff is entitled thereunder.

PARTICULARS OF LOSS AND DAMAGE

	£
Alterations to plumbing involving removal and reinstatement of washing-machines and kitchen fitments:	700.00
Replacement of flooring:	3,000.00
	3,700.00

> And the Plaintiff claims damages limited
> to £5,000 and interest under
> County Courts Act 1984, s.69.
>
> Dated this 9th February 1993
>
>   (signed)
>   Makepiece & Streiff,
>   Bank Chambers, Barset.
>
>   Solicitors for the Plaintiff, who
> To the Chief Clerk of the   will accept service of all
> Court and the above-named   proceedings on his behalf at
> Defendant.   the above address.

The court now annexes to the default summons a copy of the particulars of claim and the form of admission defence and counter-claim. As the defendant is a limited company there is a special rule as to service of documents on the company as we have seen earlier. By section 725 of the Companies Act 1985, documents may be served on a limited company by ordinary post at its registered office or at any local office which has a connection with the transaction. If sent by first class post the documents are then deemed to be received on the second working day after posting.

On February 26, Messrs. Makepiece receive from the court a copy of the defence filed by the defendants. The Company's defence is signed on behalf of the Company by a Director. In reply to the question: "What are your reasons for disputing the Plaintiff's claim?," the Defendants state:

> "The work under the contract was carried out as set out in the scheme approved by the Plaintiff. The scheme did not include any work to the existing sink waste pipe, which appears to have caused the trouble. This was entirely the responsibility of the Plaintiff. The Defendants deny that they were negligent in carrying out any of the work under the contract. They contend that they are not liable for the damage alleged by the Plaintiff."

Mr. White telephones Mr. Greene to tell him of his development. It seems that the case will proceed to trial and it will be necessary to get together the evidence for the trial.

Mr. Greene had already contacted a firm of specialist plumbing and heating engineers who had assessed what was required and given him an estimate. He has also obtained an estimate for replacement of the damaged flooring on which the figures in the particulars of claim were based. Mr. White writes to this firm and asks them for a full technical report on the problems with the plumbing and to confirm that they agree that the installation was done negligently. In due course they send him a very helpful report confirming these matters.

The defendants had offered "without prejudice" to meet half the sum for alterations to the plumbing on their own estimate. It will be recalled that they estimated it would cost £1,000 and they were prepared to do the work if Mr. Greene had paid 50 per cent. of that. The nature of a "without prejudice" letter is that it is a letter offering a form of compromise and cannot be produced in court as an admission against the person who has written it. Having made this offer it is logical that the defendants will go on to consider making a payment into court. We shall explain the nature of payments into court below. Since they know that their offer to bear the cost of half the work will be unacceptable they decide that if they are to effect compromise a considerably higher offer will have to be made. Accordingly Mr. White receives notification from the court as follows:

> "TAKE NOTICE that the defendant has paid into court the sum of £800 in satisfaction of your claim in this action.
>
> If you elect to accept the payment in satisfaction of your claim you must give written notice of acceptance by hand or by post to the defendant and to the court office so as to reach them within 21 days after receipt by you of this notice but in any case not less than 3 days before the hearing of the action begins."

Mr. White informs Mr. Greene of this payment into court and explains carefully to him the nature of the legal gamble involved. (See p. 340). It is unclear exactly what the sum of £800 represents. There is no obligation on the defendant to give a "break down" of this figure and to say what amount they are offering in respect of alterations to the plumbing and replacement of flooring and what amount, if any, in respect of inconvenience and discomfort. Since the offer is very substantially lower than the actual outlay, quite apart from the element of discomfort and inconvenience, Mr. Greene gives firm instructions to reject the offer.

Mr. White writes to the defendants directly, since they have not as yet instructed solicitors and indicates that the offer will not be accepted. He points out to them that automatic directions should now be complied with. One of the difficulties of litigating against a party who does not employ a lawyer is that to some extent in order to behave scrupulously fairly to that party one may feel obliged to give routine procedural advice as to what they must do. The consequences of not doing so in the present case would simply be to incur delay and potential expense. Accordingly Mr. White indicates the nature of discovery and what is required. In fact both parties are able to say that there is very little which needs to be discovered apart from documents of which both parties already have copies, such as initial correspondence and the invoices, specification etc. Mr. White agrees to dispense with formal discovery and decides that a bundle of agreed documents can be put together to be shown to the judge at trial.

The next matter which Mr. White considers is the question of expert witnesses. The costs of calling expert witnesses can be very high, as experts, whether medical consultants, consultant engineers etc. invariably charge substantial daily fees for attending court to give evidence about the subjects of their expertise. In the present case, as we have seen, Mr. White has obtained an expert's report on the defects in the plumbing and the work necessary to put those defects right. The defendants will themselves have experts who work for them in these areas and no doubt will be calling such experts at trial. In order to cut down the expense of calling expert evidence, as we have seen, the automatic directions provide that each party must exchange a copy of its experts' written reports in the hope of agreeing the matters in contention and, that if these matters cannot be agreed, both parties are limited to the number of experts they can call. In the present case the parties agree that one expert each will be sufficient on the relevant matters.

In due course therefore Mr. White and the defendant company exchange their expert reports. It is quite apparent that these cannot be agreed because they are substantially in dispute. The company's expert contends that the problem was due to the existing sink waste pipe which was no responsibility of theirs. Mr. White nonetheless hopes that the defendants will be so impressed by the thoroughness and professionalism of the report which he has commissioned that the defendants will conclude that a judge is more likely to accept the evidence of his expert witnesses and therefore the defendants will be prepared to compromise the claim.

Mr. White and the defending company then agree a bundle of the necessary documents, *i.e.* invoices, letters of complaint, etc., to be put before the judge, and over the telephone it is also possible to agree that the trial will last approximately four hours, that being each party's estimate of the time that the judge will take to hear the evidence. There is in fact very little in the way of legal dispute in the present case it being entirely a matter for the judge to decide whether the terms of the contract implied that the defendants were to be responsible for the whole of the plumbing arrangements. Mr. White obtains from his expert witness and from Mr. Greene details of holidays when each would be unavailable but fortunately neither intends to go on holiday for several months to come. Mr. White also corresponds with the defendants to ascertain whether any particular hearing date would be inconvenient for them and obtains their agreement that the trial should be called on as soon as possible. Consequently Mr. White writes to the court requesting that a date of trial be fixed, estimating the length of hearing as four hours and indicating the number of witnesses to be called by both parties. Eventually both Mr. White and the defendants receive notification from the court that the matter is listed for hearing in the judge's court at the Court House, Barchester in about six weeks time. Mr. White finds that Mr. Amity has a particularly busy week in the week of trial and therefore that the case will have to be conducted for Mr. Greene by a barrister. Accordingly he telephones the barristers' chambers with which his firm usually deals to confirm the availability of a barrister for that week and the barrister's clerk tells him that Mr. Adam Bede is available. Mr. White indicates something of the nature of the case and they are able to agree a fee for Mr. Bede's appearance on that day. Mr. White then carefully prepares a brief for the barrister.

THE CONTENTS OF THE BRIEF

When preparing a brief for a barrister it is important to include all conceivably relevant matter which the barrister should have before him for the proper conduct of the client's case. If Mr. White had been able to use the principal of his firm Mr. Amity, then he would have explained matters to Mr. Amity face to face as well as probably giving him a full written note. Where a barrister is to be employed, then a full written brief is prepared rather than having a face to face meeting to explain the nature of the case. Mr. White encloses all the necessary documents, in particular the statement of Mr. Greene and of his wife explaining the circumstances and the inconvenience and discomfort that will be caused by having the work done when they will not be able to use the kitchen for some days. In addition he encloses copies of the pleadings, experts' reports, and the agreed bundle of documents, *i.e.* invoices, specifications and letters of complaint. Mr. White then prepares a full brief, that is a lengthy narrative of the relevant matters in the case giving details of the factual situation, the evidence necessary to prove Mr. Greene's case, and commenting on any points of law which arise. Mr. Bede is instructed to ask for the full cost of the necessary work to the plumbing and floor replacement together with a substantial sum of damages for distress and inconvenience. The brief is delivered about a fortnight before the trial. In principle the brief fee is payable as soon as the brief is delivered even if the case should be settled between the parties the next day. This is because the brief fee includes a substantial element for the work of the barrister in preparing the case thoroughly which he might undertake immediately he receives the brief.

It is not uncommon for negotiations to continue even up to the very day of trial but in this case there are no more offers forthcoming from the defendant. Of course since there has been a payment into court there is always an element of bluff and double bluff in such negotiations and the defendants are no doubt still hopeful that the case can be compromised. Mr. White however scents that the defendants may be less than confident given the strength of his own expert's report and the fact that they have made a payment into court.

On the day of the trial Mr. Greene, Mrs. Greene, the expert witness who prepared the report, a Mr. Trollop, and Mr. White meet Mr. Bede the barrister at court about half an hour before the case is due to start. This is known as a "conference" and provides an opportunity for Mr. Bede to discuss the case with Mr. Greene whom he will not have seen before. He is also able to discuss the case with the expert witness and to clarify one or two points to as to the very full instructions which he has received from Mr. White.

Not very long before trial Mr. White had received notification from the defending company that they were instructing a firm of solicitors to represent them. This firm has in turn briefed a barrister from another set of chambers in Barset to appear at the trial. Mr. Bede has a word with his opponent to see whether any offer of compromise will be forthcoming and in fact his opponent does offer an increase to £1,500 together with interest and costs. He puts this proposal to Mr. Greene and although this would represent a substantial improvement on the amount of money paid into court Mr. Greene, perhaps rightly, believes that this demonstrates the lack of confidence the defendants have in their case and insists on fighting on into court. It is by no means unusual however for plaintiffs to be very susceptible to offers of compromise made "in the corridor" outside court especially where there is likely to be a strong conflict of evidence on the facts, and a large percentage of cases are settled at this late stage.

The case is then called into court. Mr. Bede makes a brief opening speech and hands the agreed bundle of documents to the judge. He then calls his witnesses Mr. Greene and Mrs. Greene to explain the basis of the contract, and his expert witness to explain the points in dispute in relation to the plumbing and the costs of replacement of the floor. These witnesses are cross-examined by the barrister for the defendants but he is unable to shake their evidence substantially.

The defendants then call their contracts manager who negotiated the contract but his evidence seems a little vague and uncertain as to the exact responsibilities which the defendants were supposed to undertake in totally refitting this kitchen. When Mr. Bede rises to cross examine the defendant he is able to procure further damaging admissions of uncertainty as to the precise terms agreed upon. The expert witness whom the company have brought is likewise less impressive than the expert witness called by the plaintiffs, and Mr. Bede is able to expose a certain lack of technical knowledge in the witness when compared with the very impressive performance put up by his own expert.

At the end of the evidence, defence counsel addresses the judge on the facts and the law and, if he should be unsuccessful, on the measure of damages for distress and inconvenience. The plaintiff's counsel then has the last word and he rehearses for the judge the strong salient points in his own side's evidence and makes his submissions as to what awards should be made in terms of damages.

Quite commonly the judge would retire to consider matters and perhaps to review any authorities cited. However, in the present case there are no substantial points of law and the judge feels able to give his decision on what is a relatively straightforward factual dispute then and there. He announces that he accepts the evidence of the plaintiff and his expert witness and finds for the plaintiff on all material points. He awards the plaintiff the full costs of repairs and floor replacement. He does not however award the plaintiff interest because he has not as yet had the work done and therefore has not expended the money. He then considers the question of general damages for distress and inconvenience and awards the plaintiff the sum of £600 in respect of this to take into account both the inconvenience and discomfort suffered so far, and the further discomfort which will be caused when the plumbing is shut off entirely for the time necessary to effect the repairs. As part of the discomfort has already been suffered the judge quantifies this amount at £400 and awards interest on that sum from the date when the proceedings were issued at the rate of 15 per cent. per annum.

The judge then asks if there were any other matters to be drawn to his attention. The counsel for the plaintiff, Mr. Bede, rises and tells the judge that there has been a payment into court in the sum of £800 and he asks that this amount should be paid out to the plaintiffs in part satisfaction of the sum which the judge has just awarded. The defence barrister has no objection to this course of action. The interest accrued on that money in court, although it belongs to the defendants is also to be paid out to the plaintiff in part satisfaction of his claim. The judge then makes an order for the balance of the sum due to be paid within 14 days to the plaintiff. Mr. Bede then asks for costs on the appropriate scale which in the present case is scale 2 and the judge makes that order.

Following the judgment, the money standing in court is then paid out to the plaintiff's solicitors and Mr. White receives a cheque from the defendants about 10 days later for the balance. In the letter which accompanies this cheque the defendants ask if Mr. White would like to try and agree costs in the matter rather than going through the procedure of taxation in an effort to bring the case to a conclusion. Mr. White states that he is happy to do so and puts forward his proposals for costs by letter to the defendant's solicitors. The defendant's solicitors telephone him a few days after receipt of the letter saying that they have taken their client's instructions on the letter. A certain amount of negotiation then takes place on the telephone as a result of which Mr. White is able to agree an inclusive figure for costs that is for his firm's own profit charges, together with counsel's fees, the expert witnesses fees and other necessary disbursements. Shortly after, a cheque for this sum is received direct from the defendants.

Mr. White had asked Mr. Greene for a substantial payment on account of legal costs before the litigation was undertaken, this being a normal and prudent step in litigation. As the defendants have now paid almost all the costs of the case Mr. White is in the happy position of being able to send on to Mr. Greene the amounts of damages which he has received together with the re-imbursement of almost all the amount which Mr. Greene had lodged with Makepiece and Streiff on account of costs. Only a small amount need to be retained to cover the elements of work for which Mr. White has been unable to persuade the defendants in the case to pay.

If, following the judgment the defendants had not paid the amounts due in time, or at all, then Mr. White would have had to proceed to enforcement of judgment in one of the ways considered later at page 361. If it had not been possible for him to have agreed the costs then he would have had to proceed with the lengthy and time consuming procedure for taxation of costs which would inevitably have taken several weeks longer before Mr. Greene's full entitlement and liability could have been determined.

THE FIXED DATE SUMMONS

Any claim for a sum of money is made by what is called a "default summons" as we have seen. There is one alternative form of summons, called the "fixed date summons" which is available only for a small minority of cases in which the claim is for, or includes, a non-monetary remedy. This might be for example for the return of goods unlawfully withheld, or for an injunction or for the recovery of possession of land. (CCR Ord.3 r.2).

The name fixed date summons is appropriate because the summons notifies the defendant of a return date, that is, a date on which a hearing is to take place. In most cases this will be the date of the pre-trial review. The main exception to this is where the claim is for the recovery of possession of land, coupled perhaps with a claim for rent arrears or monetary payments. In this case, the return date will be for the hearing of the action by the judge in court (C.C.R., Ord. 3, r. 3(4)).

As we have seen, the default summons procedure has several possible outcomes, depending on whether the defendant puts in a defence, or perhaps only a colourable defence, or admits the claim but asks for time to pay, and so on. In the fixed date action there is always a hearing, except that if the defendant files an admission the plaintiff can apply to the court for judgment on the admission—whether it is of the whole claim or only part—without waiting for the return day. This option is not, however, available when the claim is for the recovery of land (C.C.R., Ord. 9, r.4).

PAYMENT INTO AND OUT OF COURT

After the solicitor for a defendant has collected the evidence about a case and knows enough about the strength of his clients and the plaintiff's relative positions, then if he feels his client's position is less than secure he may well consider advising the defendant to make a payment into court. This is an extremely valuable tactic in defence because it puts the plaintiff under a considerable pressure as to costs. The reason is that where a defendant pays a sum into court funds and the plaintiff does not accept this sum within 21 days the case will go on to trial. At the trial the fact that a payment into court has been made, and the amount of the payment into court, is not disclosed to the trial judge until he has decided all questions of liability and quantum of damages. What will happen then depends upon the figure which the judge awards as damages. There are three possible outcomes:

1. If the judge decides that the defendant has actually won on liability then the payment into court is irrelevant and the money is paid back from court funds to the defendant.

2. If the plaintiff succeeds and a judge awards a plaintiff a larger sum than the amount paid into court then again the payment into court is irrelevant. The court will order that the money in court be paid out to the plaintiff in part satisfaction of his claim and that any further sums due for the defendant be paid to make up the amount awarded by the judge.

3. If the judge has awarded the plaintiff the very same figure as, or

a lower figure than, the amount paid into court, then the true significance of the payment in becomes apparent. In such a case the usual principle that the winner of litigation is awarded his costs payable by the loser does not apply. In such a case the judge will award the plaintiff his costs to be paid by the defendant only up to the date when the plaintiff received notification of payment into court. From that time on the judge will then order that the plaintiff must pay the defendant's costs until the end of the trial.

The nature of the legal gamble represented by a payment into court is thus clear. If the defendant's solicitor has calculated the amount accurately and made a payment in early in the case the plaintiff will be at great risk of having to bear a substantial part of the costs of the case even though he wins and is awarded something. Indeed, since the heavier costs in litigation are usually incurred as trial approaches the earlier the payment in is made the greater the proportion of the costs will be borne by the plaintiff. He will not only have to pay the defendant's costs from the date when he declined the offer which is represented by the payment into court but he will also of course have to bear his own costs for that period since no one else will be paying them! If the payment in is well calculated and made early in the case then the results of this drastic costs order, which is known as a "split" order may well totally wipe out any monies which the court awards the plaintiff in the litigation. It is a very real way therefore for the defendant to bring pressure to bear on a plaintiff especially in cases where there is likely to be some factual dispute, such as an allegation of contributory negligence which may make the eventual amount that the plaintiff is likely to be awarded very uncertain. It would be a very strong minded (or possibly rash!) plaintiff who did not accept a payment in of say 90 per cent. of what he hoped to get at trial. He would be gambling quite a lot in such a case to press on in the hope of getting the further 10 per cent. that he wanted. Whether the tactic of payment into court works depends on many factors including the strength of the evidence, the certainty with which damages can be calculated, the stage of the proceedings at which the payment in is made, and undoubtedly the strength of character of the plaintiff in resisting the psychological pressures applied by this tactic.

METHOD OF PAYMENT INTO COURT

A defendant wishing to make a payment into court should pay either cash, postal order or solicitor's cheque made payable to H.M. Paymaster General for the amount which he wishes to put forward (together with interest on that amount calculated up to the day of payment into court) and in addition produce the summons and a covering notice stating that he pays the amount into court in respect of the whole of the cause of action in respect of which the plaintiff claims. If a plaintiff has sued for more than one cause of action then the defendant must specify whether he is making the payment into court in respect of each or all of them.

The court will then issue a receipt and prepare a notice of payment into court which will be sent to the plaintiff in Form N242. The plaintiff as we have seen then has 21 days in which to accept the money. If he decides that he wishes to accept it outside the 21 days period the plaintiff will have to apply to the court for permission to do so and the court will undoubtedly impose a term that the plaintiff pays the defendant's costs from 21 days after he received the notice of payment into court up to the date on which he is allowed to accept the money.

Where a defendant has made a payment into court quite early in a case and this has not been accepted by the plaintiff it need not be the defendant's last tactical throw. As indicated above, informal negotiations between the solicitors may continue right through even up to the court room door. The defendant can however put further pressure on the plaintiff if he thinks that his first payment into court has been too low by "topping up" the payment by a further payment into court. The further payment in is made in the same way as the first one and the notification of the further payment in by the court to the plaintiff. The plaintiff then has a further 21 days to accept the whole of the money now in court. If he does accept the whole of the money in court he is entitled to legal costs as well up to the date he gives the court notice of acceptance of his payment in. This effectively brings the case to an end.

USING COUNSEL

A solicitor has full rights of audience in the county court so the decision to employ counsel is entirely at the discretion of the client as advised by his solicitor. This decision will be based on a variety of considerations financial, practical and professional. For example how much is at stake, the importance of the matter to the client, the legal and factual complexity, the firm's own internal advocacy resources and the solicitors' commitments and so on. The quality of the advocacy may well be crucial. Since barristers specialise in advocacy it may therefore be better to employ a barrister even though the firm has solicitors who are available to take the case. Moreover, an important consideration is that it is often actually more cost effective to employ a barrister. Barristers can be engaged for a fixed fee no matter whether the case lasts the whole day or just half an hour. Moreover, in the county court it is often difficult to predict exactly at what time of day a case will start. It may well be unremunerative for a senior solicitor to spend much of his day waiting in the court corridors to start a case which will take an hour and for which he will then need to charge the client his time at the full hourly rate. It may be better to employ a barrister at a fixed fee even though someone from the firm must accompany that barrister. The decision as to whether or not to use a barrister in a case calls for considerable knowledge and experience of tactics. It is often taken at the early stage of drafting the pleadings. If the case is of sufficient complexity to require a barrister to draft the pleadings then instructions to the barrister are drawn up with all relevant documents and sent to him. Once a barrister has drafted the pleadings (which bear the barrister's name when filed at court) it is almost inevitable that the same barrister will be used at the trial if the case goes that far. As we have seen in the case of *Greene* v. *Matchless Kitchens Ltd.* Mr. White himself prepared the pleadings and indeed did so very competently. However because the firm's own advocacy resources were stretched it was decided to employ a barrister late in the day.

One consideration when deciding when to use a barrister is the extent to which costs will be allowed on taxation because it is not automatic that the costs of counsel are allowed. In particular, counsel's fees are not allowed on interlocutory applications unless the judge or district judge certifies that the case is of sufficient difficulty to be fit for counsel. So, for example, suppose that there had been some difficulty with the automatic directions in the case of *Greene* v. *Matchless Kitchens Ltd.* and that Mr. White had had to apply to the District Judge for some interlocutory order relating to discovery. Mr. White would certainly have been able to attend and conduct such an interlocutory application himself most competently, and had he employed a barrister to do so there is no doubt that the District Judge would have disallowed the barrister's fees when a taxation of costs took place at the end of the case. As we know, in the case in question, costs were agreed between the parties, but the same principle applies because the defendants would certainly not have agreed to pay a barrister's fees for attending on such an interlocutory application notwithstanding that all other items of costs might have been accepted.

Where the decision to have a barrister is taken it is necessary to choose one. In practice the choice of a barrister is guided by knowledge of the kind of work a barrister does, the level of his fees in relation to the importance in monetary value of the matter in hand, and simple questions of availability and accessibility. A firm which regularly instructs a particular set of chambers usually knows the competence and areas of specialisation of the barristers in that set of chambers and instructs the same person for the same type of work. For a modest county court claim of the nature described in *Greene* v. *Matchless Kitchens Ltd.* it would obviously have been quite unnecessary to brief a highly experienced and expensive Queen's Counsel and had the firm done so there is no doubt at all that they would not have succeeded in recovering the whole of the barrister's fees for the case. Accordingly a relatively junior member of those chambers was chosen.

Because practising barristers obtain their work exclusively through solicitors they are wholly dependent on the solicitors' instructions properly to obtain all the information they require. Thus any work sent to a barrister commences with written instructions, that is, copies of all relevant papers accompanied by a statement of the firm of solicitors of the issues arising and ending with instructions as to what counsel is to do. The whole of these instructions are traditionally enclosed in a cover or "back sheet" and tied with pink tape. These are then sent to the barrister's chambers.

If the instructions are to draft pleadings or give advice on liability or the law or evidence or quantum of damages the instructions will say so and be titled accordingly. If the client is legally aided this must also be indicated on the back sheet.

Where the instructions are to appear in court as in *Greene* v. *Matchless Kitchens Ltd.* the instructions are called a "brief" and are usually marked by the solicitor with a fee agreed between him and counsel's clerk, except in legal aid cases where counsel's clerk merely puts forward a fee note which is then assessed by the taxing officer of the court. Depending on what has been done by counsel already on the case the brief papers will comprise all that counsel will need at the trial including the pleadings, witness statements and other documents in the order in which they will be provided to the judge and the other parties. The delivery of the brief must be decided with a careful eye as to tactics since as we have seen the fee for the brief is due on delivery of the documents to counsel's chambers even if the case is settled the next day and before the barrister has even opened the papers. Of course, whilst this is the theory if the case is in fact settled before the barrister has looked at the papers, it is usually possible to persuade the barrister's clerk to agree a reduced fee. It is often prudent when one is about to deliver a brief to one's choice of barrister to notify the opponents that this is about to take place so that they may have the opportunity to put forward any last minute offers. If they delay past the stage of delivery of the brief they will know that any terms of settlement that can be agreed will inevitably involve them having to pay counsel's fees.

In claims which result in judgment of less than £3,000 there are upper figures for counsel's fees prescribed in the County Court Rules. Where claims involve more than £3,000 however there is no upper limit but certain norms for barrister's fees in various types of work become accepted, and these are increased from time to time within the discretion of District Judges. Accordingly, it is always important to agree a fee which is reasonable within the usual range for that type of work, if one hopes to recover the whole of the fee from one's opponent if one is successful. There is a wide discretion in the court on the question of what fees should be allowed since the importance and complexity of matters dealt with and the skills, common knowledge and state of experience of barristers vary infinitely. Moreover, the amount involved in a claim is only one of the various criteria to which the court will have regard in deciding what fees are proper for barristers. It is, for example obvious that there may be as much legal and factual complexity in a claim involving, say, £3,000 as in one involving 50 times that sum.

AFFIDAVITS

Usually at a trial in open court, evidence must be given by calling a witness to testify orally on oath. As we have seen, if evidence is "agreed" as in the case of experts' reports then there may be no need to call the witness but the facts can either be admitted or a document produced to show what the experts have said. There is a further kind of evidence which is commonly used in hearings before the district judge

in chambers. This is affidavit evidence. A person may swea
vit for use in proceedings. The person who swears the ɛ
known as a "deponent." The affidavit is subject to most of tʰ
evidence so that the deponent must swear to the conter
affidavit either from his own knowledge entirely or he must s
he swears the affidavit based on information and belief and statι
he obtained that information or belief. The form of the affidɛ
closely regulated by the rules. It must be expressed in the first peι
drawn up in numbered paragraphs and start with the deponent's naι
residence and occupation. We have seen a very common form ι
affidavit already, namely the affidavit of service by the process serveι
John Doe in the case of *William Dunbar & Co.* v. *Cowper.* It will be
noted that having set out the substance of the affidavit, the words at the
bottom left which are called the "jurat" must follow the signature of
the deponent and the jurat must be signed by the deponent and the
person before whom the affidavit is sworn.

A solicitor or commissioner for oaths who takes a deponent's oath is
entitled to a fee. Affidavits may be sworn without fee before a judge,
registrar, Justice of the Peace, or an officer of the court appointed by
the judge for the purpose.

Where an oath is taken in the normal way, the person taking it gives
the deponent a New Testament and asks him to hold it in his raised
right hand and repeat after him "I, John Smith, do swear by Almighty
God that this is my name and handwriting and that the contents of this
my affidavit are true [and that these are the exhibits therein referred
to]."

The person administering the oath to the deponent of an affidavit for
use in proceedings must not be a party to the proceedings, or the
solicitor for the party on whose behalf it is being used, or his partner,
clerk or his agent (R.S.C., Ord. 41, r. 8).

A document referred to in an affidavit and forming part of the facts
sworn to by a deponent, is called an exhibit and will be marked by the
solicitor or commissioner for oaths before whom the affidavit is sworn
so as to identify it as the document referred to. It is referred to in the
affidavit as "the letter [or as may be] dated [etc.] now produced to me
and marked JS 1 [or other suitable mark]." The solicitor or commissioner marks the document JS 1 and endorses it: "This is the letter [or
as may be] marked JS 1 referred to in the affidavit of John Smith sworn
before me the   day of   ."

(signed).

PERSONAL INJURIES

A RUNNING DOWN ACTION

Henry Fielding v. *Wm. Green & Co. Ltd. and T. Smollett*

The facts of the collision giving rise to this action are not in dispute and are set out in the following statement made by the plaintiff, following his discharge from hospital, when he comes in by appointment to discuss the accident with Mr. White:

Henry Fielding of 23 Meadow Close, Barset, states:

I was born on 23rd April 1953. I am a civil engineer and am unmarried. On November 18th, 1992, I was driving my green Audi 2000 saloon motor car XYZ 100K along New Road, Barset. The road was clear and there were no vehicles parked along the kerb on my nearside. My speed would be between 30 and 35 mph. I was alone in the car.

As I approached the T-junction with Old Street, I was aware of a motor van approaching along Old Street toward the junction. The van appeared to be moving fairly slowly and was slowing down. I now know the van belonged to Wm. Green & Co. Ltd. and was driven by a Mr. T. Smollett. I momentarily thought the driver would halt at the broken white line marking the junction, in order to allow me to pass safely. My view of the approaching van was clear as there is no building on the New Road frontage immediately before the junction.

To my amazement and alarm, just as I was passing the junction the van emerged from Old Street into my path and struck my Audi by the nearside front door, tearing the door off and severely damaging the bodywork of the rear door and wing. My windscreen was shattered. I am insured for third party risks only. My insurance company is Fidelity Motor Insurers, Policy No. 39215436.

I was not wearing my seat belt, although the Audi has front seat belts, which are in good order.

I was jolted out of my driving seat and forced against the buckled door pillar on my nearside.

I had instantly braked when I saw the van pass over the white line in the road but I lost control when I was knocked out of the driving seat and the car swerved across the road and came to rest against the offside pavement some distance down New Road.

I felt severely shaken and suffered considerable pain. A passer-by called the police and a police patrol car and an ambulance came a few minutes later. I was too shocked to say anything to anybody. At the Barset District Hospital the doctor who examined me said "You are in a mess." They took numerous X rays and told me I had a fracture of the left upper arm. I had 21 stitches in the left half of my face and my arm was put in a tight bandage across my chest. I was later admitted to the orthopaedic department because the specialist I saw was not happy about my back. I was discharged by the hospital on December 8th. My arm was still in the tight sling and I was still getting backache. I was told to go to my own doctor which I did. He gave me a certificate for one month to January 5th.

I had to attend the physiotherapy department at the Hospital to have exercises to mobilise my left shoulder joint. The back pain has gradually subsided. I am now able to move the arm at the shoulder but I get pain in the joint and some backache still.

I was away from work for six weeks. My Department sick pay scheme provides for six month's full pay period, so I have no loss of earnings.

Statement taken by E. W.
Makepiece & Streiff,
Bank Chambers, Barset,
11th January, 1993.

In reply to Mr. White's question, Mr. Fielding states he has been visited in hospital by a policeman who took a statement from him. This was about a week after the accident.

Mr. Fielding produces a letter he received from Wm. Green & Co. Ltd.'s insurers, Invicta Assurance Limited, quoting their insured company's policy number, stating that they had received a report of the accident to the Company's Ford Van PQR 001W and requesting him to forward their letter to his insurers or alternatively to give particulars of his policy. Mr. Fielding has replied, giving this information, and at the same time has sent a copy to his own insurers, Fidelity Motor Insurers, with his account of the accident. He hands his copy correspondence and report to Mr. White, which includes a copy of the sketch plan forming part of the report to his insurers. He also produces to him a reply from Fidelity Motor Insurers stating that he was not covered through them for the damage and injury he had suffered as his policy was for third party, fire and theft only. As the position appeared to be that the accident was due solely to the negligence of the van driver, they did not propose to take any action. If Mr. Fielding brought proceedings, in the unlikely event of a counterclaim being made, they would make a proper contribution to the legal costs incurred by Mr. Fielding in resisting the counterclaim. They asked to be kept informed of developments and, in due course, of the settlement of the claim.

Mr. Fielding also hands to Mr. White a receipted account from Barset Motors Ltd. detailing the repairs carried out to the Audi, costing £780, including incidental expenses of towing.

Mr. Fielding informs Mr. White that when the police visited him in hospital they did not say if anyone was to be prosecuted.

He asks Mr. White to take any necessary steps to recover from the Company or its insurers all his losses, including general damages for his injury.

Immediately following the interview, Mr. White writes to the Chief Constable to inquire whether the police intend to take any action following the accident and whether they are in a position to supply their reports of the occurrence. He also writes to Mr. Fielding's consultant physician at the hospital to request a medical report and prognosis to enable him to arrive at a figure for the claim for general damages. He undertakes to pay the consultant's fee.

As Mr. White thinks that there was a strong prima facie case of negligence on the part of Mr. Smollett, he considers that without waiting to receive replies to his letters he is in a position to assert the liability of William Green & Co. Ltd., although not fully to assess the damages. He, therefore, writes to The Manager, William Green & Co. Ltd.:

MAKEPIECE & STREIFF

Solicitors

Clement Amity   Bank Chambers
Anthony Adverse   Barset
                                                      Tel: 00 765 4321

Our ref: EW/90407   11th January, 1993.

William Green & Co. Ltd.,
26 Market Square,
Barset.

Dear Sirs,

Motor Accident 18th November 1992 involving your Ford Van
PQR 001W

We have been consulted by Mr. H. Fielding regarding this accident, about which we believe you are already aware.

It is clear that your driver, Mr. T. Smollett, was solely to blame in that he failed to stop at the junction of Old Street, along which he was driving toward the junction with the major road, New Road.

Our client was detained in hospital for a fortnight. He has had considerable pain and suffering which continues to be experienced. He is attending the physiotherapy department in order to improve the mobility of his joints. It is impossible to say whether he will have any permanent result from his injury. His Audi was badly damaged and has been repaired at a cost of £780.

Our client claims damages against your Company and Mr. Smollett, which will be substantial. We understand your Company is insured with Invicta Insurance Limited and you should pass this letter to them to deal with.

Yours faithfully,

(signed)

Makepiece & Streiff

About 10 days later a reply is received from the claims manager of Invicta Insurance Ltd. stating that the letter of January 11, has been passed to the insurance company's solicitors Messrs. Rime and Reason who will be replying. The following letter is then received:

RIME & REASON

Solicitors

C. Reason
N. Wisdom, BA.
R.E. Verse.

Invicta House,
Market Street,
Barset.
Tel: 00765 1234

Your Ref: EW/90407
Our Ref: N.O./76131

27th January 1993.

Messrs. Makepiece & Streiff,
Bank Chambers,
Barset.

Dear Sirs,

Motor Accident 18th November 1992.
Our client: Wm. Green & Co. Ltd. & T. Smollett
Your Client: H. Fielding

Your letter of 11th January to Wm. Green & Co. Ltd. has been passed to us by Invicta Insurance Limited, together with the reports in their possession. We confirm that we shall be acting for Wm. Green & Co. Ltd. and Mr. Tobias Smollett.

On the basis of the information received by us, we are quite unable to accept that the accident was entirely due to the negligence of the van driver, Mr Smollett, or indeed that it was in any way caused by his negligence. We, therefore, repudiate liability on behalf of the Company and Mr. Smollett. If proceedings are commenced against our clients we will accept service on their behalf.

Yours faithfully,
(signed)
Rime & Reason.

In early February, Mr. White receives the report from the consultant physician, Dr. J. Weissmantel, which follows:

BARSET DISTRICT HOSPITAL

Dr. J. Weissmantel, MD., FRCP.
Consultant Physician

3rd February, 1993.

re: Henry Fielding

I examined Mr. Fielding whom I have attended as an inpatient from shortly after his admission as a casualty patient on November 18th last. I was told he had been involved in a car accident on that day, in which he sustained a fracture of the left humerus, lacerations on his face and severe shock. He is 39 years of age. He returned to work on January 5.

His present complaints are occasional backaches, some restriction in the movement of the left shoulder joint and occasional slight pain.

Physical examination showed no abnormality in back, hips and legs. Movement of both shoulder joints was free and nearly equal. Movement of the left arm produced some pain at the limit of movement up, forward and back. Movement of the neck was free and painless.

> *Opinion*: This is a case of traumatic fracture of the left surgical neck of the humerus, treated by immobilisation followed by physiotherapy. In spite of the patient's symptoms there is no residual disability and his symptoms are expected to disappear in a few weeks. There will be no permanent scarring of his face.
> *Prognosis*: Good.
>
> (signed)
Consultant

With this information Mr. White can conclude that the damages as a whole cannot possibly exceed £50,000, and indeed are likely to be very substantially less than that figure. Accordingly he has no option to commence proceedings in the High Court and must commence in the county court. He prepares a default summons against the defendant and particulars of claim. The particulars of claim are as follows:

IN THE BARSET COUNTY COURT   Case No. 930631
BETWEEN

Henry Fielding

Plaintiff

and
William Green & Company Limited (1)
and
T. Smollett (Male) (2)   Defendants

PARTICULARS OF CLAIM

1. At all material times the Plaintiff was the owner and driver of an Audi saloon motor car registered number XYZ 100K and the first named Defendants were the owners of a Ford motor van PQR 001W driven by their servant or agent the second-named Defendant.

2. On 18th November 1992 the Plaintiff was driving his said motor car along New Road, Barset in the County of Barsetshire when the second-named Defendant drove the said motor van out of Old Street and into collision with the Plaintiff's said motor car.

3. As a result of the matters aforesaid the Plaintiff's said motor car was damaged and the Plaintiff suffered personal injury, loss and damage.

4. The said personal injury, loss and damage were caused by the negligence of the second-named Defendant as servant or agent of the first-named Defendant.

PARTICULARS OF NEGLIGENCE

The second-named defendant as the servant or agent of the first-named Defendant was negligent in that:

(a) he failed to keep any proper look-out
(b) he drove at too fast a speed
(c) he drove out of a minor road and on to a major road when by reason of the presence of the Plaintiff's motor car it was unsafe so to do
(d) he failed to slow down, stop or otherwise control the said motor van so as to avoid the said collision.

PARTICULARS OF INJURY

Concussion, lacerations to the face and left arm, fracture of left upper arm, injury to the back. Severe shock, pain and suffering.

PARTICULARS OF SPECIAL DAMAGE

Cost of repairs to motor car	£780
Towing	£20
	£800

AND the Plaintiff claims damages and interest thereon pursuant to s.69 County Courts Act 1984.

Dated this 8th day of February 1993.
(signed)

To: The Chief Clerk of the Court, and to the above-named Defendants.	Makepiece & Streiff, Solicitors for the Plaintiff who will accept service of all proceedings at Bank Chambers, Barset, on behalf of the Plaintiff.

Mr. White instructs Joan to issue the summons. Joan takes it with two copies of her particulars of claim and the court fee to the court office. The case number is entered on the particulars of claim. Joan has indicated that the documents are to be served by her firm and the form of summons stamped with the court seal together with one copy of the particulars of claim duly stamped and the Admission, Defence and Counterclaim are returned to her for service. These are now sent by post to Rime and Reason with a covering letter. The service of the summons is acknowledged by post in three days' time. Messrs. Rime and Reason must of course also return their form of defence to the court within the 14 days allowed for this.

On February 11, Mr. White receives from the police a reply to his letter. This states that after due consideration of the reports received it has been decided that no prosecution will be taken arising out of the accident. It is, therefore, possible to provide the copies of statements and reports in connection with the accident as requested and these are enclosed. They include the pro forma Road Accident Report form completed by the constable who attended at the scene of the accident, the statement made by Mr. T. Smollett at the police station immediately after the accident and the statement made by Mr. Fielding to the police officer in hospital. There is a fee for this information, which Mr. White sends.

For the plaintiff's case, Mr. White finds that the material parts of the statement to the police by Mr. Smollett are the following:

"I was driving my company's Ford van PQR 100W along Old Street, Barset, in the direction of New Road at 7.25 p.m. on 18th November, 1992. My speed along the road was not more than 25 mph at the most and it was probably nearer to 20 mph. I am very familiar with this road, which I use frequently and am well aware of the "give way" sign at the junction with New Road. I had every intention of stopping at the junction. I could see a car approaching along New Road towards the junction from my off side. It was going fast, probably in excess of 40 mph.

"I braked in what would normally be ample time to bring the van to a halt before reaching the intersection, when I felt a softness of the brake pedal and the footbrakes seemed to have lost power. I grabbed at the handbrake and braked as hard as I could. The van was drawing to a halt as the approaching car (which I now know was the Audi motor car XYZ 100K, driven by Mr. Fielding) passed the junction but the front of my van passed over the dotted white line and would have come to a halt perhaps two feet or so out from the kerb line. The Audi was travelling close in to the kerb and the driver made no attempt to pull out slightly to avoid my van. If the driver had been going at no more than the limit of 30 mph he would have had no difficulty in taking the evasive action necessary to avoid the impact. I had a clear view of the Audi as it approached and its speed seemed to me to be excessive."

Mr. White appreciates that this places his client's claim on an entirely different basis. It will be necessary to amend his particulars of claim, by the addition of a paragraph alleging failure to maintain the van properly. However, he also appreciates the need to obtain direct evidence as to the condition of the braking system on the van. As the accident happened over two months previously, he knows this may not be easy. He telephones Mr. Fielding, tells him of this development and says he will get all available information about the condition of the hydraulic system of the van and will endeavour to obtain an independent engineer's report. He expresses the view that there is still sufficient prima facie evidence of negligence to justify the allegation of liability and he is authorised by his client to proceed with the action.

Mr. White, since he knows that the case will be more complicated than anticipated, telephones the defendant's solicitors Rime and Reason and tells them of this new development. He asks if he may have facilities for having the van inspected and agrees meanwhile that there may be an extension of time for filing the defence until March 8. He confirms this by letter. Mr. White then has the van inspected on February 24, 1993 by a motor engineer, Mr. Lucas Sparkes, F.I.M.I., who reports that he found the hydraulic braking system in proper working order. However, immediately after the accident a loose connection was discovered in the system. This was where the fluid pipe runs back from the master cylinder to the slave cylinders. The pipe is attached to the master cylinder by a nut and this nut was found to be loose and fluid was seeping through. Nothing was found wrong with the nut but as a precaution the pipe and junction had been replaced. He was able to inspect the discarded nut, and could himself detect no fault with it. He is unable to account for the slackening of the nut, but he has no doubt that this was the cause of loss of braking power.

He further reports that the van is six years old and is showing its age. The mileage on the clock is under 50,000, but this is clearly not the mileage in that period. He has been told that the van does local journeys only and averages 12,000 miles per year.

It is apparent from this report that objective evidence of negligence in respect of maintenance will be very difficult to obtain: the facts are all within the exclusive knowledge of the defendants. Mr. White appreciates that the case will be more difficult to fight than had been envisaged.

His first consideration is to amend the particulars of claim. He therefore prepares amended particulars, the amendment consisting of the addition to the particulars of negligence of a new paragraph in red ink:

---

5. The first-named Defendant Company was guilty of negligence in that they:
1. allowed a defective motor-vehicle to be used on the road without ensuring that it was roadworthy and safe to drive;
2. failed to detect a defect in the braking system of such magnitude that it resulted in failure of the brakes;
3. failed to ensure that the vehicle was properly inspected for defects and maintained in a safe and roadworthy condition.

A copy of the amended particulars of claim dated March 1, 1993, is filed at the court and a further copy is sent direct by post to the defendant's solicitors. The covering letter enclosing this tells the solicitors for the defendant that it is appreciated that further time may be required for preparation of the defence in the light of the new allegations and a further extension is granted up to March 31. At the same time Mr. White, knowing that under automatic directions he will be required to disclose the contents of his consultant's report to the defendants sends a copy of the consultant's report and requests confirmation that subject to liability they agree it. He also encloses the receipted account from Barset Motors Ltd. requesting that they agree this item also to avoid the need to call a witness from Barset Motors Ltd. at the trial.

On Monday March 31, 1993 Mr. White receives from the court the defence as follows:

IN THE BARSET COUNTY COURT Case No. 930631

[Heading as before]

PARTICULARS OF DEFENCE OF FIRST AND SECOND DEFENDANTS

1. Paragraph 1 of the amended Particulars of Claim is admitted.
2. Save that on the date alleged the Plaintiff suffered an accident no admissions are made as to any of the matters alleged in paragraphs 2–4 of the amended Particulars of Claim and the Defendants and each of them deny that the said accident was caused by their negligence as alleged, or at all.
3. Further or in the alternative the said accident was caused or contributed to by the negligence of the Plaintiff in that he:
   (a) drove his Audi motor car at an excessive speed and exceeded the speed limit;
   (b) failed to keep a proper look out;
   (c) failed to see the First Defendant's motor van in sufficient time to avoid colliding with it or at all;
   (d) failed to slow down, stop, take evasive action or otherwise avoid the said collision;
   (e) further, or in the further alternative such injury as the plaintiff sustained in consequence of the said accident was caused wholly

---

or in part by his own negligence in failing to make any proper use of the seat belt with which his vehicle was equipped.

4. The First Defendant admits that the braking system of its said van was defective in so far that a slack nut permitted the escape of brake fluid from the system, but asserts that this was a latent defect which was not detected in spite of proper standards of maintenance and could not have been detected by inspection before the occurrence of the accident.

5. The First Defendant denies that it failed to ensure that the vehicle was properly inspected for defects or that the vehicle was not properly maintained.

6. The Defendants deny that the failure of braking power of the vehicle was the primary cause of the accident.

7. No admissions are made as to the alleged exceeding of the speed limit or any injury and/or loss and/or damage alleged to have been suffered by the Plaintiff.

8. Save as hereinbefore specifically admitted the Defendants deny each and every allegation contained in the amended Particulars of Claim as though the same were herein set out and traversed *seriatim*.

Dated this 28th day of March 1993
(signed)
Rime & Reason,
Invicta House,
Market Street,
Barset.

To the Chief Clerk
of the Court and to the
above-named Plaintiff
and his solicitors.

Solicitors for the Defendants who will accept service of all proceedings at the above address on behalf of both Defendants.

The following day Mr. White receives from Messrs. Rime confirmation that the hospital consultant's report and repairs account are agreed.

Mr. White now sees that the case raises difficult issues of evidence and law and that a high level conference is necessary. He therefore consults his principal Clement Amity who will be likely to undertake the advocacy and suggests a conference with the client. This is arranged for April 6.

At this conference the difficulties of establishing particular omissions to inspect and maintain the van are explained to Mr. Fielding. Mr. Fielding asks whether the motor engineer who inspected and reported on the van should be called as one of his witnesses. Mr. Amity states that this would entail obtaining the leave of the court and it would be given on condition that a written report with his views should be supplied to the defence before the hearing. It would be likely to lead to a situation where experts would have to be called on both sides with the possibility of a conflict of opinion. In view of Mr. Lucas Sparke's inability to suggest how the nut could have worked loose, he doubts the wisdom of involving him further. On the credit side, he will be able to present the case on the basis that the existence of a defect, admitted by the defendants, raises a presumption of negligence which it is their duty to rebut. They will, therefore, have to bring witnesses to establish that they properly maintained the vehicle, when and how it was inspected and so on. It is difficult to see how they can satisfy the court of this because a nut cannot suddenly loosen itself. Whilst the case is a difficult one it is clear that justice (in the abstract, of course) is on the plaintiff's side and the sympathy of the court will almost certainly be with him. Mr. Amity discounts the allegation of contributory negligence on the part of Mr. Fielding in the matter of driving since this depends on the production of an independent witness as to Mr. Fielding's speed at the time. Whether it is contributory negligence not to have worn a seat belt is more difficult. Had Mr. Fielding been thrown up through the windscreen then the defendants would have been entitled to a substantial discount (usually up to 25 per cent.) on the injuries thus caused, because of the failure to wear a seat belt. But where the impact is from the side it is far from clear whether any such discount should be allowed. However, since it appears that Mr. Fielding was thrown clear of the driver's seat and hit the near-side door pillar it is highly possible that wearing a seat belt would have saved some or all of the injuries. Nevertheless, it is for the defendants to prove that wearing a seat belt would have saved the injuries. Mr. Fielding is content to let the case proceed. Mr. White asks Mr. Amity whether there is any particular order in addition to automatic directions which is required. Mr. Amity agrees with Mr. White that as the medical report and special damages are agreed there is no need to do more than proceed to set the case down for trial. Accordingly Mr. White corresponds with the defendant's solicitors to agree an estimate for the length of hearing and indicate the number of witnesses whom they propose to call. Mr. White passes on this information to the county court by letter and requests that a hearing date be arranged. The court notifies both sides that the hearing date has been fixed for June 8, 1993. The requirements of the automatic directions or, if there is one, the district judge's order on a pre-trial review must be scrupulously complied with; *e.g.* documents must be produced and exchanged, correspondence must be agreed, etc. Documents to be put in evidence must be put in date order in bundles and copies made for the court and all other parties. Mr. White therefore prepares for the trial by arranging an appointment with Mr. Fielding when his statement on the file can be gone through, brought up to date and expanded to cover any points not already fully covered.

At the hearing the case is presented by Mr. Amity and defended by Mr. C. Reason. The judge has before him only the filed papers reproduced or referred to above. Mr. Amity, therefore, in opening the case for the plaintiff gives a detailed account of the events giving rise to the claim and describes the injuries suffered by Mr. Fielding.

The formal steps taken subsequent to the submission of the defence require in this case little comment. Mr. Amity hands up a copy of the hospital consultant's report and proceeds to inform the judge that there is, as he understands it, no dispute as to the facts of the accident and that the special damages and the hospital consultant's report are agreed. Mr. Amity's submission, that the admitted existence of the mechanical defect leading to a loss of braking power raises a presumption of negligence which it is the duty of the defendants to rebut, is accepted by the court and this throws the weight of Mr. Amity's advocacy into the cross-examination of the defendants' witnesses.

The course of the presentation of the case and defence are sufficiently indicated from the judgment, which follows:

The Judge: In this case I am asked to decide on an issue of negligence in unusual circumstances. (Describes the accident and the defect in the van braking system leading to it.)

I accept that the facts raise an inference of negligence on the part of the defendants and I have to decide whether on the evidence they have presented to me they have proved that the defect arose and remained undetected without any fault on their part. The plaintiff's solicitor undertook a very difficult burden of proof in so far that the whole of the facts are within the exclusive knowledge of the defendants and their employees. The defendants also had a considerable burden to show that they had no knowledge and no means of knowing of defects that suddenly caused a loss of braking power. Mr. Amity was unable to find any weakness in the general system of maintenance as presented by the defendants' witnesses. However, he did secure the admission that the brake fluid was low in the reservoir after the accident and that the seepage of fluid was still observable the next day by the mechanic who carried out the removal and replacement of the pipe. The defendants' fitter, who carried out the servicing and said he serviced the vehicle 10 days before the accident, agreed that it was not put up on a ramp and that the light in the inspection pit was poor. I am unable to accept that such a defect would not reveal itself over a period both by a drop in the level of the fluid in the reservoir and by the fluid around the pipe and nut. I cannot accept the submission, which I regard as impossible that the defect occurred suddenly at the time of the accident and without warning. In the outcome, therefore, I do not consider that the defendants have discharged the evidential burden resting on them, which is to rebut the presumption of their own negligence.

With regard to the issue of failure to wear a seat belt although it is clear to me that the injury to his left shoulder was as such caused by his failure to wear a seat belt in that he was thrown bodily across the car and collided with the near side door pillar, I consider that with an impact of this severity it is quite clear that he would have sustained injuries, probably of a "whip lash" type anyway by being thrown backward and forward had he been wearing his seat belt. The issue is a difficult one and no clear evidence has been presented but I am satisfied that it is for the defendants to show me that the extent of the plaintiff's injuries would have been significantly less had he been wearing a seat belt and whilst the issue is far from clear cut I consider that they have not discharged the burden upon them to show this. I am therefore not minded to make any deduction from damages for that allegation of contributory negligence.

He has made virtually a complete recovery and since the medical evidence is accepted it is clear that there will be no future disability nor any future loss of earnings. I therefore assess his damages for personal injuries in the sum of £3,000. The judgment is therefore for a total sum of £3,780. In addition I award interest at the usual rates on general damages from the date of service of the summons and on special damages from the date of the accident. Is it possible for the precise figures to be agreed?

(Mr. Amity and Mr. Reason briefly confer. Mr. Amity had prepared a preliminary calculation of interest based on the likely awards of damages and although the judge has awarded slightly less than the figure for which he was hoping he shows his calculation to Mr. Reason. Mr. Reason agrees the method of calculation and the interest rates applicable in such a case which are set by judicial precedent of which both are aware. After a few words to avoid the need to work out exact figures with calculators they are able to agree a round sum figure for interest of £35.)

Mr. Amity: "We have managed to agree a round sum figure to avoid wasting the court's time whilst we compute a precise one in the sum of £35 Your Honour."

The Judge: "Very well there will be judgment for the plaintiff in a total sum of £3,815."

Mr. Amity: "With costs on scale 2 Your Honour?"

The Judge: "Yes very well and order for costs on scale 2."

Note:

Although in this case there was no claim for loss of earnings because Mr. Fielding did not lose any since his employers have a generous sick pay scheme, in many cases employers have a term in a contract of employment where there is such a sick pay scheme, that if an individual is off work due to an accident in respect of which a claim is to be made from some other person that the sick pay is to be treated as an interest-free loan and therefore if a claim can be made from that other person for the amount of earnings lost, reimbursement of the amount of the loan should be made to the plaintiff's employers. This is obviously a sensible provision, because otherwise the employers will of course have no right of action directly against the person who caused such an accident to recover the amount of sick pay they will have paid to the plaintiff for the period when he was off work.

PERSONAL INJURIES CLAIMS

Personal injury cases often receive a great deal of publicity. However, those that get to court are only a tiny percentage of all the claims that are brought. In the vast majority of cases, perhaps as many as 96 per cent., litigation is settled before there is any trial. Many indeed are settled even before court proceedings need to be issued at all. The remainder are settled by negotiation during the course of proceedings or sometimes dropped if it becomes clear that the claim is bound to fail if pursued; there is after all no point in throwing away good money after bad on hopeless cases. The success of the solicitor in negotiations as in the proceedings themselves depends as much on his tactical skill in exploiting every advantage, procedural and psychological, as on his knowledge of the law. The foundation for success lies in careful attention to detail in the assembly of facts. When for example an injured client comes in after an accident, the solicitor must inquire into every detail of the accident to extract all the circumstances that could show the fault of the person responsible, without neglecting possible weaknesses in his client's case. He will wish to know the names and addresses of witnesses, to have a plan with measurements of the scene of the accident and possibly photographs. He will inquire into the client's earnings and how they are likely to be affected by the accident. In the case of a factory accident, he will want to know about the system of working, the arrangements for supervision, the particulars of machinery and so on. He will inquire what the losses, past and prospective, are likely to be. His course of action after receiving these instructions will depend on the infinite variety of circumstances that can surround any accident, but he will lose no time in writing to the prospective defendant and, unless liability is admitted, which is rare at this stage, will probably see the benefit of commencing the action. What Samuel Johnson said about hanging could be said of the receipt of a writ or a county court summons: it powerfully concentrates the mind.

PREPARATION FOR THE HEARING

It is in the interests of all parties to keep the hearing as short as possible. As we have seen, the pleadings are concerned with defining the issues in dispute and eliminating those that are not.

As soon as notice of the date of the hearing is received from the Chief Clerk, the legal executive responsible must ensure that all his witnesses are warned to attend. Witnesses may be required simply for the oral evidence they can give or for the original documents they are able to produce, or both. It is important that a document is produced by the right person, namely the person in whose possession or control the document properly is and who is able to give evidence of its genuineness. (The rules have been relaxed in certain cases, *e.g.* bank accounts and bank records.)

Where there is doubt about the willingness of a witness to attend, a witness summons must be issued. It may be applied for by attendance at the court office or by post. In the High Court the summons is called a *subpoena* and there are two forms, of verbal evidence (*ad testificandum*) and to produce documents (*duces tecum*). In the county court only one form of request for summons to a witness is used, in which reference is made to any documents to be brought to court. A separate request is filed for each witness, but if the decision on whom to call is in doubt or a witness's name and address have not yet been ascertained, it can be issued in blank and served by the solicitor for the party applying for it (C.C.R., Ord. 20, r. 12). It is now usual for witness summonses to be served by the party concerned. In such a case the party usually employs a process server and this has the virtue of speed and certainty. It is possible to serve a witness summons by post but, save in cases where one is absolutely certain that the witness will acknowledge receipt and abide by the summons, because of the difficulties of potentially unwilling witnesses claiming non-receipt, it is more normal to serve witness summonses personally. The limited expense involved in instructing a process server will almost always be allowed as a legitimate disbursement on taxation of costs. The court bailiff service, however, can also be used for service of the witness summons if necessary.

The witness must be served with the summons together with "conduct money" which is a modest amount for subsistence and reasonable costs of travel to and from the court on the day in question. The witness may subsequently be able to claim loss of earnings for the day in court but these do not need to be tendered at the time of service of the witness summons.

A legal executive who has the conduct of a case must of course brief the solicitor who is to be the advocate. This is a vital part of his work, because if he fails to communicate any detail of the material he has collected for the case, the solicitor's position may be undermined and the client's position placed in jeopardy. It is to be expected that, when it is known that a case may go to trial, consultation between the legal executive and the solicitor who will represent the party in court will take place and that this will continue during the remaining stages of the preparation up to the hearing. This is, of course, one of the great advantages of carrying the case through without using counsel.

JURY TRIAL

Jury trial is uncommon in the county court and in some kinds of proceedings it is excluded; in some there is a general right for either side to ask for a jury, *e.g.* malicious prosecution cases or where the applicant is accused of fraud. Otherwise, it is at the discretion of the judge. A county court jury consists of eight members and a majority verdict of seven members can be accepted (C.C.A. 1984, ss.66).

THIRD PARTY PROCEEDINGS

It is always up to a plaintiff to decide whom to sue. If he sues defendant X then defendant X has no way of saying that the plaintiff should have sued Y instead and bringing in Y as a co-defendant. However, in certain situations whether or not a defendant is legally liable, he can ensure that someone else is brought into the action to stand trial at the same time. This is where a defendant institutes third party proceedings.

Example

A pedestrian P is walking on the pavement when he is injured by a car driven by D which mounts the pavement. P naturally sues D.

However, D wishes to show that he was not in fact to blame for mounting the pavement but did so only in order to avoid a car which was approaching him on the wrong side of the road driven by T. Accordingly D will defend P's action claiming that he was not in fact negligent. However to insure himself in case he is found to be at all negligent he will issue third party proceedings against T to bring him into the action so that T may be called upon to contribute to any damages awarded to P.

In cases involving third parties automatic directions do not apply and there is always a pre-trial review. This is because procedurally the case is rather more complex than the routine cases to which automatic directions are appropriate. The District Judge will give directions to all parties concerned with a view to ensuring that the whole issue comes before the court in the most convenient and expeditious manner. It is often appropriate in situations in tort where P has sued D, who in his turn has issued third party proceedings against T, for P to go on to consider amending his summons and particulars of claim to allege that T may also be liable as an alternative second defendant.

THE INJUNCTION

Justice for a successful plaintiff sometimes calls for a remedy going beyond the award of a sum of money damages and costs or the return of the plaintiff's property. The law provides such a remedy in the injunction, which compels the defendant to do or to refrain from doing some act. This is an aspect of law enforcement that is readily lighted on by the press: the property owner who has to pull down a newly constructed building because it interferes with his neighbour's right to light; the husband who has to be restrained from molesting his estranged wife, and so on. Injunctions are more readily associated in the public mind with high court proceedings than with the county court. Generally, an injunction can only be had in the county court if it is "ancillary," *i.e.* incidental, to some other remedy the court has inherent jurisdiction to grant such as damages. This restriction has now been relaxed to enable the court to grant injunctions as the principal or only remedy in actions concerned with the ownership, use and enjoyment of land (C.C.A. 1984, s.22). Most applications in the county court continue to be applications which are part of proceedings for one of the remedies the court more commonly provides.

Normally application for an injunction is made after the issue of the summons and it can be made at any time up to and after judgment. Application is on notice, but in cases of real urgency can be made *ex parte* and even before any other form of proceedings is started in the court. If made *ex parte* the application must be supported by evidence on affidavit. In such circumstances, the injunction granted is likely to be *interim*, *i.e.* an order which will remain in force only pending the trial of the substantive issue between the parties by the normal processes of the court.

The essence of an injunction is that it is effective against the person concerned; failure to comply is contempt of court for which the penalty is imprisonment. The imprisonment continues until the contempt is purged by compliance with the terms of the injunction.

AFTER THE TRIAL

EXECUTION

William Dunbar and Co. v. John Cowper

In this case related above (pp. 302), judgment has been entered on behalf of the plaintiffs. The defendant has seven days to discharge the whole of the debt and costs. In the hope of avoiding having to take enforcement action, Mr. White writes to Mr. Cowper referring to the service on him of the form of judgment and draws attention to the time allowed for payment. If payment is not made by due date he states, execution will be levied on his goods and this will add substantially to the costs.

No payment having been received in this period, Mr. White decides to ask the court to issue a warrant of execution, which will lead to the seizure and sale of goods from Mr. Cowper's home if the amount, together with additional costs is not paid. Mr. White thinks it likely that the threat represented by the issue of the warrant will be enough to persuade Mr. Cowper to make payment, or at least to reveal his financial position and make proposals for payment over a period. To set the process in motion, he prepares the request for warrant of execution.

This is taken to the court office by Joan, with the plaint note and fee. The court now prepares the warrant of execution against goods of the defendant which gives the bailiff authority to remove and sell them if payment is not forthcoming.

This is passed by the court office to a bailiff, one of whose functions it is to execute warrants. The date of the levy will depend on the availability of a bailiff to undertake it and his ability to meet with the defendant and to gain entry to his premises. Requests for execution are generally taken in the order in which they are received and issued. The notice of levy, which will be handed to the person who admits him to the premises, contains a note explaining its effect and the procedure to be followed.

The bailiff executing the warrant in this case calls at Mr Cowper's house. Mr Cowper is at work and the shock of receiving the notice of levy is taken by Mrs. Cowper. The bailiff must manage to gain entry by peaceable means. Once inside he may go over the house and require entry to any room for this purpose. He explains his mission and gives Mrs. Cowper the notice of levy, drawing attention to the explanatory notes. She telephones her husband. She tells the bailiff that her husband regrets that he has not complied with the court order hitherto, but thinks that if he can have 14 days to pay, he can raise the amount. The bailiff points out that it is his duty to levy and remove goods of such sale value as will realise a sum to cover the amount due under the warrant, including the court fee and the cost of issuing the warrant. In what he selects he will omit clothes and bedding to the value of £100 and tools of trade to the value of £150. The goods are taken to be sold by auction and if there is any surplus after the judgment debt, costs and the expenses incurred by the court in effecting the sale, the court will account to Mr. Cowper for the balance. He explains that as an alternative to taking the goods away (which he refers to as "entering into close possession") it will be possible, with Mrs. Cowper's co-operation to select the goods to be seized but to leave them on the premises for, say, a week in which time Mr. Cowper may have found the money to pay off the debt. This procedure he refers to as "taking walking possession." He asks whether Mr. Cowper will agree to his entering into walking possession of their motor car. After again telephoning her husband, Mrs. Cowper agrees. The bailiff then, having confirmed with Mrs. Cowper that the car is fully paid for and is owned by Mr. Cowper (and not, say, Mrs. Cowper), inspects it, takes particulars and completes and signs a form adapted to show that the motor car has been left in the garage, but under conditions laid down in the agreement. He also completes a form of request to hold walking possession and an authority to re-enter, which he asks Mrs. Cowper to sign.

Having obtained Mrs. Cowper's signature to the form on behalf of her husband, he hands over the inventory and leaves. On return to the office, he takes the precaution of checking the registered ownership of the car by letter to the Driver and Vehicle Licensing Centre.

As Mr. Cowper pays the debt and costs in accordance with his undertaking, no further enforcement action is called for.

SALE OF JUDGMENT DEBTOR'S EFFECTS

Goods seized under a warrant of execution must be deposited by the bailiff in some fit place or safeguarded in such other manner as the district judge directs (C.C.A. 1984, s.90).

Unless they are perishable, or the debtor requests in writing, they cannot be sold for at least five days after seizure (C.C.A. 1984, s.93). As sale is invariably by public auction, the arrangements usually take longer. The Chief Clerk is required to deliver or send to the debtor an inventory of the goods removed and to give him at least four days' notice of the date, time and place of sale (C.C.R., Ord. 26, r. 12). The proceeds following the sale must usually be held for 14 days to cover the contingency that bankruptcy proceedings may be started against the judgment debtor.

It is, therefore, usually to the advantage of the judgment creditor if the threat of seizure produces a satisfactory arrangement for payment.

It is often considered that the bailiffs are not especially efficient at enforcing judgments by warrant of execution. There are certain restrictions on the bailiff's powers. In particular they can only execute judgments involving less than £5,000. In judgments involving over £5,000 a successful party who is called a *judgment creditor* at this stage must execute the judgment by instructing the High Court sheriff. The judgment must be transferred to the High Court for the purpose of enforcement. It is widely considered that the High Court sheriff is much more efficient at enforcing judgments by seizure of goods than is the bailiff. Although, as indicated above, if the judgment is for a sum larger than £5,000 a judgment creditor must employ the sheriff and not the bailiff, a judgment creditor also has the *option* of instructing the sheriff rather than the bailiff in any case where the judgment is for more than £2,000. Because of the greater speed and efficiency of the sheriff it is in fact normal for all judgment debts of more than £2,000 to be enforced through the sheriff rather than the bailiff.

OTHER METHODS OF ENFORCEMENT

For a money judgment of an amount which is moderate in relation to the likely resources of the judgment debtor, a warrant of execution is the most direct and appropriate means of obtaining satisfaction of the judgment debt. Where, on the other hand, the amount involved is unlikely to be realised by a sale of household or business effects by a warrant, or where difficulties are experienced in levying execution, other expedients can be used.

FINDING OUT ABOUT THE DEFENDANT'S MEANS

It is often prudent, especially in debt cases, to advise a plaintiff who wishes to sue for a debt to have a status enquiry report carried out by an inquiry agent before even issuing proceedings. Nothing is as frustrating for the layman as to spend money on establishing his legal rights only to find that there is no way of enforcing the judgment that he has obtained and that he has thrown good money after bad. Accordingly it is always wise advice to suggest status inquiry reports before even commencing an action unless the client is already satisfied by previous business dealings or otherwise that the defendant will be good for any amount awarded against him.

If however one has not for any reason done this and has obtained judgment then although it is often an automatic first reaction to apply for a warrant of execution, sometimes it is best to give a little consideration to whether or not some other method of enforcement of the judgment may be better. One can always instruct an inquiry agent even after obtaining judgment, but after obtaining judgment it is also possible to apply to the court for an order for oral examination. For this purpose he applies *ex parte* for an order that the debtor be orally examined by the court (C.C.R., Ord. 25, r. 3). The examination takes place in the court of the district in which the judgment debt resides or carries on business, and if necessary the proceedings must first be transferred to that court (C.C.R., Ord. 25, r. 2).

To make application for oral examination of the debtor an application is made *ex parte* to the court on payment of the appropriate fee. The court then draws up the order for oral examination and this must be served on the debtor in the same manner as a default summons is served (C.C.R. Ord. 25, r. 3(3)). In other words it is best to serve it personally, if necessary by the bailiff or process server. However, the District Judge may, before making an order for oral examination, give the person to be examined an opportunity of making a statement in writing or an affidavit as to his means (Ord. 25, r. 3(7)).

If the person to be examined fails to attend the court will adjourn the examination and make a further order for his attendance. This time the order is served personally and conduct money has to be tendered to him (C.C.R., Ord. 25, r. 3(4), (5)). Failure to attend the adjourned hearing renders the judgment debtor liable to be committed to prison.

The oral examination usually takes place before a member of the court staff appointed for the purpose and the client may be represented by a solicitor or by a suitably qualified member of his staff. The hearing is not just intended to be a polite inquiry, but to be a cross-examination and "that of the severest kind."

GARNISHEE ORDERS

A particularly effective method of securing payment of a money debt is garnishee proceedings. This is a process by which a person who owes money to the judgment debtor (the "garnishee") may be ordered by the court to pay it instead to the judgment creditor. The judgment creditor who seeks a garnishee order makes application *ex parte* accompanied by an affidavit setting out particulars of the debt owing from the proposed garnishee to the judgment debtor. The garnishee order *nisi* is issued by the court and served on the garnishee.

The garnishee order tells the garnishee that he must "freeze" the amount which he owes to the judgment debtor (often this is a credit balance in the bank account in the name of the judgment debtor) and either pay that money into court or attend the hearing of the application for a garnishee order absolute. A copy of the garnishee order *nisi* is then served on the judgment debtor himself. It is always served later on the judgment debtor than on the garnishee so that he has no opportunity to withdraw money from a bank or obtain payment of a trade debt before receipt by the garnishee of the garnishee order *nisi*. Usually a garnishee will have no interest in whether or not a garnishee order is made unless he disputes that he actually owes money to the judgment debtor. Accordingly usually the garnishee either pays the money into court or any way writes into the court and says that he does not propose to contest the application and is happy to comply with any order the court makes. If the garnishee or the judgment debtor do not successfully oppose the order at the hearing the district judge will then make an order requiring the garnishee to pay the debt to the judgment creditor (C.C.R., Ord. 30, rr. 1–3).

CHARGING ORDERS

If the judgment debtor owns land or premises then it is possible to apply for a charging order which will take effect over that land just as if the judgment creditor was a mortgagee. The application is very similar to that in the case of garnishee and proceeds in two stages. First the judgment creditor obtains a charging order *nisi* by application on affidavit identifying the judgment debt and the land of which the judgment debtor is the owner. The court will then make a charging order nisi which will bind the land until a hearing of the full application. At this hearing, if no proposals are made satisfactorily to pay the debt a charging order absolute will be made which takes effect over the land and puts the judgment debtor in the position of mortgagor to the judgment creditor as mortgagee. This is merely a way of securing the debt of course and does not in itself get the money paid. It does ensure however that if there is any dealing with the land the mortgage must be redeemed. The judgment creditor may in due course proceed anyway like any other unpaid mortgagee to obtain an order for sale in respect of the land and in that way it will be paid out of the proceeds of sale.

ATTACHMENT OF EARNINGS

The above mentioned methods are the more satisfactory at least in relation to large debts. If however the judgment debtor has a steady job but nothing worth seizing by execution and no funds worth garnishing and no land worth charging then the final alternative is usually attachment of earnings. Application for this is made by the judgment creditor and a questionnaire is then sent to the judgment debtor and often to his employer requesting details of the judgment debtors employment. This questionnaire must be returned to the court and the court will then consider making an attachment of earnings order whereby the employer is directed to deduct each week or month a prescribed amount from the wages or salary of the judgment debtor and to remit it to the county court for onward transmission to the judgment creditor. Where the amounts involved are relatively modest and especially if the judgment debtor has a reasonably highly paid job and few dependants this may be a satisfactory method of obtaining payment. If however the judgment debtor's salary is low and he has several dependants then a very low rate of payment may be ordered so that unless the debt is very modest recovery of the sum under this procedure may take years. The procedure is also of little use if the judgment debtor is in casual work or prone to frequent changes of employment.

ENFORCEMENT OF NON-MONETARY JUDGMENTS

Non-money judgments require different forms of enforcement. Thus, the recovery of land is effected by a warrant for possession (C.C.R.,

Ord. 26, r. 17). The recovery of specific goods withheld by a defendant is secured by a warrant for delivery (C.C.R., Ord. 26, r. 16). An injunction requiring the defendant to do, or refrain from doing, something is enforced by warrant of committal. Failure to comply with the warrant entails the defendant being committed to prison. A warrant of committal can also be obtained against the directors and officers of limited company which wilfully fails to carry out a judgment or order of the court. Before a person can be committed to prison, a hearing by the judge is arranged at which the defendant is called upon to show cause why the order should not be made. The notice of the hearing is served personally on the defendant (C.C.R., Ord. 29, rr. 1, 2).

Where the order is made, the defendant is committed to prison for a fixed term. A prisoner can at any time apply in writing to the court for his discharge showing that he has purged or is desirous of purging his contempt. The application has to be witnessed by a senior prison officer and notice of the application must be served on the judgment creditor at least one day before the application is made (C.C.R., Ord. 29, r. 3).

INTEREST ON MONEY JUDGMENTS

Where a county court judgment is given for a sum of less than £5,000 then it does not carry any interest. This may cause grave injustice. Thus, where it has been found that the defendant is liable to the plaintiff in the sum of, say, £4,000 and moreover because of limited means the defendant obtains an order allowing him to pay that sum to the plaintiff at, say, £20 per week, it is obvious that the judgment will take something like four years to collect in full. In all that time the value of money is falling yet there is no recompense for the plaintiff by way of interest on the amount awarded. Had the plaintiff chosen to sue in the High Court, as he perfectly well might have for that sum, then the judgment would have carried interest at the rate of 15 per cent. per annum from the time of judgment being given until it was paid in full on the balance from time to time outstanding. This is a powerful reason for suing in the High Court even in respect of quite modest sums, at least in straight forward debt cases or where the plaintiff otherwise hopes that the action will finish early and without grave complications. Moreover, even though one has to commence proceedings in the county court one can still register a county court judgment in the High Court provided it is for a greater sum than £2,000, and the judgment then becomes a High Court judgment and attracts interest at the rate of 15 per cent. per annum. Unfortunately the High Court cannot be used for attachment of earnings and therefore if that is the only method of enforcement available to a plaintiff he will have to stay in the county court even if his judgment is for considerably more than £2,000.

County Court judgments of more than £5,000 do however attract interest at the judgment debt interest rate of 15 per cent. per annum, just as in the High Court. Sadly however there are still further complications. In particular, interest ceases to run for any period during which a judgment creditor is attempting to enforce the judgment. Thus, for example, from the moment that one attempts to enforce judgment by execution against goods or by an attachment of earnings, or garnishee no interest runs. This is however so long as the method of enforcement chosen produces any payment at all, however modest. If the method of enforcement is totally ineffective then interest will run throughout that period. The unfortunate consequence of this is that if one attempts, say, garnishee proceedings which only recover a small amount, no interest runs during the period of those proceedings. This rule however does not apply in the case of enforcement by charging order. In that single case interest continues to run for the period during which the charging order procedure takes place.

It is necessary for a party wishing to claim interest under a judgment to file certificates giving computations of the interest claimed.

THE AWARD OF COSTS

The rules concerning the award of costs are complex and would require a study that is beyond the scope of this book. Here however we outline the basis of charging and the procedure for settling the amount of costs which one party must pay towards the costs of another in litigation. This procedure is called taxation of costs. The word "taxation" should not be misunderstood. It has nothing whatsoever to do with the Inland Revenue but rather is a derivation of a Norman French word meaning "assessment." It refers to the assessment by the court of the figure which it is fair for the loser to have to pay the winner in litigation. The nature of taxation has been briefly considered in the earlier chapter on The Legal Profession p. 19.

Clearly it would be quite unfair to make the loser pay the winner any sum for legal costs which the winner might choose to claim and there has to be a procedure therefore by which the court will assess any claims to costs. In the County Court there are now only three scales of costs. The first of these scales is called the "lower scale" and sets out a series of maximum items which can be claimed in various stages in a case involving less than £100. In the nature of things such cases would be very rare indeed, as such modest claims will usually be referred to arbitration where in principle only the fixed costs allowed on the summons is obtainable. The second scale is called "scale 1" and governs the amounts to be allowed in any action which resulted in an award of between £100 or £3,000. If the action fails entirely, that is, the defendant wins, then the scale is fixed by reference to the amount by which the plaintiff originally claimed. There is then "scale 2" which governs all actions involving more than £3,000.

Solicitor's charges for contentious business need to be itemised. That is, an account has to be made out detailing in chronological order the documents prepared, copies made, letters written, attendances on client and witnesses and at court, time otherwise expended on the case in preparation, reading and legal research, and in addition court fees, barristers' fees, expert witness fees and other disbursements.

It is for the solicitor for the winning party for whom costs have been awarded to prepare and file his bill within three months of the judgment or order by which costs were awarded (C.C.R., Ord. 38, r. 20). In drawing up the bill the solicitor will have regard to the appropriate scale the basis of which is set out above. In relation to lower scale and scale 1 there are various maxima described for each individual stage of the proceedings which is claimable by the winning party's solicitor. On scale 2 however there are no maxima so prescribed and the amounts to be awarded are entirely within the discretion of the District Judge. This recognises the fact that the County Court now has an unlimited financial jurisdiction and thus cases of very considerable substance, necessitating expert and detailed work at a high level, may be brought there.

The drawing up of bills of cost is sometimes undertaken by the solicitor or Legal Executive who actually conducted the litigation file in question. More usually however it is drawn up by someone called a "costs draughtsman." This is a person, who usually started out in life as a Legal Executive who eventually decided to specialise in the very difficult and time consuming work of preparing bills of costs in the detailed form in which they are required for taxation in the litigation process. Larger firms have their own "costs draughtsmen" who specialise in just this task but smaller and medium-sized firms often have recourse to outside freelance costs draughtsmen who are sent the file and then prepare the bill in the necessary format. Freelance costs draughtsmen are often paid on a commission basis on the gross total of the bill which they draw up, and thus they have every incentive to ensure they prepare the bill scrupulously and claim every conceivable item at the maximum appropriate rate allowable.

Once the bill is prepared an appointment for taxation must be obtained. The solicitor or Legal Executive who has conducted the file must lodge his bill in the court office with all necessary supporting papers and vouchers and sufficient copies for the other parties of the bill. On receipt of the documents the Chief Clerk will send a copy of the bill to every other party entitled to be heard on the taxation and give all parties not less than 14 days' notice of the appointment for taxation. It may be that the District Judge thinks an appointment unnecessary and he may then conduct a "provisional taxation" in which he goes through the bill without the attendance of the parties. He then sends a notice of the amount he proposes to allow on the bill to the parties, requiring them to inform the court within 14 days if any of them object to the amount allowed and wishes to be heard on the matter. If a request for hearing is received an appointment for taxation is given.

When the taxation appointment takes place, and a lengthy appointment may well be allocated for a substantial matter, the solicitor or Legal Executive for the winner will justify each of the items charged on his bill both as regards whether the item was proper in principle, and then as to whether he has charged an appropriate and fair amount for it in terms of the expertise which he has employed and the time expended. As each item is reached, the representative of the losing party can contest any item or the amount charged for it or the rate of method of computation of the amount concerned.

The test which the District Judge must employ at a taxation of costs is to consider whether each item charged is reasonable in nature and amount. If he finds that it is reasonable then he will allow the item in full. If he finds that it is unreasonable in principle he will delete it entirely or "tax off" the items as it is called, or simply reduce it to a reasonable figure.

Either party to a taxation however who is dissatisfied with the District Judge's decision can ask the District Judge to reconsider his award on any particular items. This may be done at the hearing itself but can equally be done by filing notice within two days of the end of the taxation. There is then a re-hearing on the items objected to and if either party is dissatisfied with the decision the District Judge then reaches, application can be made for a further review of the taxation to a Circuit Judge.

It is self evident that the taxation process may be lengthy and time consuming. For example, after a case is over, drawing up a bill will take many hours' work, or alternatively have to be sent out of the office to a freelance costs draughtsman whose fees will not in principle be recoverable from the loser. There will then be some months' delay in obtaining a taxation appointment and some time spent at court on that appointment. To avoid this delay and the associated costs and fees (for there is a substantial court fee payable for taxation based on the amount of the bill) it is very common at the end of litigation for the parties to attempt to "agree" costs. Where this happens the winning party's solicitor will put forward his suggestion informally, often by letter, to the loser and so negotiation will then ensue to attempt to fix a fair amount. Settling costs by negotiation in this way is extremely common even in litigation which has been strenuously contested up to that point. Probably 80 per cent. or more of all cases lead to costs being agreed rather than there being a taxation.

SOLICITOR AND OWN CLIENT COSTS

The taxation process discussed above determines the level of payment which the winner can obtain from the loser in Civil Litigation. However it commonly happens that the amount awarded at taxation, or the amount that can be negotiated between the parties, does not cover all the costs that a successful party's solicitor is entitled to charge that party. The winner may expect his opponent to meet his bill for all reasonable steps from the commencement of the proceedings, but the solicitor may well have done work connected with the proceedings which the court will not consider it reasonable to charge directly to the opponent. It may be, for example, that a client has been very demanding of his solicitor and has called in frequently for interviews and attendances which did nothing particularly to further the case but were rather in the nature of going over old ground or setting the client's mind at rest. The solicitor's time for those attendances will certainly have to be paid for and if the opponent is not ordered to meet that cost then the solicitor will inevitably deliver his own client a bill for the extra time for which the opponent cannot be held liable. This is known as "solicitor and own client costs" and it is important therefore to stress to a client at the outset of litigation that he, the client, must behave reasonably if he expects to recover all his legal costs from the losing opponent and that if he does not behave reasonably he will inevitably receive a bill himself notwithstanding that he has won the litigation. The several bases on which costs can be awarded are dealt with more fully in Volume II (Proceedings in the High Court).

Fixed Costs

Above we have discussed taxation of costs. In addition however there are various items of "fixed costs" which is all that the plaintiff will obtain in cases where an action ends very early without substantial opposition from the defendant, for example as we have seen in the case of *Cowper* v. *Dunbar*. If a case ends in default judgment a plaintiff is only entitled to the items of fixed costs stated on the summons. These figures are prescribed from time to time and appear in the appropriate part of the Green Book. In such a case therefore this is the only amount which can be recovered from the losing party. If there has been a good deal of preliminary work on the case before the issue of proceedings therefore the item of fixed costs will certainly not cover all the solicitor's charges and in that case he will inevitably need to deliver to his own client a bill for the extra work done.

Registration of County Court Judgments

There is a register of county court judgments of £10 and more. This is kept by a private company, The Registry Trust Ltd. at 171/173 Cleveland Street, London W1P 5PE. It is the responsibility of the chief clerk of a county court to transmit to the Registry a return of every registrable judgment. The register is open to inspection on payment of the prescribed fees. Forms of application are available at county courts.

The Regulations provide that when a judgment is satisfied, or complied with, any party to the action can apply to the registrar of the court, who on proof of the satisfaction or compliance and payment of the prescribed fee will transmit a certificate to the Company who will discharge the entry.

SOME TIME LIMITS OF GENERAL APPLICATION

Matter	Reference	Time
Admission of claim	Ord.9, r.2(1)	Within 14 days after service of summons
Admission of facts		
in writing (voluntary)	Ord.20, r.1	At any time
Notice to admit	Ord.20, r.2(1)	Not later than 14 days before hearing
Admission in response to notice	Ord.20, r.2(2)	Within 7 days after service of notice
Costs		
Application for increase certificate	Ord.38, r.9(4)	Within 14 days after order
Counterclaim		
Notice of	Ord.9, r.2(1)	Within 14 days after service of summons
Default Summons		
Reply to qualified admission	Ord.9, r.3(1)	Within 14 days after receipt
Judgment in default	Ord.9, r.6	After 14 days from service of summons
Summary judgment when no real defence— Service of Notice of application	Ord.9, r.14	Not less than 7 days before day fixed for hearing
Defence	Ord.9, r.2(1)	Within 14 days after service of summons
Documents		
Notice to Admit	Ord.20, r.3(1)	Not later than 14 days before trial
Challenge	Ord.20, r.3(2)	Within 7 days after service
Notice to produce	Ord.20, r.3(4)(nn)	Reasonable time
Evidence:		
Affidavit:		
Notice of use in court	Ord.20, r.7(1)	14 clear days before hearing
Object to use	Ord.20, r.7(1)	7 days after receipt of notice
Fixed Date Summons:		
Service	Ord.7, r.10(5)	Not less than 21 days before return day
Further Particulars:		
of claim—Defendant's request	Ord.6, r.7	After filing of defence
of defence—Plaintiff's request	Ord.9, r.11	Any time
Garnishee Proceedings:		
Service of order nisi	Ord.30, r.3	7 days before return day

Matter	Reference	Time
Interlocutory Applications: 　　Notice	Ord.13, r.1(2)	2 days before hearing
Judgment Summons	Ord.28, r.3(1)	14 days before hearing date
Payment into court 　　By defendant	Ord.11, r.1(1)	Any time before judgment
Acceptance by plaintiff 　　of lesser amount	Ord.11, r.3	(1) Notice of acceptance within 21 days after receipt of notice of payment in but not less than 3 days before hearing
	Ord.11, r.5	(2) Later acceptance at any time for the hearing begins, on terms
Taxation 　　Bill, lodging of	Ord.38, r.20(1)	Within 3 months of Order
Notice of Appointment	Ord.38, r.20(2)	14 days' notice
Witness Summons 　　Service on witness	Ord. 20, r.12(4)	A reasonable time before the hearing

Self Testing Questions

1. What is the jurisdiction of the County Court?
2. What forms of proceeding exist in the County Court?
3. What does a District Judge do?
4. What is a pre-trial review?
5. What is discovery of documents and how is it carried out?
6. What are the steps to be taken by each party between close of pleading and the trial?
7. What is a brief to Counsel and what should it contain?
8. Explain the nature of and procedure for obtaining summary judgment.
9. Explain the various procedures for enforcing a judgment for a money sum.
10. When and how can evidence be given on affidavit?

INDEX

Page numbers of forms and precedents reproduced in the text are shown in *italics*.